MANAGEMENT
IN
INDIA

To my sister Susan
—Herbert J. Davis

This volume is dedicated to my immediate and extended families in Australia and India, who are tied together by their love for, and confidence in, India
—Samir R. Chatterjee

To my wife Melanie
—Mark Heuer

MANAGEMENT IN INDIA

Trends and Transition

Edited by
Herbert J. Davis
Samir R. Chatterjee
Mark Heuer

Response Books
A division of Sage Publications
New Delhi / Thousand Oaks / London

First published in 2006 by

Response Books
A division of Sage Publications
B-42, Panchsheel Enclave
New Delhi 110 017

Sage Publications Inc
2455 Teller Road
Thousand Oaks,
California 91320

Sage Publications Ltd
1 Oliver's Yard,
55 City Road
London EC1Y 1SP

Published by Tejeshwar Singh for Sage Publications India Pvt Ltd, phototypeset in 10.5/12.5 pt AGaramond by Star Compugraphics Private Limited, Delhi and printed at Chaman Enterprises, New Delhi.

Library of Congress Cataloging-in-Publication Data

Management in India: trends and transition/edited by Herbert J. Davis, Samir R. Chatterjee, Mark Heuer.
     p. cm.
     Includes bibliographical references and indexes.
     1. Management—India.   2. Personnel management—India   3. Corporate culture—India.   I. Davis, Herbert J.   II. Chatterjee, S. R. (Samir Ranjan), 1945– III. Heuer, Mark, 1954–

     HD70.I4.M342   2005   658'.00954—dc22   2005025554

ISBN: 0-7619-3363-8 (Hb)   81-7829-593-8 (Hb India)

Production Team: R.A.M. Brown, Sanjeev Sharma and Santosh Rawat

Contents

Section Eight: Global Managers in India

Foreword

Today, India is considered one of the most exciting and vibrant emerging markets in the world. India's distinct advantage as a future economic power lies in its large pool of skilled managerial and technical manpower capable of competing with the finest in the world, a burgeoning middle class whose size exceeds the population of most countries, and an economic system which is increasingly investor friendly. Demographically too, India is an extremely young country which makes it an attractive market for consumer goods and services. India's long tradition of democracy, an independent judiciary, and a remarkably free press are all conditions for continuing economic progress. Additionally, these conditions make it an ideal destination for business investment. Hence business growth for the future might well lie in doing business in India and with India.

However, things may not always be as they seem. The business scenario in India can be deceptively simple. It is by no means an easy management system to understand either in terms of its culture or its processes. It is a business system which is in transition, dynamic, and complicated. In fact, it is almost trite to say that Indian management culture is complicated; however, it is precisely because it is complicated that one needs to understand how and why it is complicated and what its drivers are. Consequently, understanding the complexities of business and management in India begins with a solid grounding in its economic policies and laws. Additionally, the aspiring manager in India must also understand and internalize the Indian mindset, culture, approaches to leadership, values, ethics and change. These find their roots in India's history as a large, diverse, multiracial, and multireligious nation.

Following nearly three decades of often acrimonious political, social, and cultural discord, India has entered the 21st century as a globalizing economy. After independence from the British in 1947, India was a new and desperately impoverished nation. Rightfully, India's founding fathers focused on the development of basic infrastructure and human resources necessary to sustain its economy. India's first Prime Minister Jawaharlal

Nehru launched programs to establish institutions of higher learning including the Indian Institute of Technology as well as management and other engineering colleges to encourage self-reliance and indigenous development.

However, successive political leaderships maintained a socialistic orientation and focused on a centrally planned economy and capacity building even as they maintained democracy in the most diverse nation in the world. In the mid-1980s Prime Minister Rajiv Gandhi inspired new hopes and dreams of transforming the country through decentralization and technology, thereby, enabling India to more adequately provide for basic human needs. India's success, particularly, in the information technology sector, can be traced to this period in her history. Today, India is the leader in business process outsourcing with an unprecedented $150 billion in foreign currency reserves. While India's economic reform process begun in 1990 and the continuing policy initiatives of the last few years have resulted in significant inflows of foreign investments, understanding Indian managerial thinking is of critical importance for future managers in India. In recent years Indian management culture has changed substantially. Understanding the way managers in India approach issues such as human resources, their values, ethics and work goals are essential if one is to succeed in this dynamic economy.

This volume, assembled by three experienced observers and scholars of India, is therefore, an extremely significant and remarkable accomplishment. It brings together a large and diverse set of issues that often are neglected and side-stepped when one considers the Indian business scenario. More importantly, the diverse background of the contributors brings together differing perspectives which will be extremely useful to those managers who look to understand and draw their own conclusions about the human and cultural aspects of doing business in India.

This book examines a wide range of issues of management culture, all of which will play a critical role in the success of India going forward. Drawing on the talents of an outstanding team of contributors, this volume will be a landmark reference to understanding management in India. It will be a valuable read for all those who wish to do business in India as well as for management students worldwide.

Sam Pitroda
Chairman, National Knowledge Commission of India

Preface

This book is the result of a commitment made by the first two editors at least a decade ago to make a contribution to the enrichment of managerial learning about India. It took a much longer time than was envisioned. The starting point of the idea has now become overlayed with many developments propelling Indian managers to focus on global imperatives in every sphere of their work. The future drivers of economic prosperity need their logic, ideas and practices carefully considered as they broaden their visions of building dynamic world class organizations. Competing issues, challenges and explorations need to be brought into focus in making this intellectual journey meaningful.

However, it is impossible to reach a level of optimum balance in compiling a volume on the many faceted challenges facing Indian managers during this first decade of the 21st century. This volume is designed to contribute to a new genre of analytical and empirical thinking to assist this new generation of managers in India as well as expatriate managers with interest in India. Managerial culture in India has advanced to a point where 'connectedness' to regional and global challenges is critical to India's continuing business success.

This volume is designed to analyze and, therefore, better understand Indian managerial culture. In an emerging economy like India's, managerial culture is subject to extensive change and, consequently, new behaviour patterns emerge. A decade after India chose to initiate economic reforms, this volume looks at India's managerial culture to both identify and understand cultural paradigms as well as how managerial thinking has evolved in India since reforms were first initiated.

Our attempt has been to cover as many diverse issues as possible without compromising academic rigour or accessibility. We hope students, scholars and managers will find this a valuable and enriching read.

Acknowledgements

This book has been a truly global endeavour with the editors and contributors spread across many nations. We are conscious that a book attempting to cover managerial challenges in the dynamic context of contemporary India is bound to be a work in progress. While the editors accept sole responsibility for limitations and inadequacies, we express deep gratitude to the large number of contributors who have helped shape the ideas of the book.

Our special thanks to the Department of Strategic Management and Public Policy at George Washington University, USA, and the International Business Unit and the School of Management, Curtin University of Technology, Australia, for continuing support and encouragement of the project. Our sincere thanks to Mr Chapal Mehra of Sage for his professional stewardship of the book and Mr Subramaniam Ananthram, Research Associate at the School of Management, Curtin University of Technology, for his continuing research assistance and Mr Adam Korengold of the School of Business at The George Washington University for his assistance with the introduction. We have carefully followed the proper procedures in contacting relevant copyright holders for this book. However, if any have been inadvertently left out we will make every endeavour to correct them at the earliest opportunity.

We also wish to acknowledge the following copyright holders for granting permission to re-publish articles from their respective journals:

American Business Review
S. Gopalan and A. Stahl (1998), 'Application of American Management Theories and Practices to the Indian Business Environment: Understanding the Impact of National Culture', *American Business Review*, 16(2): 30–41.

Academy of Management Executive
D. Kapur and R. Ramamurti (2001), 'India's Emerging Competitive Advantage in Services', *The Academy of Management Executive*, 15(2): 20–31.

Blackwell Publishing
Sen Gupta and P. K. Sett (2000), 'Industrial Relations Law, Employment Security and Collective Bargaining in India: Myths, Realities and Hopes', *Industrial Relations Journal*, 31(2): 144–53.

Cornell University
S. Kuruvilla (1996), 'Linkages between Industrialization Strategies and Industrial Relations/Human Resource Policies: Singapore, Malaysia, the Philippines, and India', *Industrial & Labor Relations Review*, 49(4): 635–57.

Elsevier Limited
M. Tayeb (1996), 'India—A Non-Tiger of Asia', *International Business Review*, 5(5): 425–45.
K. Mellahi and C. Guermat (2004), 'Does Age Matter? An Empirical Examination of the Effect of Age on Managerial Values and Practices in India', *Journal of World Business*, 39: 199–215.

Emerald Group Publishing Ltd.
S. R. Chatterjee and C. A. L. Pearson (2000), 'Work Goals and Societal Value Orientations of Senior Indian Managers: An Empirical Analysis', *The Journal of Management Development*, 19(7): 643–53.
A. Gupta, M. Koshal and R. K. Koshal (1998), 'Women Managers in India: Challenges and Opportunities', *Equal Opportunities International*, 17(8): 14–26.

Management International Review
S. R. Chatterjee and C. A. L. Pearson (2000), 'Indian Managers in Transition: Orientations, Work Goals, Values and Ethics', *Management International Review*, 40(1): 81–95.

Palgrave Macmillan
J.P. Neelankavil, A. Mathur and Y. Zhang (2000), 'Determinants of Managerial Performance: A Cross-cultural Comparison of the Perceptions

of Middle-level Managers in Four Countries', *Journal of International Business Studies*, 31(1): 121–40.

Sage Publications
S. Kakar, S. Kakar, M.F.R. Kets de Vries and P. Vrignaud (2002), 'Leadership in Indian Organizations from a Comparative Perspective', *International Journal of Cross Cultural Management*, 2(2): 239–50.

Springer
M. Thakur, and B. N. Srivastava (2000), 'Managing Alliance Intricacies: An Exploratory Study of U.S. and Indian Alliance Partners', *Asia Pacific Journal of Management*, 17: 155–73.

Springer
P. N. Khandwalla (2002), 'Effective Organisational Response by Corporates to India's Liberalisation and Globalisation', *Asia Pacific Journal of Management*, 19, 423–48.

Springer
S. K. Chakraborty (1997), 'Business Ethics in India', *Journal of Business Ethics*, 16(14): 1529–38.

Introduction

Approximately one out of every three people on Earth lives in India or the People's Republic of China. India's orientation to the West (as a British colony) and to the East (owing to its relationships with key Asian economies) positions it as a major economic player in the developing world as well as in the global economy.

India's intellectual capital is formidable as evidenced by an annual output of half a million engineers, a quarter of a million medical doctors, and some one hundred thousand management school graduates. An entrepreneurial culture has taken root at the village level, a competitive strategy orientation is making increasing demands on traditional quality concepts, and a vast internal market provides a sustainable basis for increasing market development. India's legal framework, banking infrastructure, maturing accounting systems, established financial markets, and both marketing and management professions provide India with a distinctive advantage. Additionally, India's population estimated at well over one billion, and its relative youthfulness (seventy percent under the age of thirty-five) makes it both an attractive market and a continuing source of intellectual and professional resources. India therefore rivals China as among the world's largest markets.

Just as Western observers have long viewed China as the world's largest market, the emergence of India as another nation of over one billion people has targeted it as a major opportunity for business. While large segments of the population are highly educated, both in the West and domestically, at the same time dramatic deficiencies in poverty are being alleviated along with improvements in literacy, and education at all levels.

The relative size of India's economy compared to China presents a growth opportunity. As China's economy continues to expand and factor prices rise, India is positioned to take on a larger share of foreign direct investment (FDI). India's overall GDP is less than half of China's and inflows of foreign direct investment to India remain negligible relative to China. In 2003, for example, FDI to India was only six per cent of that to China. However, total FDI to India has risen more than tenfold since the beginning of reforms (from $1.7 billion in 1991 to $22.3 billion in 2001).[1] Consequently, India now stands on the cusp of becoming one of the world's most attractive destinations for foreign direct investment.[2]

Overall Economic Growth

In nominal terms, India is the world's twelfth largest economy with an estimated 2004 gross domestic product (GDP) of $500 billion.[3] Measured by purchasing power parity, India's economy is the fourth largest in the world.[4] Annual GDP growth slowed from between 7 and 7.5 per cent in the mid-1990's to 4.3 per cent in 2002.[5] In 2004, India failed to meet its target growth rate of 8.1 per cent annually due to destructive monsoon rains in the latter half of the year; however, growth recovered to approximately 6.5 per cent from the 2002 figure.[6]

This inability to meet the requisite growth targets due to a destructive monsoon indicates a strong dependence on agriculture. Fifty eight per cent of the population depends on agriculture[7] which accounts for 25 per cent of total GDP.[8] While the manufacturing and services components of the economy have experienced growth in recent periods, the susceptibility of the agricultural portion of the economy to changes in weather patterns or other uncontrollable factors has contributed to the volatility of the overall economy.[9]

Industry and Policy Overview

A watershed in Indian economic policy took place in the 1990's with India's market based transformation. Reforms began in the 1990s resulted from a balance of payments crisis as a result of oil price shocks that resulted from the Persian Gulf War, the collapse of the former Soviet Union, and the emergence of China as an economic power. This prompted a program of International Monetary Fund (IMF) assistance conditioned on extensive economic reforms. Before the crisis, annual economic growth was under 3 per cent, national budget deficits were over 7 per cent of GDP, and foreign direct investment stood at approximately $100 million annually.[10] Spurred by the IMF, the government in Delhi undertook two key reforms: trade liberalization and the elimination of restrictions on foreign and domestic investment.[11]

The present government under prime minister Manmohan Singh has sought to increase the share of foreign investment in GDP from approximately 25 per cent (half the figure for China).[12] According to the consulting firm A.T. Kearney's annual survey of corporate leaders concerning foreign direct investment, India is now the third most favoured destination for foreign direct investment in the world, based on the quality of its workforce, management talent, legal regime, lack of cultural barriers, and favourable legal and regulatory environment.[13] India's pre-1991 trade policy, which focused on import substitution, has given way to a stronger emphasis on international trade. India has been a member of the World Trade Organization (WTO) since 1995 during which time both imports and exports have risen steadily. According to the WTO, trade now comprises 29.8 per cent of Indian GDP. Its trade volume ranks within the top twenty per cent of countries, tenth in the world for services exports, and eighth for services imports.

Monetary Policy, Money, and Finance

The Reserve Bank of India (RBI) policy has emphasized a managed depreciation of the rupee. It has increased the money supply between 10 and 16 per cent each year since 2000, and has maintained steady interest rates as the commercial bank lending rate has fluctuated between 11.5 and 12.5 per cent between 1999 and 2003.[14]

The IMF has not provided funds to India since the reforms of 1991. India's external debt represents a significantly smaller share of GDP (approximately 10 per cent, compared to 28 per cent) than it did at the time of the IMF intervention in 1991.[15] The rupee has depreciated significantly against the euro (see chart), depreciated more steadily against the British pound and the dollar during the past several years, and remained comparatively stable against the Japanese yen.[16]

Foreign Exchange Rates, 1999–2003

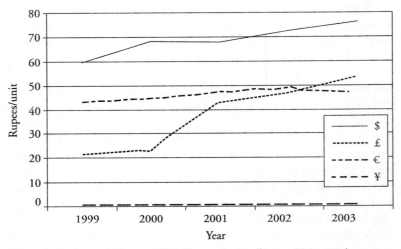

Year

Source: India Country Report 2004, Economist Intelligence Unit, 2004.

Foreign exchange reserves have not been depleted to maintain the exchange rate; on the contrary, they have steadily increased since 1999.[17] In May 2003, reserves stood at $113 billion, representing the fifth highest position among emerging markets and the sixth largest in the world, and providing approximately fourteen months of import cover.[18]

Development Indicators

India has made tremendous strides in its economic development since the initiation of market-based reforms in 1991. In particular, access to sanitation and potable water greatly improved in the last decade of the twentieth century. However, nearly one quarter of the population was still undernourished in 2000, and government expenditures for education were still only about 4 per cent of GDP.[19] There is still a large segment of the Indian population which has restricted access or no clean water, food sanitation or health services. Questions of human development and growth still persist in India as do those of economic equity and opportunity. India's needs for energy, clean water, sanitation and education, in the coming decade, will pose a major obstacle to continued growth.

Development Challenges and Accomplishments, 1990–2000

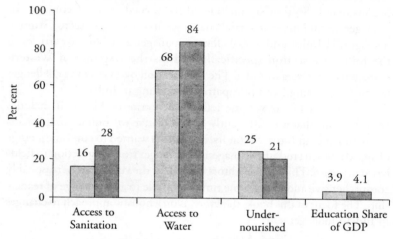

Change from 1990 (light column) to 2000 (dark column)

Source: United Nations Development Programme.

Conclusion

Since 1991 Indian business and industry have been forced to accept and simultaneously compete in a globally competitive marketplace. The initial reaction to this competition was a sense of panic and then a slow but steady embrace of globalization. With the introduction of economic liberalization Indian managers and their underlying managerial culture has begun to change. Indian corporations and their managements increasingly view themselves as members of a wider global economic community. This volume brings together the diverse issues of leadership, culture, ethics, gender, and globalization to map the trends and transitions in Indian management. The first section provides an overview of the changing contexts of Indian management and then proceeds to examine the cultural values affecting the shape of organizations and behavioural patterns in India. Section two explores the specific patterns of managerial culture to a considerable depth. Section three considers the conceptual and empirical perspectives of managerial leadership in India. Section four continues the broad leadership discussion in the area of human resources and industrial relations. In section five the critical area of ethics is considered. Section six includes three special areas of concern for managers including; managerial challenges in the services sector, woman managers in India, and global alliance management. The two articles in the following section specifically address the response of Western managerial practices in India. The final section overviews the challenges facing the growing band of expatriates working in India.

The content of the volume reflect three criteria. Firstly, it includes contributions that are sufficiently broad relative to contemporary management issues in India. Secondly, the editors wanted to combine a range of approaches in studying managerial challenges from abstraction to field-based evidence. Thirdly, the editors wished for the volume to be reasonably comprehensive and at the same time accessible to a wide range of readership. The focus of this book, therefore, is on a holistic approach to changes in Indian management.

Notes

1. Jha, Rhaghbendra. "Recent Trends in FDI Flows and Prospects for India." Australian National University, South Asia Research Centre. Internet: http://ssrn.com/abstract=431927 (4 June 2005).
2. Jha, Rhaghbendra. "Recent Trends in FDI-India." ASEAN Analysis. Internet: http://www.aseanfocus.com/asiananaylsis/article.cfm?articleID=672 (4 June 2005).
3. India Country Commercial Guide FY 2004. U.S. Commercial Service, U.S. Department of Commerce. Internet: http://www.doc.gov.
4. "Indian Economy Overview." EconomyWatch.com. Internet: http://www.economywatch.com/indianeconomy/indian-economy.overview.html (23 April 2005).
5. Ibid.
6. Back to earth: India's economy. *The Economist* (18 September 2004): 76.
7. "Indian Economy Overview."
8. India Country Commercial Guide.
9. International Monetary Fund. Staff Report of India Article IV Consultation. IMF Country Report No. 05/86 (March 2005).
10. Morrison, Wayne and Alan Kronstadt. "India-U.S. Economic Relations." U.S. Congressional Research Service (10 February 2005).
11. Singh, Nirvikar and T.N. Srinivasan. "Indian Federalism, Economic Reform and Globalization." Stanford Center for International Development (September 2004).
12. International Monetary Fund.

13. FDI Confidence Index. A.T. Kearney Global Business Policy Council (October 2004).
14. *India Country Report 2004.* Economist Intelligence Unit (2004): 48. (International Monetary Fund statistics.)
15. Ibid, 42.
16. *India Country Report 2004.* Economist Intelligence Unit (2004): 57.
17. Ibid, 57.
18. Ibid, 42.
19. India Human Development Report. United Nations Development Programme. Internet: http://hdr.undp.org/statistics/data/cty/cty_f_IND.html (24 April 2005).

Section One

UNDERSTANDING INDIAN MANAGEMENT AND CULTURE

1 Understanding Indian Management in a Time of Transition

Samir R. Chatterjee and Mark Heuer

In many ways, business and management culture in India has always been a reflection of the complexity and diversity that characterises the country as a whole. Today, the contours of Indian management also reflect contemporary processes of social and economic change that are now re-shaping the very 'idea' and image of India. Several developments over the last few years, particularly attempts by the government to re-structure the economy by opening it up to international competition, have brought India to the threshold of a major transformation in its business culture. In this sense, India is a nation in transition. Moving away from a government-controlled, inward looking 'command' economy, India has begun to embrace the global market in the hope of achieving rapid economic development. As a result, Indian management systems are moving towards a new global orientation and operational context. Family dominated business conglomerates and large public sector enterprises continue to dominate the Indian economy but these are beginning to give way to innovative, globally oriented, corporate players—particularly within the booming Information Technology (IT) industry.

The significance of these structural transitions cannot be under-estimated. As many of the contributors to this current volume note, several 'traditional' characteristics of management in India remain in place—notions of authority and hierarchy, the role of familial networks, indigenous ethical-philosophical frameworks and community boundaries; the importance of continuity and stability in institutional and individual norms and practices; and, finally, a general acceptance of ambiguity.

The degree to which these 'typical' features of Indian management systems are likely to be transformed by a new global context is, in some respects, the crux of contemporary debate about the evolution of Indian management systems. As suggested by the broad range of arguments and perspectives presented by these selected readings, such debates can perhaps never be resolved with complete satisfaction. Nonetheless, it is possible and plausible to suggest that India is moving towards developing a unique 'hybrid' form of management that seeks to remain grounded in selected 'traditional' patterns of behaviour, while embracing many of the best practices of global management systems.

India's Potential in a Global Context

For certain observers, the story of India in the latter period of the 20th century is a tale of unfulfilled potential. As the convenors of a 2003 conclave on India's future have noted, there is an 'unacceptable performance-potential gap' with India making up 16 per cent of world population but accounting for a global GNP share of only 1.5 per cent, while its share of total world trade is a mere 0.7 per cent (Purie, 2003, p. 9). An unresolved question, therefore, is whether the 21st century will mark India's emergence as a 'global giant' or whether it will be a nation characterised by stunted growth and frustrated ambitions.

By other measurements, however, there are indications that India is beginning to emerge as a significant global economic player. In a very long-term historical sense this may even be characterized as a global *re-emergence* since as the first Indian empire under Chandra Gupta Maurya (325 BC) India was once possibly the single largest economy in the world. Over two thousand years later, the world's 10 largest economies accounted for two-thirds of the gross world product (Table 1) and, by this measurement, India ranked as the fourth largest economy, confirming its increasing significance as a global economic force.

In 1980, China and India both had around 3 per cent of the share of the world product. By 2000, India had a per capita income of $2,390, a population of over a billion people, and accounted for over 5 per cent of the world product. According to World Bank estimates, in terms of GDP, the decades of the 1980s and 1990s witnessed a remarkable change in relative national product shares and ranking. During this period, China jumped from being the ninth largest economy in the world to second place

Table 1: Income of the World's 10 Largest Economies in 2000

	Per Capita Income ($)	Population (m)	Gross Domestic Product ($b)	Share of Gross World Product (%)	Ranking
United States	34,254	282	9,646	21.7	1
China	4,297	1,289	5,540	12.5	2
Japan	26,430	127	3,354	7.6	3
India	2,394	1,016	2,432	5.5	4
Germany	24,988	82	2,054	4.6	5
France	24,448	59	1,440	3.2	6
United Kingdom	23,568	60	1,407	3.2	7
Italy	23,362	58	1,348	3.0	8
Brazil	7,306	170	1,245	2.8	9
Russia	8,022	146	1,168	2.6	10
Rest of World	5,332	2,766	14,748	33.2	11–206
World	7,331	6,054	44,382	100.0	1–206

Source: World Bank's World Development Report 2002.

and India advanced to become the fourth largest from the eighth position. Russia was the biggest loser contracting from the third to the tenth rank.

A scenario built on recent World Bank models indicates the continued upward movement of India into third place by 2010. During the third period of this scenario (2026–50), India is projected as joining China as the two largest economies. This study suggests:

> with 18 percent of world income each, the economies of the two Asian giants are three times larger than that of the United States, whose share in the world income has fallen to six percent, half the share of China in 2000 (Hooke, 2003, p. 103).

Furthermore, this model suggests that between 2051–2100, India would emerge as the largest economy in the world with 16 per cent of the world income, followed by China with 15 per cent. However, regional groupings like ASEAN, NAFTA, and the EU were also predicted to become more important than specific countries.

It is prudent to sound a note of caution on measurements based solely upon gross domestic and world products, and predictions that suggest the inevitability of uninterrupted patterns of rapid economic expansion. Certainly, however, the Indian economy had demonstrated a steady, if not always spectacular, growth by the end of the 1990s. After decades of relative insularity in terms of the broad thrust of economic policy and industrial development, the new global orientation of the economy has also generated intense interest among international investors and analysts over India's long-term potential.

Historical Context of Transition

In the decades after independence in 1947, India, under the political leadership of Jawaharlal Nehru and his daughter Indira Gandhi, pursued a development policy based upon the promotion of a highly planned, state interventionist 'command' economy. Although there were many notable successes during this period, criticism of this approach began to accelerate. In particular, many critics felt that India had become locked into relatively stagnant rates of national economic expansion of around 3.5 per cent per annum, a so-called 'Hindu rate of growth' that could only improve by adopting a more competitive, outward oriented economy. Other critics argued that India's massive public sector and excessive government intervention was constraining private industries. From a managerial perspective, it was certainly evident that India's policy settings over many decades had given rise to something of an insular and 'closed' managerial mindset.

Since 1991, the Indian economy is increasingly being reformed in line with contemporary global imperatives, which is creating fundamental shifts in managerial culture. Significant progress has been recorded in industries like computer software and hardware; automobiles and auto-components; agriculture; mining; banking and insurance; and, the media and entertainment industries. Despite these improvements, India's ranking in the IMD World Competitiveness score, A.T. Kearney's FDI confidence index, or Standard and Poor's Transparency Indicators, has been relatively disappointing. For a country that is so large, culturally diverse, and rich in natural and human resources, to be 135th out of 173 countries on the UN Human Development Index hardly signals India's true potential.

India's managerial heritage is of considerable relevance in understanding the more general economic and cultural transformations currently being witnessed in Asia. This is because India has a deeply felt, sophisticated, and very durable cultural heritage that has shaped and re-shaped itself over thousands of years—a heritage that has also had a defining influence on many 'neighbouring' countries of the Asian region. At the same time, India is also one of the most amenable of Asian nations to 'global' information and cultural flows. It has a British inspired institutional underpinning, a vigorous democratic political system and a highly educated, somewhat 'Westernised' and/or English speaking social elite.

In spite of this, a 'negative' work culture and relatively insular managerial perspectives have often been identified as significant inhibitors of progress. As some scholars have pointed out, 'India's low "efficiency orientation" can be interpreted in terms of the level of power-distance, a low risk taking propensity and the importance of familial and social networks' (Sparrow and Budhawar, 1997, p. 235). Such statements made in isolation, however, may lead those who are unfamiliar with India to develop an overly negative image of the country as static and unchanging. In fact, India's history demonstrates that it has an extraordinary capacity to absorb and accept change while maintaining deep-rooted traditions.

Reforms in the 1990s and into the 21st Century

During the decade of the 1990s India underwent significant transformation. In 1991, a Congress party government introduced a series of important structural economic 'reforms'. Although these policies were a response to a pressing economic crisis, it was also related to a long-term shift towards more 'liberal' trade and economic policies that had begun in the 1980s under the political leadership of Indira and Rajiv Gandhi. As a result, by the early 1990s India was ready to embark upon a program of 'liberalisation', including, among other policy measures, the gradual removal of 'protectionist' trade barriers, the deregulation of domestic production, the promotion of foreign investment, and the pursuit of long-term policy goals such as financial sector restructuring, governmental fiscal restraint, and public sector 'disinvestment'. Significantly, however, many of these policy agendas remain incomplete today—a fact that has generated ongoing debate as to the pace and the consequences of 'liberalisation' in India.

The gradual dismantling of the so-called 'licence permit raj' saw the states and sub-regions of the country assuming a much more prominent role as economic actors in terms of investment and policy formation. The 1990s, therefore, are best characterized as a time of tumultuous national, regional and local level political and social change in India as these fundamental changes to policy settings began to filter through the economy at regional and local levels. Another critical aspect of the changing face of India was the new importance in economic policy formation, managerial culture, and popular consciousness, accorded to *international* forces. It is this new global context that perhaps represents the greatest transition for Indian management over this period.

India's Changing Corporate Structure

Internationally competitive costs and an available pool of highly skilled local labour have contributed to a new image for India as a nation moving away from a traditional agrarian base and heavy industries towards a 'knowledge-driven' society. While these images of generalised social transformation are often wildly exaggerated, this type of discourse has undoubtedly been, in part, responsible for leading MNC's locating major R&D facilities in India in recent years. Indeed, in doing so, knowledge-based corporations such as Microsoft, Motorola and General Electric have professed their faith in India's long-term potential to become a leading agent in the global information revolution.

Similarly, the launch of the Government of India's national IT task force in 1998 represented a new strategic paradigm. The task force announced the bold goal of making India an IT superpower within 10 years and aimed to provide a new vision of economic development for the information age. Acting on the recommendations of the task force, the Government of India introduced a range of measures designed to stimulate the sector. These policy measures included: reducing tariffs and duties on imported IT-related equipment, easing foreign investment and exchange controls, tax and regulatory/bureaucratic exemptions, and providing the industry with greater access to finance (Economic Analytical Unit, 2001, p. 105). In many respects, the emergence of the Indian IT sector in the 1990s marked a new cooperative spirit between the public and private corporate sectors and helped to develop a revitalised sense of confidence in the country.

By the year 2001, the IT sector's total output had reached about US $10 billion and, until the meltdown in the global knowledge sector, software exports had risen to around US $6 billion—nearly 10 per cent of total national goods and services' exports. Sectoral growth rates were phenomenal. Between 1994–95 and 2000–01, the Indian IT industry grew at an average annual rate of 46 per cent. Using 1994 as a base year, software revenues had increased by 785 per cent by 2001 (Economic Analytical Unit, 2001, pp. 100–103). More than 800 firms within the sector were working with a clear vision to begin with small, feasible IT-related projects and then slowly climb up the value chain as the reputation of the company and the consequential image of the country as an IT centre became established. As some scholars have noted: 'By 2000, more than 200 of the fortune 1,000 companies were outsourcing their software requirements to Indian software houses, and in software services, "made in India" was becoming a sign of quality...' (Kapur and Ramamurti, 2001, p. 21). Moreover, the rapid growth of the Indian IT sector may well stimulate much needed inputs in terms of developing fundamental communication infrastructure (for instance, improvements in telephony systems and number of lines) that will allow for the Indian information 'revolution' to proceed to the next level. In this way, the international acclaim India has received for its excellence in the high-tech service sector within the short period of a decade also offers some potential for this success to be replicated in other affiliated sectors of the economy.

It is also important to note that the wider Indian corporate sector is undergoing a period of unprecedented change. Well-established corporate champions of the past have sometimes found it difficult to adapt to a much more ruthlessly competitive business climate, while a select group of companies, particularly within the 'knowledge' sector, have recorded phenomenal rates of growth. As Table 2 indicates, over the course of a decade, there has been a great deal of change in terms of the market valuations of leading companies, with new IT-related players such as Wipro and Infosys displacing formerly important manufacturing concerns.

Again, a snapshot of the value of leading Indian companies in 2011 is likely to be quite different to Table 2 and may well include a number of new corporate 'players'. In this respect, it is apparent that the relative stability that formerly characterized the Indian corporate scene has now given way to a more uncertain and volatile business climate.

Moreover, the growth of the IT industry is slowly beginning to shift the geographic centre of power within India's business culture. Whereas many of the diversified family conglomerates are headquartered in the Western 'megacity' of Mumbai (Bombay), the location of IT-related industries and their executive management headquarters are more dispersed.

Table 2: Ten Leading Indian Companies in 1992 and 2001
by Market Capitalization (US $ Billion)

Company	1992	Company	2001
Tisco	2.21	Hindustan Lever	10.30
ITC	1.20	Reliance Industries	8.84
Telco	1.14	Wipro	6.65
Century Textiles	1.13	Infosys Technologies	5.79
Hindustan Lever	0.89	Reliance Petroleum	4.65
Reliance Industries	0.77	ITC	4.29
Grasim	0.74	Oil & Natural Gas	4.05
GSFC	0.71	Indian Oil	2.73
ACC	0.67	State Bank of India	2.26
Colgate	0.57	HCL Technologies	2.22

Source: 'The Plot Thickens: A Survey of India's economy', *The Economist*, 2 June 2001.

As indicated in Table 3 industry appears to be developing in three major geographic 'hubs': Western India (Mumbai-Pune), a small section of the North (New Delhi-Noida) and, most significantly, in the states

Table 3: Leading Software Companies in India, 2000–2001

Firm	Location of HQ	Per cent Share of Industry Revenues
Tata Consulting Services	Mumbai	8.3
Wipro	Bangalore	5.2
Infosys Technologies	Bangalore	4.9
HCL Technologies	Noida	3.4
Satyam Computer Services	Secunderabad	3.4
IBM India	Bangalore	2.2
Cognizant Technology Solutions	Chennai	1.9
NIIT	New Delhi	1.8
Silverline	Mumbai	1.7
Pentasoft	Chennai	1.7
Total		34.5

Source: Economic Analytical Unit (2001, p. 103).

and cities of South India (Bangalore-Chennai-Hyderabad). Regional governments in these southern states have also played a significant role in corporate development through the establishment of state-of-the-art software technology parks. Bangalore's 'Electronic City' and Hyderabad's 'Cyber City' are not only comparable to global benchmarks but also link directly to leading educational institutions. A number of leading global IT companies, such as Microsoft and IBM, have invested in these regions because of proactive government policies at a state level. These regionally concentrated investments are only likely to intensify over forthcoming years.

Managerial Culture in Transition

Understanding culture and the values and social norms it enshrines is crucial in a rapidly globalizing context. Managers in India retain a strong orientation towards the cultural legacy of an ancient but continuously living and evolving civilization. However, superimposed on this legacy is the impact of changing technological and organizational systems. In India, cultural factors deeply influence many aspects of organizational, social, familial and religious life at the micro level, while, at the macro level, these cultural systems are beginning to adjust to the unavoidable realities of economic reform, communication technology and global-ization. In terms of their capacity to cope with these dramatic transform-ations, it is perhaps relevant that Indian managers have been noted for their ability to tolerate high levels of uncertainty and ambiguity—as indicated by research that shows that India is one of five countries with the lowest scores of 'uncertainty avoidance' out of an extensive sample of nations (Hofstede, 1991).

Almost five decades after gaining independence, a new generation has come into its own in India and has assumed a position of corporate and familial leadership. The worldview of this generation is much less ideology-driven than that of its predecessors, who were, typically, reared on stories of the sacrifice and idealism of heroic figures from the Indian nationalist movement. Several developments have caused a break with continuity, shifting values from selfless service and the pursuit of salva-tion to a 'here and now' approach, which is more focused upon individual self-interest and advancement (Chatterjee, 1998). In contrast with previous decades, entering a commercial profession is now seen to be the first, rather than the last, preference for many of India's 'best and brightest' graduates. In part, this is due to a widening gap between public and private sectors in terms of salary remuneration (Lawler et al., 1995). More generally, this change in perceptions is also due to a more general aspiration among the so-called 'great Indian middle class' towards entrepreneurial success and 'conspicuous' consumption.

In fact, the size and the quality of India's highly educated middle class, across a range of industry sectors, is a notable source of international competitiveness. As some observers have noted:

> None of the large Western companies investing in India are doing so simply for cheap labour, China's main lure. The more important attractions are India's large and increasingly open domestic market and the enormous pool of the skilled labour. More engineers graduate each year in India than in China and South Korea combined. That is why Motorola is planning to make India what it calls a "brain centre" for engineering and design work, and why Digital Equipment Corporation, Japanese subsidiary chose Indian software engineers, over its own Japanese employees, to write the tricky computer programs that translate English code into Japanese characters (*Forbes*, 1994: 132).

Moreover, there has also been a discernible shift in India towards valuing professional/technical personnel and inputs within the workplace. Thus, even the oldest of 'family' conglomerates are now keen to stress that their business operations are driven by dedicated teams of specialized professionals who have obtained their positions through their technical or managerial expertise. This trend has also been strengthened by the share-market listing of corporations, meaning that professional organizational and managerial structures and standards of corporate governance are subject to greater scrutiny.

In addition, Indian corporations and managers are beginning to create synergistic links with the social networks of the so-called Indian 'diaspora' living abroad. Overseas Indians and their associated social networks have become increasingly important and influential contributors in setting the managerial culture that predominates in various industries in India today. Again, the IT sector is leading the way in forging new technical and investment linkages. In particular, there are close connections between the IT industry in India and extensive networks of overseas Indians living, studying, and working in technology hubs in the United States such as Silicon Valley and key centres of higher learning. The growth of the IT sector in India, therefore, could be another indication, and even an agent of change, in relation to the growing influence of 'Anglo-American' models of management and corporate governance in India. In reviewing the development of the Indian economy in 2001, the *Economist* noted:

> Software engineers in Bangalore disport themselves on pristine campuses, fitted out with state-of-the-art gymnasiums. Call centres near Delhi equip themselves with spare telephone lines, back-up generators, and back-ups for the back-ups. Their quality standards, management styles and ideas of corporate governance owe more to western, especially American, models than to the traditions of Indian firms. The gleaming campus in Bangalore of Infosys, India's third-biggest information technology firm, has a golf green and a Domino's Pizza as the staff canteen. You might as well be in Silicon Valley. ('The Plot Thickens: A Survey of India's Economy', *Economist*, 2001).

As indicated, an increasing number of foreign businesses and MNCs are now establishing major operations in India. Again, their entry has introduced a new 'global' dynamic within Indian management culture as employees and local managers learn to operate within the broader context of the unique corporate cultures of these transnational business giants. Nonetheless, very often there is also an equivalent need for these corporations to adapt their marketing and management strategies to the local Indian context. This gradual adaptation often takes place through a painful process of 'trial and error' as international businesses identify the unique problems and opportunities of operating in an Indian context. Among others, these challenges include problems with infrastructure (power, telecommunications, transport); forging partnerships with government agencies; developing effective quality control and assurance programmes; and, perhaps most notably, accommodating differences between 'foreign' and Indian cultural norms and management styles.

With reference to the interplay between indigenous and international influences, some prominent scholars of Indian management strongly advocate that a paradigm shift in managerial values and assumptions does not necessarily imply a rejection of 'traditional' wisdom, ethical frameworks, and values (Chakraborty, 1998). These scholars suggest that, like the Japanese, Indian managerial values and goals need to arise out of deeply rooted social and ethical traditions. While 'tradition' is unmistakably observable in the daily lives of managers and employees across the country, work organizations appear to be at the crossroads. At least amongst senior-level Indian managers, there appears to be a parallel emergence of 'global' value paradigms (Chatterjee and Pearson, 2000a; Chatterjee and Pearson, 2000b).

Similarly, scholars of business culture have been debating theories of 'convergence' and 'divergence', as the influence of globalization takes hold. The convergence theorists argue that the emergence of a Western market-oriented economy inevitably leads to the adoption of values and culture associated with it (Bond and King, 1985; Webber, 1969; Child, 1981). In contrast, the divergence theorists argue that if the culture of the indigenous location is sufficiently powerful, it will retain its uniqueness in spite of the impact of broader factors of homogenization (Laurent, 1983; England and Lee, 1974). In contrast, anthropological 'acculturation' theorists suggest that the dynamic interaction of all of these influences often allow for the emergence of 'hybrid' forms of culture (Beals, 1953). Several research surveys of Asian managers have also contended that these business leaders are able to maintain a duality of values, one field of value formation is drawn from their own cultural heritage, while the other impacts on them through the wider forces of internationalization (Bedi, 1991). In the Indian context, it is thus possible to suggest that a hybrid blending of values is creating neither convergence nor divergence but a unique Indian managerial value system.

Managerial Challenges in Tomorrow's Economy

Many first wave peasant economies are still at the bottom. Second wave cheap labour, mass-manufacturing countries are in the middle. A single advanced Third wave country is on top. A third floor has been built on what until now was a two storied structure. Where in that three level house will India fit? That is the central question facing India (Toffler, 2003, p. 21).

In answering this rhetorical question, futurologist Toffler suggests that the managerial challenge before India is to expedite the application of

Third wave knowledge to the First and Second wave sectors for example, the application of genetics to the production of cotton, and the application of lasers, satellites, and computers thereby radically transforming agricultural outputs. In the areas where India has been successful in the last decade, including the IT sector, cheap labour has been the critical success element not managerial vision. Cheap labour as a source of success does not provide a secure future because of its substitutability by another country at anytime, the inevitable protectionist responses it encourages, and because the lower wage advantage is always at the mercy of technological breakthrough. The challenge of an economy moving away from 'cheap labour' is not merely in having an educated workforce. A knowledge economy requires opportunities to apply such knowledge. Global quality, for example, cannot be achieved unless quality is both recognized and institutionalized in the home market.

In tomorrow's economy, dominated by the Third wave mindset, managers will have to have a completely different approach to their functions and roles. Grand strategy-making and resource allocation will be insufficient without inspiration, empowerment, innovation, entrepreneurship and learning.

> Frontline managers, heading small, disaggregated and interdependent units focused on specific opportunities, are the company's entrepreneurs. They are the builders of the company's performance by continuously strengthening those business. Like coaches who leverage the strengths of individual players to build a winning team, senior level mangers link these separate businesses into a coherent, winning company (Ghoshal et al., 2001, p. xxiv).

As global linkages take hold across the organization, managerial challenges will have to be driven by learning and innovation. Capability for a world-class organization essentially emerges from the values, competencies and mindsets of new generation of managers. The challenge of upgrading employee skills and reorientation of mindsets is a formidable challenge for Indian managers with broad macro-level implications for a realignment of India's overall educational system.

> Japan's heroes work for Toyota, Sony and Honda; German heroes work for BMW, Audi and Mercedes. While we did not have national heroes in

our traditional exporting businesses, we did begin in the nineties to make
our software into national icons. People like Narayana Murthy and Azim
Premji increasingly became role models for the young. This is a welcome
development (Das, 2002, p. 262).

Mapping Transitions in Indian Management: Some Highlights

The articles in this book attempt to chart the fundamental and often
difficult transitions that are taking place in Indian management systems
today. The selected readings in the early part of the book consider in
depth many of the questions posed in our introduction—What is the
influence of cultural context and social norms? Have value orientations
begun to shift among Indian mangers given the new global context of
economic activity and social and informational flows? and, Is it possible
to facilitate cultural and organizational transitions that will nurture organizational innovations, individual leadership, and a new culture of entrepreneurial activity and energy in India?

Specific articles in this volume examine the critical issue of the culturally
embedded and yet, dynamic, ethical frameworks underpinning Indian
management systems. In some respects, the readings included in this
section are among the most provocative and thought provoking in the
entire volume. They also speak directly to one of the core themes outlined
in the introduction—What is unique about the evolving pattern of Indian
management?

An issue of paramount importance in India is the role of trade unions.
Unlike many East Asian countries, labor unions in India (as in many
other South Asian countries) exert considerable influence in determining
the work culture of both private and public sector organizations. Typically,
unions are organized on an industry-wide basis and often have local,
regional and national affiliations with powerful political parties.
The article by Anil Gupta and P. K. Sett examines the collective bargaining
environment in India and its implications. Articles eight and nine present
a range of views on the present state of human resource management,
training, and development in India. The article by Gupta, Koshal, and
Koshal addresses one of the most notable developments in Indian business,

the increasing participation and prominence of Indian women in business and managerial hierarchies.

All of the articles in this volume demonstrate, in different ways, the importance of a greater degree of vitality, responsiveness, vision, leadership, ethical commitment, organizational learning, and innovation on the part of Indian management culture if India is to truly achieve greater international competitiveness in the coming years.

References

Anon. 2001. 'The Plot Thickens: A Survey of India's Economy', *Economist*, 2 June.

Beals, R. 1953. 'Acculturation', in A. L. Krober (ed.), *Anthropology Today*, Chicago: University of Chicago Press.

Bedi, H. 1991. *Understanding Asian Managers*, Sydney, Australia: Allen & Unwin.

Budhawar, P. 2001. 'Doing Business in India', *Thunderbird International Business Review*, 43(4): 549–68.

Bond, M.H. and A.Y.C. King. 1985. Coping with the threat of westernisation in Hong Kong. *International Journal of Intercultural Relations*, 9, 351–64.

Chakraborty, S.K. 1998. *Values and Ethics for Organizations: Theory and Practice*, New Delhi: Oxford University Press.

Chatterjee, S.R. 1974. 'Some Aspects of Authority Patterns in Indian Organisations', *Indian Journal of Commerce*, December, pp. 1–20.

Chatterjee, S. R. and C. Pearson. 2000a. 'Indian Managers in Transition: Orientations, Work Goals, Values and Ethics', *Management International Review*, 40(1): 81–95.

Chatterjee, S.R. and C.A.L. Pearson. 2000b. 'Work Goals and Societal Value Orientations of Senior Indian Managers: An empirical analysis', *Journal of Management Development*, 19(7): 643–53.

Chatterjee, S. 1998. *Work Related Value Orientations of Indian Managers: An Empirical Investigation*, Management Centre for Human Values, Indian Institute of Management, Calcutta.

Child, J.D. 1981. 'Culture, Contingency and Capitalism in the Cross-National Study of Organisations', in L.L. Cummings and G.M. Staw (eds), *Research in Organisational Behaviour*, Greenwich: JAI Publications.

Chowdhry, K. 1966. 'Social and Cultural Factors in Management Development in India', *International Labour Review*, 92(2): 132–47.

Das, G. 2002. *The Elephant Paradigm: India Wrestles with Change*, New Delhi: Penguin Books.

Economic Analytical Unit 2001. *India: New Economy, Old Economy*, Canberra, Department of Foreign Affairs and Trade, Commonwealth of Australia.

England, G.W. and R. Lee. 1974. 'The Relationship between Managerial Values and Managerial Success in the United States, Japan, India and Australia', *Journal of Applied Psychology*, 59: 411–19.

Forbes. 1994. *Now We are our own Masters*, May 23, 153(11): 128–38.

Ghoshal, S., G. Piramal and C.A. Bartlett. 2000. *Managing Radical Change: What Indian Companies must do to become World-class*, India: Viking.

Ghoshal, S., G. Piramal and S. Budhiraja. 2001. *World Class in India: A Casebook of Companies in Transformation*, New Delhi: Penguin Books.

Gopinath, C. 1998. 'Alternative Approaches to Indigenous Management in India', *Management International Review*, 38(3): 257–75.

Hofstede, G. and M. Bond. 1988. 'The Confucian Connection: From Cultural Roots to Economic Growth, *Organisational Dynamics*, 16(4): 5–21.

Hofstede, G. 1991. *Cultures and Organisations*, McGraw-Hill, London.

Hooke, G. 2003. Asian Economics in Coming Decades, Unpublished Report, University of International Business and Economics, Beijing.

International Institute for Management Development. 2000. *The World Competitiveness Scoreboard*, Lausanne, Switzerland.

Kakar S. 1977. 'Authority Patterns and Subordinate Behaviour in Indian Organisations', *Administrative Science Quarterly*, 16.

Kapur, D. and R. Ramamurti. 2001. 'India's Emerging Competitive Advantage in Services', *The Academy of Management Executive*, 15(2): 20–33.

Laurent, A. 1983. 'The Cultural Diversity of Western Conceptions of Management'. *International Studies of Management and Organisations*, 13, 75–96.

Lawler, J. J., H.C. Jain, C.S. Venkataratnam and V. Atmiyanandana. 1995. 'Human Resource Management in Developing Economies: A Comparison of India and Thailand', *International Journal of Human Resource Management*, 6(2): 319–46.

Lithgow, L. 2000. *Special Blend: Fusion Management from Asia and the West*, New York: John Wiley and Sons.

Paul, A. 2002. Can India catch up? *Fortune*, 9: 32–40.

Purie, A. 2003. 'Global Giant or Global Pygmy'?, *India Today*, 17 March (Special Issue).

Ralston, D.A., D.J. Gustafson, F.M. Cheung and R.H. Terpstra. 1993. 'Difference in Managerial Values: A Study of U.S., Hong Kong and PRC Managers', *Journal of International Business Studies* 10(1): 249–75.

Singh, J.P. 1990. 'Managerial Culture and Work-related values in India', *Organizational Studies*, 11(1): 75–101.

Sinha, J.B.P. 1991. *Work Culture in the Indian Context*, New Delhi: Sage.

Sparrow, P.R. and P.S. Budhawar. 1997. 'Competition and Change: Mapping the Indian HRM Recipe Against World-Wide Patterns', *Journal of World Business*, 32(3): 224–42.

Toffler, A. 2003. *Tomorrow's Economy*. India Today, Special Conclave Issue. March 17, pp. 20–22.

Webber, R.H. 1969. 'Convergence or Divergence', *Columbia Journal of World Business*, 4(3): 75–83.

World Bank. 2001. *World Development Report*, New York: Oxford University Press.

2 The Influence of Indian National Culture on Organizations

Mark Heuer

Most observers would agree that the national culture of India differs fundamentally from the Euro-American baseline often used for evaluating business strategy and performance. But how and why is India different? And do India's cultural differences matter in terms of economic growth and participation in the globalization of the world economy?

An initial observation would be that India, in the parlance of national culture researchers, is more collective and accepts higher power distance than the US and many European countries (Hofstede, 1980). Why is this? The immediate explanation could be that Indians retain a stronger identity to family and religious values, which cause Indian society to retain traditional ties. But how does that explain the success of the increasingly sophisticated software industry in India and the educational system in India that provides a large supply of highly trained technical personnel? On the other hand, depending on the Indian state involved, employers in smaller businesses reportedly still accrue and delay wages of employees in order to make them highly dependent on their bosses (Sinha, 2000).

There are many pieces to this puzzle. The purpose of this article is to explore the dynamic nature of India's national culture and how the organizational culture, values and management practices are evolving in response to environmental influences, such as economic liberalization and globalization. For example, different types of organizations, such as MNCs, as well as private and public Indian organizations, may accept or synthesize cultural adjustment differently than others. Certain industries, such as software, experience rapid growth and integration into the global marketplace while others retain indigenous management practices. These issues will be explored here, followed by an attempt to explain the influences on Indian management culture from the perspective of three management theories: resource dependence, resource-based view of the firm and institutional theory.

National Culture: An Indian Perspective

Despite the importance of cross-cultural management issues, most past studies have not been concerned with cultural distance at both the national and organizational levels. Following Pothukuchi, Damanpour, Choi, Chen and Park (2002), this article evaluates culture at both levels by operationalizing national culture in terms of values and organizational culture in terms of management practices.

Hofstede's (1980) values dimensions are a common approach for operationalizing national culture in terms of values. While Pearson and Chatterjee (2001) argue that Hofstede's five dimensions of national culture may no longer be suitable because they were developed in an era with different environmental imperatives, this article uses Hofstede's measures as a baseline for comparison due to the widespread recognition and application of these dimensions. Hofstede's four dimensions (along with a fifth which was later identified) can be described as follows:

- **Individualism-Collectivism:** the extent to which ties between individuals are loose versus a society in which people are integrated into strong, cohesive groups. Individualism implies a loosely knit social framework in which people are expected to take care of their immediate families and themselves, while Collectivism involves a tight social framework in which people expect those in the in-group (family and organizations) to look out for them in exchange for strong loyalty.
- **Power distance:** the extent to which people believe that power and status are distributed unequally and accept an unequal distribution of power.
- **Masculinity-femininity:** the extent to which society values achievement versus affiliation. Masculinity characterises a society in which assertiveness and merit-based reward practices are commonly

accepted and supported, as opposed to a more feminine society in which quality of work life and interpersonal relationships receive more emphasis in the workplace.

- **Uncertainty avoidance:** the extent to which people are threatened by uncertain, unknown or unstructured situations. Career stability, formal rules and procedures, attainment of expertise and belief in absolute truths are characteristic of a society with high uncertainty avoidance. Newman and Nollen (1996) indicate that uncertainty avoidance may be an artifact of the time during which Hofstede did his research and may not be relevant in Asian countries.

- Hofstede and Bond (1988) also identified **Long-term orientation** as an additional dimension. It refers to the extent to which a society values patience, perseverance and a sense of obedience and duty towards the larger good.

National culture can be described as the collective programming of a group of people with common experiences, such as political and educational systems, at the national level. Hofstede (1991) refers to this as software of the mind. For Indian managers, as well as those wishing to manage multinational corporations or other concerns in India, national culture is important in understanding what factors will motivate employees in India in order for organizations to enjoy sustainable performance. Neelankavil, Mathur and Zhang (2000) argue that understanding differences in values and values dimensions has a profound impact on effective cross-cultural management. They reason that values dimensions such as individualism relate to a variety of constructs in the social sciences, such as self-actualization and security needs, and are crucial to explaining cross-cultural differences in management. This argument is valid both in terms of using national culture value dimensions as a baseline approach, as well as in understanding a rapidly changing environment and the implications this has on values measurements (Pearson and Chatterjee, 2001)

On a foundational level, comparisons of national culture dimensions should assist managers assess the risks inherent in a 'one size fits all' approach to global human resource management. From a more fine-grained perspective, such comparisons can be useful in understanding how to motivate personnel in individual countries and to track and adjust for possible changes. For example, Neelankavil et al. (2000) evaluate national culture similarities and differences in a study of middle-level managers in India, China, the Philippines and the United States. A key factor in this study is that while India, China and the Philippines are Asian, the amount of Western influence in each is markedly different. The differing degree of Western influence allows the examination of culture on job evaluation and motivation using the US as a benchmark.

The measurement of individualism-collectivism provides a key result of the study, with China and the US on opposite ends and with India and the Philippines in between. India, the Philippines and the US rank relatively close on uncertainty avoidance (40, 44 and 46 respectively, based on a 0–100 scale), while China is at 69. Masculinity-femininity is also similar with India, the Philippines and the US at 56, 64 and 62 respectively, while China is at 45. Neelankavil et al. (2000) explain this result based on China's weaker exposure to Western management practices, while India and the Philippines show a mix of Asian traits and Western management practices in their results. In the case of India, in particular, Neelankavil et al. reason that national culture has evolved into a hybrid approach toward management practices. They reason that India is rooted in a framework of transcendent ideology. As a result, there is a primary mode of behaviour supported by the traditional Indian approach, as well as a secondary mode supported by Western influence. This leads to unique superior-subordinate relationships, work behaviour and management practices in India. In essence, this study shows that Asian countries are not all the same despite some geographic similarities based on input from middle-level managers.

Additionally, in a study comparing Indian CEOs with US CEOs, Kakar, Kakar, deVries and Vrignaud (2002) raise the issue of whether the Westernisation of Indian firms has a significant impact on the leadership practices of the Indian executive. Their research utilises a Leadership Practices Inventory to identify how Indian hybrid organisations differ from its US counterparts. They reason that power distance, viewed as the tendency to idealize the leader of an organization, remains a significant difference between Indian and US organisations.

So, what does this mean for managers? The results suggest that managers are socialised by their own national culture, regardless of management level in an organization, and tend to develop values, beliefs, behaviours and practices that are compatible with the main features of that national culture (Gopalan and Rivera, 1997). As an example, Gopalan and Rivera (1997) cite a cross-national study of US and Indian salespersons

in which US salespersons responded negatively to organisation formalization and bureaucratic structures, whereas Indian salespersons reacted
favourably by demonstrating a higher level of work commitment and
reduced work alienation. The study theorises that differences in the socialization process may explain the response, as American salespersons are
socialised in a culture characterized by low power distance and a high
degree of individualism. They dislike authority, conformity and close
supervision. Conversely, Indian salespersons are raised in an environment
emphasizing high degrees of collective dependence and power distance and
respond favourably to tighter control and supervision (Agarwal, 1993).

Similarly, Tan and Khoo (2002) note that as the expansion of India's
economy heralds the mass adoption of Western technology, knowledge
and management systems, cultural management has to be considered
because knowledge of a host country's culture-related values are crucial
for managing the best results from every employee. It also reduces the
potential for misunderstanding and conflict between management and
the workforce. Cultural management is particularly important in India,
as it is a deeply religious nation where its people display behaviours that
are highly influenced by religious norms, values and beliefs.

Indian society demonstrates a high power-distance culture. This means
that workers prefer authoritative and hierarchical forms of management.
They also respond favourably to close supervision. Bosses are expected
to demonstrate powerful personalities and be authoritative. Managers
who demonstrate a high 'power figure' type of behaviour are more likely
to gain the respect of subordinates. Clear and direct orders are preferred
(Tan and Khoo, 2002). According to Sinha and Kanungo (1997), the
lack of clear job descriptions and expectations, fluid timeframes, or
ambiguity in job objectives, affect negatively the work behaviour of Indian
employees. In order to create worker enthusiasm and motivation, clear
job descriptions and detailed instructions need to be provided.

The meaning of work for Indian workers is more than what one
accomplishes in one's job. Indian workers greatly value good relationships
between superiors and subordinates. Such relationships are highly power-
based with leaders or managers as the power figures. It is common practice
in India for subordinates to show reverence and respect towards their
superiors. In return, subordinates expect their leaders' protection, concern
and support (Sinha and Kanungo, 1997).

The Western-style manager, on the other hand, places the highest importance on driving the workforce towards developing self-initiative, creativity and intrapreneurship in their jobs (DeVries, 1998). Indian workers may view the democratic management styles adopted by charismatic-type Western leaders as a sign of managerial weakness or incompetence (Gopalan and Rivera, 1997).

Environmental Influences of National Culture

The traditional American relationship vis-à-vis nature has been one of dominance although there is an increasing emphasis on conservation and ecological awareness, suggesting a trend towards living in harmony with nature. In this dominance approach, the majority of Americans believe that natural resources and elements can and should be utilised for the benefit of mankind. Science and technology are considered allies used to minimise or mitigate the effects of disease, pestilence, drought, floods and earthquakes. This dominance over nature and other elements has resulted in most Americans having an internal locus of control. Responsibility and accountability lie with the individual and outcomes cannot be shifted to an unknown supernatural force. This tendency towards an internal locus of control carries over to goal-setting practices in organizations along with a belief that individuals with a strong internal locus of control are more likely to actively pursue, and thus achieve, their goals than are those with an external locus of control (Gopalan and Stahl, 1998).

Traditional cultures such as those found in India socialise people to be predisposed towards an external locus of control. Individuals with an external locus of control believe that humankind is basically helpless in influencing life's events, which are largely controlled by fate and/or by supernatural forces that are largely beyond human control. Even if individuals in the Indian corporate environment can intellectually relate to and understand the basic premise behind goal-setting practices, to what extent will they be effective in implementing such practices over the long run if it is not positively reinforced by societal values? Can advanced education neutralise and overcome the force of fatalism? Will exposure to international management practices neutralise the effects of national culture allowing Indian employees to develop a strong internal locus of control? Although India has one of the largest pool of well qualified and talented scientists, technicians and other professionals in the world, it lags behind several countries in both basic and cutting-edge research in many areas. While some may attribute this phenomenon to lack of resources and other structural issues, an alternative explanation may be that it could be due to a lack of adequate positive reinforcement from society. It is reasonable to hypothesise that Indian scientists and other professionals working in the US and other Western countries are able to have a high level of achievement not only because of access to superior resources, but also because of the prevailing mindset that encourages and nurtures an internal locus of control (Gopalan and Stahl, 1998).

Organizational Culture: The Link to Management Practice

Newman and Nollen (1996) note that the key competitive advantage derived from correctly adapted management practices comes from align-ment between key characteristics of the external environment (national culture in this case) and internal strategy, structure, systems and practices. For managers of MNCs, the implications are that adaptation to local cultural conditions is necessary to achieve high-performance outcomes. Corporate initiatives that are created at headquarters and promoted worldwide run the risk of conflicting with unreceptive national cultures. The US, with its extreme values of individualism, is a particular example as management practices such as employee participation, merit-based systems and individual responsibility are likely to be unwise in countries culturally unlike the US. In essence, Newman and Nollen (1996), in their study of financial results of work units in 18 countries on three continents, found that management practices should be adapted to the local culture to be most effective.

In practice, Mendonca and Kanungo (1996) note that organizations in developing countries—traditionally those in the private sector and, more recently, public sector organizations—have invested considerable resources, time and effort to adopt state-of-the-art human resources man-agement practices developed in Europe and North America. While the poor management practices, bureaucratic inefficiencies and low produc-tivity evident in many of the organizations creates pressure to adopt quick solutions, the effectiveness of this approach is open to serious questions.

Mendonca and Kanungo point to mounting evidence against the indiscriminate transfer to developing countries of techniques and practices based on Western thought and value systems.

Socialization of Work Relationships

As mentioned in the discussion on individualism-collectivism, Indians are socialized in a culture where an individual derives his/her identity based on family and caste membership. It is not uncommon to see Indians sacrifice or defer their individual goals for the collective goals of the family or a larger collective entity. Additionally, age and seniority are given great respect in India (Gopalan and Stahl, 1998). Conversely, socialization practices in the US stress independence over dependence and ascendancy of individual rights over group goals and aspirations (Gopalan and Stahl, 1998).

Developing this relational context further, Gopalan and Rivera (1997) draw on the five categories of value orientations based on Kluckhohn and Strodtbeck (1961). While Hofstede's value dimensions deal with society in general, Kluckhohn and Strodtbeck can be used to relate national culture to organizational culture in a context more specific to India. These value orientations are:

Human Nature

Most Indians are socialized to believe that their present nature and current state of affairs are unchangeable and a result of their actions and lifestyles in previous births. Qualities and personality traits possessed by individuals are ascribed to the particular caste that they are born into. Consequently, less effort is focused on improving one's present situation than in Western cultures.

Man-Nature

A widespread belief is that life's events are predetermined and controlled by supernatural forces external to an individual. Consequently, most Indians tend to have an external locus of control and subjugate themselves to nature. This disposition may negatively impact qualities such as ambition, work ethic and persistence. In contrast, many Westerners believe they can control nature and their own destiny.

Time

Indians are oriented towards the past and view time as an infinite entity. This orientation toward time causes tremendous pressure to conform to traditional practices and beliefs. This view contrasts with the Western focus on the future which translates into a preference for planning, scheduling and a sense of urgency.

Relational

As discussed in terms of power dominance, most Indians prefer hierarchical relationships, which may be a consequence of the caste system. These relationships, supported by the caste system often extend to business in which there is strong mutual support based on caste membership. This can lead to hiring in a company or industry based on caste. Whereas other cultures tend to hire more based on skill sets dominating a particular industry.

How, then, do value orientations influence employee motivation and organizational culture as a whole? Western management practices support the belief that employees are motivated when they are given a greater degree of autonomy, responsibility and control over their work and they lose motivation when placed in a highly bureaucratic, structured and controlled environment.

As mentioned previously, Mendonca and Kanungo (1996) suggest there is mounting evidence that argues against the indiscriminant transfer to developing countries of techniques and practices based on Western thought and value systems. Programmes that are highly successful in the industrialized, developed countries of the West can, and often do, fail in the developing countries because of incongruence with the internal work culture. Thus, while an employee's job performance will benefit in any culture from goal-setting, performance feedback and valued rewards, the manner in which these practices are carried out is where problems arise (Mendonca and Kanungo, 1996). In particular, management practices that are favoured in the US, such as employee participation, individual responsibility, merit-based rewards, and short-term approaches, are likely to be unwise in countries such as India that are culturally unlike the US. A mismatch between work-unit management practices and national culture is likely to reduce performance. As mentioned previously, Newman and Nollen (1996) note that the issue of fit is especially salient for US managers because the US has extreme values for both individualism and long-term orientation cultural dimensions. They conclude that the competitive advantage derived from correctly adapted management practices comes from alignment between key characteristics of the external environment and internal strategy, structure, systems and practices.

The globalization of business will have a tremendous impact on life-styles and role relationships in developing countries such as India. For example, as MNCs establish operations in what are previously 'closed economies', they will begin to affect tradition and culture (Gopalan and Stahl, 1998). As there is a striking difference in culture and values espoused by large tradition-bound organizations and new global organizations, Chatterjee and Pearson (2000a) reason that the core beliefs and values of an ancient and complex society with a massive rural population need to be sharpened to make them context relevant rather than be replaced by wholesale imported values. Indian managers are combining traditional values and dimensions of the contemporary global market imperatives in a unique way. In fact, Chatterjee and Pearson reason that Indian managers may encompass the 'crossvergent values' concept developed by Ralston, Holt, Terpstra and Kai-Cheng (1997), which occurs when both national culture influences and economic ideology form a unique value system. In fact, for many Indian managers, cross-vergence means that the modern technological and globalized world does, in fact, exist, but does not extend beyond the boundaries of their professional role. Indian managers may not synergise divergent values in a terminal sense but may rearrange their work goals and related values in different layers at different points of time (Chatterjee and Pearson, 2000a). In a study of over 400 senior Indian managers from the public and private sector, Chatterjee and Pearson (2000b) found that managers participating in the study viewed their society as being in transition, and the focus is on how to be successful in a market economy and less on goals that were important prior to economic reform. In particular, the study found that an emphasis on learning and market responsiveness is displacing goals of stability, tradition and security.

India in a Global Business Context: Organizational Responses

As discussed in this article, Indian management practices are undergoing a significant shift in response to economic liberalization and global business integration. The response to these forces appears to differ based on type of organizations, industry segment and geography. Additionally, perceptual differences may be apparent based on the managerial level of the individuals (e.g., middle or senior management). In this final section the differences will be discussed while also providing a theoretical context to explain, on an exploratory basis, the reasons for the differences.

Indian organizations, from an organizational perspective, can be broadly grouped under three categories: Western industrialized firms, which include joint ventures/subsidiaries of MNCs; hybrid firms, which are medium-to-large, family-dominated firms and may be involved in joint ventures with Western firms; and, indigenous firms, which include small-to-medium enterprises and may provide ancillary support services to larger firms (Gopinath, 1998). Additionally, public and private organizations in India should be differentiated in terms of organizational culture. In all cases, the multiplicity of languages prevalent in India must be recognized. There are 15 major languages in India with distinct scripts, traditions and literature. This poses challenges for the cross-fertilization of management ideas in India and may contribute to differing degrees of convergence in terms of management practices (Gopinath, 1998).

Gopalan and Stahl (1998) suggest that as MNCs (Western industrialized firms) establish operations in previously 'closed economies', such as India, they will affect tradition and culture. Compared to domestic firms (hybrid and indigenous firms), MNCs may be more inclined to hire women, pay higher salaries and promote them to managerial positions. They also speculate that as the use of English, use of the Internet and familiarity with Western modes of education become more widespread, Indian managers will develop a hybrid or crossvergence approach to management that will combine indigenous and imported methods. In particular, Gopalan and Stahl identify loyalty, an integral Indian value, as a management value that may be retained because it maintains and fosters an environment of trust necessary to build effective business relationships. On the other hand, equal employment opportunity practices may lead to hiring the most qualified person for a job, as opposed to preferential hiring of family members or relatives, which is more of an established practice in indigenous firms.

Another impact of liberalization and the greater involvement of MNCs is an increased level of competition of Indian firms with the MNCs. This has raised concerns about total quality management, workforce skills and pressure to change from indigenous, costly and probably less effective technology to more effective technology applications (Sparrow and Budhwar, 1996). Nevertheless, Hofstede (1993) asserts that development cannot be pressure-cooked. Liberalization and globalization require a cultural infrastructure, which takes time to develop. Hofstede concludes that local management must be part of this infrastructure; it cannot be imported in package form.

In contrast to larger (hybrid) organizations, which are more able to influence their environments, smaller organizations are affected by their environment, by the community as well as the values, beliefs and assumptions prevalent in their environment. This environment often involves pervasive poverty, inadequate infrastructure facilities, a weak industrial base and underdeveloped human resources (Sinha, 2000).

Kamdar (2002) also identifies regional differences in Indian work culture, such as Maharashtra, where worker unions are known for their aggressive stance; Kerala, where employees are highly literate; and Gujarat, where the society's norm of relaxation spills over into the work culture for at least three hours during the afternoons. The regionalization issue contributes to the growth of industries in certain areas. For example, India's software industry has been growing at a 50 per cent rate for the better part of a decade with more than 800 firms located in cities like Bangalore, Hyderabad, Pune, Chennai and New Delhi providing a range of software services, mostly targeted at foreign customers (Kapur and Ramamurti, 2001).

Pertaining to industries, Kapur and Ramamurti (2001) pose the question: how has a country whose economic achievements were otherwise modest, managed to develop a reputation for excellence in this rapidly growing high-tech sector? Software makes extensive use of resources in which India is at a comparative advantage. India produces the second largest annual output of scientists and engineers in the world, behind only the US. The cost of an Indian software engineer is one-half to one-fourth that of an American engineer. Additionally, Indian engineers are trained in English, which gives them a decisive advantage over their Chinese counterparts.

India's success with software has spilled over into other knowledge-based industries such as pharmaceuticals and biotechnology, attracting investments from MNCs, while also serving as a source of talent abroad, where technical workers may collaborate with others back home in India. Both of these developments provide the opportunity for building competitive advantage through intellectual capital.

Challenges and Opportunities for Growth through Resource Advantages

From the perspective of the organization, India seems to be straddling two currents of economic development which can be explained by strategic management theory. One is that of resource dependence, or the need to access needed resources through strategic interactions (Andrews, 1971) in order to nurture ongoing growth. Another is the Resource Based View of the Firm (Barney, 1991), which involves developing resources and capabilities into a sustainable competitive advantage. As discussed previously, various types of organizations have responded differently to economic liberalization and globalization. The Resource Based View of the Firm suggests that Indian firms able to develop sustainable competitive advantages build rare, unique combinations of capabilities and resources. The resources could be accessed through alliances or joint ventures with MNCs, and can bridge opportunities with Indians working abroad with entrepreneurial and technical capabilities. In essence, resource dependence involves accessing needed resources and capabilities from external sources, while the Resource Based View of the Firm involves developing the resources into unique combinations internally. For the computer software industry, India already possesses a resource advantage through an available pool of trained technical specialists with lower labour costs than the US and other developed countries. Additionally, Indians working overseas may offer the intellectual resources needed to address resource gaps. Other industries, however, are limited by a lack of access to resources. These constraints come in many forms, not all of which are economic.

Acting as a potential constraint or facilitator of these firm-level efforts are the more macro issues of government, social tradition and national culture. These forces have the potential to provide opportunities or constraints to Indian firms and managers in their efforts to adjust to liberalization and globalization. From an institutional theory perspective, Meyer and Scott (1983) note that shared belief systems and relational frameworks come together in complex and shifting ways, in that they may be mutually supportive or they may work in opposition.

Taken together, resource dependence, the Resource Based View of the Firm and institutional theory provide the theoretical support to evaluate organizational culture and Indian management practice. While in the medium to long term, India may emerge as a leading provider of knowledge-based tradable services, there remains the politics, Indian style, described by Kapur and Ramamurti (2001) as 'cacophonous and fractious, playing itself out in one of the most socially heterogeneous societies in the world, with sharp social inequities, a corrupt and inefficient bureaucracy, and poor accountability of political actors.' As an indication, there have been four general elections and six prime ministers in the last decade. On the plus side, India has systemic stability anchored by deep-rooted, democratic institutions, which is one of the reasons why coalition politics both nationally and in the states is so evident. Also, there is the large and sophisticated network of educational institutes which supply the human capital required by the software industry. Many of these graduates migrate to the US for higher education and jobs and form a part of the social network that nurtures the Indian software industry (Kapur and Ramamurti, 2001). The factors that support growth of industries in India rely on cultural adaptiveness. The upgrading of India's roads, ports, power supply and rail transportation has not been able to support growth for other industries in the way that telecommunications links and air have been able to support software. Finally, from a corporate culture perspective, the IT sector has affected Indian capitalism, because the corporate culture and business practices of India's IT firms are vastly superior to those of India's traditional business houses. Conversely, Indian IT firms have been at the forefront of improved corporate governance.

From the perspective of organizational culture and management practices, India is a country in transition with vast potential and challenges, very significant accomplishments, but also respect for the past and social traditions. Future research could build on propositions involving resource dependence, the Resource Based View of the Firm and institutional theory as a way to identify various strands of Indian national culture and their influence on organizational culture and management practice. Comparisons of various industries from the perspective of these theoretical approaches could differentiate among the industries and help better understand the challenges ahead during this transition period.

References

Agarwal, S. 1993. 'Influence of Formalization on Role Stress, Organizational Commitment, and Work Alienation of Salespersons: A Cross-national Comparative Study', *Journal of International Business Studies*, 24: 715–39.

Andrews, K.R. 1971. *The Concept of Corporate Strategy*. Homewood, IL: Irwin.

Barney, J.B. 1991. 'Looking Inside for Competitive Advantage', *Journal of Management*, 9(4): 49–61.

Chatterjee, S.R. and C.A.L. Pearson. 2000(a). 'Indian Managers in Transition: Orientations, Work Goals, Values and Ethics', *Management International Review*, 1: 81–95.

———. 2000(b). 'Work Goals and Societal Value Orientations of Senior Indian Managers: An Empirical Analysis', *Journal of Management Development*, 19(7): 643–53.

De Vries, M.K. 1998. 'Charisma in Action: The Transformational Abilities of Virgin's Richard Branson and ABB's Percy Barnevik', *Organizational Dynamics*, 26(3): 7–21.

Gopalan, S. and J.B. Rivera. 1997. 'Gaining a Perspective on Indian Value Orientations: Implications for Expatriate Managers', *International Journal of Organizational Analysis*, 5(2): 156–79.

Gopalan, S. and A. Stahl. 1998. 'Application of American Management Theories and Practices to the Indian Business Environment: Understanding the Impact of National Culture', *American Business Review*, 16(2): 30–42.

Gopinath, C. 1998. 'Alternative Approaches to Indigenous Management in India', *Management International Review*, 38(3): 257–76.

Hofstede, G. 1980. *Culture's Consequences*, Beverly Hills: Sage.

———. 1991. *Cultures and Organizations: Software of the Mind*. Berkshire, England: McGraw-Hill.

———. 1993. Cultural Constraints in Management Theories, *The Academy of Management Executive*, 7(1): 81–94.

Hofstede, G. and Bond, M.H. 1988. 'The Confucius Connection: From Cultural Roots to Economic Growth', *Organization Dynamics*, 16: 4–21.

Kakar, S., S. Kakar, M.F.R. Kets de Vries and P. Vrignaud. 2002. 'Leadership in Indian Organizations from a Comparative Perspective', *International Journal of Cross-Cultural Management*, 2(2): 239–50.

Kamdar. (2002). 'Patterns of Work Culture: Cases and Strategies for Culture Building', *Asia Pacific Journal of Management*, 19(1).

Kapur, D. and R. Ramamurti. 2001. 'India's Emerging Competitive Advantage in Services', *The Academy of Management Executive*, 15(2): 20–33.

Kluckhorn, C.L. and E.L. Strodtbeck. 1961. *Variations in Value Orientations*. Evanston, IL: Row, Peterson and Company.

Mendonca, M. and R. Kanungo. 1996. 'Impact of Culture on Performance Management in Developing Countries', *International Journal of Manpower*, 17(4–5): 65–73.

Meyer, J. and R. Scott. 1983. *Organizational Environments: Ritual and Rationality*, Beverly Hills, CA: Sage Publications.

Neelankavil, J.P., A. Mathur and Y. Zhang. 2000. 'Determinants of Managerial Performance: A Cross-cultural Comparison of the Perceptions of Middle-level Managers in Four Countries', *Journal of International Business Studies*, 31(1): 121–41.

Newman, K.L. and S.D. Nollen. 1996. 'Culture and Congruence: The Fit Between Management Practice and National Culture', *Journal of International Business Studies*, 27(4): 753–79.

Pearson, C.A.L. and S.R. Chatterjee. 2001. 'Perceived Societal Values of Indian Managers: Some Empirical Evidence of Responses to Economic Reform', *International Journal of Social Economics*, 28(4): 368–76.

Pothukuchi, V., F. Damanpour, J. Choi, C.C. Chen and S.H. Park. 2002. 'National and Organizational Culture Differences and International Joint Venture Performance', *Journal of International Business Studies*, 33(2): 243–66.

Ralston, D.A., D.H. Holt, R.H. Terpstra and Y. Kai-Cheng. 1997. 'The Impact of National Culture and Economic Ideology on Managerial Work Values: A Study of the United States, Russia, Japan, and China', *Journal of International Business Studies*, 28(1): 177–207.

Sinha, J.B.P. 2000. '*Patterns of Work Culture: Cases and Strategies for Culture Building*', New Delhi: Sage Publications.

Sinha, J.B.P. and R.N. Kanungo. 1997. 'Context Sensitivity and Balancing in Indian Organizational Behavior', *International Journal of Psychology*, 32(2): 93–105.

Sparrow, P.R. and P.S. Budhwar. 1996. 'HRM in the New Economic Environment: An Empirical Study of India', *Management Research*, 19(4–5): 30–35.

Tan, K.C. and H.H. Khoo. 2002. Indian Society, Total Quality and the Rajiv Gandhi National Quality Award, *The Journal of Management*, 21(5–6): 417–27.

Section Two

INDIAN MANAGEMENT CULTURE IN TRANSITION

An Overview of the Culture of Management in India

In spite of the converging forces of globalisation, local contextual imperatives still remain a major managerial challenge for cross-national work organisations. The cultural uniqueness of a country is a variable in the development of a major strategic platform for any industry or any company with ambition to expand beyond national boundaries. This is specifically relevant to a high-context society like India where the various macro-level initiatives need unique cultural understanding for diffusion to the 'meso' and 'micro' levels. There has been a continuing debate on the cultural influences not only in terms of conceptual validity but also in terms of characteristics such as industry type, social and administrative heritage, educational and demographic profiles, etc. The complex, multi-faceted construct of 'culture' can only be categorised and compared from a very limited range of theoretical frames in management literature.

An alternative understanding of the diversity across cultures and their meaningful conceptualisation may be obtained through the experiences of large-scale economic reform and managerial reorientations as local adaptations and resilience are studied. The globalisation advantage postulates cultural diversity as a source of potential benefit that enhances the building of a global mindset. The two articles of this part underpin the essential competencies of 'learning' and 'adapting' as the deeply contested notion of corporate globalisation takes hold and a distinctive Indian brand of management emerges.

The chapters by Neelankavil, Mathur and Zhang included in this section emphasise 'learning' in the specific context of India's recent transformations and the dynamics of the institutional forces that strongly influence these. The chapter by Tayeb (Chapter Four) demonstrates the 'adaptability' of ideas of the determination of managerial performance in three Asian countries. Here, Tayeb presents a number of illustrations of positive developments in India's economic competitiveness in recent years. The paper contends forcefully that the human resource quality and the infrastructural investment by the government have been able to provide the pre-requisite to building the strategic success of many national and global companies. Some commentators have described India more as an 'elephant' economy which is large, strong and intelligent, but not as agile and dynamic as the smaller Asian 'tiger' counterparts.

The article by Tayeb extends beyond an analysis of the strategic foundations initiated in recent decades by the government. Besides an emphasis on innovative physical and social infrastructure and the adoption of forword-looking fiscal and monetary policies, ensuring the continuity and stability of such policies across successive democratically elected governments has been a remarkable feature of governance in recent years. Against this background of macro-level reform agenda, the weakness of managerial level internalisation has been a serious criticism of the Indian progress. Neelankavil et al. on the other hand explore this common criticism by introducing a research study on the perceptions of middle-level managers in India, China and the Philippines as a contrast to USA in terms of the determinants of managerial performance. Confirmation of the postulation can be found in many research studies of recent years. For example, a well known scholar and executive distilled his thoughts as,

My experience as a consultant to a dozen Indian companies during the past decade is that while many have acquired a reasonably robust strategy, they implement poorly. I am also associated with a venture capital fund that has invested in fifteen Indian companies in information technology, and its experience is the same—the best successful firms are not the ones with the best business model that those with execution ability (Das, 2002; pp. 139–40).

Numbers of scholars, management consulting firms and social commentators have been highlighting the paradox demonstrated by Indian managers evidenced through a glaring gap between the sophisticated skills in strategy development as against its implementation. The trend of global companies working closely with their Indian counterparts has been accelerating this process. Neelankavil et al. highlight that in order to achieve success as a company, industry or country, competencies and values, performances of managers need to be aligned to gain a quantum synergy. This is particularly relevant to the lack of national accountability of the under-performing public sector. In spite of emerging national consensus in terms of global market orientation, the reality is that more than 80 per cent of the top 25 companies in India are still in the public sector domain.

The two chapters of this part provide an overview of where the journey of transformation began, what some of the recent trends have been and some indication of how the managerial mindset of performance orientation may be taking shape in India. It is to be noted that a decade ago India had about the same GDP as China while it is almost double for China today. Is this sudden tearing away of the Chinese due to a performance focus? Or, does it have the cultural context as an explanation?

Reference

Das, G. (2002). *The Elephant Paradigm: India Wrestles with Change*, Penguin Books, pp. 139–40.

Determinants of Managerial Performance: A Cross-cultural Comparison of the Perceptions of Middle-level Managers in Four Countries

James P. Neelankavil, Anil Mathur and Yong Zhang

Introduction

The rapid growth of international business has led to unprecedented demands on firms' ability to manage their diverse cross-border activities. Success in such activities necessitates a thorough understanding of the process of cross-cultural management. Despite the rapid rise of globalism with the attendant drive toward standardization and the predominance of Western management theories, the belief that what works in the West should also work in other parts of the world has met with growing skepticism (Newman and Nollen, 1996; Adler and Jelinek, 1986; Black and Porter, 1991; Hofstede, 1994; Laurent, 1983, 1986; Traidis, 1989, 1990; Earley and Erez, 1997). Researchers and practitioners have long argued over what factors motivate managers in different countries and how managers can effectively manage a firm's international activities. Some believe that these factors differ significantly across countries and are heavily influenced by national cultures (e.g., Bigoness and Blakely, 1996). As a consequence, firms need to adapt their management practices to suit the national cultures in which they operate in order to achieve a high level of managerial performance.

However, the research community offers only limited guidance on how management practices should be adapted. The field of international management is still considered to be in a nascent, pre-paradigmatic stage with a dire paucity of theory-driven studies in the "hypothetico-deductive category" (Adler, 1983; Kyi, 1988; Black and Mendenhall, 1990). Research findings often offer mixed recommendations when attempting to match approaches to the management of international activities to the conditions companies might face. For example, under what conditions should companies transfer their effective management practices across cultures, rather than subscribe to the "cultural relativity" theory as argued by some researchers (e.g., Hofstede, 1994) and adapt their managerial approaches? The situation is further exacerbated by caveats in studies that have dealt with the influence of culture on management practices. For example, studies have often focused on countries that were not significantly different from one another, used samples that were not representative of the target population, or involved only limited numbers of firms and industries (Heiskanen, 1985).

The current study studies management practices through the study of managers themselves. We surveyed 784 middle-level managers from four countries (China, India, the Philippines, and the United States) with diverse cultural and industrial backgrounds to identify what managers themselves consider to be important determinants of managerial performance. The central thesis of the present study is that cultural influences are important factors affecting the process and outcome of management. Effective cross-cultural management is a function of a country's cultural peculiarity, and for that matter, its similarity with other cultures.

In the sections to follow, we will review the literature, describe our research, and finally, discuss the implications of the findings and directions for future research.

Literature Review

Research In Cross-cultural Management

Studies of international management have dealt with the issues from several perspectives: managerial values, value dimensions, comparative management, and managerial factors/determinants. Studies on *managerial values* have focused on the differences in managerial values in different countries (England and Lee, 1974; Ralston et al., 1992; Bigoness and Blakely, 1996) and tried to explain how such value difference account for managerial differences. For example, Ralston et al. (1992) compared

Western-developed measures (such as machiavellianism, locus of control, intolerance of ambiguity and dogmatism) with Eastern-developed Chinese Value Survey (such as Confucian dynamism, human-heartedness, integration, and moral discipline) and found that both culture and the business environment interact to create a unique set of managerial values in different countries.

Research on *value dimensions* (See Chinese Culture Connection, 1987; Hofstede, 1980 and 1994; and Punnett and Yu, 1990) took a more in-depth approach in studying how dimensions of value differ and how such differences affect cross-cultural management. Dimensions such as "individualism" and "moral discipline" relate to a variety of constructs in the social sciences, such as self actualization and security needs from Maslow's hierarchy of needs. These value dimensions were found to be crucial in explaining cross-cultural differences in management (Hofstede, 1980, 1994).

Understanding differences in value and value dimensions has profound impact on effective cross-cultural management. Earley and Erez (1997) effectively argue in their book, *the Transplanted Executive*, that there is a direct relationship between culture and managerial beliefs/ practices, and cultural value shapes the meaning of varied aspects of the work-place. Managerial practices that work effectively in one culture often work poorly in others. They alert the global managers to the danger of assuming that effective management practice is universal. Synthesizing the works of various scholars in cross-cultural research, they suggested a framework with two essential elements: self-knowledge and cultural values.

Earley and Erez (1997) posit that the cornerstone of successful cross-cultural management, is "knowing thyself," particularly understanding the relative importance of three self-motives: (a) self-enhancement, the desire to maintain a positive self-image, (b) self-growth, the desire to feel competent in the face of challenge, and (c) self-consistency, a desire to experience coherence in their lives. The second element consists of the cultural values that influence a manager and his subordinates. The authors used two principal dimensions of cultural difference: the self- vs. group-focus (more commonly referred to in the psychological liter-ature as individualism-collectivism) and power differential (the amount of power a person can acceptably exercise over others, c.f., Hofstede's 'power distance'). The self- vs. group-focus dimension of culture has a direct bearing on the self-motives. The extent to which managers with self-focused values are driven or satisfied by each motive is largely determined by internal standards, whereas the relative strength of the self-motives for those who are group-focused is socially determined (Adler, 1998).

The study of *comparative management* (such as Bartlett and Ghoshal, 1992) suggests that multinational companies should focus on individual managers and the cultural context in which they operate. Studies in this stream of research have investigated cross-cultural factors in the identification of managerial potential (Evans, Sculli, and Yau, 1987), managerial job attitude (Kanungo and Wright, 1983), and cross-cultural training effectiveness (Black and Mendenhall, 1990).

Studies in the area of *managerial factors* have focused on issues such as human resources management (HRM) (e.g., Lengnick-Hall and Lengnick-Hall, 1988; Milliman, et al., 1991). In their research of strategic human resources management, Lengnick-Hall and Lengnick-Hall found a reciprocal interdependence between a firm's business strategy and its human resource strategy. Issues dealt with include gender and training of managers for foreign assignment (e.g., Edstrom and Lorange, 1984; Tung, 1984), managerial satisfaction (Gomez-Mejia and Balkin, 1987), compensation and motivation (McCelland and Burnham, 1995; Morais, 1993).

Differences in National Cultures and Their Influences on Managerial Practices within Organizations

Culture exists at various levels, in a group, in an organization, and in a nation. Many researchers shared the view that organizations exist within cultural contexts. As a result, management assumptions, organizational structure and functions are influenced by national culture (e.g., Hofstede, 1980). Each culture has its own unique set of beliefs, value systems, attitudes, and related behaviors. Such uniqueness precedes organizational values and any role-centered managerial skills (Chakraborty, 1991). For example, the potential effectiveness of various management practices and motivational techniques used within an organization depends on the prevailing cultural values and norms. Management practices that reward personal competition may be highly valued in individualistic cultures such as America, but not in collectivistic cultures such as China. A middle-level manager who encourages open criticism will be appreciated by employees in a culture of low power differential where employees feel more free to exchange ideas with their bosses, but may instead raise the suspicion of employees in a culture of high power differentials. As a consequence, it is not surprising to find that the authoritarian style of the Japanese manager (high power differentials) is often met with resistance and resentment from U.S. (low power differentials) auto workers in the United States (Earley and Erez, 1997). Therefore, managers from different national cultures vary widely as to their basic conception of what constitutes effective managerial practices. Each culture must be studied within its own unique context in order to understand the important determinants of managerial performance in a particular organization.

National culture is a complex, multi-faceted construct. One of its most basic dimensions is the individualism-collectivism distinction in which countries differ (Hofstede, 1980). Evidence suggests that differences along this dimension of culture account for major differences in managerial assumptions and practices. For example, Laurent (1986) indicated that for American managers, "ambition and drive" were seen as crucial to managerial career success. This reflects a pragmatic and individualistic achievement-orientation. In contrast, their French counterparts viewed "being labeled as having high potential", a more social/collective element, as the most critical element. Such deep-seated managerial beliefs are strongly shaped by national cultures, and a thorough understanding of individualism/collectivism dimension of culture will shed light on differences in managerial perceptions and performance.

Hofstede (1980) defines individualism-collectivism as the relationship between the individual and the collectivity that prevails in a particular society. Many countries differ in this important cultural characteristic. In Europe and North America, individuals prefer independent relationships to one another, and individual goals take precedence over group goals (Hofstede, 1980). But in many countries in Asia, Africa, and Latin America, people are more likely to have an interdependent relationship with each other. Such collectivistic cultures embrace interdependence, family security, social hierarchies, cooperation, and low levels of competition (Triandis, 1989, 1990).

China is often considered a country with a collectivistic culture. As such, the Chinese society has historically focused on social interests and collective actions, and de-emphasized personal goals and accomplishments (Oh, 1976; Li, 1978). In the Chinese society, harmony and conformity not only tend to govern all interpersonal relations, but these qualities also enjoy social and cultural approval (Hsu, 1981). Some researchers have observed that differences on the collectivism and individualism dimension reflect a fundamental difference in China's cultural orientations (Ho, 1979).

On the other hand, the United States is ostensibly a country known for its "rugged individualism." The concept of individualism is the belief that each person is an entity separate from the group and, as such, the individual is endowed with natural rights (Spence, 1985). In sharp contrast to cultures that are characterized by self-sufficiency and inter-dependency, the Americans view rugged individualism as a desirable trait worth striving for. They embrace the belief that an individual is not only self-sufficient as a matter of fact but that he must strive toward it as an ideal. Thus, individualism is considered central to the American character (Spence, 1985). American values such as individual achievement orient-ation and encouragement of the attainment of material prosperity are rooted in individualism. This is also evidenced by theories of ego and moral development which hold that the highest stage a person can attain is one in which the individual rises above the acceptance of and conformity to the society's standards to an autonomous level (Loevinger, 1976).

Somewhere in between these two extremes along the individualism-collectivism dimension are India and the Philippines. While the Indian society reflects certain characteristics of collectivism as do many Asian cultures, the basic cultural orientations of India is profoundly rooted in Buddhism, Vedantic and Yogic Psychology, derivative epic and Pauranic literature (Chakraborty, 1991, p. 19). The Indian value system is set within the framework of transcendent ideology (such as "Chitta-shuddhi" or purification of the mind; self-discipline and self-restraint; and renun-ciation and detachment) which is the cutting edge of India's deep cultural structure. Such cultural uniqueness is reflected in Hofstede's survey on culture's dimensions (Hofstede, 1980). While China's score (using Taiwan as a surrogate) on individualism dimension is 17 and the United States' is 91, India is somewhat neutral with a score of 48. The Philippines is similar to India in several aspects. For example, the score for the Philip-pines on the Hofstede's cultural value dimension survey is 32. Although Filipinos exhibit many Asian traits in family and other social interactions, in business management they tend to mix Asian traits with Western management philosophies. For example, in their work place, Filipino managers maintain very close personal relationships with their peers and subordinates, reflecting a collectivistic cultural trait. It is also not uncommon for Filipino managers to become God-parents to the children of their subordinates and to act as sponsors at the weddings of staff members. Yet, they are ardent believers and practitioners of Western, and especially American, management methods in their business activities. Filipino managers value formal business education and utilize Western management methods.

Such western influences in both India and Filipino businesses are also reflected in other dimensions of culture (Hofstede, 1980). For example, both India and the Philippines had scores (40 and 44 respectively) similar to the U.S. (46) on the uncertainty avoidance measure, while China had a score of 69. Uncertainty avoidance measures the extent to which people in a society tend to feel threatened by uncertain, ambiguous, risky or undefined situations. On the measure of masculinity, the same pattern holds. Masculine cultures are characterized by assertiveness, valuing achievement and abhorring failure while feminine societies favor nurturing roles, interdependence between people and caring for others. The scores of India, the Philippines, and the United States were 56, 64, 62 respectively while China's was 45.

Such differences in cultural orientation are bound to influence managerial styles (defined as the overall set or pattern of behavioral characteristics that distinguish the country's general approach to management) in each country and reflect an important dimension of organizational culture (e.g., Wagner and Moch, 1986). Researchers argue that the impact of cultural differences along the individualism/collectivism dimension of culture on managerial styles should be treated more specifically and explicitly in management research because of its implications for organizations.

Therefore, we would expect significant differences in the perceptions of the most important determinants of managerial performance between managers from the four countries. Specifically, perceived importance of factors that determine managerial performance would show a high degree of cultural influence with managers from the People's Republic of China and those from the United States exhibiting the most amount of difference. In fact, we expect that China and the U.S. would represent bipolar extremes on a continuum with India and the Philippines placed somewhere in between. Although India and the Philippines are hypothesized, *a priori,* to be closer to each other on the continuum and exhibiting less cultural influence, Indian and Filipino managers are also expected to show differences in what they believe to be the most important determining factors of managerial performance.

Differences among Eastern Cultures

This study also focuses on the differences within Eastern cultures. Relatively few studies have dealt with differences among Eastern cultures and none, to our knowledge, on what local managers themselves perceive as important determinants of managerial performance in the three Asian countries. Since cultures and levels of economic development vary more widely across regions, researchers tend to focus on major differences between the East and the West, and across countries with different levels of economic development, such as between the developed and developing countries (e.g., England and Lee, 1990; Welge, 1994). Major differences within such groupings tend to be overlooked. For example, Asian countries are not necessarily very similar despite geographical proximity and economic similarity. In addition, few studies have compared less developed countries in the region.

Although China, India, and the Philippines are all Asian countries facing similar sets of issues in their economic development, they are far from being homogeneous. Significant differences exist between them with regard to their cultural heritage and managerial philosophy. While both India and the Philippines had considerable Western influences in managerial philosophy, it is only quite recently that the Chinese managers began to be exposed to Western management concepts. Further, although management practices in both India and the Philippines had similar origins, they have progressed and developed differently in modern times. Modern Indian management practices evolved from the British system prior to India's independence and adopted similar practices in the "management agency system" since independence (e.g., Bhagwati and Desai, 1970; Jones, 1989). Similarly, a significant number of multinationals who came to the Philippines since World War II provided a rich source of managerial skills (Tiglao, 1992). However, while the Philippines continued to benefit from multinational presence and westernized education (Tiglao, 1992), Indian management practices have developed a distinct Indian flavor. For example, Indian companies are still run very paternalistically with personal relationships playing a critical role in the management of a business organization (Garg and Parikh, 1986). It is, therefore, both meaningful and important for companies to develop a better understanding of the differences in managerial practices between India and the Philippines.

Thus, this study seeks to compare middle-level managers among three developing countries, i.e., China, India, and the Philippines, in addition to comparisons with the United States. The recent renewed interest in these developing countries as potential markets for both exports and foreign investment makes this study worthwhile. Researchers have called for increased efforts directed toward studying such markets (e.g., Thomas and Philip, 1994).

The Study

This study focusses on middle-level managers (distinct from senior executives and entry-level managers) because of the critical role they play in the daily operations of a company. It is increasingly recognized that middle managers play an important role in the implementation of corporate strategy (Bourgeois and Broadwin, 1984; Hart, 1992). Middle managers, by virtue of their pivotal position within a company, function as a conduit between policy/strategy makers and entry-level managers. They are suppliers of information to top management and consumers of decisions made by top management (Westley, 1990). When representing and implementing strategic and tactical decisions of top executives, they must remain extremely sensitive to the nature and requirements of lower-level managers and other members of the organization.

Method

Data Collection

Data for this study were collected directly from middle-level managers in the four countries using self-administered questionnaires. Initial contacts were made with the chief executives of publicly-held companies in all countries except China. Upon contact, CEOs were told the purpose of the study and their cooperation was sought in collecting data from their subordinate managers. They were requested to distribute questionnaires to middle managers in their organizations. For this study, middle managers were defined as those below the rank of vice-president with at least three years of managerial experience. Potential respondents were contacted by their CEOs for participation. Completed questionnaires were returned to the researchers directly, thus ensuring the anonymity of the respondents. In China, due to the lack of a sufficient number of publicly-held companies, samples were obtained from a Cadres Training School in southern China. Trainees were all middle-level managers sent to the school for management training by their respective companies located throughout the region.

A total of 784 responses were received from all four countries, 204 from China, 184 from India, 220 from the Philippines, and 176 from the US. These responses came from 79 Indian companies, 36 Philippine companies, 56 American companies, and 38 Chinese companies. Demographic and other characteristics of the samples are given in Table 1.

The majority of the respondents were male and relatively young (under 45 years). A closer examination of the data revealed sufficient variability in the demographic characteristics (age, education) and work-related variables (functional responsibilities, number of subordinates, hours worked, years with the present employer, and years on the present job). Such within-sample variability ensures that each sample represented a wide cross-section of middle-level managers in the country so that the opinions expressed by the respondents are independent of variables such as types of companies, functional areas, or specific industries. Analyses also suggest sufficient sample compatibility across countries in age, gender, weekly work hours, number of subordinates, and area of expertise.

Measures

The development of the measures followed a two-step process. Prior research suggested various determinants of managerial performance, such as leadership ability, communication skills, planning, controlling, etc. (Grimsley and Jarrett, 1973). The starting point of the measure development was a list of 46 items used by Johnson, Neelankavil, and Jadhav (1986) to assess the importance of various performance factors. In their study, Johnson, et al. (1986) identified five key performance factors for middle managers: problem solving, ability to work under pressure, integrity, organizing, and planning. Responses to the 46 statements representing

Table 1: Demographic Profiles of the Four Samples

Characteristics	Philippines (N = 220)	India (N = 184)	USA (N = 176)	China (N = 204)
Sex				
Males	67.3%	89.7%	63.6%	66.8%
Females	32.7%	10.3%	36.4%	33.2%
Age				
Under 35	29.3%	53.6%	28.9%	47.5%
35–44	42.3%	27.8%	39.9%	28.3%
45–54	20.5%	14.8%	24.8%	15.6%
55–64	7.9%	3.8%	6.4%	8.6%
Functional responsibility				
Data processing/computer	3.2%	7.1%	9.1%	2.0%
Engineering/research	8.7%	13.6%	10.0%	13.2%
Finance/accounting	14.6%	16.3%	22.7%	25.9%
Marketing/sales	21.9%	15.8%	18.2%	11.2%
Personnel/HR	7.8%	9.2%	8.0%	13.7%
Production/maintenance	11.4%	15.2%	3.4%	10.6%
Others	32.4%	22.8%	26.7%	23.4%
Number of direct subordinates (Mean)	12.5	8.3	7.8	19.7
Average number of hours spent on the job/per week	45.0	49.8	50.4	42.8
Time with the present company (number of years)	11.6	8.3	11.6	9.8
Time in the present job (number of years)	5.5	4.0	3.4	5.6
Number of years of formal education				
Less than 13	9.6%	61.1%	6.3%	43.6%
13–17	77.6%	27.2%	46.3%	53.0%
18 or more	12.8%	11.7%	47.4%	3.4%

the five dimensions were reviewed by a sample of middle-level managers. They indicated whether the statements were clear and easy to understand and whether the statements represented key determinants of managerial performance. Based on the feedback, some statements were reworded and redundant statements were removed. Finally, 40 statements were used in the survey instrument. In addition to measuring determinants of managerial performance, the survey questionnaire asked for demographic and work-related (e.g., length of experience) information from the respondents. The study reported here is part of a large-scale, global study which tracks managerial value and performance in various countries.

Respondents from Indian, Filipino, and American companies received an English version of the questionnaire. Those from Chinese companies received a Mandarin Chinese version of the questionnaire. A cross-cultural consulting firm was hired to translate the original questionnaire into Chinese. The translated version was validated through the back-translation technique and was properly tested for consistency with the original version. To ensure accuracy of the translation, the entire process was closely monitored by one of the principal investigators who is proficient in both languages. Discrepancies in the translations were resolved with translators from the consulting firm. The final version of the questionnaire was prepared professionally.

Analysis and Results

Prior to testing the main prediction of this study and to justify the pooling of data from the four countries, factor analyses were conducted to determine whether data from the four countries share similar data structure. Items that had dual loadings or very low loadings were dropped from the analysis to purify the data. This process resulted in retaining 18 items that are shown in the appendix.

Subsequent factor analysis produced five factors in Chinese, Indian, and Philippine sub-samples, and 6 factors in the American sub-sample. There were striking similarities in the factor solutions from the four countries that warrant further factor analysis.

In the subsequent factor analysis, the number of factors to be retained was first constrained to be five, next six, and finally seven (independently for each country). Factor structures that emerged from these analyses were compared across the four countries. The six-factor solution showed striking similarities across the four samples and is reported in Table 2. These six factors represented the following dimensions of managerial performance: planning and decision making ability; self-confidence and charisma; educational achievements; communication skills; past experience; and leadership ability. This analysis suggests that the underlying dimensions of managerial performance perceived by the middle managers were very similar across the four countries. Therefore, data from the four countries were pooled in subsequent analyses.

Table 2: Factor Loadings for the Four Countries and Combined Samples

Item #	Factor 1					Factor 2					Factor 3					Factor 4					Factor 5					Factor 6				
	P	I	U	C	4	P	I	U	C	4	P	I	U	C	4	P	I	U	C	4	P	I	U	C	4	P	I	U	C	4*
1.																				.33					.43	.86	.77	.79	.47	.84
2.	.31										.31	-.43				.84	.81	.84	.32	.82		-.34	.55			.59	.37		.78	.46
3.																.83	.79	.84		.80									.54	
4.			.32														.36												.40	
5.	.58	.55	.45	.33	.55	.31															.31							.39	.39	.33
6.	.71	.71	.56	.35	.66														.67		.31							.56		
7.	.80	.73	.66	.66	.77														.72											
8.	.60	.79	.78	.80	.76														.38											
9.	.70	.59	.74	.84	.71		.36																							
10.											.86	.80	.79	.85	.88															
11.											.83	.84	.82	.86	.85															
12.											.37								.55		.81	.68	.61	.54	.56	.44				
13.											.49	.50				.31				.57	.83	.72			.82					
14.	.50					.57	.69	.77	.67	.67																				
15.						.74	.44	.62	.48	.63																				
16.						.77	.71	.86	.82	.79														-.33		-.45				
17.	.37					.77	.82	.88	.83	.84																				
18.	.33					.69	.42			.46				.32					.48		-.35			.80		-.30				

Note: Table entries are factor loadings. Loadings of less than .30 are not printed for clarity.
* P = Philippines, I = India, U = USA, C = China, and 4 = full sample.

The second phase of the analysis focused on identifying similarities and/or differences across these countries based on the importance attached to the factors of managerial performance. For this purpose, data from the four countries was pooled and factor analyzed. For this analysis too, the number of factors was constrained to six. The resulting factor structure was similar to the one reported in the earlier analyses and the interpretation of the factors was also similar. Factor scores for these six factors were used in subsequent analyses.

To test the prediction of this study, MANOVA analysis was carried out to see if there are any differences across the four countries in terms of managerial performance factors. For this test, factor scores for the six-factor solution were used as the dependent variables. This analysis revealed that there are significant differences across the four countries (Multivariate $F = 20.616$, $p < .001$). Univariate tests for the six-factor scores revealed that significant differences do exist for all the six factors. Mean factor scores for the four countries and corresponding univariate F-statistic are shown in Table 3, along with the results of post-hoc pair-wise comparisons. While Filipino managers attached great importance to planing/decision making ability (mean factor score = .218), Indian managers attached least importance (mean factor score = −.220). The mean scores for American and Chinese managers were close to the overall mean (.006 and −.038 respectively). As far as self confidence/charisma is concerned, Chinese managers felt it is very important with a mean factor score of .214, and American managers felt it was least important with mean factor score of −.228. The scores for Filipino and Indian managers were close to the overall mean (.039 and −.070 respectively). Educational Achievements were rated very highly by Filipino managers (mean factor score = .310) and very low by American managers (mean factor score = −.513). Indian and Chinese managers rated this near the overall mean (.078 and .040 respectively).

While Filipino and Indian managers rated communication to be important (factor scores of .141 and .121 respectively), Chinese managers rated it to be low (mean factor score = −.340). Both Filipino and American managers rated past experience to be important (mean factor scores = .399 and .232 respectively), while Chinese rated it to be rather low (mean factor score = −.625). Finally, Filipino and Indian managers rated leadership ability to be high (mean factor score = .193 and .214 respectively), while Chinese managers rated it to be rather low (mean factor score = −.470).

Table 3: Comparison of Managerial Performance Factors
Across the Four Countries

Factors	Philippines	India	USA	China	F-Value
1. Planning/decision making ability	.218	−.220	.006	−.038	6.677[a]
Philippines					
India	***				
USA	***	***			
China	***				
2. Self-confidence/charisma	.039	−.070	−.228	.214	6.703[a]
Philippines					
India					
USA	***				
China		***	***		
3. Educational achievements	.310	.078	−.513	.040	25.095[a]
Philippines					
India	***				
USA	***	***			
China	***		***		
4. Communication skills	.141	.121	.090	−.340	11.109[a]
Philippines					
India					
USA					
China	***	***	***		
5. Past experience	.232	.033	.399	−.625	46.950[a]
Philippines					
India	***				
USA		***			
China	***	***	***		
6. Leadership ability	.193	.214	.075	−.470	22.588[a]
Philippines					
India					
USA					
China	***	***	***		

Note: Table entries are mean factor scores for the four samples. Asterisks (***) indicate significant differences across countries.
[a] Significant at $p < .001$.

Post-hoc pair-wise comparisons of the four countries on the six dimensions of managerial performance revealed an interesting pattern of similarities and differences. On three out of six dimensions (communication skills, past experience, and leadership ability) Chinese managers were clearly different from those from the others. With respect to the remaining three dimensions, Chinese managers were closer to some than to others. For example, on educational achievement, Chinese managers were similar to Indian managers but different from American and Filipino managers. With respect to self-confidence, Chinese managers were similar to Filipino managers but different from Indian and American managers. Finally, with respect to planning and decision-making, Chinese managers were similar to Indian and American managers but different from Filipino managers. Overall, these results indicate that Chinese managers were most unique in their perceptions, as if representing an extreme position or viewpoint.

Although American, Filipino, and Indian managers tend to be similar on some factors (leadership ability and communication skills) there are many differences across these countries. For example, on educational achievements and planning/decision making ability, managers from these three countries had quite different views. With respect to past experience, while American and Filipino managers tend to agree, they responded differently from Indian managers. Finally, with respect to self-confidence, while responses of American and Filipino managers were different, no such differences were found between American and Indian managers as well as between Indian and Filipino managers. These findings indicate that there are significant differences that are critical for understanding management performance in these countries.

Table 4: Overall Distance Across the Four Countries in Terms of Managerial Performance Factors

	Philippines	India	USA	China
Philippines	.000			
India	.297	.000		
USA	.838	.580	.000	
China	1.576	1.239	2.035	.000

Note: Table entries are squared Euclidean distances based on factor scores.

Finally, to determine the overall pattern of similarities and differences across the four countries, mean factor scores for the four countries were used to compute an overall distance matrix. The distance matrix is given in Table 4. As shown in the table, the distance between India and

Philippines is the least (.297) indicating these two countries are most similar in terms of the overall managerial performance factors. Also, India and Philippines are both closer to the US than either is to China (distances of .580 and .838 respectively). Finally, China is the most dissimilar of the four countries as indicated by its distance from the other three countries. These results are discussed in greater detail in the discussion section.

Discussion

This study set out to assess the perceptions of Chinese, Indian, Filipino, and U.S. middle-level managers with respect to the importance of various factors in contributing to managerial performance. An understanding of such differences is important for effective management across cultures because these perceptions play a critical role in determining the effort and focus of the managers.

This study revealed that there are clear differences in the perceptions of managers across the four countries with respect to the importance they attached to various factors of managerial performance. This finding is consistent with the framework proposed by Tayeb (1988, 1995) and Misumi (1985). Tayeb (1988) suggested that many companies, driven by common task environments, tend to develop similar structures across cultures. However, culture plays a role in determining how these structures are developed. Similarly, Misumi's (1985) findings suggest that certain underlying supervisory behaviors are genotypic or task oriented (independent of cultural influence), but they might be expressed differently in different cultures due to cultural influence. We found that the perceived importance of performance factors differ across all four countries as a result of cultural differences.

Differences between China and the U.S.

A unique result of the present study is the mapping of cultural distances between the four countries. On the basis of middle managers' perceptions regarding managerial performance factors, our study found that the U.S. and China are the most dissimilar pair. These two can be taken to represent the two extremes of a continuum. A review of the underlying pattern reveals that these two countries differed on all factors of managerial performance except for planning and decision making. Managers from both China and the US rated this factor close to the overall mean, indicating that they did not hold extreme position on this issue. But the similarity on this factor does not undermine the significance of the vast differences across the two countries along the other factors.

These differences are not surprising given the widely acknowledged cultural differences between these two countries. The Chinese society had long been closed to Western influences until the "Open Door Policy" was instituted in the late 70's. Deep-seated cultural values and customs and a central planning system led to substantial differences in management styles. Despite recent gradual abandonment of such a practice and the corresponding shift to a market-oriented economic structure, many Chinese managers are still new to modern management theory and techniques. Remnants from the old economic system are bound to influence managers' perception and practices.

Differences between India/Philippines and U.S.

A complex pattern of similarities between the perception of managers from India, Philippines, and the US tends to support the notion that India and Philippines might be between the two extremes represented by the US and China. While the differences across these countries suggest that India and Philippines themselves do not assume polar positions, similarities between India/Philippines and the US suggest that these countries might be closer to the US rather than to the Chinese end of the continuum. Further, the fact that there are substantial differences between the perceptions of managers from India and Philippines, suggests that these two countries do not occupy the same position on the continuum along the theoretical framework expounded by Hofstede.

Collectively, these results suggest that India and Philippines are somewhere between these two extremes. Although we did not attempt to establish any direct relationship between the cultural orientation of middle managers and their perceptions regarding managerial performance factors, empirical evidence suggests that cultural orientations could have played a role in these perceptions. These results are consistent with those of Hofstede (1980). While a theoretical perspective suggests that the U.S. and China would be on the two ends of the Collectivism—Individualism continuum, Hofstede found it to be empirically true. Also, consistent with Hofstede's findings we found that India and the Philippines are between the two extremes. The results of this study were in line with the theoretical prediction of Hofstede's results. From these findings, it appears that cultural orientation toward individualism/collectivism has some influence on the perceptions of managers.

Differences between China, India, and the Philippines

Conventional comparisons of the Eastern and the Western countries have either implicitly or explicitly assumed that all Asian countries are similar and therefore can be culturally grouped and labeled the Eastern or Oriental culture. Contrary to this assumption, sufficient differences in managerial perceptions across these countries prevent us from making such an assertion, particularly with regard to managerial practices. For example, we found that Filipino managers showed marked differences from Indian and Chinese managers with respect to planning/decision making, educational achievement, and past experience. Also, perceptions of Chinese and Indian managers differed on four out of five factors: self-confidence/charisma, communication skills, past experience, and leadership skills. Differences in perceptions across these Asian countries can be accounted for by the historical contexts within which these cultures have evolved. While the Chinese culture was isolated from outside influence for a very long time, both Indian and Filipino cultures have had outside influence for a very long time. Furthermore, the nature of outside influences experienced by India and Philippines were also quite different, as discussed earlier.

Taken together, this study supports the view that cultural values, such as collectivism/individualism, impact managerial perceptions, attitudes, and behaviors. Therefore, anyone attempting to do business in a global setting should pay special attention to cultural factors.

Equally important in the study of managerial differences are the similarities shared by the managers across the four countries. Such similarities can be further examined in the context of their organizational, historical, and cultural backgrounds. Despite significant cultural differences, managers need not assume that the determinants of success will always differ across all countries and at all times. For example, the middle managers from our four countries considered similar factors as determinants of their performance. As mentioned, this might be driven by the similarities in their roles (as middle managers), tasks performed (motivating, training, evaluating, communication, controlling, etc.), and organizations (structure, etc.). The importance of these factors testifies to the notion that certain non-culturally dependent variables relate to managerial success. However the relative importance of these factors may be culture-bound. These findings should be helpful to global and international companies in planning their human resource recruitment and training efforts. As the globalization of business continues, placement and management competent middle-level managers across national boundaries and cultures become increasingly critical.

Implications and Conclusion

The findings of this study have important implications for researchers interested in understanding cross-cultural differences in managerial practices as well as for practitioners interested in doing business in the four countries. First of all, this study supports the notion that culture has a significant impact on managerial practices particularly between vastly different countries such as China and the United States. Secondly, for researchers interested in cross-cultural comparisons of managerial practices, this research contributes to our understanding of the differences in seemingly similar countries. Many differences exist among countries and managers of international business enterprises should take note. Asian countries are not necessarily similar to one another in their managerial orientations, despite cultural relatedness. Similar cases can be made about Latin American or other regional clusters. This study serves as a basis for conducting further comparative studies involving these countries/cultures.

For managers in the studied countries, the findings provide insight into the factors that lead to effective managerial practices and successful job performance. The managers should, on the one hand, develop sufficient self-knowledge to become an effective manager. He should ask himself what his own cultural values are and whether his subordinates share those values. If not, how to create an environment which is conducive to effective management. This is particularly important to companies in selecting, training, and motivating expatriate managers for assignments in India, Philippines, and China. For example, by understanding the processes of how people are driven and motivated in a culture, we can gain important insights into why our subordinates work and react the way they do. We can also determine the most effective way to manage employees who come from diverse cultural backgrounds. Self-enhancement or a desire to feel good about oneself and the desire to maintain a positive self-image may be universal. But what is important but less obvious is that the source of what makes people feel good differs according to their general cultural value. An American worker may feel that "I have made it all by myself" while a Chinese worker may feel that "I couldn't have made it without others," when mesmerizing the joy of achievement.

This information is also valuable for evaluating the performance of expatriate managers. A thorough understanding of managerial perceptions as moderated by cultural differences enables companies to adopt a more effective global human resource strategy and better prepares an expatriate upper-level manager for dealing with middle managers in those countries. The findings suggest that a manager might have to rely more on his/her leadership ability in India and the Philippines compared to China to achieve success. On the other hand, while in China he/she may need to rely more on personal charisma/self confidence compared to in India or Philippines.

All in all, culture plays an important role in global business, and to achieve success in cross-cultural management, managers should understand both themselves and others. This entails understanding one's self knowledge and the cultures of those he manages. He must also understand what constitute effective managerial practices in a particular cultural context and what is considered acceptable work behavior. The competitive advantage derived from correctly adapted management practices comes from appropriate alignment between the external environment and a firm's internal strategies, structures, and managerial practices. The congruence between managerial practices and the national culture is likely to produce better performance outcomes.

However, limitations of the study should be kept in mind. First, no direct attempt was made to measure the cultural orientation of individual managers. Although desirable from a methodological standpoint, it is considered trite given the large volume of literature attesting to such differences. This study is based on the *a priori* assumption that significant cultural differences exist between the four countries. Yet, future research may try to measure the cultural orientation of the managers when assessing the influence of culture. Second, only four countries are studied. The inclusion of more countries is certainly desirable in the quest for better knowledge of culture's impact on managerial performance.

References

Adler, Nancy J. 1983. Cross-cultural management research; The ostrich and the trend. *Academy of Management Review*, 8: 226–232.

Adler, Nancy, J. & Mariann Jelinek. 1986. Is 'organization culture' culture bound? *Human Resource Management*, 25: 73–90.

Adler, Semour. 1998. The Transplanted Executive. *Personnel Psychology*, 51 (4) Winter: 1009.

Bartlett, Christopher A. & Sumantra Ghoshal. 1992. What is a global manager? *Harvard Business Review*, September/October: 124–132.

Bhagwati, Jagdish & Padma Desai. 1970. *India: Planning for industrialization*. London: Oxford University Press.

Bigoness, William J. & Gerald L. Blakely. 1996. A Cross-National Study of Man agerial Values. *Journal of International Business Studies*. 27(4): 739–752.

Black, J. Stewart & Mark Mendenhall. 1990. Cross-cultural training effectiveness: A review and a theoretical framework for future research. *Academy of Management Review*, 15(1): 113–136.

Black, J. Steward & Lyman W. Porter. 1991. Managerial behaviors and job performance: A successful manager in Los Angeles may not succeed in Hong Kong. *Journal of International Business Studies*, 22(1): 99–113.

Bourgeois, L. J. & D. R. Brodwin. 1984. Strategic Implementation: Five approaches to an elusive phenomenon. *Strategic Management Journal*, 5: 241–264.

Chakraborty, S. K. 1991. *Management by values—Towards cultural congruence*. Delhi, Oxford University Press. 1991.

Chinese Culture Connection. 1987. Chinese values and the search for culture-free dimensions of culture. *Journal of Cross Cultural Psychology*, 18: 143–64.

Earley, P. Christopher & Miriam Erez. 1997. *The Transplanted Executive*. Oxford University Press. New York.

Edstrom, Andrea & Peter Lorange. 1984. Matching strategy and human resources in multinational corporations. *Journal of International Business Studies*, 15(2): 125–137.

England, George W. & Robert Lee. 1974. The relationship between managerial values and managerial success in the United States, Japan, India, and Australia. *Journal of Applied Psychology*, 59: 411–419.

Evans, W. A., D. Sculli, & W. S. L. Yau. 1987. Cross-cultural factors in the identification of managerial potential. *Journal of General Management*, 13(1): 52–57.

Garg, Pulin K. & Indira J. Parikh. 1986. Managers and corporate cultures: The case of Indian organizations. *Management International Review*, 26(3): 50–66.

Gomez-Mejia, Luis & David B. Balkin. 1987. The determinants of managerial satisfaction with the expatriation and repatriation process. *Journal of Management Development*, 6(1): 7–17.

Grimsley, Glen & Hilton F. Jarrett. 1973. The relation of past managerial achievement to test measures obtained in the employment situation: Methodology and results. *Personnel Psychology,* 26(Spring): 31–48.

Hart, Stuart L. 1992. An integrative framework for strategy making process. *Academy of Management Review,* 17(2): 327–351.

Heiskanen, Tuula A. 1985. How steel workers in different countries see their work. *Journal of Occupational Behavior,* 6: 273–92.

Ho, D. 1979. Psychological Implications of Collectivism: with Special Reference to the Chinese Case and Maoist Dialectics, in L. Eckensberger, W. Lonner & Y. Poortinga, editors, *Cross-Cultural Contributions to Psychology.* Amsterdam: Swets & Zeitlinger.

Hofstede, Geert. 1980. Motivation, leadership, and organization: Do American theories apply abroad? *Organizational Dynamics,* 9: 42–63.

Hofstede, Geert. 1994. Management scientists are human. *Management Science.* 40(l): 4–13.

Hsu, F. L. K. 1981. *American and Chinese: Passage to Differences.* Honolulu: University of Hawaii Press.

Johnson, Richard A., James P. Neelankavil, & Arvind Jadhav. 1986. Developing the executive resource. *Business Horizons,* 29(6): 29–33.

Jones, Stephanie. 1989. Merchants of the Raj. *Management Accounting-London,* 67(8): 32–35.

Kanungo, Rabindra N. & Richard W. Wright. 1983. A Cross-cultural comparative study of managerial job attitudes. *Journal of International Business Studies,* 14(Fall): 115–129.

Kyi, K. M. 1988. APJM and comparative management in Asia. *Asia Pacific Journal of Management,* 5: 207–224.

Laurent, Andre'. 1983. The cultural diversity of Western management conceptions. *International Studies of Management and Organizations,* 8: 75–96.

Laurent, Andre'. 1986. The cross-cultural puzzle of international human resource management. *Human Resources Management,* 25(1): 91–102.

Lengnick-Hall, Cynthia A. & Mark L. Lengnick-Hall. 1988. Strategic human resource management: A review of the literature and a proposed typology. *Academy of Management Review,* 13(3): 454–470.

Li, Dun J. 1978. The Ageless Chinese. New York: Charles Scribners.

Loevinger, J. 1976. *Ego Development: Conceptions and Theories.* San Francisco: Jossey-Bass.

McClelland, David C. & David H. Burnham. 1995. Power is the great motivator. *Harvard Business Review,* (January–February): 126–39.

Milliman, John, Mary Ann Von Glinow, & Maria Nathan. 1991. Organizational life cycles and strategic international human resource management in multinational companies: Implications for congruence theory. *Academy of Management Review.* 16(1): 318–39.

Misumi, Juji. 1985. *The Behavioral Science of Leadership: An Interdisciplinary Japanese Research Program*, Ann Arbor, MI: University of Michigan Press.

Morais, Richard. 1993. The global boss' pay: Where and how the money is. *Forbes*, (June 7): 90–98.

Morris, Michael H., Duane L. Davis and Jeffrey W. Allen. 1994. Fostering Corporate Enterprenueurship Cross-cultural Comparisons of the Importance of Individualism Versus Collectivism. *Journal of International Business Studies*, 1st Quarter: 65–89.

Newman, Karen L. & Stanley D. Nollen. 1996. Culture and Congruence: The Fit between Management Practice and National Culture. *Journal of International Business Studies*, 27(4): 753–779.

Oh, Tai K. 1976. Theory Y in the People's Republic of China. *California Management Review*, (19): 77–84.

Punnett, Betty Jane & Ping Yu. 1990. Attitudes toward doing business with the PRC: A comparison of Canadian and U.S. companies. *International Studies of Management and Organization*, 20: 149–160.

Ralston, David, David J. Gustafson, Fanny M. Cheung, & Robert H. Terpstra. 1992. Eastern values: A comparison of U.S., Hong Kong and PRC managers. *Journal of Applied Psychology*, 77: 664–71.

Spence, Janet. 1985. Achievement American Style: the Rewards and Costs of Individualism. *American Psychologist*, 40(12): 1285–95.

Tayeb, Monir H. 1988. *Organizations and National Culture: A Comparative Analysis*, London: Sage.

Tayeb, Monir H. 1995. Supervisory styles and cultural contexts: A comparative study. *International Business Review*, 4(1): 75–89.

Thomas, Anisya S. & Annamma Philip. 1994. India: Management in an ancient and modern civilization. *International Studies of Management & Organization*. 24(1,2): 91–115.

Tiglao, Rigoberto. 1992. Focus: Philippines—New, upwardly mobile tycoons. *Far Eastern Economic Review*, 155(35): 44–45.

Triandis, H. C. 1989. The Self and Social Behavior in Differing Cultural Contexts. *Psychological Review*, 96(3): 506–520.

Triandis, H. C. 1990. Cross-Cultural Studies of Individualism and Collectivism, in J. Berman, editor, *Nebraska Symposium on Motivation*. Lincoln: University of Nebraska Press.

Tung, Rosalie L. 1984. Strategic management of human resources in the multinational enterprise. *Human Resource Management*, 23(2): 129–143.

Wager, John and Michael K. Moch. 1986. Individualism-Collectivism: Concept and Measure. *Group & Organization Studies*, 11 (3): 280–304.

Welge, Martin K. 1994. A comparison of managerial structures of German subsidiaries in France, India, and the United States. *Management International Review*, 34(Special Issue): 33–49.

Westley, Frances R. 1990. Middle managers and strategy: Microdynamics of inclusion. *Strategic Management Journal*, 11(5): 337–351.

Appendix: Items Used To Measure Managerial Performance

1. The ability to lead a group to accomplish a task without arousing hostility
2. The ability to modify approach or behavior tendencies in order to reach a goal
3. The ability to effectively present an oral report to a conference group
4. The ability to effectively express ideas in writing
5. The ability to effectively organize the work effort
6. The ability to effectively plan and follow through on those plans
7. Consistently making decisions in a timely manner
8. The ability to sort out all the relevant facts related to a problem or situation
9. The ability to solve problems effectively
10. The reputation of the college or university where a degree was obtained
11. Level of formal educational achievement in terms of degrees and grades
12. Degree of experience, either on the job or in related jobs or fields
13. A track record of favorable results on previous assignments
14. Degree of self-confidence
15. Level of charisma
16. Level of self-esteem
17. Level of self confidence
18. Having an optimistic outlook on life

4 | India: A Non-Tiger of Asia

Monir Tayeb

Introduction

The newly industrialized countries of Central and South East Asia are becoming an increasingly competitive and formidable force to be reckoned with. They have made inroads in the markets which have hitherto been regarded as the domain of Japanese and Western companies. In the race to catch up with, and in some cases even to surpass, the advanced industrialized nations, they have left their other fellow Asian countries far behind, even though at some stage in the race they were all on the same line. Why didn't the other runners make it? The present paper takes India as an example of the non-Tigers of Asia and compares it with the Tigers in an attempt to start answering this question. In doing so the paper seeks to understand the "why" of the phenomenon under study, and is therefore an explanatory paper rather than a prescriptive one.

Competitive Advantage of Nations

We know that nations which succeed in the international market are those which not only have competitive advantage on certain factors of production, but also are able to manage these factors in such a way as to translate their potential advantage to an actual one. This point can specially be noted in Porter's seminal study (1990).

In his national "diamond", Porter considers four sets of conditions/ characteristics as playing determinant roles in a nation's international success:

1. *Factor conditions.* The nation's position in factors of production, such as skilled labour or infrastructure, necessary to compete in a given industry.
2. *Demand conditions.* The nature of home demand for the industry's product or service.
3. *Related and supporting industries.* The presence or absence in the nation of supplier industries and related industries that are internationally competitive.
4. *Firm strategy, structure, and rivalry.* The conditions in the nation governing how companies are created, organized, and managed, and the nature of domestic rivalry.

Porter placed his emphasis on industry advantages, rather than on the national advantage as a whole. It is argued here, in line with Francis's argument (1992), that there are national differences in competitiveness and not just differences in where competitive advantage lies. None of the countries that Porter included in his sample was a non-runner. That is to say, had he included also countries like Pakistan and Bangladesh he would have observed that these latter nations are not competitive internationally at any level, be it firm, industry or nation (Tayeb, 1995), whereas "Porter's countries" are major players in the international market. The present paper builds on Porter's model, by concentrating on a non-runner country, India. In comparing India with some of the more successful Asian countries, the paper attempts to explain why she has not been able to turn her potential competitive advantages into success in the international market.

National Performance

On nearly every measure of a nation's well-being, both material and non-material, India has lagged behind. The latest report by the World Bank classifies Hong Kong, Singapore, Taiwan and South Korea as high ($7911 or more) and upper-middle ($2556–7910) income nations and India as a low income one ($635 or less). India, according to the same report fares poorly on the annual GNP growth rate. Table 1 illustrates the positions held by these countries.

On non-financial measures such as commercial energy consumption per capita, infant mortality rate, population per physician ratio, and life expectancy at birth, India has a much worse record than its successful Asian counterparts.

Table 1: Average Annual Growth Rate of GDP

	1970–1980	1980–1990
Hong Kong	9.2	6.9
Singapore	8.3	6.6
South Korea	9.6	9.6
Thailand	7.1	7.9
Malaysia	7.9	5.7
India	3.4	5.4
Indonesia	7.2	5.6

Source: World Bank Development Report, 1993.

In 1991 Singapore's per capita energy consumption was over 6000 kg of oil equivalent, Hong Kong's just over 1400, South Korea's over 1900, Malaysia's over 1000, and India's was 337. As Table 2 shows these countries' records in this respect were, expect for Singapore, very similar in 1970.

Table 2: Commercial Energy Consumption Per Capita (kg of Oil Equivalent)

	1970	1991
Hong Kong	973	1,438
Singapore	3,863	6,178
South Korea	495	1,936
Thailand	150	438
Malaysia	452	1066
India	113	337

Source: World Bank Development Report, 1993.

Table 3 shows that Indian people's state of health also compares poorly with that of their fellow Asian nations. Infant mortality rate, life expectancy at birth and population per physician ratio have improved greatly for all the nations under consideration, but India's progress has been much slower on all these criteria than the other nations over the period between 1970 and 1991.

Table 3: State of Health

	Infant Mortality Rate (per 1000 live births)		Population Per Physician		Life Expectancy at Birth (years)			
					Female		Male	
	1970	1991	1970	1990	1970	1991	1970	1991
Hong Kong	19	7	1510	NA	73	80	67	75
Singapore	20	6	1370	820	70	77	65	72
South Korea	51	16	2220	1370	62	73	58	67
Malaysia	45	15	4310	2700	63	73	60	68
Thailand	73	27	8290	5000	61	72	56	66
India	137	90	4890	2460	49	60	50	60

Source: World Bank Development Report, 1993.

Competitive Advantage in Human Resources

A major production factor which the Asian Tigers have been able to turn successfully to their competitive advantage is their human resources. They have done so through the management of this resource at both firm level, through management styles, and national level, through government policies, especially education and economic ones. Indeed, these nations have hardly any natural resources other than their people. Not surprisingly, the pattern of development in these economies reflected their competitive advantage in cheap labour.

Typically, rapid growth began in the agricultural economy. Rising incomes in the countryside created a surplus of investable resources and a market for domestic manufacturers. The industrial take-off came next, led by labour-intensive manufacturing. As demand for labour went up, so did urban and rural wages. The economy began to rise out of poverty. In other words, a "magic mix" of human resource management and economic policies catapulted these nations from a state of underdevelopment to that of highly competitive players in the international market.

The following sections discuss these two factors, human resources and government policies, in India and explore the reasons why she was unable to follow the same pattern as her fellow Asian nations. But let us first examine in some detail where the Asian Tigers stand on these and other related factors.

The Tigers

The South East Asian Tigers are former LDCs (less-developed countries) that have achieved their aspirations through mainly export-led development and openness to foreign direct investment. These are Hong Kong, South Korea, Taiwan, Singapore, Indonesia, Thailand, and Malaysia. They are sometimes referred to as the Asian Dragons, Asian Tigers, and are included in various combinations in wider regional clusters such as the Pacific Rim, the Asia–Pacific and the ASEAN.

There were several factors which gave these countries a comparative advantage in many manufacturing and service areas and contributed to their spectacular economic take-off. First, they achieved their growth through export. Taiwan and South Korea, for instance, have few natural resources, little arable land, and the highest population densities of any country except for Bangladesh and the city-states of Hong Kong and Singapore. The one policy that both have pursued is to be export-orientated. This simply means that they did not handicap their exports in world markets. Almost all developing countries do this, by bans, quotas or tariffs on imported goods. One of the disadvantages of trade restriction is that it both makes the home market more attractive to a would-be exporter, and also raises the cost of their imported input, so hampering them if they try to sell abroad.

In partnership with Japan, South Korean and Taiwanese firms have penetrated new markets. In the period from 1989 to 1990, when the value of world trade expanded by an annual average of 13%, Thailand increased its exports by 31%, Malaysia by 23%, and Indonesia by 15% (*The Economist*, 8 September 1990).

Second, some, but not all, of the NICs (newly industrialized countries) adopted an open approach towards foreign direct investment. Unlike many of the LDCs, they actively encouraged foreign direct investment without foreign ownership in their economies. Singapore's offer of generous tax breaks to foreign investors three decades ago lured major oil refineries. These have made the country the world's third largest refining centre, after Houston and Rotterdam, even though the island republic produces no petroleum of its own and consumes only 10% of its refinery output (*Time*, 30 July 1990). This policy is still pursued to date.

The primary attraction of Thailand, Malaysia and Indonesia for foreign investors was these countries' low-cost production sites and highly skilled workforces. South Korea, however, only recently decided to open up its territory to foreign direct investment and to allow a very limited entry as of January 1992. No single investor can hold more than 5% of a South Korean company, and total foreign ownership in any company is limited to 10%. Major industries such as steel, electricity and finance are closed to foreign investors altogether.

Third, cultural, political and economic characteristics, such as a strong commitment to public education and a neutral role for religion have been major reasons behind the success of Asian Dragons and their would-be imitators in the region (Schlossstein, 1991). These countries have a highly skilled, committed and loyal workforce who are prepared to sacrifice themselves for the good of their company to a far greater extent than are their counterparts in other LDCs (and indeed in Western advanced countries). As West (1989) puts it,

> "East Asia can point with pride to the more accurate measure of economic vitality, their increasing rates of productivity. Here we confront the East Asia edge as a reflection not of trade surpluses but of ideas about work, loyalty to their country, and notions about the future. East Asia cultures have turned on its head the long-held claim that successful modernization was somehow linked to the "particularistic" values associated with Western thought" (p. 5).

Herman Kahn stated it boldly in 1979 when he said the Confucian ethic was playing a "similar but more spectacular role in the modernization of East Asia than the Protestant ethic played in Europe" (see also Weber, 1930). These "non-Confucian countries", Khan added, "now outperform the West" (quoted in Solomon, 1979, p. 185).

Fourth, as industrialists, these nations are very entrepreneurial, aggressive and competitive, and keep an eye for new opportunities and new markets. For instance, Thailand, which has the region's most flexible and vigorous private sector, was very quick to react to the Persian Gulf crisis in late 1990 and early 1991. With a characteristically sharp eye for a good opportunity, the country's Prime Minister exhorted Thai businessmen to sell fruit juice to Coalition soldiers stationed in the Persian Gulf (*The Economist*, 8 September 1990).

Fifth, as late developers, the NICs utilized modern techniques and high technology in their efforts to pursue their policies and to achieve their economic objectives. Singapore is typical of the Tigers. Lacking in major natural resources, Singapore must trade to survive. The information technology industry makes a crucial contribution to those export efforts and, in the process, it has modernized the entire business infrastructure. Indeed, Singapore owes its strategic position in the international trading network to its electronic links to global markets. To capitalize on the full potential of information technology, Singapore formed a National Computer Board in 1981. Its objective was to establish Singapore as an international computer software services centre. Singapore has also poured millions of dollars into its utilities and infrastructure (e.g. modern highways, an excellent underground system) and has underwritten R&D and office/science parks.

Finally, political stability in these countries in the past three decades or so has also played a significant role in their economic success. Their governments have pushed through development policies single-mindedly and with resistance to special interest groups. Land reforms, for instance, were carried out in Taiwan by a dictator (Chiang kai Shek), and in South Korea by a government carried along by a wave of public anger at collaborators with the Japanese colonizers.

These countries, even though they have the appearance of a democracy, and now respect civil liberties, have pursued an authoritarian regime throughout the period of their industrialization and economic take-off. It was only in 1987 that the South Korean street riots drove the military out of office. Taiwan's gradual political reform started in the early 1980s and culminated in the end of martial law and a much freer electoral system as recently as 1988. Singapore is still a virtual "benign autocracy". It is interesting to note that political reforms in these countries began only after they had achieved a high level of prosperity and growth.

The Non-Tiger—India

India, like many other developing countries which were until a few decades ago the colonies of major imperial powers, is suspicious of foreign powers and attempts to avoid domination at all costs. For this reason, she considers economic growth and industrialization as her top priority, and is willing to sacrifice everything to this end. But has she been successful? The answer seems to be an emphatic "no". India has not achieved the level and growth rate of per capita output that its endowments of productive inputs and institutions would seem to warrant (Trinque, 1993).

In the 1960s, when India's approach could still be deemed promising, its industrial output went up on average by 5.5% a year. Its manufacturing output (a narrower measure) went up more slowly, at 5.2% a year. By developed-country standards this looks impressive. At such a rate of growth, industrial output would double every 12 years. However, by the standards of India's Asian neighbours, it was decidedly unimpressive. Industrial output in Pakistan grew almost twice as fast, at 10.8% a year. Thailand managed 11.5%, Taiwan 13.2%, and South Korea, 16.5%. In the 1970s these gaps widened substantially and India fell even further behind. In the 1980s India's industrial output grew as quickly as elsewhere in Asia, thanks to modest liberalizing reforms that began early in the decade—but it was satisfactory growth from, by then, an anomalously small base. Judging performance over the past 30 years by the narrow priorities that India set itself, its development strategy has been an unambiguous failure. Nowhere else, not even in communist China or the Soviet Union, is the gap between what might have been achieved and what has been achieved as great as in India (*The Economist*, 4 May 1991).

Two factors which are arguably most crucial and which have contributed to the economic take-off of the Asian Tigers are their human resources and their economic policies.

The following sections discuss these two factors in India and explore the reasons why she was unable to follow the same pattern as her fellow Asian nations. The discussion is summarized in Fig. 1.

Indian Human Resources

The country is rich in human resources, which matter most for economic advance, as well as other natural resources. A review of the literature on the Indians show that they are resourceful and hard working, have a keen sense of responsibility, are thrifty and entrepreneurial, and are ambitious and materialistic. And as many of us who live in Western societies observe in our day-to-day life, a vast majority of the Indian immigrants who have settled in these societies have done very well in various walks of life, be it academia, business or other professions. As an Indian industrialist put it "Overseas Indians have successfully faced competition in their host countries. There is no reason why Indians can't do the same in their own country if they are given the same opportunities" (*Time*, 10 January 1994, p. 27).

Figure 1: The Twin Contributions of Human Resource Management
and Government Policies to India's Position in the
International Market

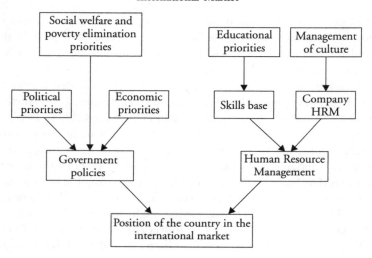

A likely explanation for why Indian people do not succeed in their
own home country as much as they do abroad, is that India, or rather
her leaders, have systematically mismanaged her valuable, but at the same
time, low-cost human resources.

The extent of employee productivity is one of the criteria by which
one can judge a country's performance in the management of human resources. Table 4 demonstrates the different rates at which Indian and
South East Asian employees contribute to the economic performance of
their respective countries.

Table 4: Gross Output Per Employee (1980 = 100)

	1970	1988	1989	1990
Singapore	73	122	129	135
South Korea	40	177	193	204
Thailand	77	109	112	113
Malaysia	96	NA	NA	NA
India	83	175	179	NA

Source: World Bank Development Report, 1993.

Human Resources and Educational System

Education, of course, plays a crucial role in the development and management of human resources. India has many excellent universities, and one of the biggest cohort of technically trained manpower in the world.

At the lower end of the system, however, India has done less well. According to the 1981 census, only 36.17% of the total population of India are literate. The figure for Malaysia and China is 60% and 70%, respectively. According to the *Financial Times* (26 June 1992) India has highest illiteracy rate in the world. This will, of course, hinder her economic growth.

The Indian educational system is experiencing several problems. The basic educational objectives of universal primary education, and equality of access and expansion of opportunity, which are enshrined in the Constitution of the country, have yet to be achieved (Mehta, 1989; Rao-Seshadri, 1993). Out of 179 million children in the age group of 5–14 years—about 27% of the total population in 1981—only 38.45% of those in the age group of 5–9 years and some 50% in the age group of 10–14 were actually enrolled in schools. It was worse in rural areas where two in every three children in the age group of 5–9 years and six in every ten in the age group of 10–14 years were not attending school. Children of scheduled castes and scheduled tribes, and girls in general were the worst sufferers (Census of India, 1981).

India's record in this respect, as Table 5 shows, compares poorly with her Asian competitors. Moreover, Indian schools are marked by a high degree of infrastructural constraints. In the mid-1980s (the latest date for which data are available), of the total number of primary schools in the country, only 47% were housed in permanent buildings, 59% of the schools were without drinking water facilities; 85% without a lavatory; 40% without blackboards; 53% without playgrounds and 71% of the primary schools had no library facilities (Krishna, 1985). Given such conditions it is not surprising that more than seven out of every ten children enrolled drop out without completing their schooling (Ministry of Education, 1985: p. 36). One obvious reason for this state of affairs is the amount of money that the government is willing or can afford to spend on education. Table 6 compares India with Asian Tigers; she does not compare well with them.

Table 5: Percentage of Age Group Enrolled in Education

	Primary		Secondary	
	1970	1990	1970	1990
Hong Kong	117*	106*	36	NA
Singapore	105*	110*	46	69
South Korea	103*	108*	42	87
Malaysia	87	93	34	56
Thailand	83	85	17	32
India	73	97	26	44

*For some countries with universal primary education, the gross enrollment ratios may exceed 100% because some pupils are younger or older than the country's standard primary school age.
Source: World Bank Development Report, 1993.

Table 6: Central Government Expenditure on Education
(Percentage of Total Expenditure)

	1980	1991
Singapore	14.6	19.9
South Korea	17.1	15.8
Thailand	19.8	20.2
India	1.9	2.5

Source: World Bank Development Report, 1993.

Of those Indian children who do get a chance to receive some form of education, only a small elite gets the best. There are four types of schools in India: the English style public schools, independent private schools, state run and controlled schools, and centre schools whose curricula and administration come under Central Government authority. The first two categories care for the children of a very small elite and constitute a negligible percentage of all the schools in the country. They usually provide the students with a variety of means of learning such as laboratories, libraries, games and sporting facilities. For the rest of the schools, the only method of learning, apart from lectures given by teachers, are textbooks whose publication and contents are controlled by the State or Central governments.

Textbooks have been primarily responsible for killing the interest of young minds in learning. There is, therefore, no scope for innovation when children's studies are confined to textbooks. Another major characteristic of the system is an emphasis on conformity. The system does not seem to encourage creativity, self-discovery, curiosity, divergent opinions, self-expression and reading books other than those related to school books.

A third major characteristic of the educational system is its tradition-orientated policies. The emphasis is on learning for certificates and degrees and not on development of the mind.

As a consequence of the problems which beset the educational system, as Rao-Seshadri (1993) argues, the general perception of the functioning of the system is low, as demonstrated by widespread student unrest and strikes; the level of educated unemployment is high, indicating that the usefulness of the certification awarded by the system is negligible for many students; and "brain drain" or the export of Indian-trained scientists and technicians to the West also continues to be high, which means that the economic, scientific and industrial climate in India is such that those who can are choosing to leave.

Some remedies have been adopted by the government in its 5-year educational plans to improve this situation. (a) There has been increased investment in education, leading to an impressive expansion in educational facilities; (b) policies such as reservation of seats, scholarships, etc. have been adopted to increase participation of women and minorities; (c) manpower planning and vocational-technical education have been receiving increased attention in an effort to make education more relevant to the workplace; (d) privatization of primary education has been suggested in order to elevate the quality of education; and (e) the non-formal sector is also being encouraged and given more credibility in an effort to increase access to education (Rao-Seshadri, 1993). The impact of these plans on the present and future generations of young Indians remains to be seen.

Management of Cultural Characteristics

India has a complex and varied culture and it is dangerous to talk about an Indian culture. However, there are certain characteristics that many researchers and writers on the subject agree are shared by the diverse peoples of India (Koestler, 1966; Segal, 1971; Parekh, 1974; Mehta, 1989; Tayeb, 1988), such as, arranged marriage, fatalism and expression of emotions. Of the characteristics which are most held in common by

Indian people, collectivism is one which can be readily identified as related to work organization, and which India shares with the Asian Tigers. It would therefore be useful to examine how this trait is being managed in these countries.

South Eastern Asian cultures, as was noted earlier, are characterized by collectivism. Many writers on cross-cultural management attribute the hard work and high degree of commitment of the employees in the region to their collectivism. On the basis of this argument, one would expect the Indians also show high commitment to and involvement in the interests of their work organizations. In a survey of a large sample of Indian employees, Tayeb (1988) found that this was not the case.

The explanation may lie in another aspect of the culture of the country, i.e. the nature and size of the in-group. An example can clarify this point. Let us take three cultures, Iran, India, and Japan. These societies are characterized by, among others, a strong sense of group and community. A typical Japanese, Indian or Iranian person is very loyal to his or her own group or team, and places the interest of the group before his or her own interests. On the face of it, one would expect to see this characteristic—collectivism—to have been carried over into their work organizations, in the form of, for instance, hard work and a high degree of commitment, dedication and emotional attachment to the company. But a closer examination of societal cultures, employees' attitudes and values, and the management structure of work organizations in these countries (Tayeb, 1979, 1988, 1990) reveals that it is only in Japan that the collectivism of Japanese culture has been carried over into its companies. The Iranians and Indians as employees are as detached from their work organizations and have as individualistic a relationship with their workplaces as any individualistic nation.

Now if one goes beyond collectivism and look into the in-groups, the focus of loyalty and commitment, in these three cultures, one notices striking differences. In Iran, the in-group consists of the immediate family, i.e. parents, siblings, spouses and children. In India, the in-group includes other members of the extended family as well: the grandparents, grandchildren, uncles, aunts, cousins, close friends, and relatives. There are even different names by which different members of the extended family are referred to, depending on their age. For instance, the elder brother is *dada*, the elder sister is *didi* and so forth, signifying the importance of each family member. The workplace does not seem to have any place in Iranian and Indian in-groups. It belongs to the out-group. One is quite prepared to put the interest of the in-group above that of the out-group. The employee's low commitment to the work organization observed in Iran (Tayeb, 1979) and India (Tayeb, 1988) and the corruption, which bedevils Indian public administration (Mehta, 1989), are manifestations of the position of the workplace within the in-group-out-group division. In contrast, in Japan one's workplace appears to be decidedly a part of one's in-group, and it is therefore a focus of the employee's commitment and loyalty.

It is true that the high degree of employee commitment in Japan and other South East Asian countries, and the low commitment in India and Iran have other explanations beside culture (Briggs, 1988; Tayeb, 1988, 1990), but culture plays a significant part.

As mentioned earlier, other characteristics such as resourcefulness, hard work, risk aversion, and emotional dependence have also been attributed to Indian people (see for instance Parekh, 1974; Hofstede, 1980; Tayeb, 1988). These characteristics are not unique to the Indians. They can certainly be attributed to their Central and South East Asian counterparts as well, among others. But what is interesting to note is that the Japanese and other Asian Tigers appear to have been able to build on the cultural characteristics of their people and incorporate them into their organizational culture: quality circles thrive on collectivism (Tayeb, 1990), *ringi* decision making cushions employees against individual risk taking (Hofstede, 1980), and close management-subordinate relationships provide an atmosphere of emotional support (Tung, 1984, 1988). Indian managers do not appear to have succeeded in incorporating the cultural characteristics of their employees into their organizational culture.

Trade Unions and Industrial Relations

There are no craft unions in India. Trade unions are either plant-based or national organizations which are run locally in each state and focus their activities on the interest of their immediate members at the plant or local industry level. There are provisions for setting up works committees in factories and workers participation in decision making at shopfloor and plant levels. However, these committees, and indeed any other form of workers participation, have not been successful (Chaudhuri, 1981). There are various acts of Parliament which secure minimum wages, regulation for payment of wages, working conditions, equal remuneration for men and women and several schemes providing security to the workers against contingencies, such as industrial accidents. Generally, industrial relations legislation is pro-worker and aims at protecting their employment and general well-being. For instance, the regulations are such that it is virtually impossible for management to sack a worker or reduce his or her wages even if he or she has seriously breached the terms of their contract (Tayeb, 1988).

There is obviously a dilemma here. If one continues with the existing practices, the inevitable result will be inefficiency, overmanning and low productivity. If one decides to change the rules and, for instance, dismiss the under-performing worker (more often than not a villager who sends a large proportion of his wages to his family back home), one deprives not only the worker of livelihood and means of survival but also his extended family.

It is also important to mention that, in contrast to the situation in the Asian Tigers, Indian Industrial relations is prone to conflict (Johri, 1992), and mistrust and hostility bedevils the relationships between the two sides of the industry from time to time (Tayeb, 1988).

The Role of the State

Politics

India is sometimes referred to as the world's largest democracy, unlike most other developing countries which have centralized non-democratic governments. The system, however, can more realistically be considered as a peculiar mixture of 'democracy' and 'non-democracy'.

Take freedom of expression and the party political system, for example. The All India Radio and Doordarshan (television network) are directly run and controlled and manipulated by the government. The advent of satellite and cable television has, however, increased the Indian viewers' choice and the government-controlled television and radio are having to adapt to the new circumstances.

Films shown in public movie halls are heavily censored for scenes and dialogues that the officials consider immoral. Newspapers, however, enjoy freedom of expression, and criticize government bodies, politicians and other public figures freely. The Indian press, unlike radio and television, is not a monolithic body, and represents a wide range of social and political values and views. Indeed, India is probably the only society outside the Western world where issues of public importance can still be debated freely in the press.

Also, there is the Parliament and the party political system, whose characteristics make them very different from many other democracies, especially those in Western societies. First, the government machinery is very centralized and the Centre has far more substantial powers in relation to the states than exists in any other similar federations (Segal, 1971). For instance, the central government can declare a state of emergency, not only in times of war but even to maintain law and order and proper government in the states, and it can assume extraordinary powers over constituent states and over individual citizens whose fundamental rights may be disregarded. Finance is centrally controlled, but agriculture, irrigation, power, education, health and road transport are in the hands of the states which make up the current political and geographical map of the country.

Second, the opposition has until recently been fragmented into many small groups. Since independence, virtually only one party, the Congress Party, has been in power. This dominance of the Congress Party over the political scene has resulted in an almost single-party system and the electorate is not given a meaningful national choice.

Third, because of the dominance of the government by the Congress Party, at the time of elections, Congress politicians make extensive use of government facilities and officials to organize their campaigns and this puts them at an enormous advantage compared to their financially and otherwise weaker rival candidates (see for example Segal, 1971; *Time*, 27 June 1994).

Fourth, the elections are in most cases far from free and fair. Party workers usually spend a great deal of money and organize lunch and dinner sessions for villagers or distribute food items among them to induce them to vote for their candidates. There are also cases of violation of rules and fraud. The efforts by independent election commissioners in their fight against such practices has in recent times met with vehement opposition from the Congress Government and other interested parties.

In a democracy such as this, powerful interest groups such as farmers in rural areas, the middle classes in towns can and do derail policies which may otherwise be beneficial to the country as a whole.

Compare this with the situation in East Asian Tigers. In considering the development of political institutions and their role in economic change and industrialization in East Asia, one of the most crucial features is the extent to which state agencies and controllers are able and willing to develop policies independently of powerful economic and social groups and then have the capacity to implement them (Whitley, 1992). This is commonly discussed in terms of the "autonomy" of the state to pursue objectives that do not simply reflect the demands or interests of social groups, classes or society and have been evaluated in terms of the background of bureaucratic elite and their ties to the dominant landed, commercial and industrial classes (Skocpol, 1985; Wade, 1990). An important aspect of state autonomy here is its capacity to implement its policies, either through direct control of economic institutions and resources or through indirect manipulation and guidance (Whitley, 1992).

A related significant feature of political system is the overall commitment of the political and bureaucratic elite to state-led industrialization (Samuels, 1987) and their perception that state legitimacy rests significantly upon rapid economic development.

State autonomy, as Whitley (1992) points out, needs to be combined with a political commitment to economic development led by state institutions, of course, if it is to play a major role in the industrialization process and structure the sorts of successful forms of business organization that develop. This commitment was quite high in Japan, South Korea and Taiwan for much of the post-war period, although less tied to direct state control of resources and enterprises in Japan than South Korea and Taiwan. In Hong Kong, however, it was much more muted and expressed in relatively indirect ways. Broad elite support for industrialization and economic growth here did not imply a leading role for the state.

The Economy

Although India has become an industrial power in its own right (ninth in the world), agriculture is still the mainstay of its economy—it is by far the largest single employer in the country and accounts for around 40% of the country's gross national product (*Financial Times*, March 24, 1982). Seventy percent of the population still lives in the rural areas (*The Economist*, 4 May, 1991).

A major characteristic of all developing countries is the all-pervasive and crucial role that their governments play in the management of the economy as well as in politics. Almost all of these countries pursue protectionist industrial and economic policies. India is no exception. India's may be described as a mixed economy with protective interventionist policies where the private sector is allowed to operate under governmental guidelines and direct control, and where the government also owns and manages manufacturing and service industries. Like many other third world countries, the government's objectives in economic planning are mainly: removal of poverty; creation of employment; attainment of self-reliance; reduction of inequalities in income and wealth (through high taxes and setting a low upper limit for wages and salaries); and attainment of balanced regional developments.

The government tries to achieve these goals by exerting its hold over the economy through such means as carrying out 5-year economic plans, issuing licences for setting up factories, discriminative licensing policies for different industries according to the country's needs, giving priorities to applicants who set up factories in the "centrally noted backward areas", strict import control to protect domestic industries, restricting establishment and expansion of capital intensive high technology industries, and setting up social goals, such as employment and prosperity of backward areas, before profit for private industries (Mehta, 1982). Although in the past few years government has eased its hold on the economy, especially the private sector, and relaxed its import policies, the economic policy is still highly protectionist and far from being one based on a free market.

Consequences of a virtually closed and insular economy are enormous, the most serious of which are the neglect of industrial modernization and the phenomenon of industrial sickness (Johri, 1992). One manifestation of this industrial sickness can be seen in both state-owned and private organizations. The government's enterprises are run with extraordinary inefficiency. Various BICP (India's Bureau of Industrial Costs and Prices) studies of state-owned steel plants, coal mines, shipyards, machine-tool factories and so on have found the same management failures every time: under-use of capacity, poor materials planning, excessive inventories, egregious over-staffing, obsolete technology, inadequate maintenance and inappropriate products. The costs are simply passed on to India's private sector, in the form of either higher prices (especially to private industrial customers) or higher taxes.

In the private sector, the restriction on imports and foreign investment in the name of building up national industries and economic self-reliance, has resulted in coddled, inefficient enterprises that find it difficult to compete with the outside world. According to an Indian top trade official, until recently, India was just off the map as far as world trade and investment are concerned. The figures back him up: the world's second most populous nation accounts for less than 0.5% of global commerce (*Time*, 10 January 1994). IMF figures available for 1950–1994 show a downward trend in the period from just over 2% to just over 0.05% of world exports (*The Economist*, 21 January 1995). Moreover, because of lack of competition, consumers have a limited choice. There is also no incentive for producing high quality products.

In a comparative study of English and Indian firms, the author (Tayeb, 1988) found that the English electronics companies which participated in research had a market share of not larger than 3 or 4%, thanks to their German, American and Japanese rivals. But their Indian counterparts had between 50 and 90% share of their domestic market in the absence of foreign competitors. As a result, the English companies had specialized departments for R&D in order to meet the challenges posed by their competitors. But none of the Indian firms felt the need for such a specialist function. At the most, they would send their senior managers to attend international exhibitions and conferences in order to learn and come back with new ideas.

This may be sufficient for a domestic captive market; but it cannot do for the international market

The protectionist policies of the government have shielded producers from competition and left them free of any pressure to control costs or innovate. Protected markets have allowed workers in the large companies to demand, and receive, high wages. As a result, Indian products cannot compete in the international market either on quality or on price. The scene is changing gradually and slowly. Since 1991 the government has started a process of limited liberalization. Reforms such as the dismantling of the restrictive import licensing system, removal of many of the barriers to foreign investment and reductions in tariffs are designed to open up the Indian economy to overseas trade and investment (Crompton and

Rodriguez, 1992). Until 1992, for instance, foreign firms were not allowed to control more than 40% of a domestic enterprise; now they may acquire as much as 51% and, with special government permission, even 100%. But the government bureaucracy and the private sector vested interests are slowing the process down.

In 1993 the central government approved $2.5 billion in foreign investments, including funding for five large power stations, as well as dozens of $5 million to $10 million investments by foreign companies seeking to gain toeholds in a potentially lucrative market. Since government follow-through remains slow and complicated, however, less than $450 million of the approved amount has flowed into the country. That is small change compared with Thailand, for example, which in 1993 attracted $1.5 billion in foreign investment, or China, which got nearly $20 billion (*Time*, 10 January 1994).

The businessmen, although understanding the need for liberalization, seem reluctant to carry it out, as they have a stake in the present system. The most successful have learned to manipulate the rules and the bureaucrats in charge, and have invested heavily to that end. Moreover, protection means less competition and safe profits. Businessmen may be waking up to what this approach has done to the economy as a whole, but they are bound to fear that they themselves will lose out if real reform ever happens (*The Economist*, 4 May 1991).

There are also oppositions to the government's economic reform programmes from trade unions and some politicians (*Financial Express*, 20 February 1992; *Wall Street Journal*, Eastern Edition, 17 January 1994).

An active role played by the government in the management of economy, is not, of course, unique to India. But it is the nature and the direction that this role takes that make a difference. Whereas India's policies in effect encourage inefficiency, and suffocate innovation and competition, those of its fellow Asian countries achieve quite the opposite.

Taiwan, for instance, had one of the largest public enterprise sectors outside the Communist bloc and sub-Saharan Africa from the 1950s to the 1970s (Wade, 1990). According to Whitley (1992), state support and connections are often a crucial aspect of business activities in South East Asian societies, particularly in South Korea (Amsden, 1989; Jones and Sakong, 1980), and form a key component of their dominant business systems. This support does not, though, usually extend to the granting of monopoly powers or toleration of sustained inefficiency. Rather, it tends to reward success and punish failure and so "accelerate market forces" (Abegglen and Stalk, 1985: pp. 136–144).

In South Korea, primarily through credit rationing and control of the banking system, but also through the tax system, control over licences and other administrative devices, state agencies have exercised decisive influence on the strategic choices and investment decisions of the favoured conglomerates, or chaebol (Amsden, 1989; Jones and Sakong, 1980; Kim, 1988; Wade, 1990). The oligopolistic pattern of industrial structure in many heavy manufacturing industries is largely the result of state co-ordination of economic activities and encouragement of particular developments. Through cheap loans and other inducements certain chaebol have been pushed into new sectors of activity, while others have been discouraged from entering these areas (Zeile, 1989). Generally, the state ensured that at least two chaebol had firms in each of the new industries it wanted to develop but restricted the total number to ensure significant profits and opportunities for expansion.

The Taiwanese state has pursued "developmentalist" policies, in the sense that it has systematically encouraged industrialization and export sectors since the 1950s (Cumings, 1987; Gold, 1988; Haggard, 1988). Tax incentives and selective assistance for exporters have directed entrepreneurs' attention to particular sectors, such as plastics and electronics (Amsden, 1985; Hamilton, 1989; Orru, 1991), and the state has tended to use public enterprises as the preferred instrument for sector development (Whitley, 1992).

Social Welfare Through Economic Policies

India, like many other third world countries, lacks an extensive and well-developed national welfare state. People largely depend on their families and other relatives for help when they get old, or are sick or are without a job. Social issues such as poverty, unemployment and even ethnic problems are tackled through economic plans via business organizations.

Generally, labour-intensive technologies are encouraged in order to increase the level of employment. Quotas are set for the companies to recruit workers from among lower castes and migrants from rural areas. As was mentioned earlier, all firms, whatever their size, are encouraged to put themselves in "backward areas". They are told what to produce (for example, textile mills had to supply a quota of cheap cloth for the poor) and, in many cases, how much to charge. Despite various measures such as tax breaks, cheap credit and subsidies and regulated freight prices, costs tend to be higher in the backward areas. Unions, protected by stringent labour laws, keep wages high, and there is high resistance to job shedding. There are also regulations and measures which make it almost impossible for managers to sack their manual workers or deduct from their wages even if they do not carry out their tasks properly.

Partly to avoid making employees redundant and causing their families to suffer, the protection of inefficient firms has gone to such an extent that failed (the so-called 'sick') firms cannot under existing laws close down. Most sick firms are kept alive with subsidies, tax relief and credit extended by the state banks. Nearly 20% of the outstanding loans of India's financial institutions are loans to sick enterprises (*The Economist*, 4 May, 1991).

In spite of the welfare through enterprise and other developmental policies, successive governments have failed to reduce the widespread poverty in the country.

Poverty

Since independence in 1947, the Indian state has intervened extensively in the countryside with a plethora of policy packages in order to promote rural development, advance social justice and improve the conditions of the poor. However, the "achievements" of over four decades of such planned "deliberate development" fall far short of the goals and aspirations. While relative inequalities have not increased, the conditions of the majority of the populace has not improved. Today, as much as 45–50% of India's populace continue to live under variously drawn poverty lines, a proportion that has not changed in India (Sharma, 1992). Sharma argues that the roots of poverty are fundamentally political. That is, the poor masses of the country are effectively disenfranchised when it comes to making authoritative decisions affecting their plights. In competition over resources and the fruits of development they lose out to dominant interests because these exercise hegemonic control over the discourse of development and its resources, organizations and programmes.

Trinque (1993) sees the poverty as a result of the mismanagement of the economy. He argues that the country's disappointing economic performance is the result of economic incentives that bias investments towards the perpetuation of a relatively stable, slow-growth equilibrium. Trinque then attributes the long history of slow growth to a relative neglect of agriculture, particularly in the eastern region. This neglect stems from economic incentives unfavourable to the provision of the necessary physical infrastructure. Failure to utilize fully India's agricultural potential is responsible for the widespread poverty that has hindered the growth of the country's other economic sectors.

Whatever reasons one might believe to be behind the massive poverty in India, the fact remains that it slows down the country's economic growth and competitiveness in the international market.

Concluding Remarks

This paper attempted to explore why a country like India, which has ample natural resources and a reasonably trained low-cost workforce, has been unable to match the spectacular achievements of some of its fellow Asian nations, notably the so-called East Asian Tigers. It was demonstrated that on significant indicators of national performance, such as rate of GDP growth, per capita energy consumption, infant mortality, life expectancy, and health provisions, India compares poorly with Central and South Eastern Asian Tigers.

The paper discussed the socio-political, economic and cultural factors which have played a significant role in the Tigers' current status in the international market. India was then compared with these countries. Two major factors, human resources and the role of the state, were discussed in detail. It was argued that the country's human resources have been mismanaged, thanks to both macro and micro level policies. Education, politics and economic/trade policies of the government were especially singled out as areas whose mismanagement contributes most to the country's inability to benefit from its potential comparative advantages, and compete in the international market successfully.

The countr' has not achieved its aim of providing universal primary education for its citizens. The system suffers from serious problems, such as underfunding, poor infrastructure and inadequate teaching practices.

It was also argued that Indian people in general compare equally well with their fellow Asian counterparts on such work-related cultural characteristics as hard work, entrepreneurial spirit, collectivism and willingness to accept responsibility. However, the economic, political and business climate of the country has been unable to provide them with opportunities to realise their full potential.

The largely insular and protectionist industrial and economic policies of successive governments since independence are considered to be responsible for inefficient private and state-owned enterprises and their lack of competitiveness in domestic and international markets.

Changes are however taking place. A process of restructuring and reorientating of the educational system is currently underway. There is also a change of direction on the economic policies front. Privatization of state-owned enterprises, removal of trade restrictions, and exposure of domestic firms to competition from foreign firms are gradually taking place. It remains to be seen how far the reforms will be allowed to progress, given the immense political will that is needed to accompany it, and the opposition to it from some quarters.

One thing is clear. These reforms will have major implications for Indian organizations. They have to adapt to a competitive and changing market, where customers can no longer be taken for granted. They need to invest in employee training and in technology in order to improve their productivity and efficiency. In their attempt to flourish in the new dynamic market they have to carry their employees with them. A different style of management-employee relationship is called for, one which will be based on cooperation and teamwork, instead of hostility and division.

As for foreign firms, India offers new opportunities, albeit not totally risk-free. Many multinationals have already set up subsidiaries and joint-venture partnerships there. The future for India is bright, if the opportunities thus created are utilized and expanded judiciously. If India's economic reforms gain strength and turn around the country's fortune in the international market, those developing countries which have not yet done so can take heart and embark upon a similar enterprise.

References

Abegglen, J. C. and Stalk, G. (1985) *Kaish: The Japanese Corporation.* Basic Books, New York.

Amsden, A. H. (1985) The Division of Labour is Limited by the Rate of Growth of the Market: The Taiwan Machine Tool Industry in the 1970s. *Cambridge Journal of Economics*, Vol. 9, pp. 271–84.

Amsden, A. H. (1989) *Asia's Next Giant.* Oxford University Press, Oxford.

Briggs, P. (1988) The Japanese at Work: Illusions of the Ideal. *Industrial Relations Journal,* Vol. 19, pp. 24–30.

Census of India (1981) *1981 Key Population Statistics Based on 5% Sample Data.* Series I, Paper 2, New Delhi: Registrar General of Census.

Chaudhuri, K. K. (1981) *Workers' Participation in India: A Review of Studies,* 1950–1980. Working paper No. 41, Indian Institute of Management, Calcutta.

Crompton, P. L. and Rodriguez, G. R. (1992) Implications of Recent Trade and Industrial Reforms in India. *Agriculture and Resource Quarterly,* Vol. 4, No. 4, pp. 542–553.

Cumings, B. (1987) The Origins and Development of the Northeast Asian Political Economy, in Deyo, F. C. (Ed.), *The Political Economy of the New Asian Industrialism.* Cornell University Press, Ithaca, NY.

Francis (1992) The process of National Industrial Regeneration and Competitiveness. *Strategic Management Journal,* Vol. 13, pp. 16–78.

Gold, T. B. (1988) Entrepreneurs, Multinationals and the State, in Winckler, E. A. and Greenhalgh, S. (Eds), *Contending Approaches to the Political Economy of Taiwan,* M. E. Shape, Armonk, NY.

Haggard, S. (1988) The Politics of Industrialization in the Republic of Korea and Taiwan, in Hughes, H. (Ed.), *Achieving Industrialization in East Asia.* Cambridge University Press, Cambridge.

Hamilton, G. (1989) *The Organizational Foundations of Western and Chinese Commerce.* Paper presented to the International Conference on Business Groups and Economic Development in East Asia, University of Hong Kong, 20–22 June.

Hofstede, G. (1980) *Culture's Consequences.* Sage Publications, California.

Johri, C. K. (1992) *Industrialism and Employment Systems in India.* Oxford University Press, Delhi.

Jones, L. and Sakong, I. (1980) *Government, Business and Entrepreneurship in Economic Development: The Korean Case.* Harvard University Press, Cambridge, MA.

Kim, K.-D. (1988) The Distinctive Features of South Korea's Development, in Berger, P. L. and Hsiao, H.-H. M. (Eds), *In Search of an East Asian Development Model.* Transaction, New Brunswick, NJ.

Koestler, A. (1966) *The Lotus and the Robot,* Danube edition. Hutchinson, London.

Krishna, K. (1985) India's Primary Schools: The Funding of Desperate Needs. *Monthly Commentary on Indian Economic Conditions,* Vol. 26, No. 9, pp. 69–74.

Mehta, P. (1989) *Bureaucracy, Organisational Behaviour, and Development.* Sage Publications, New Delhi.

Mehta, V. R. (1982) "Centre and Periphery" in Indian Politics, *Government and Opposition,* Vol. 17, pp. 164–179.

Ministry of Education (1985) *Challenge of Education—A Policy Perspective.* Publication Division, New Delhi.

Orru, M. (1991) Business Organizations in a Comparative Perspective: Small Firms in Taiwan and Italy. *Studies in Comparative International Development,* 26.

Parekh, B. (1974) The Spectre of Self-Consciousness, in Parekh, B. (Ed.), *Colour, Culture, and Consciousness*. George Allen and Unwin, London.

Porter (1990) The Competitive Advantage of Nations. Macmillan, London.

Rao-Seshadri, S. (1993) *An Evaluation of the Effectiveness of Educational Programs: The Indian Experience*. Unpublished Ph.D. thesis, Pennsylvania State University.

Samuels, R. J. (1987) *The Business of the Japanese State*. Cornell University Press, Ithaca, NY.

Segal, R. (1971) *The Crisis of India*. Jaico Publishing House, Bombay.

Sharma, S. D. (1992) *The Policies and Politics of Rural Development and the Limits to Reform and Redistribution: The Case of Post-Independence India*. Unpublished Ph.D. thesis, University of Toronto.

Skocpol, T. (1985) Bringing the State Back In: Strategies of Analysis in Current Research, in Evans, P. B. *et al*. (Eds), *Bringing the State Back In*. Cambridge University Press, Cambridge.

Solomon, R. (1979) *Asian Security in the 1980s: Problems and Policies for a Time of Transition*. Rand Corporation, Santa Monica.

Schlossstein, S. (1991) *Asia's New Little Dragons*. Contemporary Books, Chicago.

Tayeb, M. H. (1979) *Cultural Determinants of Organizational Response to Environmental Demands: An Empirical Study in Iran*. M. Litt. thesis, University of Oxford.

Tayeb, M. H. (1988) *Organizations and National Culture: A Comparative Analysis*. Sage Publications, London.

Tayeb, M. H. (1990) Japanese Management Style, in Daily, R. (with contributions from Keenan, T. and Tayeb, M.) (Ed.), *Organisational Behaviour*, pp. 257–282. Pitman, London.

Tayeb, M. H. (1995) The Competitive Advantage of Nations: The Role of HRM and its Socio-Cultural Context. *International Journal of Human Resource Management*, Vol. 6, pp. 588–605.

Trinque, B. M. (1993) *Challenge–Response Mechanism and Unmodal Strategy; Inertia and options in India's Economic Development*. Unpublished Ph.D. thesis, The University of Texas at Austin.

Tung, R. L. (1984) *Key to Japan's Economic Strength: Human Power*. D. C. Heath, Lexington, MA.

Tung, R. L. (1988) *The New Expatriates*. Ballinger, Cambridge, MA.

Wade, R. (1990) *Governing the Market*. Princeton University Press, Princeton, NJ.

Weber, M. (1930) *The Protestant Ethic and the Spirit of Capitalism*. George Allen & Unwin, London.

West, P. (1989) Cross-Cultural Literacy and the Pacific Rim. *Business Horizon*, March-April, pp. 3–17.

Whitley, R. (1992) *Business Systems in East Asia*. Sage, London.

Zeile, W. (1989) Industrial Policy and Organizational Efficiency: The Korean Chaebol Examined. Program in East Asia Business and Development Research Working Paper No. 30, Institute of Governmental Affairs, University of California, Davis.

Section Three

MANAGERIAL VALUES AND LEADERSHIP

Emerging Trends in Work Values and Leadership in India

Section Three includes three field-based explorations of managerial conceptualisations of leadership, work-related values and related issues. In a country where roles, responsibilities and goals of managers are often intimately linked by tradition, heritage and a strong belief system, empirical analysis can provide a significant glimpse of workplace re-orientation of contemporary leadership approaches. In their research on a comparative perspective of organisational leadership in India, Kakar and Kakar's, Kets de Vries and Vrignaud's perceptions of five leadership practices, namely, challenging, inspiring, enabling, modelling and en-couraging are evaluated amongst both CEOs and 'followers' in large organisations where both Indian and Western managerial approaches are in practice. The chapter examines the extent to which the widely held 'culturist' propositions of leadership are still valid in such large and 'hybrid' forms in the corporate context. The interesting conclusion is that in spite of the global linkages and reorientation of the competitive managerial mindset, traditional values and idealizations still strongly influence the domains of leadership behaviour in India

In Chapter Six, espousing work goals and societal value orientations, Chatterjee and Pearson provide empirical evidence suggesting a strong convergence of learning orientation and strategic outlook amongst senior managers while there is a new gap in terms of a diffusion of social vision amongst corporate leaders, creating a wide chasm between national reform goals and micro-level managerial visions.

Chapter Seven by Mellahi and Guermat deals with the demographic variations in managerial values in the Indian context. This is a significant issue given that 70 per cent of Indians are under the age of 35. The emerging generational shift in values therefore needs to be considered carefully.

The recent large-scale research in the area of cross-national leadership and value orientations has been provided by a project called Global Leadership and Organizational Behavior Effectiveness or GLOBE. The project involved 200 researchers from 62 countries and underpinned an exploration into the debate of 'culturally endorsed' and 'universal' aspects of values in leadership. The two culturally endorsed attributes that received wider acceptance were value-based charismatic and participative leadership. In terms of societal practices in performance orientation, India was surprisingly placed with a moderately high score. The scores on future focus, humane orientation, industrial sector influence all tended to see the leadership platform in India in a very positive light. There is an implicit thread of leadership and value shift towards more global skills, cosmopolitanism, inter-cultural dexterity, learning emphasis, commitment to performance, and future orientation that cuts across the three chapters in this section.

The focus of this section is to discuss the managerial challenge of establishing a fine balance of holding on to a long-held traditional value system while adopting a new layer of values, assumptions and belief systems necessary to make a mark in a globalising world. The empirical evidence contained in chapters here point to a clear shift away from a paternalistic orientation to more thoughtful and inclusive values. The strong value-based leadership role observed in organisations such as Infosys has had a strong transformational impact on the managers of

Indian corporations. Such nurturing of leadership can instill not only world-class quality, excellence and performance, but also a new and enriching connection between organisations and their people.

Reference

House, R. J. Paul J. Hanges, Mansour Javidan, Peter W. Dorfman and Vipin Gupta. (2004). *Culture, Leadership and Organizations: The GLOBE Study of 62 Societies*. London: Sage Publications.

5 Leadership in Indian Organizations from a Comparative Perspective

Sudhir Kakar, Shveta Kakar,
Manfred F.R. Kets De Vries, and Pierre Vrignaud

The proposition that a people's cultural tradition, comprising beliefs, values, attitudes, and social practices, strongly influences their behavior in modern business organizations, thus leading to diversity in management around the world, has enjoyed considerable theoretical and empirical support (Haire et al., 1966; Hofstede, 1980; Laurent, 1983; Tayeb, 1988; Lincoln and Kalleberg, 1990; Schneider and Barsoux, 1997). In the last three decades, this 'culturalist' thesis has continued to provide the dominant paradigm for the study of management and leadership styles in Indian business organizations (Chakraborty, 1987; Elhance, 1984; Garg and Parikh, 1995; Kakar, 1971; Singh and Bhandarker, 1990; Sinha, 1972, 1979, 1995; Virmani and Gupta, 1981). According to this paradigm, there are certain culture-specific expectations, shared by leaders and followers alike, that arise from socialization patterns within the family (Garg and Parikh, 1995; Kakar, 1978; Sinha, 1972).

These culture-specific expectations are said to play a significant role in shaping the context of organizational leadership in India. Among the patterns that have been identified in the literature, the following are the most relevant to the present research.

- A strong preference for an authoritative (not authoritarian) leader who is strict, demanding but also caring and nurturing—very much like the *karta*, the paternalistic head of the joint family in India. Sinha (1979) has called this type of leader the 'nurturant-task' (NT) leader, who is strict in getting the task accomplished and tries to dominate the activities of the subordinates. He is, however, not authoritarian but nurturant in the sense of functioning as a benevolent guide to the subordinates and taking a personal interest in their wellbeing and growth. Among the subordinates, on the other hand, there is a complementary tendency to idealize the leader and look on him as a repository of all virtues, deserving of faith and respect. He is thus a role model with many facets—high integrity, system builder, humane father-figure (Virmani and Gupta, 1981). The modeling function of leadership, then, has a high salience in Indian organizations.

- The cultural preference for the NT leader is related to a strong desire for power combined with dependency needs—wishes that are manifested in a search for proximity to the leader (Nandy and Kakar, 1980; Sinha, 1972). There is thus a pervasive use of ingratiating behavior towards the leader in Indian organizations, the ingratiators tending to exaggerate the power distance, showing their dependency and thereby seeking to evoke nurturant behavior from the leader (Pandey, 1981).

- There is a tendency to centralize power and control and a high status orientation (Virmani and Gupta, 1981; Singh and Bhandarker, 1990), making a collaborative team effort difficult—a pattern further reinforced by difficulties in giving and receiving negative feedback.

- There is a high preference for a personalized mode of relating across functions and tasks and thus a greater influence of informal networks on organizational decision-making (Dayal, 1988; Garg and Parikh, 1995).

Given the current state of the country's industrialization and integration with respect to the global economy, the question arises whether the culturalist thesis is still adequate to explain leadership in Indian organizations. One need not completely subscribe to its polar opposite, the 'universalist' thesis, which argues that since modern organizations are essentially based on Western technology, the fundamental problems of management are invariant and independent of the organization's cultural location (Hickson and Lammers, 1979; Negandhi, 1979, 1985), to recognize some of the problems in the culturalist thesis that generally takes a country or nation as its unit of culture. In the case of India, the culturalist dilemma may be posed in the form of a basic question: is there an Indian culture? The answers to this question have been varied (Ramanujan, 1990). One answer may state that there is no single Indian culture. There are historically rooted and contemporary traditions, ancient and modern, rural and urban. Each regional, linguistic, religious and caste group has its own culture. A contrary approach may be that under the apparent diversity, there is a real cultural unity in India that lets us speak of the Indian culture with some confidence. Another answer may be that what we see of Indian culture is nothing special to India. It is nothing but pre-industrial, feudal, agricultural, or whatever other category of social evolution we might care to use. Others, of course, may argue that mere is a unique Indian way that imprints and patterns all things that enter the subcontinent, including modern Western organizational forms.

Apart from the problem of taking India (or any other large, heterogeneous country) as a unit of culture, the culturalist paradigm must also confront the problem of cultural change. In other words, cultures are not static but dynamic. This is especially true of Indian management culture which, among all of India's various cultures, is arguably the most exposed to forces of modernization and globalization and therefore to the processes of cultural assimilation, transformation, reassertion and recreation which, too, are inherent in all cultural encounters.

Perhaps the most important fact, then, that demands a modification of the culturalist thesis in its original form is the rapid social and economic change that has taken place in the last three to four decades and which has recently picked up pace with the liberalization of the Indian economy and its increasing integration with the global marketplace. This change has been especially marked in the sub-culture of modern business organizations which have been in close contact with other, chiefly Western, management cultures through easy access to Western management literature, joint ventures and participation of Indian managers in management development programs mounted by local, regional and national chambers of commerce and management associations and also by the universities. Depending on the type of modern business organization, one would thus expect leadership practices, especially of chief executives who are the most exposed to these influences, to approach closer and closer to those of their Western colleagues.

From the viewpoint of leadership, modern business organizations in India can be grouped under four categories. First, there are the subsidiaries of multinational companies, some of the successors to the British-managed firms before Independence, which follow the management practices of their parent organizations. Second, there are the medium to large firms, family managed, which often have collaborations and joint ventures with Western (but now also a few Japanese and Korean) companies, where the management style is a 'hybrid' (Gopinath, 1998) of traditional Indian and Western practices. In addition, put into the category of 'hybrid' are those companies where top management has been exposed through management training (MBA and advanced management programs) to Western practices. Third, there are the indigenous firms, small to medium enterprises, which are family controlled and follow the traditional Indian, paternalistic management style. And, fourth, there are the entrepreneurial ventures run by young professionals, many of them small in size but with a large market capitalization, such as the ones in the fields of information technology, whose leadership styles have still to be systematically explored. It is the leadership of the hybrid firm, where significant changes in the management culture have taken place in the last two decades, which is the focus of our study.

The Hybrid Firm

The hybrid firm, which dominates the Indian industrial economy today, is a further development of the private company that was generally owned and managed by a family belonging to one of the traditional business communities, notably the Gujaratis, Parsis, Sindhis and Marwaris. The reason for the domination of these communities was their particularly high level of internal trust, mutual co-operation and close network of channels for business, loans, information and other resources (Tinberg, 1979). Homogeneous in their composition of top and middle management, the community's traditional culture and family socialization patterns were particularly salient for a study of its leadership practices.

As some of these family businesses grew and ventured into large-scale, complex enterprises, often in partnership with Western companies, the need for professionalization of the organization became imperative, their leadership now reflecting a juxtaposition of divergent and heterogeneous elements of two separate cultures (Garg and Parikh, 1995). Many of these companies are still not fully professional in the sense that the top leadership positions, especially that of the CEO, are occupied by members of the owner's family. But these family members have almost always been professionally trained in well-known institutions of higher learning in India or in universities in Europe, the UK and the US.

Besides the professional qualifications of the top management, another important change bearing on these firms' management culture has been in the composition of their employees, especially at the middle and senior management levels. Most of these executives come from upper and middle classes of urban India and do not necessarily belong to the traditional business community of the owners. Most have also physically grown up in nuclear families (although they may have been inculcated with the ideology and values of the extended family). The cultural predispositions deriving from traditional socialization within the extended family do not inform their organizational expectations and behavior quite as emphatically as postulated by the culturalist thesis. Further, these employees have also been educated at colleges, universities, and especially institutes of management set up after the 1960s which have exposed them to Western management values that may sharply differ from the accepted Indian cultural values (Boer and van Deventer, 1989).

In spite of these changes in the background and socialization of those occupying managerial positions in Indian organizations, there is still a debate on the degree to which an Indian manager is westernized. Whereas some see increasing convergence of management practices (Filella, 1981; Das and Manimala, 1993), others believe that this westernization is a surface phenomenon that does not touch the core personality of the Indian manager who, when push comes to shove, reverts to cultural detours to get things done (e.g. Sinha, 1995). Yet, whatever the pervasiveness and dominance of 'core' Indian values is in the rest of society, a recent study of a large sample of senior level managers suggests that such traditional values as close interpersonal relations at work are increasingly receding in importance and that 'there is an emergence of global value paradigms' (Chatterjee and Pearson, 2000: 94).

The question remains whether the westernization of Indian firms has a real impact on the leadership practices of the Indian executive. Do the encroaching Western practices really make a difference? To explore this question the study reported in this article examines the dimensions on which the top leadership of modern Indian business organizations, of the hybrid variety, differs from its Western, chiefly US, counterparts. By top leadership, we mean the CEOs of individual firms (or their equivalent in large corporations), a group which is vital for the study of business leadership but is rarely willing to collaborate in organizational research. We were thus interested in comparing the leadership practices of Indian and American CEOs, as described in their direct reports and reports from their subordinates.

Method

Sample

The Indian part of the study was carried out in the summer of 1999 in 23 family-owned 'hybrid' companies based in Delhi, Ahmedabad, Bombay and Bangalore. Twelve of them were engaged in various forms of collaboration with Western firms. One hundred and twenty people were surveyed and interviewed. We collected data from 16 CEOs[1] (direct report), and 104 of their subordinates (observer reports). Each CEO was described by an average of four observers. The companies were medium- to large-scale enterprises in different sectors of industry, such as automotive, textile, chemicals, and computers, with an annual turnover that ranged from 20 million to 1.1 billion US dollars and a workforce ranging from 250 to 18,000 employees. Except for two, all the CEOs were members of the owner families. The average age of the Indian CEOs was 50 years. All the Indian CEOs were men and came from Punjab, Delhi, Gujarat, Bengal, Maharashtra, Tamil Nadu, Uttar Pradesh and Rajasthan.

Measures

For the assessment of leadership practices, each CEO and four to five senior managers reporting directly to the CEO were asked to complete the Leadership Practices Inventory (LPI) for that CEO. The LPI, comprising 30 descriptive statements, is perhaps the most widely used 360-degree instrument for leadership evaluation in the organizational world today. In this instrument, feedback is sought on five leadership practices which have been identified as common to extraordinary leadership achievement: challenging the process (also called envisioning), inspiring a shared vision (i.e. creating a 'buy-in' for the vision), enabling others to act (i.e. team building), modeling the way ('walking the talk'), and encouraging the heart (giving constructive feedback). We chose to use the LPI because this instrument is widely used for evaluation of managers. The sound psychometric properties of the LPI have been proven in large-scale samples (Posner and Kouzes, 1988, 1993; Kouzes and Posner, 1995). For their database of 43,899 American managers, including CEOs' self-reports (n = 6651), and their subordinates' reports (n = 37,248), Posner and Kouzes state that the Cronbach alpha coefficients are respectively 0.81, 0.87, 0.85, 0.81, 0.91 for the five scales: challenging, inspiring, enabling, modeling, and encouraging (Kouzes and Posner, 1995: 343). A factor analysis (principal axis factoring followed by varimax rotations) of the data in this same data base shows that five factors explain 60.5 percent of the variance, and that the saturations of the items on these five factors are consistent with the five scales of the LPI (Kouzes and Posner, 1995: 344–45).

The Subscales

Each scale is measured by six items that are on a five-point Likert scale ranging from 1 (= strongly disagree) to 5 (= strongly agree). Therefore for each scale, the minimum score is six and the maximum 30. Following are descriptions of the scales, including sample questions.

1. *Challenging*—six items

   - I seek out challenging opportunities that test my own skills and abilities.
   - I challenge people to try out new and innovative approaches to their work.

2. *Inspiring*—six items

   - I talk about future trends that influence how our work gets done.
   - I describe a compelling vision of what our future could be like.

3. *Enabling*—six items

   - I develop cooperative relationships among the people I work with.
   - I actively listen to diverse points of view.

4 *Modeling*—six items

- I set a personal example of what I expect from others.
- I follow through on promises and commitments that I make.

5 *Encouraging*—six items

- I praise people for a job well done.
- I find ways to celebrate accomplishments.

Such 360-degree instruments are particularly interesting because the CEOs' responses can be compared with those of observers. Using the questionnaire in such a manner, the test-taker not only does a self-assessment, but also receives feedback from colleagues, subordinates, superiors, and others who are familiar with his or her leadership style. Such a feedback process on these various dimensions of leadership will give the test-taker a more balanced view of how his or her leadership style is perceived. Note that Kouzes and Posner did not find a significant difference between 'self' and 'observer' responses (Kouzes and Posner, 1995: 345–6).

The LPI has also been shown to be valid for intercultural studies. It has been successfully used for these kinds of studies both in English (the language in which the instrument was originally created) as well as in Spanish and French translations (see a review of this work in Posner and Kouzes, 1988, 1993; Kouzes and Posner, 1995). These studies did not show a significant difference between American and European managers, between Americans and Mexicans, or Americans and French Canadians. A similar study was done with managers from four Pacific Rim countries (Korea, the Philippines, Taiwan and Malaysia), and it showed similar results.

Results and Discussion

Reliability Analysis

Before proceeding with a comparison of averages, we verified the reliability of the scales by calculating the Cronbach alpha coefficients. The values of these coefficients are respectively: 0.68, 0.80, 0.81, 0.78 and 0.91 for the five scales: challenging, inspiring, enabling, modeling, and encouraging. These values show an acceptable validity given the small size of the data sample; they are in fact similar to the values generally observed for LPI scales within specific small-scale professional categories (Posner and Kouzes, 1993; Kouzes and Posner, 1995). We then compared the averages of the direct reports in our Indian group ('self') with the observer reports on the five scales; and did not find any significant differences. We therefore decided to aggregate the data for the responses as a whole.

Comparison of Data on Indian Leaders to the US Norms

In order to test the hypothesis of the existence of cross cultural differences, we compared the parameters of the Indian sample group with the group of American managers who made up the population that constituted the database of Kouzes and Posner's (1995) validation study for the LPI. We retained the aggregated data from the direct and observer reports (n = 43,899).

Table 5.1 shows the results of the subjects in the Indian sample group, as well as those of the American managers to which they are compared.

The differences in the averages (Table 1) vary from 2.90 to 1.02 in absolute value. For the dimensions of challenging, inspiring, enabling, and modeling, the differences are negative (the averages of the Indian group are higher than those of the American group). On the other hand, for the dimension of encouraging, we observed a positive difference' (the average of the Indian group is lower than that of the American group). These differences are all significant as assessed by Student's tests (p<.001). In order to evaluate the effect size we calculated Cohen's d (the ratio between the difference in means and the standard deviation of the reference population). Based on the levels generally adopted to judge the size of this effect (Cohen, 1992; Corroyer and Rouanet, 1994), we considered the differences on the challenging, inspiring and modeling scales to be a medium-size effect, and the differences on enabling and encouraging to be a low-size effect (note that the scores of the Indian group are lower than those of the American norm on this last scale). In sum, the Indian group is characterized by scores that are higher than the American norm for the challenging, enabling and modeling dimensions, and lower for the dimension of encouraging. In their comparison of different groups, Kouzes and Posner (1995) examined not only differences in averages, but also the ranking of the dimension averages, which—according to them— shows the relative importance afforded to leadership in each of these dimensions. We have observed, from a descriptive point of view only, that the order of the dimensions in the Indian groups (enabling, modeling, challenging, inspiring and encouraging) is different than that of the American group (enabling, challenging, modeling, encouraging, and inspiring). The organization of the dimensions of leadership in the Indian group is, therefore, different from the organization of these dimensions in the American group.

Table 1: LPI Scores as Assessed by Indian and US CEOs and Observers

	Indian sample		US sample[a]		Difference	
LPI Scales	Mean	SD	Mean	SD	Mean	d[b]
Challenging	24.26	3.23	22.38	4.17	−1.88***	−0.45
Inspiring	23.38	4.14	20.48	4.90	−2.90***	−0.59
Enabling	24.91	3.59	23.89	4.37	−1.02***	−0.23
Modeling	24.48	3.58	22.18	4.16	−2.30***	−0.55
Encouraging	20.81	5.30	21.89	5.22	1.08***	0.21

[a] data from LPI validation sample, $n = 43,899$, Kouznes & Posner (1995: Table A3, pp. 345–46);
[b] effect size: $d = (m_{US} - m_{indian})/S_{US}$; ***significant at .001.

Leadership Practices

In comparing the LPIs of the Indian group to the American norm, perhaps the most surprising finding is that for the top leadership of Indian organizations (as reflected in the assessments of their own and the observers' reports), scores were higher on all dimensions of leadership except that of encouraging (see Table 1).

The difference in means is significant and demonstrates a medium-size effect in favor of the Indian group in three areas. The first is inspiring, which concerns the leader's capacity to envision the future and enlist the support of others. The second is modeling, in which the leader is rated on his success in building teams, setting clear goals, planning small wins, setting an example and ensuring that certain values are adhered to in the organization. The third is challenging, which assesses if the leader is able to search for opportunities and to experiment and take risks. The difference in means is significant and demonstrates a low-size effect in favor of the Indian group in the area of enabling, which measures the leader's success in planning, empowerment, delegation, and building trust. The high scores of the Indian CEOs on enabling and modeling are consistent with Singh and Bhandarker's (1990) study of five Indian 'transformational' leaders who were also rated highly on these aspects of leadership. And last but not least, the difference in means is significant and demonstrates a low-size effect, but this time against the Indian group for the dimension of encouraging—which indicates a lower ability of the Indian CEOs to recognize contributions arid celebrate accomplishments.

We did consider whether or not the fact that the LPI was designed within an American cultural context would bias our study. The fact that we observed differences between the Americans and Indians is particularly interesting in this case, since, as we discussed earlier, previous intercultural studies using the LPI did not show significant differences. The LPI proved thereby to be relatively insensitive to cultural context. Also, the majority of the participants in our study had enough experience in Western business organizations to be familiar with the cultural context that frames the LPI questionnaire.

We acknowledge, however, that this assumption would be strengthened by a statistical analysis designed to verify the equivalence of this instrument in different cultural contexts. (For a review of equivalence among instruments in cross cultural studies, see Berry et al., 1992; and for a recent review see Vrignaud, in press.) Unfortunately, the size of our sample group is too limited for this kind of analysis, as the statistical methods for identifying culturally biased psychometric instruments, in particular at the item level, require samples of several hundred subjects.

A more fundamental criticism can be raised about the perspective of cultural universalism introduced by the use of the LPI as a means of cross cultural comparison despite the fact that it is based on theoretical references that are external to the culture being studied. The LPI was constructed through open-ended questionnaires and interviews of a vast sample group of managers on best leadership practices. Because the participants were North American, cultural absolutism was unavoidable.

This type of research could be broadened by interviewing managers from different cultures, thus adopting a perspective of moderate cultural relativism. We are currently developing a questionnaire for leadership evaluation that will take into consideration cross cultural variations (Kets de Vries et al., 2001).

Another possible explanation for the higher LPI scores of Indian leaders could be that because of the greater power distance in Indian organizations, as postulated by the culturalist thesis, senior managers are apprehensive about criticizing the CEO and thus do not honestly express their true opinions on the LPI questionnaire. Considering that the difference in means is not significant between direct and observer reports, which show the same difference with the US norm, the fear explanation does not seem very plausible. The perception that the leaders have a tendency to be authoritarian is also reflected in the Indian leaders' comparatively low scores on the encouraging dimension.

Another possible cultural explanation is a widely shared unconscious tendency among Indian managers to idealize the leader. This would be consistent with the culturalist postulate that, because of the socialization pattern in the family, Indians are more inclined to perceive the leader as a wise, caring, dependable yet demanding father-figure on the model of the karta of the joint family:

> In India, this automatic reverence for superiors is a nearly universal fact. Leaders at every level of society and politics, but particularly the patriarchal elders of the extended family and jati [caste] groups, take on an emotional salience independent of any realistic evaluation of their performance, let alone acknowledgement of their all too human being. When it comes to leadership in the larger social institutions of business and government in India, charisma plays an unusually significant role' (Kakar, 1978: 138)

If there is an idealization of the leader it is no longer completely blind to his deficiencies or unmindful of the organizational needs of the subordinates that the leader does not fulfill. The fact that Indian CEOs still score significantly higher on the inspiring, modeling, challenging and enabling aspects of leadership than US CEOs lends further support to the hypothesis of idealization in the case of the Indian sample. In any event, whatever the extent of idealization of the leader and its possible cultural roots, and whatever the unconscious dynamics at work, the higher LPI ratings of Indian CEOs will normally be interpreted as an indication that senior managers in India feel more committed and satisfied with the leadership of their companies than their US counterparts.

Conclusion

Our study of the leadership practices in the 'hybrid' form of modern Indian business organizations shows that, in spite of their extensive exposure to Western management concepts and practices at a time of India's increasing integration with the global economy, the influences of Indian culture on the senior managers' perception of top leadership has not disappeared. Consistent with the culturalist postulate, the Indian CEO, even when criticized as authoritarian in some aspects of his behavior, is the recipient of greater idealization from the team of senior managers than is the case with the Western sample. The Indian idealization of the leader has, of course, certain advantages such as a greater *esprit de corps* in the senior management team and in its higher degree of satisfaction with and commitment to the leadership of the organization. Yet idealization, that great construct of the imagination which is capable of conceiving with the conviction of a known fact a more perfect and valuable reality while ensuring that what is idealized is inevitably admired and held in awe, distorts the perception of the CEO's leadership. The leader is thus deprived of the critical feedback from his senior managers that would help him to eliminate certain dysfunctional behavior while he develops other, more effective, leadership practices.

Further research on leadership behavior in different cultures will perhaps have to grapple with the issue of the unit of culture more effectively than was possible in the present study. Civilizations as units of culture— Indian and Western—are based primarily on the criteria of political geography and secondarily on a common religious and cultural heritage, Judeo-Christian in the case of the West and (mainly) Hindu in the case of India. Such large units may be too diffuse and include too much cultural heterogeneity to be optimally useful. The same objections may also be raised if we take nations as cultural units. Considering that language is one of the main carriers of a group's culture, we may need to give linguistic groups greater importance than they have so far received as markers of cultural identity.

Note

1. In spite of our best efforts, seven CEOs did not fill out the questionnaire, although we did get observers' responses for these same CEOs.

References

Berry, J.W., Poortinga, Y.H., Segall, M.H. and Dasen P.R. (1992) *Cross-cultural Psychology. Research and Applications.* Cambridge: Cambridge University Press.

Boer, M. and van Deventer, F. (1989) *India, Culture and Management*. Rotterdam: Erasmus University.

Chakraborty, S.K. (1987) *Managerial Effectiveness and Quality of Work Life—Indian Insights*. New Delhi: Tata-McGraw-Hill.

Chatterjee, S.R. and Pearson, C.A.L. (2000) 'Indian Managers in Transition: Orientations, Work Goals, Values and Ethics', *Management International Review* 40(1): pp. 81–95.

Cohen, J. (1992) 'A Power Primer', *Psychological Bulletin* 112: 155–59.

Corroyer, D. and Rouanet, H. (1994) 'Sur l'importance des effets et de ses indicateurs dans l'analyse statistique des données (On the Importance of Effects and Their Indicators in Statistical Data Analysis)', *L'Année Psychologique* 94: 607–24.

Das, H. and Manimala, M. J. (1993) 'Roles Indian Managers Play', *Indian Journal of Industrial Relations* 29(2): 133–54.

Dayal, I. (1988) 'Managing Hi-tech Organizations', in P. Khandwalla (ed.) *Social Development: A Role for Organizational Sciences*. New Delhi: Sage.

Elhance, D.N. (1984) 'Professional Management and the Indian Scene', in J.S. Mathur and J. Prakash (eds) *Indian Management Scene*. Allahabad: Kitab Mahal.

Filella, S.J. (1981) 'The Indian Manager', in P.N. Singh *Profile of an Asian Manager*. Bombay: Xavier Institute of Management.

Garg, P. and Parikh, I. (1995) *Crossroads of Culture*. New Delhi: Sage.

Gopinath, C. (1998) 'Alternative Approaches to Indigenous Management in India', *Management International Review* 38(3): 257–75.

Haire, M., Ghiselli, E.E. and Porter, L.W. (1966) *Managerial Thinking—An International Study*. New York: Wiley.

Hickson, D.J. and Lammers, C.J. (1979) 'Are Organizations Culture-bound', in C.J. Lammers and D.J. Hickson (eds) *Organizations Alike and Unlike: International and Inter-institutional Studies in the Sociology of Organizations*, pp. 402–19. London: Routledge & Kegan Paul.

Hofstede, G. (1980) *Culture's Consequences*. London: Sage.

Kakar, S. (1971) 'Authority Patterns and Subordinate Behavior in Indian Organizations', *Administrative Science Quarterly* 16(3): 298.

Kakar, S. (1978) *The Inner World*. Delhi: Oxford University Press.

Kets de Vries, M.F.R., Vrignaud, P. and Florent-Treacy, E. (2001) 'The Global Leadership Life Inventory', INSEAD Working Paper.

Kouzes, J.M. and Posner, B.Z. (1995) *The Leadership Challenge*, 2nd edn. San Francisco: Jossey-Bass.

Lincoln J.R. and Kalleberg, A.L. (1990) *Culture, Control and Commitment*. Cambridge: Cambridge University Press.

Laurent, A. (1983) 'The Cultural Diversity of Western Management Practices', *International Studies of Management and Organizations* 8: 75–96.

Nandy, A. and Kakar, S. (1980) 'Culture and Personality', in U. Pareek (ed.) *A Survey of Research in Psychology*. Bombay: Popular Prakashan.

Negandhi, A.R. (1979) 'Convergence and Divergence in Organizational Practice', in C.J. Lammers and D.J. Dickson (eds) *Organizations Alike and Unlike.* London: Routledge & Kegan Paul.

Negandhi, A.R. (1985) 'Management in the Third World', in P. Joynt and M. Warner (eds) *Managing in Different Cultures,* pp. 69–97. Oslo: Universitetsforlaget.

Pandey, J. (1981) 'Ingratiation as Social Behaviour', in J. Pandey (ed.) *Perspectives on Experimental Psychology.* New Delhi: Concept.

Posner, B.Z. and Kouzes, J.M. (1988) 'Development and Validation of the Leadership Practices Inventory', *Educational and Psychological Measurement* 48: 483–96.

Posner, B.Z. and Kouzes, J.M. (1993) 'Psychometric Properties of the Leadership Practices Inventory—Updated', *Educational and Psychological Measurement* 53: 191–99.

Ramanujan, A.K. (1990) 'Is There an Indian Way of Thinking?', in M. Marriott (ed.) *India through Hindu Categories.* New Delhi: Sage.

Schneider, S.C. and Barsoux, J. (1997) *Managing across Cultures.* London: Prentice Hall.

Singh, P. and Bhandarker, A. (1990) *Corporate Success and Transformational Leadership.* New Delhi: Wiley Eastern.

Sinha, D. (1972) *The Mughal Syndrome.* New Delhi: Tata-McGraw-Hill.

Sinha, J.B.P. (1979) *The Nurturant Task Leader.* New Delhi: Concept.

Sinha, J.B.P. (1995) *The Cultural Context of Leadership and Power.* New Delhi: Sage.

Tayeb, M.H. (1988) *Organizations and National Cultures.* London: Sage.

Tinberg, T. (1979) *The Marwaris.* New Delhi: Vikas.

Virmani, B.R. and Gupta, S.U. (1981) *Indian Management.* New Delhi: Vision.

Vrignaud, P. (in press) 'Les biais culturels: de la nuisance psychométrique au potentiel heuristique (Cultural Bias: From Psychometric Nuisance to Heuristic Potential)', *Bulletin de Psychologie.*

Work Goals and Societal Value Orientations of Senior Indian Managers: An Empirical Analysis

6

Samir R. Chatterjee and Cecil A.L. Pearson

Introduction

Societies in Asia are undergoing considerable transformation with the increasing dominance of market ideology. The agenda for change in old, tradition-bound Asian societies, like India, has become critically linked to the work goals and values of the managerial élite, who have been seen to be responsible for ensuring the transition. The success of the market-based transformation in these societies will be an outcome of how deeply the reform ideology is shared at the managerial level. In spite of the importance of the profound changes in the economic life of these societies, cultural-based theories have dominated the managerial research framework (Hofstede, 1991; Westwood and Posner, 1997). Until the beginning of 1990s the managerial value system diversity was considered to be mostly due to systemic and cultural differentiation, and the researchers argued that different cultural and social experiences created different value premisses (Bass *et al.*, 1979; England, 1986; Hofstede, 1980). The imperatives of market ideology in a strong tradition bound society create a perplexing array of options for managers in their choice of action frames. Alleviation of this dilemma requires paradigms beyond the cultural analyses in understanding specific contexts.

In a survey of over 2,500 managers, in a five-country study, England (1978) found a high degree of pragmatism amongst the managers in all countries except India where moralistic emphasis of the managers of the

1960s and 1970s contrasted sharply with the contemporary management scene elsewhere. The results of the England study suggested that Indian managers paid much more importance to organisational stability than the managers from other countries. For instance, compared with US managers, Indian managers attached more importance to employee welfare than to the goal of profit maximisation. England's findings also showed that the Indian managers more consistently valued obedience and conformity and, subsequently, it was contended that Indian managers were strongly against any value that signified change and innovation (Sinha, 1990).

Managerial assumptions and values highlighting the country's long and complex traditions have mostly been considered by the Indian scholars (Chakraborty, 1991; Kao et al., 1995; Saha, 1992; Sinha, 1990). Some general considerations are now being given to the impact of economic reform on management practices (Gopalan and Rivera, 1997; Monappa and Engineer, 1999). It is perhaps more important to focus on work goals that the values generate as the basis of action frame during the rapid reform. While managerial values provide the basis for organisational architecture, work goals tend to provide the action frame by prioritizing the agendas of managers (Harpaz, 1990; MOW International Research Team, 1987; Pearson and Chatterjee, 1999a; 1999b; Shenkar and Ronen, 1987). The traditional conceptualisation of work in the Indian context has always been rooted to the idea of work as a duty (Saha, 1992). However, in recent decades studies in urban centres have found a displacement of these traditional values in favour of convergence with market oriented goals. Recently, for instance, Sinha (1990) reported findings that were not aligned to this duty orientation. He found, contrary to his expectations, that the individual preference for utilization of competencies, status and personal growth opportunities was more valued as work goals than social relations and a sense of duty. These studies provide evidence that the traditional values of managers in contemporary organisations are undergoing shifts. The need for balancing economic imperatives with the traditional societal context is acknowledged as:

> It is important that organizations continue to grow and evolve newer perspectives in terms of their values and redefine their linkages with the society. In doing so the organisations should acknowledge the emotional expectations and personal values of the employees which influence their

attitude to work and their behaviours. Unfortunately, these dimensions of sociocultural reality are either ignored or rarely considered in designing organisations or in socializing the employees (Prakash, 1995, p. 200).

This paper explores these issues by investigating the changing work goals of managers as they balance multiple imperatives of reform, tradition, organisational and personal priorities. The evidence of this paper, which is based on an empirical survey of senior Indian managers, suggests a striking shift is taking place in the managerial mindset. A strong inference of the data is that a considerable number of new imperatives are affecting the managerial work goals in ways that are leading to more convergence in managerial values. Significant amongst the findings is that the managers surveyed strongly expressed preferences for the goal orientations towards learning and market responsiveness. The learning focus amongst managers is evidenced across gender, rank, age, education, regional variation and other related demographic variables. This trend of "a learning goal", which is displacing previously held goals of "stability, tradition and security", signals the diffusion of reform culture at the micro level. The empirical evidence also confirms the paradox of the learning value emphasis not being associated with a clear social goal orientation.

Changing Managerial Work Values

Bass *et al.* (1979) and England (1978) have provided a seminal framework of Indian managerial work goals based on their multi-country fieldwork. Bass and colleagues administered about 5,000 scenarios on budgeting decisions as a means of interpreting managerial work values. It was reported that pragmatic managers chose not to prioritize such issues as safety, strike resolution, improvement to workforce morale, an emphasis on quality or to promote their environmental integrity ahead of budgetary constraints. This was a surprising revelation as the earlier England studies had identified Indian managers to be high on moralistic orientations. The results of the Bass *et al.* study demonstrate that shifts in managerial work values were occurring before the launching of the economic reform program in 1991.

The study reported in this paper addresses the connection between reform orientations and work goals. Work goal priorities and social orientations link the internal characteristics of an organisation to its broader macro context. A number of well-known studies (England, 1978; England *et al.*, 1974; England and Lee, 1974) have suggested that the work goal values of Indian managers were more skewed towards organisational stability, which in turn perpetuated an emphasis on status, hierarchy and security. In contrast to this view, a number of other authors (Gopalan and Rivera, 1997; Kao *et al.*, 1995) have indicated strong convergence of managerial work goals to align more with Western societal contexts. For instance, in a study of 200 UK and 400 Indian companies, Khan and Atkinson (1987) found strong similarities of Indian and UK managers in both recognition of social responsibility and potential gains in social involvement.

During the 1990s, the reform movement in India affected the senior managerial cadre in a way very different from the previous decades. Kao *et al.* (1995) summarised these emerging trends of social values, work goals and managerial priorities. They contended, first, a predominance of hierarchical perspective where juniors yielded to their seniors on all symbols and values and the seniors reciprocated with patronage and affection. This is very similar to the "*oyabun-kobun*" relationship of the Japanese context. Second, political culture of the organisations was based on patronage. Third, there was a strong preference for personalised relationships in the work organisation. Fourth, social networking through status and role was valued. Fifth, the importance of community orientation was significant. Finally, the general culture promoted a sense of worldview where work was not considered central to the society. In addition, the concept of "time" did not encourage a sense of urgency.

Given the tumultuous effect of macro-level reform movement of the 1990s, it was felt that such broad transformation of the Indian business culture can only be confirmed through the shifts in the work goals of senior decision makers in key sectors of the economy. It has often been argued that the transformation of the high tech industry in the Bangalore region has more to do with the managerial values and innovative work goals than a systematic convergence of competence and infrastructure. The "greenhouse" effect, which is evident in the emergence of high tech industry in Bangalore, diamond processing in Western India and similar other dramatic areas of clear distinctive value shift, provides interesting examples of new managerial paradigms at work. The managerial work goal shift needs to be understood against the background of dominant business family values of key sectors. In a special research survey of 50 top business family values, it was concluded that:

> . . . not one of the top 50 business houses is sending out a powerful survival signal. Only 14 of them display qualities that make for strong—albeit by no means powerful—survival signals . . . The lessons can hardly be ignored: for India's family business groups to survive, unidimensional excellence will not suffice. Only a leap on to the level occupied by world-class companies on every aspect of performance will ensure survival (*Business Today*, 1998, p. 21).

This study aims to examine the degree to which such paradigm shifts are noticeable across the general managerial mental models.

Methodology

Site and Respondents

The study was conducted with senior Indian managers who undertook management development courses conducted by the Management Centre for Human Values, Indian Institute of Management, Calcutta. Each of the study respondents either was a participant of a week-long residential programme at this most prestigious centre for value studies, or attended similar courses that were conducted by programme directors, from the Institute, at other Indian cities. A questionnaire was administered to most of the respondents by the first author, at the Institute, where he was the Sir Ratan Tata Visiting Fellow for six months. In most cases he briefed the participants, and this ensured the very high response rate of 85 per cent. A total of 421 questionnaires were completed. Generally, the participants completed the questionnaire on the first day of their seminar.

Respondent selection was a feature of the study. Most of the study participants were from public or private sector organizations that had approached the Indian Institute of Management to provide training in the area of Indian tradition and values. The increasing pressure of economic liberalisation programmes in the Indian workplace has been recognised by powerful and socially conscious Indian business leaders who are calling for the integration of the human values paradigm in Indian business. Some sources (Gopinath, 1996; *The Hindu*, 1997) contend that senior managerial cadre need to re-immerse themselves in traditional Indian values. Therefore, the sample had an element of self-selection in terms of the respondents being predisposed to incorporating value considerations in their managerial outlook.

Measures

The administered questionnaire provided demographic and perceptual data. The demographic data, which included gender, age, managerial level, educational qualifications and details about childhood upbringing as well as residence for the first 25 years of their life, were used to develop a profile of the managers studied. Demographic detail was also obtained about the company ownership, main business activity and organisational size of the respondents.

Perceptions about reform orientations and work goals were provided by the respondents. To evaluate the manager's reform orientations a 12-item instrument was designed. These items, which were aimed to cover concerns fundamental to the Indian worldview, were established after considerable consultation. To complete the reform value scale managers were required to rank each item for importance, from the most important (1) to the least important (12). In addition, 11 facets of work goals were assessed with an instrument that was employed by Harpaz (1990) in an extensive international study. The managers were required to rank each work goal item from most important (1) to least important (11).

Analysis

Frequency tables were employed to show the range of responses for the 421 managers. Means and their standard deviations were computed for each item, for the two scales of reform orientations and work goals. The reform orientations and work goal responses data were separately reduced by appropriate factor analyses. Employing polychoric correlation outputs the 12 reform items were reduced to five constructs, and the 11 work goal items were reduced to five variables. The combinations of items for each construct or variable are shown later in Table 3. The association for each bivariate pair was estimated with Spearman rho correlations. These analyses were undertaken with statistical analysis system (SAS) subroutines.

Results

The demographic profile of the managers studied is shown as Table 1. These data show that the sample was dominated by senior men who were mainly employed in large organisations. An unique feature of the sample is that 70.1 per cent of the managers were employed in senior managerial positions. A further striking feature of the sample was that almost 94 per cent of the managers held senior level university qualifications. Age and managerial level were significantly correlated ($r = 0.55$, $p < 0.0001$). Nearly one half of the managers worked in government and local government institutions, most of which were involved in financial activities (e.g. banking, accounting). Almost two-thirds of the study managers had lived in eastern and northern India for the first 25 years of their life and there was a strong relationship between the region of their birth and their vocation ($r = 0.22$, $p < 0.0001$). A great number of the participants were from joint families. From the profile of the managers (as given by Table 1) it might be predicted that the respondents would be anchored to traditional values that would encourage the maintenance of the status quo. However, the data of Table 2 indicate significant shifts from conventional foundations.

In Table 2 the ranked mean scores and standard deviations for the reform orientations and work goals are presented. The reform orientations of the study managers may be partitioned into two distinct sections. The first section, including work quality, personal integrity, team work, customer service and social responsibility, can be ascribed to be associated with features of a market orientated society. The second section, including workplace harmony, organisational learning, respect for seniority, innovation and creativity, an ordered relations structure value tradition, and wealth and material possessions may arguably be linked to a society's concept of organisational configuration. In the context of India the data surprisingly place work quality ahead of all of the other items, which are commonly stereotyped to have greater priority in the Indian context. In addition, the low ranking of tradition may also be interpreted to mean a displacement of tradition in preference to the higher ranked items. In reality, these data show a paradox amongst Indian managers in balancing these two sections of reform values. For example, personal integrity could have been linked to the second section, whereas organisational learning

Table 1: Demographic Data (%) for the Indian Managers

	Percentage
Gender	
Male	93.1
Female	6.9
Age	
<30	4.7
1–39	16.9
40–49	34.2
>49	44.2
Level	
Senior	70.1
Middle	25.4
Junior	4.5
Organisation (ownership)	
Government	46.6
National	17.3
Corporate	10.9
International	9.5
Private	7.8
Residence (first 25 years)	
Eastern	34.0
Northern	30.6
Western	17.3
Southern	16.4
Company size	
<100	8.6
100–499	11.9
500–1,000	8.8
>1,000	70.7
Education	
Postgraduate	55.6
Graduate	38.2
Diploma	6.2
Business (activity)	
Finance/banking	41.1
Manufacturing	26.4
Government	11.2
Professional	10.8
Other	10.3
Childhood (family)	
Joint	61.8
Nuclear	31.8
Hostel/boarding	5.7
Other	0.7

Note: n = 421

Table 2: Means and Standard Deviations of Reform Orientations
and Work Goals

Variable Description	Mean	Std
Reform orientations		
Work quality	3.61	2.40
Personal integrity	3.86	3.10
Team work	4.37	2.33
Customer service	4.90	2.98
Social responsibility	5.13	3.00
Workplace harmony	6.57	2.59
Organisational learning	7.16	2.45
Respect for seniority	7.17	2.45
Innovation and creativity	7.29	3.56
Ordered relations structure	8.82	2.72
Value tradition	8.94	3.83
Wealth and material possessions	10.21	2.31
Work goals		
Opportunity to learn new things	3.81	2.52
Work that is liked and interesting	4.09	2.74
Job with a variety of tasks and roles	4.33	2.37
Job that is matched abilities/experience	4.75	2.64
Social inter-relationships between colleagues		
and supervisors	5.24	2.65
Opportunity to improve and be promoted	5.62	2.59
Autonomy in decision making	6.00	3.25
Good job security	7.16	3.00
A good salary	7.60	2.78
Good physical working conditions	8.69	2.12
Convenient work hours	8.69	2.52

Notes: n = 421. The lower the mean, the higher the perceived level of importance;
Std = Standard deviations of the means

and innovation and creativity could have been associated with the first
section. Such ambivalence points to a definite shift in values and confirms
a transition in the perceptions of reform orientations amongst senior
managers.

The right hand side of Table 2 presents the assessed work goals in
their ranked order of importance. The study managers nominated the
opportunity to learn new things as their most important work goal. The
next three important work goals that were identified by the managers
were strongly associated with elements of enrichment, and the matching

of their skills and competencies with the workplace dimensional require-ments. Interestingly, the work goal of good social interpersonal relations was the fifth most important work goal, yet Indian society is considered to be a collective community (Hofstede, 1991). The study managers re-garded physical work conditions and convenient work hours as the least important of their work goals. Also of low importance was salary and job security. Not only is this observation at considerable variance with other international studies (Harpaz, 1990) where salary has always been highly ranked, but in Indian society the possession of a job and the associated income are vital. Overall, the findings for the ranked work goals indicate that the managers realise that their society is in transition and their focus is more on the attributes needed to be successful in a market economy, and considerably less importance is attached to the work goals that had greater relevance prior to the Indian economic reform (England et al., 1974).

Table 3 reports the significant relationships between the reform orientation constructs and the work goal variables. The combinations of reform orientation items that formed the five constructs, and the work goal items that clustered to form the five variables are shown on the vertical and horizontal axes respectively. The combinations of the items are intuitively appealing. For instance, the three items of the reform ori-entation construct, which was termed work culture, was the summary of the items of respect for seniority, workplace harmony, and ordered relationship structure, a set that reflect a socially, stabilising group of workplace features. Also, the work goal items of learning new things, interesting work, ability and experience, and promotion suggest a match of personal attributes that are vital for advancement in contemporary, dynamic, competitive work settings and this work goal variable was termed social capital. The combination of the questionnaire items that formed the five reform orientations constructs and five work goals variables are shown in the footnotes of Table 3. A total of 52 per cent (13/25) of the bivariate relationships of these ten constructs variables were in the range of 5 per cent to 1 per cent level of significance.

Table 3 presents an interesting set of relationships about reform norms and valued work goals. It is shown that three of the reform orient-ation constructs, that provide a blend of traditional and contemporary societal attributes, are strongly linked with three work goal variables that broadly integrate learning properties as well as context and content dimensions of current work domains. It is shown in Table 3 that a fourth reform orientation construct, which includes innovation and wealth indices, was strongly correlated with work goals with learning dimensions, convenient work hours and autonomy. A striking observation was that the relatively important reform orientation of social responsibility was non-significantly correlated with any of the five work goal variables. An inference of this finding is that the items developed in the 1980s (MOW International Research Team, 1987) and used in this study need to be extended. In order to be relevant to the context-specific issues, newer items need to be incorporated.

Table 3: Reform Orientations and Work Goal Correlations

Reform Orientations[b]	Work Goals[a]				
	Social Capital	Security	Empower-ment	Meaning-fulness	Status
Work culture	226**	277**	216**	007	144**
Market responsiveness	118*	251**	172**	014	062
Competency and character	250**	102*	166**	075	053
Strategic tension	228**	036	111*	188**	093
Social vision	012	026	027	048	002

Notes: [a] Work goals: social capital (learning, interesting work, ability/experience, promotion); security (social relations, security, salary); empowerment (convenient hours, autonomy); meaningfulness (task variety); status (physical work conditions)
[b] Reform orientations: work culture (workplace harmony, ordered relations structure, respect for seniority); market responsiveness (quality in all work, customer service, valuing tradition in change); competency and character (team work, organisational learning, personal integrity); strategic tension (innovation and creativity, wealth and material possessions); social vision (social responsibility)
Decimals omitted from correlations. * $p < 0.05$; ** $p < 0.01$; $n = 421$.

Concluding Discussion

The content of Table 3 suggests a strong causal link connecting the work cultural orientation, market responsiveness orientation and the level of competency to the goals of building social capital, security and empowering climate in work organisations. It is revealing that the strategic tensions brought about by the reform imperatives are linked to the meaningfulness variables. This may demonstrate that the new outward looking culture of corporate governance has brought about a mindset reorientation whose meaningfulness of managerial work life is expressed less through the traditional power relations and more through the strategic arena of the external context. This new work goal trend is tempered by the predictable link of status only with the work cultural issues. It is surprising that, in spite of the data suggesting the meaningfulness of work life deriving from strategic orientation, the status is still perceived to be strongly defined within the boundaries of work cultural domain. Perhaps the most striking implication of the study lies in the area of complete lack of linking to any of the work goals with the reform orientation of social vision. This disturbing finding confirms the generally held belief that Indian managers are not comfortable in the macro-micro boundary relations. This contrasts sharply with a small transitional society like Mongolia where social vision drives the micro-level work goals of managers at all levels of corporate life (Pearson and Chatterjee, 1999b).

The dramatic shift in managerial views about the meaning and importance of work goals is of considerable relevance to the diffusion of macrolevel reform ideology. Observers of Indian corporate functioning tend to attribute the general lack of systematic reform to an inward looking tradition bound culture. The study presented here refutes the idea that financial reward is a significant work goal for senior managers. This contrasts sharply with China, where managers attach more importance to financial rewards. In a four-country study of work goals in Confucian societies, Shenkar and Ronen (1987) found Chinese managers placing higher importance on autonomy and a very low importance on promotion. The decades of the party influence obviously devalued the attractiveness of promotion as a work or career goal. Instead, Chinese managers were more eager to obtain role clarity and autonomy in decision making.

International organizations like World Bank, IMF and ADB have been generally particular in imposing the conditionalities of social orientation emphasising the environmental domain over the recent years. The findings of this study suggest that such conditionalities have yet to be accepted as work goals by senior managers in spite of their overwhelming interest in learning new ideas. In a collectivistic society like India, contrary to expectations, it appears that managerial values are not necessarily linked to social visions. The collectivism in the Indian context refers mostly to family and kinship groups. It does not extend to work organisations automatically. Therefore, organisations need to understand that while India may have a collectivistic orientation at one level it does not extend to all situations. The broadening of the corporate performance model needs to be embedded in the work goal organisations of senior managers in providing a sustainable future for the reform movement in India (Wartick and Cochran, 1985; Wartick and Wood, 1998).

The findings presented in this paper are of interest for several reasons. First, they demonstrate the convergence of traditional and reform values through a new emphasis on learning. This has significant implications for management and training approaches in India. It appears that corporate education for the twenty-first century needs to emphasise values much more than competencies. Second, the findings point to the social value orientations and contemporary market imperatives in a unique divergent direction where tradition and modernity have a possibility of higher ground in the corporate arena. Finally, given the quest of Western corporate, social and political leaders to know more about the emerging trends in societies like India, the study results offer some basis for their understanding. These findings not only have considerable implications and consequences for Indian society, but also suggest, by inference, present complex and difficult challenges for any nation undergoing reform.

References and Further Reading

Bass, B.M., Burger, P.C., Doktor, R. and Barrett, G.V. (1979), *Assessment of Managers: An International Comparison*, Free Press, New York, NY.

Business Today (1998), "India's business families: the strategic response", Special Anniversary Issue, January/February, p. 1.

Chakraborty, S.K. (1991), *Management by Values: Towards Cultural Congruence*, Oxford University Press, Delhi.

Chatterjee, S.R. (1998), "Work-related value orientations of Indian managers: an empirical investigation", *Monograph, No.6*, Management Centre for Human Values, Indian Institute of Management, Calcutta, Monograph No. 6.

England, G.W. (1978), "Managers and their value systems: a five-country comparative study", *Columbia Journal of World Business*, Vol. 13, pp. 33–4.

England, G.W. (1986), "National work meanings and patterns—constraints on management action", *European Management Journal*, Vol. 4 No. 3, pp. 176–84.

England, G.W. and Lee, R. (1974), "The relationship between managerial values and managerial success in the United States, Japan, India and Australia", *Journal of Applied Psychology*, Vol. 59, pp. 411–19.

England, G.W., Dhingra, OP. and Agarwal, N.C. (1974), *The Manager and the Man: A Cross-Cultural Study of Personal Values*, The Kent State University Press, OH.

Gopalan, S. and Rivera, J.B. (1997), "Gaining perspective on Indian value orientations: implications for expatriate managers", *The International Journal of Organizational Analysis*, Vol. 5 No. 2, pp. 156–79.

Gopinath, C. (1996), "Relevance of Gandhian leadership for business", available at: http://www. hindubusinessline.com/bline/1996/09/30/BLFP05.html

Harpaz, I. (1990), "The importance of work goals: an international perspective", *Journal of International Business Studies*, Vol. 21 No. 1, pp. 75–93.

(The) Hindu (1997), "Essentials of an Indian manager", 30 August, p. 23.

Hofstede, G. (1980), *Cultures Consequences: International Differences in Work Related Values*, Sage, Beverly Hills, CA.

Hofstede, G. (1991), *Cultures Consequences: Software of the Mind*, McGraw-Hill, London.

Kao, H.S.R., Sinha, D. and Ng, S.H. (Eds) (1995), *Effective Organisations and Social Values*, Sage, London.

Khan, A.F. and Atkinson, A. (1987), "Managerial attitudes to social responsibility: a comparative study in India and Britain" *Journal of Business Ethics*, Vol. 6 No. 6, pp. 419–32.

Monappa, A. and Engineer, M. (1999), *liberalisation and Human Resource Management: Challenge for the Corporations of Tomorrow*, Response Books, London.

MOW International Research Team (1987), *The Meaning of Working*, Academic Press, New York, NY.

Pearson C.A.L. and Chatterjee, S.R. (1999a), "Work goal characteristics and organisational reform: an empirical study of senior Indian managers", *Asia Pacific Journal of Economics and Business*, Vol. 3 No. 1, pp. 1–28.

Pearson, C.A.L. and Chatterjee, S.R. (1999b), "Work goals in a country in transition: a case study of Mongolian managers", *International Journal of Manpower*, Vol. 20 No. 5/6, pp. 324–33.

Prakash, A. (1995), "Organizational functioning and values in the Indian context", in Kao, H.S.R., Sinha, D. and Ng, S.H. (Eds), *Effective Organizations and Societal Values*, Sage, New Delhi.

Saha, A. (1992), "Basic human nature in India and its economic consequences", *International Journal of Sociology and Social Policy*, Vol. 12 No. 1/2, pp. 1–50.

Shenkar, O. and Ronen, S. (1987), "Structure and importance of work goals among managers in the People's Republic of China", *Academy of Management Journal*, Vol. 30, pp. 564–76.

Sinha, J.B.P. (1990), *Work Culture in the Indian Context*, Sage, New Delhi.

Wartick, S.L. and Cochran, P.L. (1985), "The evolution of the corporate performance model", *Academy of Management Review*, Vol. 10 No. 4, pp. 758-69.

Warwick, S.L. and Wood, D.J. (1998), *International Business and Society*, Blackwell, Oxford.

Westwood, R.L. and Posner, B.Z. (1997), "Managerial values across cultures: Australia, Hong Kong and United States", *Asia Pacific Journal of Management*, Vol. 14, pp. 31–66.

7 Does Age Matter? An Empirical Examination of the Effect of Age on Managerial Values and Practices in India

Kamel Mellahi and Cherif Guermat

1. Introduction

A growing body of literature indicates that the increasing globalization of economic transactions in emerging economies since the early 1990s has been generating new sets of managerial values, especially among young managers (Birnbaum-More, Wong, & Olve, 1995; Ralston, Carolyn, Egri, Terpstra, & Yu, 1999; Ralston, Gustafson, Terpstra, & Holt, 1998; Mellahi, 2000; Viega, Yanouzas, & Buchholtz, 1995). Despite the growth of empirical research on emerging managerial values of young managers in emerging economies, research has been criticized for not examining managerial practices and the impact of managerial values on practices (Ralston, Holt, Terpstra, & Yu, 1997). Based on a survey of Indian managers, this paper provides an exploratory study into the possible impact of emerging managerial values in India on managerial practices. Managerial values are used here to refer to preferences for socially desirable modes of work behavior (Meglino & Ravlin, 1998; Ravlin & Meglino, 1987, 1989). They are general orientations that can be displayed in work settings and represent how the work 'ought to be' done (Meglino & Ravlin, 1998). 'Ought to be' refers here to what the individual thinks is right rather than what the organization requires. Managerial practices are what managers do in practice (Hayes, 1999).

The impact of age on managerial values in emerging economies has been investigated recently by several scholars (Birnbaum-More et al.,

1995; Ralston et al., 1998, 1999; Viega et al., 1995) but has received scant empirical study. In developed western countries, however, and in the United States of America in particular, extensive comparative research has been carried out on the so-called Baby Boomers (born between 1946 and 1964) and Generation X-ers (born mid-1960s till late 1970s) (Smola & Sutton, 2002). In particular, these studies have looked at the relationship between age, values and behavior and specific attitudes, such as job satisfaction, commitment, work values, and feeling and behavior toward authority. In general, research in developed economies demonstrates a significant linkage between age, managerial values and practices (Cannon, 1991; Cherrington, Condie, & England, 1979; Kacmar & Ferris, 1989; Kalleberg & Loscocco, 1983; McEvoy & Cascio, 1989; Rhodes, 1993; Rosen & Jerdee, 1976; Smola & Sutton, 2002; Tang & Tzeng, 1992; Zeitz, 1990). The available literature on managerial values and practices and age provides two important insights. Firstly, there appears to be a basis for exploring relationships between age and managerial values and practices. Secondly, there is a lack of research on the impact of age on managerial values and practices in emerging economies. Thus, an assessment of the impact of age may provide additional understanding into emerging managerial values and practices in India.

As an initial step towards filling this gap in the literature, we seek in this study to assess (a) whether old managers perform different levels of managerial practices, (b) whether old and young managers hold different managerial values, and (c) whether managerial values have an impact on managerial practices.

India is chosen for this study for two main reasons. First, since the announcement of the New Industrial Policy (NIP) in 1991, the Indian government initiated a number of measures to deregulate the economy and encourage foreign investment. The latter resulted in increased openness to international trade and capital flows, which could have resulted in a shift in managerial values and practices. Prior to 1991, foreign firms were allowed to invest only if they could contribute technology unavailable in India. Second, the importance of India in the global and regional economy is substantial. India attracted more than 75% of the total Foreign Direct Investment (FDI) inflow to South Asia in 1995. According to the latest World Bank global debt figures, India attracted $1.2 billion of the $2 billion in FDI inflows to the region.

2. Research Framework

2.1. Age and Managerial Practices

Situational norms place different demands on people (Cherrington et al., 1979). Young managers are expected to be under more pressure than old managers to conform to old management practices for a number of reasons. First, in a high power distance society, such as India, where respect for elders is highly valued, it is fair to assume that older managers have more power than younger managers (Hofstede, 1980). Therefore, younger managers are expected to adjust their practices more than senior managers to accommodate corporate cultural norms and norms of social control. We also expect that young managers are likely to adjust and display their behavior to be more appropriate with the expected social and managerial norms as set by old managers.

Second, according to Schneider's (1987) "attraction-selection-attrition" framework, similarity in attitudes is a major source of attraction between individuals in organizations. Consequently, managers prefer to recruit, promote and work with managers who share or appear to share similar attitudes to theirs. Other managers, lacking or not willing to adopt these attributes will either be less likely to be recruited and promoted, or, if selected, will feel pressured to display similar managerial attributes. Thus, according to the "similarity-selection-attraction" framework, less powerful people in the organization, if they want to be recruited and promoted to top management jobs, will try to exhibit similar managerial attributes by acting and behaving according to what they think powerful managers expect them to do. The key reference group that could influence decision-making is likely to be the one that is the most powerful in the organization such as the founder (Schein, 1985) or a group of powerful members (Schneider, 1987). In India, Negandhi (1973) reported that the owners' and founding families' authority and influence on the running of the firm is much higher than what was prevalent in firms operating in western countries. Conformity pressures such as coercive persuasion exercised by powerful people can serve to exert a great deal of social influence as young managers seek inclusion to the power circle.

In India, noting that around 60% of all business activities are conducted by firms that are family owned or family controlled (Ramaswamy,

Veliyath, & Gomes, 2000), managers are appointed, promoted and rewarded according to their working relationships with the controlling family. Ramaswamy et al. (2000) found that CEOs in India are invariably appointed to the post largely on the basis of social connections and often are members of the inner family circle. Invariably, Indian families prefer to have someone who shares or appears to share similar values and attitudes to theirs (Piramal, 1996). This may be due in part to the strong distrust of outsiders in India. Ramaswamy et al. (2000) noted that by definition powerful people in Indian organizations seek a direct control in the running of the company. In addition, the power play in Indian organizations tends to be very personal, wherein those who are close to the superior are bestowed with all kinds of favors, while those who are not, tend to be distanced and discriminated against (Sahay & Walsham, 1997). Roland (1984) described the relationship towards powerful people in Indian organizations as submissive and accommodating to avoid conflicts. In a similar vain, Jain and Dwivedi (1990) noted that rules of paternalism and powerful superiors govern Indian organizations.

Third, socialization researchers argue that, as a result of the socialization process, managers' change their behavior according to new work situations (Van Maanen & Schein, 1979). Socialization involves the long-term internalization of the values, norms, and culture of an organization (Meek, 1988). When new managers join an organization, they are often thrust into the social milieu of the organization and exposed to the organization's cultural paradigm that assists them in interpreting their work experiences and guide their behaviors. This experience accompanied by new skills, behaviors, and attitudes, regularizes managers' behaviors (DiMaggio & Powell, 1983). Van Maanen and Schein (1979) note that people must not only acquire new skills but also adopt the social norms and rules that govern how they should conduct themselves in new work situations by conforming to the appropriate mannerisms, attitudes, and social rituals. Failure to adapt to the work situation not only diminishes one's effectiveness in the new role but may also cause the individual to lose the right to enact the role (Leary & Kowalski, 1990). In contrast, acting the role facilitates passage through a firm's "inclusion boundaries" (Van Maanen & Schein, 1979).

Young managers therefore are under more pressure than older managers to adjust their behavior to suit the situation in which they find themselves.

Compared with old managers, they are more concerned about fitting in and are more willing to go along with expected social norms and behaviors as set by older managers. In brief, taken together, the above literature assumes that because young managers' career prospects and status are significantly improved by demonstrating conformity and adherence to the expected appropriate conduct—which is set by the older and most powerful managers within the organization—they will act according to what is expected of them regardless of what they think is right. In contrast, senior managers are less malleable and under less situational pressure to adjust and expect younger managers to behave in similar ways.

Following the above discussion we hypothesize,

Hypothesis 1: Other things being equal, there is no significant difference between management practices of young and old managers.

2.2. Age and Managerial Values

Prior to the economic reforms in the early 1990s, India adopted a socialist socio-economic policy after her independence from Britain. Saha (1992) noted that the adoption of socialism, which is to a very large extent compatible with Indian values and norms, aimed to preserve the Indian social values, norms and values characterized by contentment, absence of desire, undesirability of material goods, and stability and harmony. Social relations tend to be hierarchical and people are status conscious, finding it easier to work in superior–subordinate relationships. Sinha and Sinha (1990) listed caring for subordinates, showing affection, taking personal interest in the well being of employees and commitment to their growth as the key characteristics of Indian managers. England's (1978) seminal study found that Indian managers put more emphasis on organizational stability than their counterparts from other countries; pay more attention to employee welfare than to the goal of profit maximization; and value obedience and conformity.

Chatterjee and Pearson (2000) noted that the recent radical economic reforms and the imperatives of globalization have impacted on Indian managerial mindsets with a set of new values creating tension between traditional indigenous Indian values and the new values (hybrid values) (see also Kao, Sinha, & Ng, 1995; Khandwalla, 1996). They added that the new emerging generation of managers is influenced to a very large extent by the market culture and reforms since the early 1990s rather than the traditional Indian managerial values. They listed "technological education, consumerism, electronic mass media, trade union culture, foreign investment, changing infrastructure and urbanization of values" among the most important factors creating the new changes in values. Chatterjee and Pearson (2000) noted that recent studies in India observed a displacement of traditional Indian values in favor of convergence with market-oriented goals. In a study of young and old Indian managers' perceptions towards ethical concerns, older managers scored equal or higher than their younger counterparts in all ethical business practices (Viswesvaran & Deshpande, 1998: 29). Viswesvaran and Deshpande (1998) concluded that "the trend observed in age groups reflects changing value systems" in India.

While personal values such as honesty are less affected by socialization attempts and pressures because they are more stable over time, and less susceptible to social influences (Fazio & Zanna, 1981), managerial values are social-preference values and therefore are highly influenced by social desirability (Dose, 1997). In India, several writers (see for example Chakraborty, 1991) noted that the market economy and globalization imperatives have not affected the core traditional Indian values (deeply held and widely shared values) but have had a strong impact on situational values (role dependent values contingent upon situational elements of macro-environmental policies and corporate culture) and, to a lesser extent, on individual managerial values (work values, ethical values and other such values anchored to the core tradition but also in the process of transition). Similarly, Chatterjee and Pearson (2000) noted that while the traditional values still dominate the consciousness of the Indian society and institutions, managers are able to work with global market economy values such as individualistic values at their individual managerial levels. Thus,

Hypothesis 2: Other things being equal, there is a significant difference between the management values of young and old managers.

2.3. The Impact of Managerial Values on Managerial Practices

The above two hypotheses do not examine the possible link between values and practices. As they stand, the hypotheses cannot confirm whether or not managerial practices are influenced by management values. All that these hypotheses tell us is whether old and young managers hold similar or different managerial values and practices.

There are two main conflicting schools of thought on the effects of values on managerial behavior. A juxtaposition of the two main bodies of literature on the determinants of managerial behavior suggests that the findings are inconsistent. On the one hand, a large number of studies advocate that managerial practices are a product of managers' values (Rokeach, 1973; Schwartz & Bilsky, 1987), and that values have a strong influence on leadership style (Adler, 1991) and the decision making process (Ravlin & Meglino, 1987; Rokeach, 1973). On the other hand, a preponderance of evidence strongly supports the view that managerial practices are a product of situational factors and not managerial values. Mintzberg (1973) argues that some managerial tasks and roles are imposed on managers and not chosen by them. Tsoukas (1994) noted that the key issue is not what managers want to do, but rather what they are *capable* of doing. Similarly, Meglino and Ravlin (1998) noted that values should have their greatest impact in the absence of strong situational variables that affect behavior in other ways. Therefore managers might be acting according to what the situation dictates rather than what they believe they ought to be doing. Recently, several theorists and researchers advocated a middle ground. Chatman and Barsade (1995) noted that several researchers in organizational behavior now accept that behavior is a function of both personal values and beliefs and the situational characteristics. According to this body of research, values used in the decision making include not only the personal values of the decision maker, but also the situation such as the values of those to whom the decision maker must respond such as powerful people in the organization.

In India, a large body of literature suggests that managerial behaviors are determined to a very large extent by the situation rather than internal attributes (Miller, 1984; Sinha & Kanungo, 1997). Miller (1984) noted that whereas Americans explained others' behavior predominantly in terms of traits, Indians explained comparable behaviors in terms of social roles, obligations, the physical environment, and other contextual factors. Miller's work suggests that attributions for social events are largely the product of culturally instilled belief systems stressing the importance of either dispositional or situational factors in producing social behavior. Sinha and Kanungo (1997: 96) attribute the strong influence of situational factors to the high "context sensitivity" of the Indian culture. Context sensitivity is "a thinking principle or a mind-set that is cognitive in nature and determines the adaptive nature of an idea or behavioral context."

Sinha and Kanungo (1997: 49) noted that "some of the top men in Indian organizations are not quite consistent in their behavior patterns and values." In contrast to western managers who are expected to react in consistent and individually different ways in different situations, Indian managers' reactions depend more on the desh (place), kal (time), and patra (person) (Sinha & Kanungo, 1997: 96). They noted that "some behavior that is judged appropriate for a given place, time, and person(s) may not be appropriate for other times, places and persons." Similarly, Gupta, Surie, Javidan, and Chhokar (2002), based on the Globe study (see *Journal of World Business* special issue 37(1)) found that significant differences between what Indian managers do (As Is) and what they thought they ought to be doing (Should be). To sum up, research on India indicates that values have little impact on managerial practices. Thus, the third hypothesis is as follows:

Hypothesis 3: Other things being equal, the values of managers have no impact on their managerial practices.

3. Research Design and Methodology

The 44 managerial tasks items questionnaire used in this research has been widely used in developing and emerging economies (see Lubatkin, Ndiaye, & Vengroff, 1997; Lubatkin & Powell, 1998). The list of managerial tasks are based on the work of Montgomery (1985, 1986), and has been used for the purpose of hypothesis testing by, among others, Lubatkin et al. (1997), and Lubatkin and Powell (1998). For an extensive description of the instrument and its appropriateness in developing and emerging countries, see Lubatkin et al. (1997). It must be pointed out however, that the fact that the instrument was not developed specifically to examine Indian values and practices may fail to capture some idiosyncratic Indian values and practices.

The difference between young and old managers in attitudes, values and preferences, and other reactions to their work situations could simply be the result of spurious effects of other variables that co-vary with age (Furnham, 1990), thus confounding the comparisons. Consequently, we controlled statistically for the effect of such variables. Specifically, we used a stratified sampling design consisting of Indian top managers, two sectors of activity, both genders, and age to draw inferences about the validity of the proposed hypotheses. Furthermore, all participating companies were small or medium size firms (SMEs), thus, size was excluded from the analysis. We identify small firms as firms employing no more than 100 employees and medium firms as firms employing no more than 250 employees. The research excluded micro firm (very small firms) that employed less than 50 employees. We deliberately avoided adopting the official definitions of SMEs proposed by official Indian bodies such as the Industry Policy Statement of 1990 (see Datt & Sundharam, 2000: 615, for the a review of the different official definitions of small firms in India). Official definitions do not fit with the aim of this study because they are developed to serve administrative purposes such as helping SMEs to have access to financing from institutional bodies. We selected SMEs for two reasons. First, SMEs are now the driving force behind a substantial share of export growth and future economic prosperity in India (Datt & Sundharam, 2000: 616) and other emerging economies (OECD, 1997; United Nations, 1993). The nature of SMEs activities has also changed. Datt and Sundharam (2000: 616–17) report that in India the sector has progressed from "the production of simple consumer goods to the manufacturing of many sophisticated and precision products like electronics control systems, micro-wave components, electro-medical equipment, TV sets, etc." Second, most SMEs have a flat structure and it is likely that individual managers hold multiple positions and roles. Being generalists, SME managers often deal with several management functions. Given that managers' functional experiences are one of the most important background characteristics that affect managers' values and practices (Hambrick & Mason, 1984), using SMEs is expected to limit the impact of functional variations and different positions on managerial values and practices.

We categorized managers into two different generation–age groups. Generation is defined as "an identifiable group that shares birth years, age location, and significant life events at critical development stages"

(Smola & Sutton, 2002: 364). We used an age of 40 years as the cutoff point between older and younger managers for two main reasons. First, we took into consideration the liberalization of the Indian economy as the key factor for differentiation between pre-liberalization (old) and post liberalization managers (young) (Gopalan & Rivera, 1997). Therefore, assuming that most people join the world of management in their 30s, most people who entered the world of work after the liberalization of the Indian economy, which took place in 1991, are less than 40 years old. Second, the previous research that examined age differences tend to use the age of 40 as the cutoff between the two age groups (see Ruegger & King, 1992).

We use the perceptions and attitudes of Indian managers about their employment situation as a means of measuring managerial practices and values. Specifically, respondents were asked how frequently they engaged in each of the 44 managerial routines on a 3-point scale (low, medium, and high). The resulting 44 items reflect the perception of Indian managers on how things "are or appear to be" (Lubatkin et al., 1997). These are used as a proxy for managerial practices. Respondents were also asked how frequently they believe they "ought or they think it's right" to be engaged in the 44 managerial practices. These responses are also measured on a 3-point scale (low, medium, and high) and are used as a proxy for managerial values. This method is similar to the Globe method used by investigating "as is" to represent what leaders do and "should be" to what they think they ought to be doing (Gupta et al., 2002).

The survey was conducted in English, which is a commonly used business language in the three cities targeted for this research (Bombay, Delhi, and Calcutta). Given the low response rate for postal surveys in India (Sharma, 1992), we used a network of Indian managers to obtain a larger sample. Eight Indian managers filled in the questionnaire and agreed to distribute the questionnaire to top managers in their respective region. The eight managers were used as pilots to make sure the items are clear and reflect what Indian managers do. The 44 skill items were mailed to the eight managers in early 1999 and all responses were obtained by summer 1999. A total of 104 usable responses were obtained.

In this research, we adopt the Probit methodology. Probit models are specifically suited for limited dependent variables. Suppose we are measuring a variable by two states: high and low. Let $y_i = 1$ when the ith individual's response is high and $y_i = 0$ otherwise. Suppose also that the variable may be influenced by two factors, x and z. The Probit model then consists of estimating a model, using maximum likelihood, based on the utility index given by

$$I_i = \beta_0 + \beta_1 x_i + \beta_2 z_i \tag{1}$$

where I_i is the utility index. The probability of a positive response (in this case 'high', i.e., $y_i = 1$) is given by $F(I_i)$ where F is the Normal cumulative distribution function. A significant slope parameter (that is either β_1 or β_2 in model (1)) would indicate a significant influence of a particular variable on the respondent's response.

The binomial Probit is readily generalized to an ordered Probit, which models variables with more than two states. Suppose we have three states: low ($y_i = 0$), average ($y_i = 1$), and high ($y_i = 2$). The Probit model now involves one additional parameter, μ, called the threshold parameter. Thus we have the utility index given by

$$I_i = \beta_0 + \beta_1 x_i + \beta_2 z_i \tag{2}$$

and we observe

$$y_i = 0 \quad \text{if } I_i \leq 0;$$
$$y_i = 1 \quad \text{if } 0 < I_i \leq \mu; \text{ and}$$
$$y_i = 2 \quad \text{if } \mu < I_i$$

The probabilities are given by:

$$P(y_i = 0) = 1 - F(I_i);$$
$$P(y_i = 1) = F(\mu - I_i) - F(-I_i);$$
$$P(y_i = 2) = 1 - F(\mu - I_i)$$

3.1. Model Considerations

The two main variables considered in this paper are managerial practices and managerial values. Each variable is represented by 44 questionnaire items, and the interest is centered on the impact of age and other independent variables on these 44 items jointly rather than individually.

The technique for estimating two-dimensional relationships is called panel data. The advantages of panel data models are discussed in Baltagi (2001). In panel data the variability of a given variable is measured in two dimensions, the time and the cross-section dimensions. In the present paper we also have two dimensions, but with the difference that the time dimension is replaced with the 'item' dimension. Thus, by using the panel data approach we can obtain an 'average' effect that takes into account both the respondent effect (cross-section dimension) and the item effect.

Ideally, one would pool the 44 questionnaire items in a single model of panel data. However, the 44 items may reflect practices that do not exhibit the same pattern. Thus, pooling them is problematic. Usually, in panel data models, heterogeneity is dealt with by using a fixed effect or a random effect model, and even this would only be applied on the intercept term. In Probit models, this becomes more complicated, even for the intercept fixed or random effect (Hartzel, Agresti, & Caffo, 2001). One way of resolving this heterogeneity of items is to derive their dimensions and cluster them into homogenous clusters.[1] Factor analysis is therefore used to obtain the latent dimensions generating the 44 items, and these dimensions are the basis for clustering items into distinct types of practice. By using this procedure, the items within each dimension are homogenous enough to justify pooling the data in a single panel model.

Factor analysis of managerial practices resulted in four significant factors or dimensions, explaining a total of 99.56% of the total variation in the 44 items. The four factors explained 44.92%, 23.84%, 17.87%, and 12.91% of the variation, respectively. The factors were then optimized using the Quartimax rotation method. This rotation method minimizes the number of factors that explain each variable, which helps us identify which item belongs to which dimension.

Table 1 presents the four dimensions and their loadings, or impact, on the 44 items. In deciding which items belong to which dimension, the highest loadings were used. Although the majority of items have positive loadings, some do have negative ones. A negative loading suggests that the item in question is negatively related to the dimension and, thus, has a different direction compared with other positively loaded items. For example, a manager who thinks of himself or herself as having a strategic role would have positive loadings for strategic tasks such as item 25— "anticipating local conditions" and negative loadings for operational tasks such as item 41—"using technical skills in unit operations." The latter

Table 1: Managerial Practice Dimensions: *What Managers "Do"*

		Loading
Dimension 1: Strategic and Operational Tasks		
1	Promoting a positive image of the organization	0.898
4	Supervising subordinates while recognizing their individuality	0.815
5	Determining priorities on assigned tasks	0.954
6	Recruiting employees	0.936
8	Delegating authority to subordinates	0.898
17	Monitoring the impact of programs/projects on local and national level	0.815
18	Adjusting implementation actions as needed	0.756
21	Ensuring the timely and accurate flow of information	0.815
22	Conveying organizational goals to the outside world	0.936
23	Analyzing policy options	0.839
24	Setting goals for an organization or unit(s)	0.946
25	Anticipating local conditions and structures programs accordingly	0.946
26	Structuring programs/projects to reflect national or corporate · goals	0.941
27	Trying new ways to improve performance or sole problems	0.905
36	Applying detailed rules and regulations relevant to unit operations	0.839
38	Identifying key aspects of an issue for the purpose of decision-making	0.756
39	Using time effectively	0.967
42	Considering organizational directions in light of economic trends	0.939
43	Analyzing data	0.807
19	Organizing the acquisition of goods and services in a timely fashion	−0.898
41	Using technical skills (other than administrative) in unit operations	−0.868
Dimension 2: HR and Stakeholders Tasks		
11	Make sure that you are followed and listened to by subordinates	0.813
12	Managing conflicts and competition within a unit or organization	0.698
14	Developing good working relationship with the local community	0.776
20	Writing clear and concise official reports	0.705
34	Negotiating with representatives of other organizations	0.950
10	Coordinating among individuals and/or organizational units	−0.962
15	Keeping accurate records of financial transactions	−0.950
16	Handling contracts for goods, services and labor	−0.902
30	Organizing resources and services to minimize operating costs	−0.851
31	Handling monetary resources to stay within projected costs	−0.950
33	Negotiating intra-organizational differences	−0.954

(Table 1 contd.)

(*Table 1 contd.*)

		Loading
Dimension 3: Management of Internal and External Partnerships		
2	Dealing with politicians	0.870
3	Involved in local social activities	0.826
7	Encouraging subordinates to perform effectively	0.819
9	Organizing training in order to correct detected deficiencies	0.712
28	Detecting and resolves situations where individuals violate goals or rules	0.883
32	Managing resources efficiently to transform project inputs into outputs	0.660
40	Planning specific tasks to achieve assigned goal	*-0.887*
44	Initiating actions	*-0.870*
Dimension 4: Public Relations		
13	Maintaining cordial relationships between organizations	0.690
35	Negotiating with representatives of foreign organizations	0.853
29	Coping with unexpected conditions and events	*-0.747*
37	Using extralegal means to meet objectives	*-0.870*

item is not compatible with strategic roles of managers. Thus, the more s/he believes that his or her roles should be involved in strategic roles the less s/he is expected to carry out operational roles such as item 41.

It is therefore necessary to pool items of the same sign together within each dimension. As can be seen from Table 1, most loadings for the first dimension are high and positive and only two items have negative loadings. In the second dimension there are six negative items and only five positive items. Dimensions 3 and 4 have a total of eight and four items, respectively, two of which are negative.

Each dimension is named on the basis of its constituent items, namely Strategic and Operational Tasks (SOT), Human Resources and Stakeholders Tasks (HRST), Management of Internal and External Partnerships (MIEP), and Public Relations (PR), respectively. The first two dimensions are clearly the most important, accounting for 32 items between them.

Since managerial values do not necessarily stem from the same underlying process of managerial practices, extracting the dimensions of values is also required. Thus, factor analysis was carried out on managerial values, resulting in four significant dimensions. These four dimensions explain almost 100% of the total variation in the 44 items. The four factors explained 43.25%, 26.92%, 17.88%, and 11.94% of the variation, respectively. The Quartimax method was also used to optimize the factors.

Table 2 lists the four dimensions together with their respective value items and their loadings. It is quite obvious that managerial values have different dimensions from managerial practices. First, there are only 3 negative items compared with 12 in managerial practices. Second, managerial values share only a few items with managerial practices. These are shown in bold and underlined in Table 2. The distribution of items over the four dimensions in Table 2 does not make it easy to interpret these four dimensions. However, based on the majority of items within each dimension, we named the dimensions as Practicing Thoroughness (PT), Social Recognition and Strategic Control (SRSC), Influencing, Negotiating, and Conflict Solving (INCS), and Sense of Financial Control (SFC), respectively.

Table 2: Managerial Value Dimensions:
What Managers Think they "Ought" to be Doing

		Loading
	Dimension 1: Practicing Thoroughness	
1	Promoting a positive image of the organization	0.903
5	Determining priorities on assigned tasks	0.936
20	Writing clear and concise official reports	0.947
27	Trying new ways to improve performance or solve problems	0.909
30	Organizing resources and services to minimize operating costs	0.946
38	Identifying key aspects of an issue for the purpose of decision-making	0.994
39	Using time effectively	0.950
43	Analyzing data	0.952
	Dimension 2: Social Recognition and Strategic Control	
3	Involved in local social activities	0.916
6	Recruiting employees	0.904
8	Delegating authority to subordinates	0.882
14	Developing good working relationship with the local community	0.926
16	Handling contracts for goods, services and labor	0.856
17	Monitoring the impact of programs/projects on local and national level	0.676
23	Analyzing policy options	0.668
24	Setting goals for an organization or unit(s)	0.848
25	Anticipating local conditions and structures programs accordingly	0.946

(Table 2 contd.)

(*Table 2 contd.*)

		Loading
26	Structuring programs/projects to reflect national or corporate goals	0.919
36	Applying detailed rules and regulations relevant to unit operations	0.766
42	Considering organizational directions in light of economic trends	0.728
44	Initiating actions	0.884
<u>34</u>	Negotiating with representatives of other organizations	*−0.637*

Dimension 3: Influencing, Negotiating, and Conflict Solving

<u>2</u>	Dealing with politicians	0.856
<u>7</u>	Encouraging subordinates to perform effectively	0.892
<u>9</u>	Organizing training in order to correct detected deficiencies	0.715
<u>28</u>	Detecting and resolving situations where individuals violate goals or rules	0.904
41	Using technical skills (other than administrative) in unit operations	0.670
12	Managing conflicts and competition within a unit or organization	−0.710
37	Using extralegal means to meet objectives	*−0.889*

Dimension 4: Sense of Financial Control

15	Keeping accurate records of financial transactions	0.949
19	Organizing the acquisition of goods and services in a timely fashion	0.596
22	Conveying organizational goals to the outside world	0.833
31	Handling monetary resources to stay within projected costs	0.783
32	Managing resources efficiently to transform project inputs into outputs	0.861

Thus, we require separate Probit models for each dimension and for both positively and negatively loaded items. Within each cluster (dimension/sign), the items are likely to be homogenous and can therefore be pooled together without the need for fixed or random effect. Thus, the panel-Probit model will consider the dependent variable y_{ij} for i = 1, 104 respondents, and j = 1, N items. For managerial practices, N = 19^+ and 2^-, 5^+ and 6^-, 6^+ and 2^-, and 2^+ and 2^- for Dimensions 1 to 4, respectively. The superscripts represent positively and negatively loaded items. For managerial values, N = 18^+ and 0^-, 13^+ and 1^-, 5^+ and 2^-, and 5^+ and 0^- for Dimensions 1 to 4, respectively.

The "managerial practices" items consist of practices coded as 0, 1, and 2 for 'low,' 'average,' and 'high' level of practice, respectively. These are labeled as low level practice (LLP), average level practice (ALP), and high level practice (HLP). The "managerial values" items are coded in a similar way. The labels are low level value (LLV), average level value (ALV), and high level value (HLV).

There are three independent variables, namely age, gender, and sector. These are represented by dummies taking the value of one for old managers, males and the industry sector, respectively, and zero otherwise. The panel-Probit models are estimated by nonlinear maximum likelihood, using the BFGS algorithm (Press, Flannery, Teukolsky & Vettering, 1988). The general form of the estimated model is given in Eq. (3) for the utility index 1 representing the utility for higher response (practice or value).

$$I = \beta_0 + \beta_1 \text{Age} + \beta_2 \text{Gender} + \beta_3 \text{Sector} \qquad (3)$$

The interpretation of the model is straightforward. For example, if β_1 is statistically insignificant then we would conclude that there is no difference between young and old managers and that age has no impact on the dependent variable (managerial practices or managerial values). The coefficients are tested using individual t-statistics.

4. Results

4.1. Managerial Practices

The estimation results for the four clusters of practice are presented in Table 3. The table shows the estimated values of the betas and the t-values (in parentheses) for the utility Eq. (3). Each dimension is represented by two models, one for the positively loaded items and one for the negatively loaded items. As expected, the coefficients of age, gender and sector in the two models have opposite signs in all cases. We will therefore mainly focus on the results for positive items since higher 'positive' practices imply lower 'negative' practices. We use a superscript, for example SOT[+], to indicate positive practices. Also, note that since all independent variables are dummy variables, their relative influence on the utility index, and thus on the probability of a particular response, can be compared directly.

In the first, third, and fourth dimensions, the slopes for age are highly significant and positive for positive items. This means that older managers have on average significantly different SOT, MIEP and PR practices. For the last two dimensions, the impact of age is similar for positive and negative practices, but for the SOT dimension the impact of age is by far

Table 3: Probit Estimation Results for the Panel Model
of Managerial Practices

Dimension	Items	Threshold	Intercept	Age	Gender	Sector
SOT	Positive (19)	1.83 (31.77)	-1.01 (-13.25)	0.61 (7.67)	-0.76 (-11.68)	3.31 (32.90)
	Negative (2)	9.69 (34.18)	15.24 (29.27)	-4.93 (-23.31)	-[a]	-5.53 (-32.75)
HRST	Positive (5)	5.21 (5.38)	-0.84 (-6.93)	-5.10 (-5.79)	-0.56 (-4.46)	6.83 (7.23)
	Negative (6)	5.87 (2.54)	6.31 (2.69)	10.46 (2.50)	0.77 (7.53)	-5.83 (-2.43)
MIEP	Positive (6)	1.22 (14.37)	-0.77 (-7.96)	1.46 (8.51)	2.48 (14.83)	-[a]
	Negative (2)	5.07 (7.27)	6.63 (13.88)	-1.43 (-4.59)	-1.96 (-7.70)	-[a]
PR	Positive (2)	1.26 (12.11)	0.41 (2.52)	0.94 (4.58)	1.22 (6.32)	-[a]
	Negative (2)	0.37 (6.37)	0.78 (4.59)	-0.57 (-2.34)	-0.51 (-2.64)	-[a]

SOT: Strategic and Operational Tasks; HRST: Human Resources and Stakeholders Tasks; MIEP: Management of Internal and External Partnerships; PR: Public Relations.
[a] Parameter insignificant at the 5% level.

greater on the negative items. Thus, the results suggest that age has a statistically significant impact on managerial practices. Indeed, all age coefficients are highly significant, which rejects our first hypothesis of no difference between management practices of young and old managers.

4.2. Managerial Values

A model similar to Eq. (3) was fitted using the value items. The clustering derived in Table 2 is used in the estimation. Because there are only three negative items in total, including two dimensions having no negative items, it was decided to ignore the negative cases. Table 4 presents the estimation results for the four dimensions.

As with managerial practices, the four dimensions show different patterns. More specifically, age has a positive impact in the first and third dimensions, but a negative impact in the second and fourth dimensions. Thus, while older managers put significantly stronger emphasis on Dimension 1 (Practicing Thoroughness) and Dimension 3 (Influencing, Negotiating, and Conflict Solving) values than younger managers, younger managers put significantly higher emphasis on Dimension 2 (Social Recognition and Strategic Control) and Dimension 4 (Sense of Financial Control) values (see Tables 2 and 4). Gender has an identical impact to that of age (males put more emphasis on PT and INCS, but less on SRSC and SFC). Finally, managers in the industry sector have higher levels of values in three out of four dimensions (PT, SRSC, and SFC).

The above findings confirm our second prediction that there is a significant difference between the management values of young and old managers. Older managers put more emphasis on 23 values, while younger managers put more emphasis on 18 different values. Thus, as with managerial practices, older and young managers emphasize different sets of values.

4.3. The Effect of Managerial Values on Managerial Practice

In this section, we assess whether managerial values have any significant impact on managerial practices. We have already seen that, as dependent variables, both practices and values are explained by age and other situational variables. One remaining question is therefore whether values have any additional information content to improve the explanation of

Table 4: Probit Estimation Results for the Panel Model of Managerial Values

Dimension	Threshold	Intercept	Age	Gender	Sector
PT (18)	0.63 (18.31)	−1.28 (−14.64)	0.47 (5.06)	0.20 (2.88)	2.49 (24.92)
SRSC (13)	1.18 (24.04)	−[a]	−0.48 (−4.23)	−2.03 (−17.56)	1.69 (15.80)
INCS (5)	0.17 (5.84)	−0.39 (−4.87)	1.50 (9.65)	0.62 (4.87)	−0.17 (−6.46)
SFC (5)	0.50 (10.07)	−0.68 (−4.33)	−1.01 (−6.53)	−1.36 (−9.16)	2.83 (14.56)

PT: Practicing Thoroughness; SRSC: Social Recognition and Strategic Control; INCS: Influencing, Negotiating, and Conflict Solving; SFC: Sense of Financial Control.
[a] Parameter insignificant at the 5% level. Only positive items were included in the estimation.

managerial practices. However, to proceed we need to treat managerial values as an independent variable.[2]

The effect of managerial values can be assessed by adding two dummy variables to Eq. (3). The average level value dummy variable is set to one for an average response and zero otherwise. The high level value dummy is set in a similar manner. The low level value case is therefore obtained by setting both dummy variables to zero.

The estimation results are shown in Table 5 for the four managerial practice dimensions. Removing the two value dummy columns from Table 5 provides us with a table that is almost identical to Table 3. A comparison between Tables 3 and 5 shows that all coefficients are of the same sign and magnitude. This clearly indicates that the inclusion of managerial values does not affect the fundamental process that links managerial practices with age and the other situational variables. Managerial values have statistically significant coefficients on fourteen out of sixteen cases. However, for the first, and most important, three dimensions the impact of managerial values is positive on both positive and negative managerial practice items. This suggests that while age and other situational factors may have varying effect on managerial practices, the effect of managerial values is uniform in the sense that managers with higher levels of values tend to have higher levels of both positive and negative managerial practices. Thus our third hypothesis that managerial values have no impact on managerial practices is clearly rejected. In other words, managers' internal attributes have a significant impact on managerial practices.

5. Discussion

We hypothesized that young managers in India would adopt different managerial values, but that in work situations these differences are overridden by situational factors and, thus, young managers would be expected to adopt managerial practices similar to those of old managers. The evidence found in this paper rejects our first hypothesis. The results suggest that young and old managers in India put significantly different emphasis on different managerial practices. The analysis clearly indicates that age has a significant impact on the level of managerial practices. Overall, young managers in India put significantly less emphasis on 33 out of the 44 managerial tasks examined in this research than old managers.

Table 5: Probit Estimation Results for the Panel Model of Manager Practice

Dimension	Items	Threshold	Intercept	Age	Gender	Sector	ALV Dummy	HLV Dummy
SOT	Positive (19)	1.94 (28.92)	-1.41 (-14.19)	0.57 (7.09)	-0.69 (-9.07)	3.36 (25.95)	1.14 (13.21)	0.35 (4.96)
	Negative (2)	10.68 (12.81)	16.25 (12.34)	-3.76 (-29.19)	0.25 (1.68)[1]	-14.12 (-11.47)	—[a]	8.57 (13.48)
HRST	Positive (5)	5.30 (5.46)	-0.91 (-8.11)	-5.13 (-4.95)	-0.56 (-4.92)	6.61 (6.28)	0.41 (3.23)	0.57 (4.60)
	Negative (6)	5.75 (15.17)	5.82 (13.29)	14.61 (12.61)	2.67 (11.21)	-8.35 (-13.17)	1.78 (21.67)	3.92 (14.76)
MIEP	Positive (6)	1.23 (15.08)	-0.88 (-8.65)	1.28 (7.60)	2.48 (15.56)	—[a]	0.25 (1.83)*	0.43 (3.83)
	Negative (2)	5.33 (3.33)	3.90 (5.46)	-1.62 (-5.91)	-2.05 (-8.92)	—[a]	2.44 (3.07)	3.18 (4.57)
PR	Positive (2)	1.79 (10.75)	1.27 (4.32)	2.23 (11.38)	1.84 (9.44)	—[a]	-0.69 (-2.99)	-2.64 (-13.46)
	Negative (2)	0.44 (6.23)	0.74 (4.25)	-1.12 (-4.83)	-1.18 (-4.80)	—[a]	—[a]	1.38 (6.85)

SOT: Strategic and Operational Tasks, HRST: Human Resources and Stakeholders Tasks, MIEP: Management of Internal and External Partnerships, PR: Public Relations.
[a] Not significant at the 5% level.
* p-value less than 0.10.

Thus, we argue that young managers are departing from old practices by putting less emphasis on one set of practices and more emphasis on another set of practices. On reflection, this result may not be too surprising. Young managers may be departing from old practices for several reasons. Old managers who, according to the socialization perspective, exercise power to converge young managers to old managerial practices might be more supportive and, in the current global economy where new managerial practices are needed, perhaps identify more with young managers' practices than their own. This may well have led them to put less pressure on young managers to adopt similar practices. Whatever the underlying reasons, the findings of this study do not support the core proposition that young managers will embrace old managerial practices for the reasons advocated by the socialization perspective.

Our second hypothesis, that is young and old managers hold different managerial values, is strongly supported by the data. This paper found differences in terms of managerial values and preferences indicating that young managers, in comparison with older managers, hold different managerial values. This confirms our second prediction that young managers' values are indeed different from those of older managers. More importantly, these differences are not monotonic. Young managers emphasize 23 values *less* than old managers, but at the same time put more emphasis on 18 values. Thus, we could argue, albeit indirectly, that our findings suggest that young managers are departing from old values by putting different emphasis on the four value dimensions. These results lend credence to those who argue that young managers in emerging economies are moving away from old managerial values and embracing new values (Mellahi, 2001; Ralston et al., 1997).

Finally, the strong statistical significance of the model relating managerial practices with age, situational variables and managerial values rejects our third hypothesis. The fact that 42 out of the 44 practices are positively related to managerial values makes it clear that, overall, those who have higher values tend to have higher levels of practice, regardless of whether the practices are positively or negatively correlated with their underlying dimensions. These results provide evidence to suggest that managerial values have an impact on managerial practices. That is, managerial practices are not the sole product of situational contingencies. This could be explained by the fact that as managers in emerging economies are becoming more individualistic and power distance is becoming less important, managers are basing their actions on both internal attributes and social contingencies.

6. Research Implications

Our results have a number of implications of interest to both scholars and practitioners. For scholars, the evidence presented here complements the increasing body of literature on the impact of age on values in emerging economies (Birnbaum-More et al., 1995; Ralston et al., 1998, 1999; Viega et al., 1995). Most prior research comparing old and young managers in emerging economies has focused primarily on whether or not new young managers are adopting new managerial values. Much less research has sought to explore the actual impact of the emerging values on managerial practices. This study makes a unique contribution to the existing literature by examining the impact of emerging managerial values on managerial practices.

The results of this study clearly tie in with previous research that found that young managers in emerging economies are adopting new managerial values (Ralston et al., 1999). It is clear that emerging economies are witnessing a broad shift in managerial values and practices, with one set of managerial values replacing another. Further, these findings are in line with the growing body of research on national (sub)culture heterogeneity (see for example: McSweeney, 2002). The basic contention of this body of research is that the assumption of homogeneity of values within countries and the notion of national culture sharedness are false (Bock, 1999; McSweeney, 2002: 92), because they do not take into consideration the heterogeneity of managerial values within a country.

There is another implication born from the prior discussion that is worthy of note. It appears that old managers in India still put more emphasis on old managerial practices. This means that recent developments in the business environment have had little impact on old managers' values and practices. If so, the implication of this finding supports the view that managerial values once developed are difficult to change. For the young generation however, the new managerial values are substantially different from that of old managers. One possible interpretation of these differences might be that they are the result of the radical changes in the business environment that has occurred over the last ten years.

For the purpose of this article, the most important result was the strong impact of young managers' values on managerial practices. This has been the missing link in the research on young managers' values in emerging economies. Previous researchers only reveal that young managers are adopting different managerial values. Our research extends their results by demonstrating that despite substantial institutional pressure to neutralize the effects of the new managerial values on managerial practices, we found that young managers' values have a strong impact on managerial practices. Contrary to expectations, our results suggest that both young and old managers' behaviors are largely mediated by the values they hold. It must be emphasized that it would be incorrect to conclude that internal attributes were the only determinants of managers' decisions. Demonstrating a significant effect of values on practices does not necessarily negate the role of situational factors, nor does it suggest that internal attributes provide a better explanation of managerial practices in India than situational contingencies. We subscribe to the person–situation interactionist model, and believe that neither the internal attributes perspective of individuals acting in isolation nor the situational deterministic view of individuals obedient to social norms and culture can adequately provide an independent explanation of managerial behavior in emerging economies.

The results of this study have implications both for Indian managers and international managers operating in India. For Indian managers, the results of this study show that different managerial values and practices are likely to coexist within the same organization. Old managers can expect to work alongside young managers who hold different values to theirs and vice versa. This heterogeneity in managerial values and practices has the potential to produce negative as well as positive outcomes. One possible negative outcome is that the presence of two demographic groups holding different values and practices in an organization could create a distance between young and old managers, which makes social integration and communication between the two groups more difficult. There is a possibility that managers from different generations will be directly confronted with each other's negative stereotypes and self-serving biases, and misunderstanding and conflict may become more pronounced. In addition, borrowing from the large body of comparative research on heterogeneous and homogeneous groups, given the divergence of values and practices of old and young managers, one would expect that the divergence of values and practices, if not managed properly, would impede teamwork, increase conflict and could lead to difficult information exchange between the two age groups (Ancona & Caldwell, 1992). It must be pointed out, however, that Indian managers are well equipped to deal with diversity given the diverse cultural, linguistic, racial and ethnic diversity present in India. In addition, this heterogeneity of values and practices could result in more formal reinforcement of rules. Being different may decrease the predictability of attitudes and behaviors, and thus managers may feel the need for formal reinforcement of rules within organizations through monitoring and control to make sure that the appropriate practices are followed. In contrast, differences between young and old mangers could lead to more innovations in management processes and output (Bantel & Jackson, 1989). Thus, a further implication is that those managers who are best able to identify the probable sources of value conflict between young and old managers, and to prepare for them, will likely be more effective than those who do not. Managers have to play a difficult balancing act, paying attention to the negative effects of divergent values and practices while simultaneously attempting to capture the benefits of heterogeneity. Dealing with such diversity requires managers in India to invest time and efforts to facilitate communication and coordinate actions between the young and old managers.

For international managers operating or planning to operate in India, the results of the study suggest that a "one size fits all" approach to dealing with, and managing Indian managers is not appropriate, and that what is expected to work well with young managers might not work with old managers. The results show that demographically different managers in India hold different values and exhibit different behaviors. Further, evidence of such divergence in managerial values and practices between young and old managers in India underscores the need to re-examine the cultural homogeneity paradigm which dominates cross cultural literature, calls into question the usefulness of national cultures labels, and highlights the risks of national stereotyping. So far, cross cultural research, and expatriate teaching and training have generally focused on differences between countries and assume cultural homogeneity within countries (see Osland, Bird, Delano, & Jacob, 2000). As a result, differences within countries are generally overshadowed by national cultures effect (McSweeney, 2002). Thus, it is conceivable that international managers, constrained by their training, cultural myopia, and sophisticated stereotyping could run into problems because of the assumption that all Indian managers hold common managerial values and behaviors. Our results show that managerial values and practices vary significantly between old and young managers within the same country, hence, it would be misleading for international managers operating in India to assume cultural homogeneity within the country. In order to work successfully in India, it is important that international managers develop an awareness of how demographic dissimilarity such as age may impact managerial values and practices and lead to within-culture differences.

7. Limitations and Future Research

Any conclusions drawn from this study must be assessed against its limitations. First, this study was restricted to three main cosmopolitan cities in India. The influence of old managers on young managers in other rural and less cosmopolitan areas could be stronger than that of the three areas studied here. In addition, it is useful to duplicate the study in other emerging and developing countries. Second, only small and medium companies were considered in this study. As explained earlier, most small and medium companies have a flat structure and it is likely that individual managers hold multiple positions and roles in these organizations. Should this research be duplicated in large organizations, researchers should pay attention to the possibility that age could be closely associated with managerial positions. Thus, one would need to partial out the effect of roles in order to ensure that the observed effect is indeed due to age and not to position. This will require collecting additional information on positions during the survey and including the position variable as an independent variable in the Logit model. Third, as with all survey type research, this study does not fully capture the richness of the interaction between old and young managers in India. A longitudinal case study approach would complement this study by providing richer insights onto the interactions between old and young managers.

We believe that this paper has only scratched the surface of the emerging managerial values and practices in emerging economies. The framework that explains the reasoning process which translates personal value into behavioral action is still underdeveloped because of the number of factors that need unpacking—and it is not the focus of this paper. However, the issues raised in this article will hopefully provide impetus for both conceptual and empirical research on emerging managerial values in emerging economies.

Notes

1. We are grateful to a referee for suggesting this alternative.
2. A more appropriate way of estimating the effect of values on practice would be to estimate a simultaneous equation model where both values and practice are treated as endogenous variables. However, to our knowledge, a simultaneous model for multinomial Probit has not yet been formulated.

References

Adler, N. J. (1991). *International dimensions of organizational behavior* (2nd ed.). Boston: PWS-Kent.

Ancona, D. G., & Caldwell, D. F. (1992). Bridging the boundary: External activity and performance in organizational teams. *Administrative Science Quarterly, 37*: 634–665.

Baltagi, B. H. (2001). *Econometric analysis of panel data*. Chichester: Wiley.

Bantel, K. A., & Jackson, S. E. (1989). Top management and innovations in banking: Does the composition of the top team make a difference? *Strategic Management Journal, 10*: 107–124.

Birnbaum-More, P. H., Wong, G. Y. Y., & Olve, N. (1995). Acquisition of managerial values in The People's Republic of China and Hong Kong. *Journal of Cross-Cultural Psychology, 2(3)*: 255–275.

Bock, P. K. (1999). *Rethinking psychological anthropology* (2nd ed.). Prospect Heights, IL: Waveland.

Cannon, D. (1991). Generation X: The way they do the things they do. *Journal of Career Planning and Employment, 51(2)*: 34–38.

Chakraborty, S. K. (1991). *Management by values: Towards cultural congruence*. Delhi: Oxford University Press.

Chatman, J. A., & Barsade, S. G. (1995). Personality, culture and cooperation: Evidence from a business simulation. *Administrative Science Quarterly, 40*: 423–443.

Chatterjee, S. R., & Pearson, C. A. L. (2000). Indian managers in transition: Orientations, work goals, values and ethics. *Management International Review, 40(1)*: 81–95.

Cherrington, D. J., Condie, S. J., & England, J. L. (1979). Age and work values. *Academy of Management Journal, 22*: 617–623.

Datt, R., & Sundharam, K. P. M. (2000). *Indian economy.* New Delhi: S. Chand and Company, Ltd.

DiMaggio, P., & Powell, W. (1983). The iron cage revisited: Institutional isomorphism and collective rationality in organizational fields. *American Sociological Review, 42*: 113–123.

Dose, J. J. (1997). Work values: An integrative framework and illustrative application to organizational socialisation. *Journal of Occupational and Organizational Psychology, 70*(2): 19–40.

England, G. W. (1978). Managers and their value systems: A five country comparative study. *Columbia Journal of World Business, 13*: 35–44.

Fazio, R. H., & Zanna, M. P. (1981). Direct experience and attitudes-behaviour consistency. In L. Bekrowitz (Ed.), *Advances in experimental social psychology* (Vol. 14, pp. 161–202) New York: Academic Press.

Furnham, A. (1990). *The protestant work ethic: The psychology of work-related beliefs and behaviours.* New York: Routledge.

Gopalan, S., & Rivera, J. (1997). Gaining a perspective on Indian value Orientations: Implications for expatriate managers. *International Journal of Organizational Analysis, 5*(2): 156–179.

Gupta, V., Surie, G., Javidan, M., & Chhokar, J. (2002). Southern Asia cluster: Where the old meets the new? *Journal of World Business, 37*(1): 16–27.

Hambrick, D. C., & Mason, P. A. (1984). Upper echelons: The organization as a reflection of its top managers. *Academy of Management Review, 9*(2): 193–206.

Hartzel, J., Agresti, A., & Caffo, B. (2001). Multinomial logit random effect models. *Statistical Modelling, 1:* 81–102.

Hayes, C. (1999). Why do managers do what they do? Reconciling evidence and theory in accounts of managerial work. *British Journal of Management, 10*: 275–374.

Hofstede, G. (1980). *Culture's consequences: International differences in work related values.* London: Sage.

Jain, R., & Dwivedi, O. (1990). Administrative culture and bureaucratic values in India. *Indian Journal of Public Administration, 36*: 435–450.

Kacmar, K. M., & Ferris, G. R. (1989). Theoretical and methodological considerations in the age–job satisfaction relationship. *Journal of Applied Psychology, 74*: 201–207.

Kalleberg, A. L., & Loscocco, K. A. (1983). Aging, values, and rewards: Explaining age differences in job satisfaction. *American Sociological Review, 2*: 78–90.

Kao, H. S. R., Sinha, D., & Ng, S. H. (1995). *Effective organizations and social values.* London: Sage.

Khandwalla, P. (1996). Effective corporate response to liberalization: The Indian case. *Social Engineer, 5*(2): 5–33.

Leary, Mark R., & Kowalski, R. M. (1990). Impression management: A literature review and two-component model. *Psychological Bulletin, 107*: 34–47.

Lubatkin, M., Ndiaye, M., & Vengroff, R. (1997). The nature of managerial work in developing countries: A limited test of the universalist hypothesis. *Journal of International Business Studies, 28*(4): 711–733.

Lubatkin, M., & Powell, G. (1998). Exploring the influence of gender on managerial work in a transitional, Eastern European nation. *Human Relations, 51*(8): 1007–1031.

McEvoy, G. M., & Cascio, W. E. (1989). Cumulative evidence of the relationship between employee age and job performance. *Journal of Applied Psychology, 74*: 11–17.

McSweeney, B. (2002). Hofstede's model of national cultural differences and their consequences: A triumph of faith—A failure of analysis. *Human Relations, 55*(1): 89–118.

Meek, V. L. (1988). Organizational culture: Origins and weaknesses. *Organization Studies, 9*(4): 453–473.

Meglino, B. M., & Ravlin, E. C. (1998). Individual values in organizations: Concepts, controversies, and research. *Journal of Management, 24*(3): 351–389.

Mellahi, K. (2000). Western MBA education and effective leadership values in developing countries: A study of Asian, Arab and African MBA graduates. *Journal of Transnational Management Development, 5*(2): 59–73.

Mellahi, K. (2001). Differences and similarities in future managerial values: A five cultures comparative study. *Cross-Cultural Management: An International Journal, 8*(1): 46–59.

Miller, J. G. (1984). Culture and the development of everyday social explanation. *Journal of Personality and Social Psychology, 46*: 961–978.

Mintzberg, H. (1973). *Managing work.* New York: Harper and Row.

Montgomery, J. (1985). The African manager. *Management Review, 262*: 82–111.

Montgomery, J. (1986). Levels of managerial leadership in Southern Africa. *Journal of Developing Areas, 21*: 15–30.

Negandhi, A. R. T. (1973). *Modern organizational behaviour.* Ohio: Kent University Press.

OECD. (1997). Globalization and small and medium enterprises (SMEs). In *Organization for Economic Cooperation and Development.* Paris: OCED.

Osland, S. J., Bird, A., Delano, J., & Jacob, M. (2000). Beyond sophisticated stereotyping: Cultural sensemaking in context. *The Academy of Management Executive, 14*(4): 65–79.

Piramal, G. (1996). *Business maharajas.* New Delhi: Penguin Books India.

Press, W.H., Flannery, S.A., Teukolsky, S.A., & Vettering, W.T. (1988). *Numerical Recipes in C.* New York: Cambridge University Press.

Ralston, D. A., Carolyn, P., S, S., Terpstra, R. H., & Yu, K. C. (1999, Summer). Doing business in the 21st century with the new generation of Chinese managers: A study of generational shifts in work values in China. *Journal of International Business Studies, 30*(2): 415–433.

Ralston, D. A., Gustafson, J. D., Terpstra, R. H., & Holt, D. H. (1998). Values of Chinese managers: Does generation make a difference? In *Third Asian International Business Symposium*. Macao.

Ralston, D. A., Holt, D. H., Terpstra, R. H., & Yu, K. C. (1997). The impact of national culture and economic ideology on managerial work values: A study of the United States, Russia, Japan and China. *Journal of International Business Studies, 28*(1): 177–207.

Ramaswamy, K., Veliyath, R., & Gomes, L. (2000). A study of the determinants of CEO compensation in India. *Management International Review, 40*(2): 167–191.

Ravlin, E. C., & Meglino, B. M. (1987). Effect of values on perception and decision taking: A study of alternative work values measures. *Journal of Applied Psychology, 72*: 666–673.

Ravlin, E. C., & Meglino, B. M. (1989). The transitivity of work values: Hierarchical preference ordering of socially desirable stimuli. *Organizational Behaviour and Human Decision Processes, 44*: 494–508.

Rhodes, S. R. (1993). Age-related differences in work attitudes and behavior: A review and conceptual analysis. *Psychological Bulletin, 93*: 328–367.

Rokeach, M. (1973). *The nature of human values*. New York: Free Press.

Roland, A. (1984). The self in India and America. In V. KavoLis (Ed.), *Designs of selfhood*. New Jersey: Associated University Press.

Rosen, B., & Jerdee, T. H. (1976). The influence of age stereotypes on managerial decisions. *Journal of Applied Psychology, 6*(4): 428–432.

Ruegger, D., & King, E. W. (1992). A study of age and gender upon business ethics. *Journal of Business Ethics, 11*: 179–186.

Saha, A. (1992). Basic human nature in Indian tradition and its economic consequences. *International Journal of Sociology and Social Policy, 12*(1/2): 1–50.

Sahay, S., & Walsham, G. (1997). Social structure and managerial agency in India. *Organization Studies, 18*(3): 415–444.

Schein, E. H. (1985). *Organizational culture and leadership*. San Francisco, CA: Jossey-Bass.

Schneider, B. (1987). The people make the place. *Personnel Psychology, 40*: 437–453.

Schwartz, S. H., & Bilsky, W. (1987). Toward a universal psychological structure of human values. *Journal of Personality and Social Psychology, 53*: 550–562.

Sharma, R. D. (1992). Management training in India: Its nature and extent. *International Journal of Manpower, 13*(2): 41–45.

Sinha, J. B. P., & Kanungo, R. N. (1997). Context sensitivity and balancing in Indian organizational behavior. *International Journal of Psychology, 32*: 93–105.

Sinha, J. B. P., & Sinha, D. (1990). Role of social values in Indian organizations. *International Journal of Psychology, 25*: 705–714.

Smola, K. W., & Sutton, C. D. (2002). Generational differences: Revisiting generational work values for the new millennium. *Journal of Organizational Behavior, 23*: 363–382.

Tang, T. L., & Tzeng, J. Y. (1992). Demographic correlates of the protestant work ethics. *Journal of Psychology, 126*: 163–170.

Tsoukas, H. (1994). What is management? An outline of a metatheory. *British Journal of Management, 54*: 289–301.

United Nations. (1993). *Small and medium-sized transnational corporations: Role, impact and policy implications.* New York: United Nations Conference on Trade and Development.

Van Maanen, J., & Schein, E. (1979). Toward a theory of organizational socialization. *Research in Organizational Behavior,* 1: 209–264.

Viega, J. F., Yanouzas, J. N., & Buchohltz, A. K. (1995, July–August). Emerging cultural values among Russian managers: What will tomorrow bring? *Business Horizons:* 20–27.

Viswesvaran, C., & Deshpande, P. S. (1998). Do demographic correlates of ethical perceptions generalise to non-American samples: A study of managers in India. *Cross Cultural Management: An International Journal, 5*(1): 22–32.

Zeitz, G. (1990). Age and work satisfaction in a government agency: A situational perspective. *Human Relations, 43*: 419–438.

Section Four

MANAGING HUMAN RESOURCES AND INDUSTRIAL RELATIONS

Trends and Transition in the Human Resource Management (HRM) Context in India

Human resource management (HRM) is approached differently in different socio-cultural contexts. In USA, the primary emphasis of HRM is to focus on worker performance and motivation through extensive analysis of individual needs, training, evaluation, reward systems, job enrichment, career development, performance management etc. In contrast, the European approach to HRM has relied on a sociological perspective and focuses more on the holistic social system, the socio-political context and stakeholders like the union, government and corporate managers. The concepts and practices of HRM in India perhaps, fall somewhere between the "instrumental" view in USA and the "social embeddness" approach in Europe. Valuing people on their loyalty, integrity and commitment as opposed to their performance is often considered more relevant in traditional organizations while the corporate ethos of the globally active organizations are increasingly anchored on measurable performance achievements.

In the first chapter of this part, Kuruvilla compares the impact of industrialization strategy for economic development on human resource policies and practices and the industrial relations context in four Asian countries including India. Students of Indian management may find this approach of regional comparative views as relevant and innovative to their understanding. Industrialization or globalization strategies at the macro level have a significant impact on the design and implementation of international relations (IR) and HR practices and they are viewed differently in different contexts.

The chapter by Sen Gupta and Sett overviews the industrial relations experiences of the past three decades in India. This synoptic alternative view provides an insightful understanding that economic progress as a nation or corporate success as an organization needs the critical support of internal stakeholders. Increasingly the role of foreign capital in India and the global ambitions of Indian companies make it essential that a deeper alignment of workplace harmony through dynamic HR policies and practices be achieved by vision-driven managers. A recent study of 59 South Asian firms in Bangladesh, India, Nepal, and Pakistan by Sett suggests that the choice of HRM practices and their implementation varies greatly between "newer" and "older" organizations in these countries. The findings of the case studies suggests that global orientation in South Asia has been witnessing a definite trend away from the old "adversalism" to newer modern HRM practices (Sett, 2004).

As global firms become more active in India and as Indian firms become more active globally, the emergence of a cosmopolitan human resource culture becomes imperative. Issues such as individual versus group performance, objective versus subjective evaluation processes, culturally contexted practices in giving and receiving feedback, job rotation, training, competence versus loyalty and integrity and other such dilemmas need thoughtful resolution. The two chapters in this section, one from a global perspective written by a scholar working in USA and the other by two scholars from India, provide a two-dimensional insight into an area of utmost importance in understanding Indian management.

Reference

Sett, P. K. (2004). 'Human Resource Management and Firm Level Restructuring: The Asian Drama', *Research and Practice in Human Resource Management*, 12(1): 1–18.

Linkages between Industrialization Strategies and Industrial Relations/ Human Resource Policies: Singapore, Malaysia, the Philippines, and India

8

Sarosh Kuruvilla

The expectation that the logic of industrialism would make industrial relations systems increasingly similar (Kerr, Dunlop, Harbison, and Myers 1964) has not withstood the test of history: today's "advanced" countries have vastly different industrial relations systems. However, industrialization continues to be a central explanatory variable in research on the transformation of industrial relations systems in "developing" countries, particularly in Asia, given that continent's rapid industrialization over the past two decades.

In this paper I argue that industrialization strategies (IS's) and industrial relations and human resource (IR/HR) policy goals are closely intertwined and mutually reinforcing. Changes in the focus of national IR/HR policies are strongly influenced by changes in IS, since IR/HR policies are important components of the industrialization strategies of countries. In Asia, the key determinants of industrial relations change are the *choice* of an industrialization strategy and the *shifts* between strategies, not the *logic* of industrialism (Kerr et al. 1964) or the *levels* of industrialization (Sharma 1985).

This paper does not fully examine the reasons different countries chose certain IS's, nor does it analyze the causes of variations across countries in the institutional arrangements adopted to meet IR/HR policy goals, although I do present hypotheses concerning these issues. The focus is largely on the relationship between IS's and IR/HR policy goals at the national level.

To support this argument, I present case studies of four vastly different Asian countries: Singapore, Malaysia, the Philippines, and India. I chose these countries for three reasons. First, all four experienced shifts in their IS's after their independence. Second, the countries are currently following different IS's. Singapore currently follows a mixed strategy of advanced export-oriented industrialization and exports of services; Malaysia is in transition between low-cost and advanced export-oriented industrialization; the Philippines is primarily a low-cost exporter; and India has long pursued an advanced import substitution industrialization strategy and is currently shifting toward an export-oriented strategy. Thus, these countries permit both longitudinal and cross-sectional analyses of the links between IS and IR/HR. Third, the four countries differ vastly in their economic and industrial relations conditions.

Relevant Literature and Argument

Space constraints disallow a long review of the large and burgeoning literature on industrialization and economic development. The literature reviewed in this section is therefore illustrative.

Previous researchers have had different views regarding the relationship between IS and IR/HR policy goals. Kerr et al. (1964) claimed that the logic of industrialism causes a convergence of industrial relations systems at both national and workplace levels: to put the case briefly, modern technology requires modern institutions. Frenkel (1993) suggested that the level of industrialization determines the influence of trade unions on workplace industrial relations, with unions in more advanced Asian countries having greater influence. Sharma (1985) and Bjorkman, Lauridsen, and Marcussen (1988) argued that different stages of industrialization reflect different regimes of capital accumulation, leading to different kinds of capital labor relations. Frenkel and Harrod (1995) concluded that industrialization does not result in convergence to any specific IR model, given differences in technology, national institutions, and political dynamics. Deyo (1989) focused on the weakness of East Asian labor movements in the context of export-oriented industrialization and suggested that this weakness is linked to structural economic factors, communities' role in engendering labor organizing and protest, the oppositional potential of workers, and the degree to which elites intervene to control labor dissent. While this literature points to the existence of a link between IS and IR/HR policies, the nature of that link is never clarified due to differences in approaches and dependent variables.

This paper draws on the work of Roemer (1981), Haggard (1990), Bradford (1990), and Gereffi and Wyman (1990) to develop a typology of industrialization. Several different patterns (or trajectories) of industrialization exist. These patterns are distinguished primarily by whether they are inward- or outward-oriented and by the sector of their focus (Gereffi and Wyman 1990). An import substitution industrialization (ISI) strategy, for example, typically focuses on the promotion of locally owned industries catering to a relatively large domestic market in order to conserve foreign exchange and to promote industrialization and local entrepreneurship. Under this strategy, domestic industries are protected from foreign competition through state regulation and high import tariffs. In some countries all sectors are protected, while in others only the state-owned sector enjoys protection. The primary outcome of ISI is the generation of a local industrial base with local capital.

Within the ISI strategy category, however, there is some variation. As Gereffi (1990) noted, primary ISI most often focuses on developing consumer goods industries, while secondary ISI uses domestic production to produce substitutes for imports of a variety of capital- and technology-intensive manufactured goods, consumer durables (for example, automobiles), intermediate goods (for example, petro-chemicals and steel) and capital goods (for example, heavy machinery). The focus of a secondary ISI strategy is to create a domestically owned diversified industrial base that will fuel future economic growth. Singapore, Malaysia, and the Philippines, during the early stages of their post-independence development, pursued a primary ISI strategy; India followed a secondary industrialization strategy until 1990.

In contrast, export-oriented industrialization (EOI) typically involves an outward-looking focus, with foreign exchange earnings constituting the basis for economic development and growth. Typically, under this strategy, appropriate incentives for export and for inward foreign investment are enacted by the state. Here, too, there is variation. In Asia, primary EOI has been characterized by labor-intensive manufactured exports (often electrical and electronic components, footwear, and garments), for which the primary source of competitive advantage is the low costs of labor and production. In several Asian countries, this export growth has been financed by foreign investments made by multinationals, although Korean EOI has been largely financed by domestic firms and the state. Secondary EOI includes the export of higher value added items that are skill-intensive and require a relatively developed industrial base. Secondary EOI includes the strategies of "industrial deepening" noted by Cheng (1990) in Korea and Taiwan. There also exist other types of industrialization strategies, such as the "heavy industries strategy" and the "small scale industrialization strategy" alluded to by Roemer (1981), as well as the commodity export strategy that predated the ISI strategies used in the countries studied here, before their independence (Gereffi and Wyman 1990).

In this paper I describe four countries' dominant strategies to illustrate how IS and IR/HR policy goals are closely intertwined. However, it must be noted that identifying a country's industrialization strategy is difficult, since several IS's can be pursued at the same time. The typology used in this paper refers to the industrialization strategy that is most prominent at any given time. It is also difficult to pin down the exact dates of strategy shifts, since shifts invariably take several years to accomplish. As the cases will show, the shift from primary to secondary EOI in Singapore took approximately three years (Rodan 1989), while in the Philippines, the shift from ISI to Primary EOI took almost 20 years, partly because of the lack of coherent IS policies (Bello and Verzola 1993).

To analyze IR/HR policy goals, I use an inductive approach, based on what governments have done. In some countries these government policy goals include political suppression of unions to keep labor costs down, and in others they include union restructuring, restrictions on the subjects of collective bargaining, or changes in wage and overtime payment systems. In the primary EOI regime, for example, the key policy goal of the government involves keeping wages and other labor costs low. Government policy goals are in some instances inferred from the actions taken by the state. In most cases, I have selected only policy goals that suggest a major change in direction. I focus on the IR/HR policy goals affecting the private sector in each country.

IS's require particular national-level industrial relations policies for a number of reasons. For example, an export-oriented industrialization strategy based on cheap labor and foreign investment requires a cheap labor force with the appropriate levels of productivity and skills, a labor movement whose structure and policies do not deter foreign investment through labor militancy or resistance to the introduction of new technology, and dispute resolution mechanisms that can quickly solve industrial conflict. The dominant actor (in these countries, the state) will ensure that appropriate industrial relations and human resource legislation is enacted to support the industrialization strategy.

Figure 1: Industrialization Strategies and National Industrial Relations/Human Resource Policy Goals: The Framework

	Import Substitution Industrialization	Export-Oriented Industrialization
Primary	IR/HR Policy Goal = Stability	IR/HR Policy Goal = Cost Containment
Secondary	IR/HR Policy Goals = Stability and Productivity Enhancement	IR/HR Policy Goals = Workplace Flexibility, Productivity, Skills Development

Note: The institutional arrangements countries choose to meet the IR/HR policy goals described here will vary as a function of the state's political choices and the previous IR/HR institutional history.

The transition to secondary EOI requires IR/HR policies that emphasize productivity, increased skills formation, and workplace flexibility (defined as the ability of the employer to quickly react to changes in the market by restructuring work organization, compensation, human resource practices, and labor relations).[1] This transition often implies fundamental changes in national-level policies.

In addition, changes in workplace practices and production organization will force employers to substitute positive human resource practices for repressive labor management strategies, and such developments at the workplace or firm level will require supporting national level IR/HR policy changes. Therefore, different IS's imply different goals for national IR/HR policy. Under primary ISI, the lack of significant external competition permits the state to pursue pluralistic IR/HR policy goals. Under secondary ISI, the requirements of different industries for productivity gains force a change in the IR/HR policy goal. The focus of national IR/HR policy under typical primary EOI will be keeping labor costs low, and its focus under secondary EOI will be flexibility and productivity enhancement.

The reasons for the adoption and even success of the IS are often idiosyncratic (see Bowie 1991 for Malaysia; Rodan 1989 for Singapore; and Bello and Verzola 1993 for the Philippines). Adoption of IS could also be linked to the need for imitating successful development strategies (Cheng 1990), may be orchestrated by either "independent" states or "dependent" states (Frenkel and Harrod 1993), or may be linked to globalization. Similarly, the adoption of particular IR/HR policies may be caused by factors other than IS. For example, Haggard (1990) and Deyo (1989) argued that suppressive labor policies were initiated in some countries for political reasons, even before the adoption of EOI. This paper focuses not on the reasons an IS is adopted, but rather on the ways in which IS and IR/HR policy goals are mutually reinforcing (see Figure 1).[2]

While there is a strong interrelationship between IS's and IR/HR policy goals across countries, the specific institutional industrial relations arrangements in each country vary tremendously. What explains these variations in industrial relations institutions within and across industrialization regimes? I would suggest that the specific institutional arrangements used to meet IR/HR policy goals are determined by the *political* choices made by the state in each country, as well as the previous industrial relations in. ititutional history in each country. The ability of the state to fully enact policies consistent with the focus of the IS is constrained by several political and social factors, such as the degree of political stability and opposition to the ruling government, the legitimacy of the government, the nature of the political system, the institutional history of industrial relations, and the strength and political influence of trade unions.[3]

Country Studies of Industrialization Strategies and IR/HR Policy Goals

This section describes the industrialization strategies and IR/HR policy goals of four countries—Singapore, Malaysia, the Philippines, and India—drawing from recent research. The date of independence is used as the starting point of the analysis in each country to ensure consistency in the comparisons. Note, however, that each of these countries had an IS even prior to independence (Gereffi and Wyman 1990).

Industrialization Strategy and IR/HR Policy Goals in Singapore

Singapore adopted an import substitution industrialization (ISI) policy after independence in 1959. Because an ISI policy requires a large internal market to be self-sustaining, Singapore reunited with the Federation of Malaya in 1961, which provided it with a large market. Despite the economic rationale for integration, however, political differences resulted in a breakaway from the Malay federation in 1963 (Huff 1987). As Huff suggested, given the lack of a large market and local entrepreneurship talent, Singapore had no choice but to adopt an outward-looking export-oriented industrialization (EOI) strategy financed by foreign investment for its economic development. Rodan (1989: 85) suggested that after the collapse of the federation and the ISI strategy, the People's Action Party (PAP, the party in power in Singapore) employed the "ideological apparatus of the state to sponsor values and attitudes that enhanced the poltical legitimacy of the PAP's right to exclusive power to determine the course ahead."

The state-sponsored primary EOI strategy adopted in 1965 initially focused on attracting foreign investment in the radio receivers and televisions industries. Attracting foreign investment required policy changes in several different areas, such as infrastructural development (the development of transport, communication, free trade areas, and export processing zones); financial and fiscal incentives (land subsidies, electricity and power subsidies, building subsidies, exemption from corporate taxes, and export duty subsidies); and industrial relations policies (Huff 1987).

During British colonial rule the focus of industrial relations policy was on the control of communist unions through the union registration process, although the colonial administration enacted laws ensuring minimum standards in wages, conditions of employment, collective bargaining, and arbitration. With the adoption of EOI, however, the focus of the state's industrial relations policy was to provide foreign investors with a "stable, cheap, and flexible industrial relations system" (Chiang 1988: 239). Stability in industrial relations was promoted through the creation of a tripartite national governance structure. The National Trade Union Congress (NTUC), aligned with the PAP, led by Lee Kuan Yew, and the Employers Federation (SNEF) were provided with representation in all important national bodies, including the National Wages Council, the Economic Development Board, the Housing Board, and the Employees Provident Fund Board, as well as various other boards in several different spheres of government (Chiang 1988). To create responsible unionism, the government provided funding to the labor movement for the education of union leaders and members regarding economic development issues (Chiang 1988).

At the local level, workplace flexibility was promoted through many IR/HR policies. One such policy was to place restrictions on the subjects of bargaining; specifically, transfers, promotions, job assignments, redundancies, layoffs, and retrenchments were deemed to fall outside the scope of bargaining.[4] To contain industrial disputes in the interest of economic development, the right to strike was prohibited in essential industries, and in nonessential industries the ability of unions to strike was circumvented through various administrative requirements.[5]

Further, to ensure cost control, the Industrial Arbitration Court was empowered to ratify all collective bargaining agreements and to reject agreements if they conflicted with Singapore's national interest (Chiang 1988; Krislov and Legget 1985). To provide employers with stability in industrial relations and labor costs, the period of collective bargaining contracts was fixed at five years. Wage increases were controlled via wage guidelines of the tripartite National Wages Council that took into account the competitive position of Singaporean exports (Chew and Chew 1995). Clearly, these workplace policies reflected the need to provide foreign investors with both stability and flexibility in industrial relations.

The low-cost foreign investment–dominated EOI strategy adopted in 1963 was largely successful. By the early 1970s, manufacturing accounted for 21.4% of employment, up from 9.3% in 1965. The contribution of manufacturing to GDP increased from 15.6% in 1965 to 23.9% in 1980. In 1980, about 20 foreign corporations accounted for 76% of manufactured output, 65% of capital formation, 28% of GDP, and 82% of manufacturing exports (Huff 1987).

By 1974–76, rising wage levels due to labor shortages in manufacturing, combined with increased competition from other low–labor cost Asian nations such as Korea and Taiwan, threatened the future of a low-cost EOI strategy. The state aggressively spearheaded a second industrialization phase toward higher value added foreign investment, primarily in computer assembly and semiconductor manufacture, beginning in 1980.[6] The shift into a higher value added EOI was assisted by the tripartite National Wages Council, which recommended wage increases that were in excess of 12% for three consecutive years between 1979 and 1981. These high wage increases drove out low-cost producers (Rodan 1989: 145).

This high tech EOI strategy required IR/HR policies providing high technology and capital-intensive investors with highly skilled labor. As Chew and Chew (1995) suggested, several policy changes were introduced to meet these needs. The education system was restructured in 1981. The new curricula emphasized secondary education, several vocational training institutes and polytechnics were opened, and a new university (the Nanyang Technical University) was established to provide foreign investors with skilled labor (Begin 1993).

In order to provide companies with greater flexibility in industrial relations (the ability to quickly make changes in workplace rules), the state altered the union structure in 1981. Although the government initially sponsored a shift toward German-style industrial unionism, arguing that industrial relations outcomes should reflect industry-specific characteristics, the diversity of foreign investment eventually led the government to accept the National Productivity Council's recommendation to implement Japanese-style enterprise unions, called "house" unions. The claim was that the house unions would increase firm level flexibility and productivity, and allow collective bargaining outcomes to reflect the financial circumstances of each firm rather than each industry (Chiang 1988).

To encourage firms to continuously invest in skill enhancement and training, the Skills Development Fund (SDF) was introduced in 1982. The SDF legislation requires firms employing 50 employees or more to pay 2% of their payroll costs into the SDF. Employers contributing to the SDF can recover 80% of their contributions, provided they invest in training (Chew and Chew 1995). Applications for funds for training can be based on either a single training program or an entire year's training calendar. This system not only provided an economic incentive for skills development, but also was able to subsidize skill formation in smaller firms that do not contribute to the fund (Chew and Chew 1995).

A final change in industrial relations policy made in 1981 to support the new advanced EOI strategy was seen in wages. The National Wage Council discouraged centralized wage setting by recommending wage increases that reflected the "profitability, performance, and progress of different industries" (Pang 1983: 32–33). Following wage freezes after the 1985 recession, the NWC resumed its drive toward increased work-place flexibility by advocating flexible wage systems that would increase the variable portion of wage increases and use lump sum payments instead of base wage increases (*Straits Times*, Nov. 19, 1993).

Although the driving out of low-cost producers in the early 1980s caused a temporary economic slow-down in the early 1980s, by 1986, the restructuring of investment incentives and the investments made in education and skills development began to pay off. Higher-quality Japanese investments appeared, expanding the manufacturing of semi-conductors, disk drives, and computer assembly. The technological depth of the foreign investments increased steadily, with many firms (for example, Motorola) locating higher-end processes and R&D services in Singapore (Salih, Young, and Rajah 1988). The influx of investment resulted in a shortage of skilled and unskilled labor, and in 1986, immigration policy was altered to allow the importation of "guest workers." By early 1987, more than 195,000 guest workers had been imported (Huff 1987).

Singapore's economic development strategy is currently undergoing a shift. By the end of the 1980s, with a skilled work force and a higher-wage economy, Singapore began to turn to the service sector for continued growth after facing increased competition from other Southeast Asian countries such as Malaysia in the manufacturing of electronics. The predominant strategic change currently under way is to emphasize the finance, banking, and ports sectors in order to make the country a regional financial center and a trading and ship repairs center (Huff 1987). The service sector now accounts for 53.8% of GDP and 30% of total employment.

Singapore's industrial relations system demonstrates both stability at the national level and flexibility at the local level. At the national level, unions have significant voice in decision-making.[7] At the local level, the enterprise union structure, coupled with the restrictions on the ability of trade unions to bargain and strike, and the efficacy of the Industrial Arbitration Court (Krislov and Leggett 1985) have completely eliminated strikes. Labor-management relations are cordial, and real wages have increased steadily since 1985 (see Table 1). The trade union movement has focused its efforts on servicing its members in different spheres through

Table 1: Economic and Industrial Relations Conditions in
Singapore, Malaysia, the Philippines, and India

Variable	Singapore	Malaysia	Philippines	India
1. Population (Millions, 1991)	2.7	18.4	63.8	862.7
2. GDP per Capita (PPP $ 1990)	15,880.0	6,140.0	2,303.0	1,072.0
3. GDP Growth Rate				
1971–75	9.4	7.2	5.7	2.4
1976–80	8.5	8.6	0.0	3.4
1981–85	6.2	5.2	−1.2	5.4
1986–90	7.9	6.1	5.1	5.4
4. Sectoral Share of GDP				
Agriculture, 1980	1.2	22.9	25.1	38.1
Agriculture, 1990	0.3	18.7	22.1	32.4
Industry, 1980	29.1	19.6	25.7	25.9
Industry, 1990	29.1	26.9	25.5	27.5
Services, 1980	44.7	22.4	26.2	36.0
Services, 1990	53.8	22.7	30.7	40.0
5. Foreign Share of Mfg. Exports, 1988	86.0	60.0	66.0	0
6. Exports as Percentage of GDP, 1990	157.0	71.0	20.0	6.0
7. Union Density (percentage of total work force):				
1979	24.5	18.0	10.9	1.06
1984	16.4	16.0	9.7	1.85
1988	17.2	9.9	9.6	2.00
1993	14.2	9.5	9.6	2.00
8. Strikes				
1960	45	37	43	1,026.0
1970	5	17	104	2,843.0
1987	0	24	62	1,799.0
1989	0	17	267	1,786.0
1992	0	17	136	1,388.0
9. Average Annual Growth Rate of Earnings per Employee				
1970–80	3.0	2.0	−3.7	0.4
1980–89	5.0	3.2	6.4	3.4

Sources: *Human Development Report* (1993); *ILO Yearbook of Labor Statistics* (1993); unpublished figures assembled by author.

the creation of union-run cooperatives for transportation, textbooks, insurance, and supermarkets, and the unions also sponsored a consumer movement (Chiang 1988). With the decline of manufacturing and the rise of services, union density fell sharply from a high of 25% in 1970 to 14.5% in 1993 (Begin 1993).

The stable yet flexible IR system that Singapore created was necessary given the country's need to attract foreign investment. The choice of the specific tripartite institutional framework, however, was facilitated by several political factors, such as the lack of significant opposition to the PAP (see Chew and Chew 1995), the ability of Lee Kuan Yew to get union leaders to buy into the tripartite arrangement, and the broad societal acceptance of the need for foreign investment and exports. Arguably, the ability of trade unions to have voice in important national level decisions through the tripartite framework more than compensated for the curtailment of bargaining subjects at the local level.

The Singaporean case also demonstrates that higher technology–intensive EOI is associated with IR/HR policy that is focused on workplace flexibility and skill development. Further, IR/HR policies were well integrated with macro policies focusing on education, immigration, and economic development. In fact, Singapore provides a model of macro policy integration that other countries such as Malaysia have tried to emulate.

Industrialization Strategy and IR/HR Policy Goals in Malaysia

Like Singapore, Malaysia embarked on a vigorous ISI strategy after independence, although its ISI phase lasted longer given its larger internal market. The first phase of ISI (1957–63) focused on infrastructural and rural development, with industrialization left to the private sector. In the second phase of ISI (1963–70) the state emerged as a leading investor, motivated by the New Economic Policy (NEP) that promised the economic advancement of ethnic Malays (relative to ethnic Chinese and Indians). The NEP was based on the premise that the primary way to accomplish this goal without ethnic strife was to enact policies that would ensure rapid economic growth, and at the same time, through regulation, reserve both investment and jobs for Malays (see Kuruvilla and Arudsothy 1995; Bowie 1991; and Spinanger 1986).[8]

During the ISI phase, industrial relations in Malaysia reflected the system inherited from the British, with legislation providing for collective bargaining and minimum standards, while the focus of government policy was to contain conflict in the interest of economic development (Kuruvilla and Arudsothy 1995). The prohibition of political strikes and restrictions on the ability of the various national labor federations to carry out trade union functions (they were registered as societies) also ensured that the Malay-dominated government had control over the labor movement (Arudsothy 1990). At the level of the workplace, the legislation was similar to that of Singapore, with restrictions on the subjects of bargaining (transfers, promotions, layoffs, retrenchments, and job assignments being deemed outside the scope of bargaining), and restrictions on the ability of unions to strike.[9] During this period, there was relatively steady union growth, while wage bargaining was largely at the industry level, particularly in the plantations sector. Since the government did not use the extensive powers it commanded to regulate industrial relations in this phase, Kuruvilla and Arudsothy (1995) have referred to this period as "controlled pluralism."

A resource crunch resulting from NEP policies, the state's failed heavy industries program, and Malaysia's increasing foreign debt (which was 30% of GNP by the mid-1980s) forced Malaysia in 1973–74 to embark on an intensive export promotion drive based on cheap manufactures financed by foreign investment (Spinanger 1986; Bowie 1991). The mechanisms used to induce foreign investment, largely in the electronics industry, were similar to those followed by Singapore, except in industrial relations, where several new policies were enacted (Kuruvilla and Arudsothy 1995).

The first direction of change in IR/HR policy reflected the need to contain costs in the export sector. By 1975, policy changes included an extension of tax and labor exemptions for foreign corporations (companies were exempted from several labor protection laws), an alteration of the definition of wages for the calculation of over-time to reduce costs in the export sector (which used overtime because of the labor shortage), and a reduction in the rate of overtime pay for working on holidays and rest days. The emphasis on cost containment could also be seen in the government's refusal to enact minimum wage legislation for the export industry, and its refusal to enact equal pay for equal work in the export-oriented electronics sector, where 78.6% of those employed were female (Rajah 1994; Grace 1990).

A second direction of change in IR/HR policy focused on union control, largely at the local level. As part of the "look east" policy of the Prime Minister in 1980, the government encouraged the formation of Japanese-style enterprise unions (currently about 30% of unions are enterprise-based) (Arudsothy and Littler 1993).[10] In the export-oriented electronics sector, unions were banned. Although the ban on electronics unions was lifted in 1988 due to international pressures (Kuruvilla and Arudsothy 1995), electronics workers were not permitted (unlike their counterparts in the electrical industries) to affiliate themselves with national or industry level federations. A combination of state policies and employer opposition (Kuruvilla and Arudsothy 1995) ensured that the electronics sector continued to be union-free (less than 10% of electronics firms are unionized). The decision to allow only in-house unions in electronics is largely attributed to pressure from foreign investors (Grace 1990), although it is also consistent with the government's pursuit of a low-cost export-oriented strategy.

The third direction of change in IR/HR, involving a more activist involvement of the government in industrial relations matters, arguably developed because of the government's role as an investor and employer as a consequence of the Heavy Industries Program. Kuruvilla and Arudsothy (1995) documented the different manifestations of the new activism, including extensive powers given to the labor minister to declare industries "essential" and to suspend trade unions acting against the "national interest," and greater involvement in union recognition cases (with increased rejection of registrations in manufacturing) and in dispute settlement, where an increased number of cases were referred to compulsory arbitration. The greater involvement of the government in industrial relations reflected efforts to contain industrial conflict in the interest of fast-paced economic development.

The low-cost EOI strategy has paid rich dividends. By 1989, the manufacturing sector accounted for 30% of GDP (up from 15% in 1970) and 40% of export earnings, and the contribution of transnational corporations to exports increased from 28% of total exports in 1971 to 58% in 1988 (Kuruvilla and Arudsothy 1995). The electronics industry, the centerpiece of the dramatic export performance, employed 16.7% of the manufacturing work force in 1988 (Onn 1989), and exports of semiconductors exceeded M $4 billion, comprising 24.8% of total manufacturing exports, in 1989 (Grace 1990). The Malaysian economy registered annual growth rates of over 6% during the 1980s.

Yet, in the mid-1980s, an impetus for changing this low-cost manufacturing export strategy came from firms within the electronics industry. While the low-cost EOI strategy attracted foreign investment, it also resulted in a labor shortage. (Currently, out of a work force of about 13 million, roughly 2.5 million are guest workers, according to government statistics, while unofficial estimates place the figure at 4 million; see Kuruvilla and Arudsothy 1995.) The consequent rise in wage costs (annual wage increases exceeded 6% during the latter half of the 1980s), combined with a world-wide recession in 1985, forced the electronics industry to restructure itself. The industry started to shift toward increased automation and adopted new forms of flexible work organization (see Rajah 1994). Competition from low-cost producers in other countries, and the need to build forward and backward linkages involving the electronics industry, motivated the state to formally announce a shift from its primary EOI strategy. The new strategy emphasized the attraction of more technology-intensive foreign investment, but also emphasized the need for Malaysia to build and deepen its industrial structure.

The new industrial strategy (revised and articulated in the state's Vision 20/20 plan) implied restructuring of investment incentives to attract higher technology-based capital investment (the attraction of R&D and higher-end processes of semiconductor manufacture were key goals) and the creation of small-scale industries (which were expected to stimulate linkages primarily as subcontractors to the electronics industry [PSDC 1993]). The new strategy also implied several macro economic and social policy changes. Immigration policies were altered to allow the import of both skilled and unskilled "guest" workers, given the labor shortage. The education sector was reformed and deregulated, leading to a mushrooming of private colleges having exchange arrangements with universities in Australia and Canada (Young and Kiat 1992). Between 1985 and 1992, enrollment in polytechnics increased by 113%, and enrollment in colleges increased by 45% (Young and Kiat 1992).

The central elements of IR/HR policy thus have shifted away from cost containment and union control to training and skills development designed to provide a better-quality work force necessary to attract higher-technology investment. More specifically, the government enacted the

Human Resources Development Act in 1992, which established the Skills Development Fund, similar to that of the Singaporean system. The 1% of payroll cost paid by all firms is matched by the government, and the SDF subsidizes training costs of all applicant firms. The tax on the firm is larger than in Singapore, however, since each firm can only take back a maximum of 60% of its contributions to the SDF (Kuruvilla and Arudsothy 1995).

At local and regional levels, skills development centers have been set up by the government to work in collaboration with business. These efforts are complemented by initiatives in the private sector, such as the new agreement between the Federation of Malaysian Manufacturers and the University of Science and Technology for skill training programs, and the initiatives taken by foreign multinationals in Penang. Although these firms are often fierce competitors in the international semiconductor market, they cooperate locally in the development of skills at the Penang Skills Development Center (PSDC 1993). Wage bargaining has been decentralized to the enterprise level in the unionized sector, although in some industries, such as banking and plantations, industry-level bargaining is still the norm (Kuruvilla and Arudsothy 1995).

The move to advanced EOI has continued to attract foreign investment of high quality. Rajah (1994) suggested that higher-end processes such as chip design, wirebonding, and research and development operations are increasingly being located in Malaysia. Work organization in the electronics industry mirrors practices followed in the advanced countries, and human resource management techniques are based increasingly on the development of skills with high pay and employee involvement in a nonunion environment (Rajah 1994).

In sum, in Malaysia, industrial relations at the workplace level in the export sector exhibits the goal of workplace flexibility. In the more traditional ISI sector, industrial relations at large state-run organizations like the Malaysian Airlines System and Proton (a car manufacturer) also shows trends toward increased joint labor-management consultation and flexibility (Rajah 1994). At the national level, however, the Malaysian government has resisted the efforts of labor federations to unite into a single federation, and the government's recent "behind the scenes" support of a rival labor federation is indicative of its intention to keep the labor movement fragmented in the interests of political stability (Arudsothy and Littler 1992). Union density has steadily declined in Malaysia from over 12% to 9.9%, and the export manufacturing sector is increasingly nonunion. The growth in real wages (average annual growth has exceeded 6% since 1987), coupled with a labor shortage and union suppression and substitution practices of employers, has successfully prevented the growth of the labor movement. In sum, a shift to a nonunion model at the local level and fragmentation at the national level is apparent (Frenkel 1993).

The Malaysian case suggests a congruence between first-stage EOI and an industrial relations system geared toward cost containment. In addition, the institutional arrangements governing industrial relations included several elements of labor suppression. During the transition to second-stage EOI, however, Malaysia's industrial relations policies have increasingly resembled Singapore's, with a clear congruence between a more advanced EOI and policies focusing on skills development. And as in Singapore, EOI based on higher skills in Malaysia is bringing about an integration between IR/HR policies and macro level policies focusing on education, immigration, and economic development. The lack of opposition to the ruling political party (the Barisan National Front, which was a coalition between the United Malay National Organization [the party of the ethnic Malays] and the parties representing the ethnic Chinese and Indians, MCA and MIA respectively), and the economic advancement of the largest section of the Malaysian population (the Malays) under the current economic development strategy, provided the state the legitimacy to enact policies that apparently trade off labor and union rights for increased foreign investments in the export sector. The demands of foreign investors also appear to have been an important factor in influencing the state's choice of institutional industrial relations arrangements in the export sector (Grace 1990).

Industrialization Strategy and IR/HR Policy Goals in the Philippines

The Philippines adopted an ISI strategy (after postwar independence) that used tax incentives and protection from foreign competition to stimulate the growth of local industry. The ISI strategy successfully fostered the growth of a new domestic industrial-capital elite, and expanded manufacturing, which experienced annual growth rates of 14% between 1949 and 1953 and 11% between 1953 and 1959 (Villegas 1988). The dependence of the Philippines on the import of capital and technology to sustain its ISI strategy, however, resulted in a balance of payments crisis in 1960 (Ofreneo 1994). The shortage of foreign exchange was alleviated by stabilization loans from the International Monetary Fund (IMF) and the World Bank, granted on the condition that the Philippines deregulate its economy and open it to foreign investment through adoption of an EOI strategy (Bello, Kinley and Elinson 1988).

During the ISI phase, the focus of IR/ HR policy was pluralistic, with little effort to tinker with inherited IR/HR institutions, which were primarily American. For example, the Industrial Peace Act of 1953 was based on the Wagner Act and promoted free collective bargaining, voluntary arbitration, unfair labor practice legislation, and business unionism. The number of registered unions increased from 435 to 839 during the 1950s, with a new generation of union leadership in ISI industries such as textiles, banking, sugar, and mines (Ofreneo 1994).

The 1962–72 period was characterized by a mixed approach to industrialization. The powerful agricultural elite continued to push for economic liberalization and free trade, while the new industrial elite argued for the continuation of protection for ISI industries that had just stabilized (Bello and Verzola 1993). Some liberalization followed, via a devaluation of the peso and removal of protections in some sectors (Villegas 1988). Social unrest resulted from the devaluation of the peso, however, and set the conditions for the declaration of martial law in 1972 (Villegas 1988; Ofreneo 1994). Martial law allowed the Marcos regime and its World Bank advisers to implement the recommendations contained in the Ranis Mission report (a World Bank–funded mission) and the World Bank Country Report of 1975, both of which argued for a full-scale export-oriented agricultural and industrial strategy based on the comparative advantage of cheap labor. To attract multinational corporate investments in export processing zones established in Bataan and Mariveles, the government accelerated the decontrol of trade; increased foreign borrowings to finance reforms in education, industry, and financial systems; simplified tariffs and customs codes; and rationalized investment incentives (Villegas 1988; Macaraya and Ofreneo 1993).

To keep costs low to attract foreign investment, industrial relations policies were transformed through a new labor code introduced in 1974 (Villegas 1988). A key change in IR/HR policy focused on guaranteeing industrial peace to foreign investors. A ban on strikes was instituted, but later modified to apply only to "vital" industries "including those engaged in the production and processing of commodities for export" (Villegas 1988: 61). The Secretary of Labor was empowered to obtain injunctions against strikes. Compulsory arbitration also was introduced through the National Labor Relations Commission. Unions were prohibited from soliciting contributions to their strike funds, and all existing strike funds were to be shifted to labor education and research purposes. In addition, Article 271 of the labor code banned foreign donations to unions. These provisions, notes Villegas (1988), significantly weakened the unions' ability to strike in non-vital industries. Unfair labor practices by employers were "decriminalized."[11] Furthermore, decree No 1458 allowed permanent replacement of striking workers (Villegas 1988).

The second direction of change in IR/HR policy focused on union structure, to facilitate a tripartite corporatist arrangement for stability in industrial relations. The highly fragmented labor movement was restructured on a "one union in each industry" principle. Unions were required to become affiliated with one recognized labor center, the Marcos-controlled Trade Union Congress of the Philippines. An employers confederation was also formed to participate in tripartism.[12]

The third direction of change in labor policy focused on the provision of cheap labor to the growing numbers of foreign investors in the EOI sectors. The National Manpower Youth Council ensured a constant supply of trained workers, and the Apprenticeship Program allowed children aged 14 and older to be employed in export industries at a fraction of the prevailing minimum wage (Villegas 1988). Although minimum wages were revised numerous times, these increases fell far short of the rise in living costs.

The final direction of change in IR/HR policy was a downward revision of existing labor standards regarding working hours, overtime, and health and safety. This change was justified on grounds that existing labor protection standards were too high and did not reflect Philippine realities (Villegas 1988).

The martial law period did not accomplish a full-scale EOI strategy, given the continuing dominance of some of the industrial elites during the period of "crony capitalism" described by several authors (for example, Macaraya and Ofreneo 1993). However, foreign investment in the low-cost electronics sector continued to increase, along with foreign aid, and both helped sustain the EOI strategy. Repeated devaluations of the peso, coupled with a financial crisis that stemmed from the political excesses of the Marcos regime, the failure of domestic industries under an export regime, and the inability of exports to offset the debt payment requirements in the 1980s (the debt had reached 93% of GNP in 1986), resulted in further dependence on World Bank financing (Macaraya and Ofreneo 1993; Bello and Verzola 1993). The result was a series of "structural adjustment" loans in 1983 and 1986.

The strategic thrust of structural adjustment was a more determined implementation of EOI and deregulation of the economy, coupled with a systematic easing out of inefficient Filipino firms (Macaraya and Ofreneo 1993; Villegas 1988). The World Bank's report on the Philippines emphasized that "priority should be given to the continued expansion of labor-intensive manufacturing taking advantage of the competitive aspect of labor costs" (Villegas 1988:70).

Foreign investment increased by 1156% after the structural adjustment policies were implemented in 1983 (Macaraya and Ofreneo 1993). The nontraditional manufactures (electronics and garments) attracted 80% of the investments, and by the end of 1983, the electronics sector accounted for 32% of total Filipino exports (Macaraya and Ofreneo 1993). However, the removal of policies protectioning domestic industries and the devaluations of the peso had a devastating impact on domestic industries. For example, the number of closures of domestic firms climbed from 831 in 1981 to 2,284 in 1984 (Department of Labor and Employment 1985).

To contain the growing strikes against martial law, the government enacted BP 130 (prohibiting strikes against the national interest) and BP 227 (allowing the use of law enforcement agencies to control strikers). In addition, procedures for terminating workers were simplified in response to employer pressures (Villegas 1988), leading to increased layoffs and terminations. During 1981–82, 65,000 workers were laid off annually, whereas during 1983–85, after the 1983 implementation of structural adjustment, the annual number of layoffs increased to 82,000 (Department of Labor and Employment 1986). At least 60% of workers in the growing export sector were still receiving less than the minimum wage in the early 1980s, and this period witnessed a decline in union membership from 12.2% to 9.3% (Villegas 1988). These developments intensified the schism that existed between the pro-government TUCP and other illegal labor centers such as the KMU and FFW that opposed structural adjustment policies. This deep schism in the Filipino labor movement still persists (Ofreneo 1994).

Structural adjustment continued under the democratic regimes of Aquino and Ramos, although labor laws were altered to expand union rights. Union formation was simplified, with mandatory representation if 20% of the employees in an establishment petitioned for representation. Collective bargaining was allowed in the public sector, and the one-union-per-industry rule enacted by the Marcos regime was withdrawn. In cases of unfair labor practices such as the firing of union activists, the mandatory 15-day cooling off period before labor action was rescinded, and a simple majority was deemed sufficient in strike ballots (a change from the previous requirement of a two-thirds majority). However, the provisions restricting strikes, such as BP 130 and BP 227, continued to be enforced more firmly than during the Marcos regime, and the government cracked down on illegal strikes (Ofreneo 1994).

In an effort to curb industrial unrest, arbitration was mandated to be the final step in all grievance cases, and the terms of collective bargaining agreements were fixed at five years. To encourage more collaborative labor-management relations, a joint labor-management consultation scheme based on the Japanese example of JCC's was introduced, and a form of tripartism was introduced under which labor centers participated in the setting of regional minimum wages. It is still too early to evaluate the effects of these changes.

Although President Aquino rolled back the more repressive elements of Marcos's labor policy, suggesting a return to the sort of pluralistic policy that the Philippines had immediately after World War II, this has not resulted in the strengthening of the labor movement, nor has it promoted more stable industrial relations. If anything, easing of the rules governing union formation has resulted in even more fragmentation of the labor movement, with 7 or 8 national centers, 155 national federations along a myriad of political lines, and more than 5,600 independent local unions organized on a "general unionism" principle (Ofreneo 1994). Inter-union rivalry ("every federation behaves like a general at war with the other generals" [Ofreneo 1994: 324]) has resulted in a weak union movement, with few union victories in representation elections. The unions rely on the minimum wage as the floor for collective bargaining, and their economic muscle is weakened by the restrictions on strikes, the government's crackdown on illegal strikes, and employers' replacement of striking workers. Further, subcontracting, casualization, and the use of contract labor have increased five-fold, and have contributed to declining union power (Ofreneo 1994). Although trade unions claim a total of 3,000,000 members, the actual number of workers covered by collective bargaining contracts is under 600,000 (Department of Labor and Employment 1993). While strikes have declined over the past two years, the number of cases pending arbitration has increased sharply, suggesting that there is still conflict in the system (Department of Labor and Employment 1993).

The Philippine case suggests a correspondence between low-cost export-oriented development and a cost containment–oriented and repressive industrial relations policy. However, in this case, almost 30 years elapsed between the announcement of the EOI policy and its full implementation. Although the focus of the cost containment–oriented labor policy was consistent with a low-cost primary EOI strategy, the institutional industrial relations arrangements varied across different political regimes. During the Marcos dictatorship labor relations policies were extremely repressive. During the Aquino and Ramos governments, in contrast, democratization led to the removal of the restrictive IR/HR policies of the Marcos era. However, the liberalization of labor regulations to make union formation easier has resulted in an increasingly fragmented labor movement. Furthermore, declines in real wages and job security, the downward revision in labor standards, and an extremely weak union movement indicate that IR/HR policies have helped sustain the low-cost development strategy. Finally, the Philippines case also suggests that pressures from external bodies such as the World Bank and IMF can strongly influence a government's industrialization strategy and consequently the industrial relations system.[13]

Industrialization Strategy and IR/HR Policy Goals in India

After independence in 1947, driven by considerations of self-reliance, India adopted an advanced ISI model under the rubric of a centrally planned mixed economy (Mathur 1993). The ISI strategy emphasized the growth and long-term development of heavy capital goods industries run by the state with largely indigenous technology (Sodhi 1993). The private sector was regulated through restrictions placed on investment and production capacity. The ISI strategy was sustained by a policy of industrial licensing that regulated the entry of new firms into economic sectors, and extensive import duties ensured the protection of domestic industry from foreign competition.[14] Forty years of ISI resulted in a slow but steady economic growth rate of 2–3% per year, a diversified industrial structure with both heavy industrial and consumer goods industries, a nuclear program, and space industries. Moreover, the insularity of the ISI strategy kept the Indian economy relatively unaffected by worldwide recessions (Singh 1994).

Industrial relations policy in India was influenced by the close ties between political parties and the labor movement forged in the struggle for independence (Ramaswamy 1983). First, labor legislation was extremely protective of labor. In terms of labor standards, India's Factories Act of 1948 is among the most advanced in the world, with maternity leave and benefits, the provision of child care in all factories, and advanced legislation on health and safety.[15]

Second, union formation is relatively simple, with any seven persons being able to form a union. Each political party sponsors its own national union federation, which ensures that a multiplicity of unions are affiliated to various political parties in each enterprise. Efforts to reform union recognition legislation to allow single bargaining agents have been resisted by the political parties (Reddy 1978).

Third, since union leadership is a stepping stone to political leadership, Indian trade union law allows "external" leaders (who are not employed in the enterprise and are normally political figures) to run union affairs. Industrial action therefore is often driven by political considerations not connected with enterprise problems (Ramaswamy 1983).

In terms of collective bargaining, industry-wide bargaining occurs in certain industries where the employers are organized, but bargaining otherwise is decentralized to the enterprise level. Although there are no restrictions on the subjects of bargaining, the Industrial Disputes Act of 1947 restricts the ability of employers to fire, lay off, or retrench employees, or to close businesses. While layoffs are costly (the employer must pay 50% of wages for the first 90 days, and layoffs are permitted only for a maximum of 180 days), retrenchment and the closure of firms require government permission, which, given the close relationship that exists between unions and politicians, is rarely given.

Industrial relations is largely conflictual (the number of man-days lost due to strikes is the highest in the world) despite restrictions on strikes (for example, the provision that a strike or lockout must be withdrawn if the dispute is referred by either party to third party conciliation [Lansing and Kuruvilla 1987]).[16] The dispute resolution system is ineffective, largely because state-appointed conciliation and mediation officers are also political appointees, which allows unions and political parties influence over the dispute settlement procedure (Lansing and Kuruvilla 1987).

The political orientation of trade unions has provided the labor movement with political influence far greater than their union membership alone would warrant. Labor is the swing vote in at least 30% of all parliamentary constituencies, although the labor movement is not large (India has about 47,000 registered unions with about 6 million members, comprising about 2% of the work force [Venkataratnam 1993]).

There is considerable agreement that Indian industrial relations is "inefficient" (see Ramaswamy 1983; Mathur 1993; Lansing and Kuruvilla 1987). The multiplicity of constantly competing unions in an enterprise hinders the development of stable labor-management relationships, resulting in a very high rate of industrial action. The power of unions, it is argued, has resulted in excess employment in the public sector, and slowed rationalization and restructuring in the private sector (Venkataratnam 1993). The protection from foreign competition afforded to Indian manufacturers, and a guaranteed internal market, created huge and inefficient industries that were not able to compete internationally once the economy was liberalized (Economist 1994).[17]

The ISI strategy and industrial relations policy goals are mutually reinforcing, although they had different roots (labor policy was adopted due to the influence of trade unions, while industrialization policy was adopted in order to attain self-reliance). A protectionist ISI strategy was congruent with a highly protectionist IR/HR system that blocked the development of collaborative and flexible industrial relations.

The best evidence of this congruence can be seen in the actions of manufacturing employers, who, when protectionism was withdrawn with trade liberalization in 1991, started calling for revisions in labor legislation to allow them to retrench workers and close unprofitable firms. Meanwhile, industrialists in other sectors have been calling for a continuation of protection from external competition to give them time to restructure and rationalize their firms (See Sodhi 1993; Venkataratnam 1993).

A balance of payments crisis in 1991 was the factor that precipitated the change in India's economic policy. For several reasons, India's foreign exchange reserves had declined from U.S. $3 billion in 1990 to less than U.S. $0.2 billion in March 1991 (Kuruvilla and Erickson 1994). In danger of defaulting on its debt payments, India approached the World Bank and the IMF for emergency assistance, which was granted on the condition that India "liberalize" its economy and change its "inward orientation."

"Liberalization" is in progress currently. Industrial policy has shifted from ISI to a form of EOI. The licensing of industries has been virtually eliminated, the rules regarding monopoly restrictions have been relaxed, the ceilings on foreign investment have been removed, and the public sector has been opened to privatization. Firms are now allowed free entry into and exit from all industries except for a few strategic ones. In addition to these reforms, trade policy has been revamped to promote exports and freer trade, the Indian currency has been made fully free-floating and convertible, and restrictions on the importation of several goods have been removed. Fiscal policy has been amended to reduce the fiscal deficit and control the underground economy (estimated to be 1/5 of the economy), agricultural subsidies have been reduced, and several price controls have been removed. Furthermore, financial markets have been liberalized, banking regulations have been reformed, and stock markets have been freed from government control (see Venkataratnam 1993; Sodhi 1993).

Economic liberalization has put pressure on industrial relations institutions to change. Both employers (who now must restructure to survive in the face of international competition) and the World Bank are strongly lobbying for changes in IR/HR legislation that would allow firms to lay off and retrench workers without government permission (Sodhi 1993).

Although labor legislation has not yet been changed, IR/HR practices are undergoing rapid change. One significant outcome of structural adjustment and liberalization has been work force reduction. Given their inability to retrench, employers have introduced voluntary retirement schemes (VRS) to shed excess labor. Although precise estimates of the number of people participating in VRS are not available, Venkataratnam (1993) suggested that a total of 5 million jobs will be lost through VRS, plant closures, and the privatization of inefficient public sector organizations.

Employers' industrial relations practices clearly have become more aggressive recently. For example, the number of lockouts has increased dramatically, even as strike frequency has declined (Venkataratnam 1993). In addition, in order to avoid unionization, employers are promoting workers into administrative and supervisory ranks to make them ineligible for unionization by shifting them outside the purview of the Industrial Disputes Act (Venkataratnam 1993). Employers are also pushing for joint consultation over productivity improvements, and recent collective bargaining contracts assert management rights more forcefully than ever. For the first time, concession bargaining has occurred in several industries (Venkataratnam 1993; Sodhi 1993).

Venkataratnam (1993) suggested that for the first time, the employers feel that government is on their side. The beginnings of a government-business coalition (in contrast to the previous government-labor coalition) are increasingly apparent. For example, in the state of Maharashtra, for the first time, the government has attempted to neutralize labor unrest by declaring several private sector firms "essential and public utilities," thereby outlawing strikes in these firms (Abreu 1994).

Economic liberalization has weakened labor's ties with political parties and forced unions to face what Sodhi (1993) calls an "existential crisis." The Congress Party, the party in power, actively supports liberalization, even though its trade union arm, the powerful INTUC, fundamentally opposes liberalization. The decline of the INTUC's political influence has further weakened a labor movement whose membership is already declining due to the spread of VRS. The excessive fragmentation of unions on political lines, a growing alienation between trade unions and their members, and the waning influence of national unions over enterprise-based unions have further weakened the union movement (Sheth 1991; Sarath 1992).

Economic liberalization has thereby called into question the economic and political basis of previous IR/HR policies. Current trends indicate a movement toward increased workplace flexibility. If and how this flexibility will be institutionalized through new legislation remains open to question.

India provides an illustration of how a country's IR/HR policy goals and its ISI strategy became mutually sustaining. The close relationship between political parties and trade unions since independence ensured that the state's choice of institutional industrial relations arrangements governing industrial relations was geared toward the protection of labor rights and labor power. With the creation of a more open economy since 1991, the existing labor policy is being questioned, and workplace practices have already shifted toward greater flexibility in industrial relations. Although employer IR/HR practices have already changed, the government is approaching reform of IR legislation slowly, and through tripartite discussions. Economic liberalization has weakened trade unions considerably, but the long history of trade union partnerships with political parties has ensured that unions retain a voice in the design of the new system.

Discussion

The four country cases demonstrate that there is a close relationship between industrialization strategies and IR/HR policy goals, as argued. Each type of IS appears to be congruent with certain IR/HR policy goals (see Figure 1). Under ISI, national IR/HR policies in all four countries have focused on stability and have been relatively pluralistic. Under primary EOI, the IR/HR policies of Malaysia and the Philippines focused on cost containment, which included a substantial amount of union repression and initiatives to keep labor costs down. Under secondary EOI, the IR/HR policies of Malaysia and Singapore emphasized skills development, workplace flexibility, and productivity. In India, a shift from second stage ISI to a more "liberalized" EOI-type economy has oriented IR/HR practice toward increased employer autonomy and productivity, while debate about policy change continues.

Events in the four countries show that changes in IR/HR policies are primarily caused by changes in industrialization strategies. For example, in Singapore, changes in national IR policy were a product of deliberate decisions taken by the state after adoption of export-oriented industrialization. As Chiang (1988) suggested, it was clear to the Singaporean state that industrial relations stability and flexibility were critical to the attraction of foreign investment, and industrial relations policy was configured to meet that need.

In Malaysia, the adoption of more repressive IR policies evolved more gradually, after EOI was adopted, and appears to have been part of efforts to attract and retain foreign investment, notably in the electronics industry. Clearly, the cost containment aspect of IR policies in Malaysia developed in response to pressures from foreign investors. In the Philippines, repressive IR policies were adopted to support export-oriented industrialization by keeping costs low. In India, the IR institutions gradually evolved under a protectionist ISI regime, and the shift to an export-oriented industrialization policy has produced pressures, mostly from employers, for IR system change.

The close relationship between IS and IR/HR policy goals manifests itself in different ways. In at least two of the four countries, IR/HR policies have been used to promote the shift from one IS to another. In Singapore, the transition to a secondary EOI was encouraged when the National Wages Council mandated double-digit wage increases in an effort to drive low-cost producers out of Singapore. In Malaysia, new forms of work organization and increases in labor costs forced the government to support a second-stage export-oriented industrialization strategy, with its attendant implications for IR/HR policy as well, suggesting that the impetus for change in IS was triggered by IR/HR developments at the level of the firm. This is further evidence of the close relationship between IS and IR/HR policy goals.

There is some evidence that the arguments made in this paper are generalizable to other Asian countries. Lee (1995), Park and Lee (1995), Levin and Hong (1995), and Brooks (1995) found evidence of a similar relationship in their respective analyses of Taiwan, Korea, Hong Kong, and Indonesia.[18]

Conclusions

The results of this paper suggest that congruence between IS and IR/HR policy goals is an important precondition for successful economic development. This paper also identifies several issues for further research. One open question is why substantial variation exists across countries in institutional industrial relations arrangements, even when the IS and IR/HR policy goals are similar. Although I have shown that changes in IS have shaped IR/HR policy goals in the four countries examined, the industrial relations institutions and practices are different across those countries, and often more resistant to change, as Figure 2 shows. The experiences in these four countries suggest that the institutional arrangements used to meet national IR/HR policy goals are dependent on the choices governments make, and these choices are constrained by political

Figure 2: Variation in Institutional Arrangements to Meet National
IR/HR Policy Goals: Singapore, Malaysia, the Philippines, and India

	ISI			EOI		
	IR/HR Policy Goal = Stability			IR/HR Policy Goal = Cost Containment		
	Political Choices			Political Choices		
1st Stage	India, 1947–1980	Malaysia and Singapore, 1955–1965	Philippines, 1945–1959	Singapore, 1955–1970s	Malaysia, 1975–1986	Philippines, 1960–Current
	-Minimum standards legislation -Free CB -Multiple unionism -Job security -Industry and enterprise level bargaining -Political unionism -Institutions to reduce conflict	-Minimum standards legislation -Collective bargaining -Emphasis on conflict reduction -Restrictions on bargaining subjects	-Minimum standards legislation -Unfair labor practices legislation -Free CB -Industry and enterprise bargaining	-Tripartism -Centralized wage determination -Restrictions on bargaining subjects and strikes	-Cost reduction through changes in overtime legislation -Ban on unionization in export sector -High government involvement in union recognition and dispute settlement	*Martial Law* -Ban on strikes -Compulsory arbitration -Downward revision of labor standards -Rationalization of union structure -Decriminalization of UFLP of employers *Democracy* -Liberalization of Marcos-era laws -Fragmented and weak unions

(Figure 2 contd.)

(Figure 2 contd.)

2nd Stage	IR/HR Policy Goals = Stability and Productivity Enhancement	IR/HR Policy Goals = Workplace Flexibility, Productivity, Skills Development		
	India, 1980–1991	*Singapore, 1978–*	*Malaysia, 1986–*	*India, 1991–*
	-Emphasis on economic unionism -Emphasis on productivity enhancement	-Education restructuring -Skills development institutions -Rational-ization of bargaining structure to enterprise level -Wage decentralization -Rules emphasizing workplace flexibility	-Education restructuring -Skills development institutions -Withdrawal of unionization ban -Less government intervention -Rules emphasizing workplace flexibility	-Labor relations legislation under debate -Job security provisions under revision -Workplace flexibility under debate

conditions (for example, the power of the ruling party and the influence of unions) as well as the previous institutional history. But more research is needed to uncover the factors causing the variation in IR/HR institutions and practices.

Although most IR scholars have viewed labor, management, and government as the primary actors in any IR system, the close relationship between industrialization and industrial relations found in the four countries analyzed in this paper suggests that several external actors can affect the IR system through their infuence on the industrialization strategy.[19] For example, in Singapore and Malaysia, foreign capital played a significant role in shaping IR/HR policies and institutions. In the Philippines, the World Bank has had a fundamental impact on industrial relations through its effect on IS. Although it is not easy to separate the effects of industrialization strategy and foreign capital on industrial relations change, external actors appear to be important, and their importance is only likely to grow as the international economy becomes more global. In addition, external organizations such as the new World Trading Organization are attempting to link trade issues more directly with industrial relations policies and practices.

It is also necessary to extend the analysis of IR/HR policy to the meso (company) and workplace levels. In another study, for example (Kuruvilla 1996b), I found that ISI sector firms in Malaysia and the Philippines typically had paternalistic, complacent, and passive IR/HR practices, whereas EOI sector firms had dynamic, aggressive, and flexible IR/HR practices. In countries where inter-firm networks are important, and when employer associations are more active, the meso level assumes great importance. Thus, it is essential that future research analyze how IS, national, and meso-level IR/HR policies are linked to work-place practices.

Finally, in contrast to the prediction of Kerr et al. (1964), the only way in which the four countries analyzed here exhibit convergence is in terms of the congruence between industrialization and IR/HR policy goals. These countries diverge widely in their industrialization strategies and corresponding IR/HR policy goals and in the institutional arrangements by which the goals of national IR/HR policies have been pursued, and thus they do not converge in IR/HR institutions and practices.

Notes

This research was partially funded by grants from the Institute of Collective Bargaining, the Center for Advanced Human Resource Studies, and the Faculty Incentive Grant Program of the New York State School of Industrial and Labor Relations at Cornell University. The author thanks Harry Katz, Rehana Huq, Christopher Erickson, Jan Hack Katz, and Stephen Frenkel for helpful comments on earlier versions of this paper.

1. My definition of workplace flexibility differs substantially from that of Standing, who uses the term "flexibility" to describe the activities that firms engage in to reduce employment during economic downturns, such as subcontracting, layoffs, and use of probationers. My use of the term "workplace flexibility" follows Katz, Kuruvilla, and Turner (1993).
2. The argument is consistent with Deyo (1989) in associating EOI with labor suppression, but differs from Deyo regarding the focus of inquiry, the dependent variable, and the relationship between IS and IR/HR policy goals.
3. Although the focus in this paper is on national IR/HR policy goals, I have also studied the relationship between IS's and IR/HR practices at the workplace level. Details of this relationship can be found in Kuruvilla (1996b).
4. This feature was introduced by the Industrial Relations (Amendment) Act of 1968.
   In British usage, layoffs are temporary and retrenchments are permanent.
5. For instance, strikes were allowed only after a 14-day notice period, and only after a secret ballot was conducted with at least two-thirds of the members voting for a strike. Political strikes were disallowed, and the government could prohibit strikes if they were deemed to be against the national interest. Since strikes were not permitted once a dispute was under conciliation or mediation by a third party, either of the parties could request mediation services of the government, which would effectively end any strike. See Chiang (1988) for a more detailed description of other policies.
6. See Rodan (1989:119) for a more detailed description of this transition.
7. See Chew and Chew (1995) for support for this statement, and Leggett (1988), who argues that the labor movement has been hobbled by authoritarian government.
8. Essentially, the New Economic Policy attempted to increase the economic power of the Malay population through legislation on affirmative action in employment and in corporate investments and shareholdings.
9. Workplace policies were virtually identical to those in Singapore, and reflect the policies of the British (Kuruvilla 1996a).
10. Essentially, the "Look East" policy of the Prime Minister focused on cajoling Malays to adopt the diligent and hardworking practices of the Japanese and Koreans.

11. Under the Labor Code introduced by the Marcos government, article 250 made unfair labor practices such as union busting into administrative offenses, punishable by fine only. Under the old Industrial Peace Act, these had been criminal offenses, punishable by imprisonment, fine, or both.

12. Tripartism was, however, never fully institutionalized, given opposition from other labor groups, and the efforts to change the union structure actually led to the rise of the KMU (Kilusang Mayo Uno) to challenge the supremacy of the TUCP.

13. For a more detailed discussion of the World Bank's influence on the Philippines, see Bello, Kinley, and Elinson (1988) and Macaraya and Ofreneo (1993).

14. For a more detailed description of the development of India's ISI strategy, see Venkataratnam (1993).

15. Factories' rules are so detailed that even the toys to be kept in child care centers, called "creches," are specified by the law.

16. The man-days lost due to strikes in 1987, 1989, and 1991 were 36,583,000, 30,440,000, and 7,640,000, respectively, and strikes in those years numbered 1,799, 1,893, and 831. Note that the figures for 1991 reflect only the period January–July.

17. For instance, Ashok Leyland, one of India's largest truckmakers, argues that it costs $14,000 to make a Ford Cargo van in India, due to high labor costs and costs of licensing and import duties, whereas the same van can be made in Britain for half the price (Abreu 1994).

18. In addition, Dombois and Pries (1994) posited a similar argument in the case of Latin America.

19. The influence of external actors on the IR system has been noted by Frenkel and Harrod (1995).

References

Abreu, Robin. 1994. "The Economy" (column). *India Today*, April 15, p. 90.

Arudsothy, Ponniah. 1990. "The State and Industrial Relations in Developing Countries: The Malaysian Situation." *ASEAN Economic Bulletin*, Vol. 6, No. 3 (March).

Arudsothy, Ponniah, and Craig Littler. 1993. "State Regulation and Fragmentation in Malaysia." In Stephen Frenkel, ed., *Organized Labor in the Asta-Pacific Region: A Comparative Study of Trade Unions in Nine Countries*. Ithaca, N.Y.: ILR Press.

Begin, James. 1995. "Industrial Relations in Singapore." In Stephen Frenkel and Jeffrey Harrod, eds., *Industrialization and Labor Relations: Contemporary Research in Seven Countries*. Ithaca, N Y.: ILR Press.

Bello, Walden, David Kinley, and Elaine Elinson. 1988. *Development Debacle: The World Bank in the Philippines*. San Francisco: Institute for Food and Development Policy, Philippine Solidarity Network.

Bello, Walden, and Roberto Verzola. 1993. *Revisioning Philippine Industrialization*. Manila: Freedom From Debt Coalition.

Bjorkman, Maja, Laurids Lauridsen, and Herbert Marcussen. 1988. "Types of Industrialization and Capital-Labour Relations in the Third World." In Roger Southall, ed., *Trade Unions and the New Industrialization of the Third World*. London: Zed.

Bowie, Alasdair. 1991. *Crossing the Industrial Divide: State, Society, and the Politics of Economic Transformation in Malaysia*. New York: Columbia University Press.

Brooks, Karen. 1995. "Economic Development and Industrial Relations in Indonesia." Unpublished Paper, Cornell University.

Cheng, Tun-Jen. 1990. "Political Regimes and Development Strategies: South Korea and Taiwan." In Gary Gereffi and Donald Wyman, eds., *Manufacturing Miracles: Paths of Industrialization in Latin America and East Asia*. Princeton: Princeton University Press.

Chew, S. B., and Rosalind Chew. 1995. "Impact of Development Strategy on Industrial Relations in Singapore." In Anil Verma, Thomas A. Kochan, and Russel Lansbury, eds., *Employment Relations in Asia*. London: Routledge.

Chiang, T. B. 1988. "The Administration and Enforcement of Collective Agreements in Singapore." In *The Administration and Enforcement of Collective Agreements— A Survey of the Current Situation in ASEAN*. Bangkok: International Labour Organization, pp. 239–46.

Department of Labor and Employment. 1985, 1986, and 1993. *Annual Yearbook of Labor Statistics*. Manila: Bureau of Labor and Employment Statistics.

Deyo, Frederick. 1989. *Beneath the Miracle: Labour Subordination in East Asian Development*. Berkeley: University of California Press.

Dombois, Rainer, and Ludger Pries. 1994. "Structural Change and Trends in the Evolution of Industrial Relations in Latin America." Paper Presented at the 16th Conference of the International Working Party in Labour Market Segmentation, Strasbourg, July.

Frenkel, Stephen. 1993. *Organized Labor in the Asia-Pacific Region: A Comparative Study of Trade Unions in Nine Countries*. Ithaca, N.Y.: ILR Press.

Frenkel, Stephen, and Jeffrey A. Harrod. 1995. *Industrialization and Labor Relations: Contemporary Research in Seven Countries*. Ithaca, N.Y.: ILR Press.

Gereffi, Gary, and Donald L. Wyman. 1990. *Manufacturing Miracles: Paths of Industrialization in Latin America and East Asia*. Princeton: Princeton University Press.

Grace, Elizabeth. 1990. *Short Circuiting Labour: Unionizing Electronic Workers in Malaysia*. Kuala Lampur: Insan.

Haggard, Stephan. 1990. *Pathways from the Periphery: The Politics of Growth in the Newly Industrializing Countries*. Ithaca, N.Y.: Cornell University Press.

Huff, W. G. 1987. "Patterns in the Economic Development of Singapore." *Journal of Developing Areas*, Vol. 21, No. 3 (April), pp. 305–25.

Katz, Harry. 1994. "The Decentralization of Industrial Relations: A Literature Review and Comparative Analysis." *Industrial and Labor Relations Review*, Vol. 47, No. 1 (October), pp. 3–22.

Katz, Harry, Sarosh Kuruvilla, and Lowell Turner. 1993. "Trade Unions and Collective Bargaining." Policy Research Working Papers, Education and Social Policy Department, The World Bank.

Kerr, Charles, John Dunlop, Frederick Harbison, and Charles Myers. 1964. *Industrialism and Industrial Man.* New York: Oxford University Press.

Krislov, Joseph, and Chris Leggett. 1985. "Singapore's Industrial Arbitration Court: Changing Roles and Current Prospects." *Arbitration Journal,* Vol. 40, pp. 18–24.

Kuruvilla, Sarosh. 1996a. "The Linkages Between Industrialization Strategies, National Industrial Relations Policies, and Workplace IR/HR Policies in Southeast Asia." In Kirsten Wever and Lowell Turner, eds., *Comparative Political Economy of Industrial Relations.* Madison, Wis.: 1995 IRRA Research Volume.

———. 1996b. "The Influence of National Industrialization Strategies on Workplace Human Resource Practices." *Human Resource Management Journal,* forthcoming.

Kuruvilla, Sarosh, and Ponniah Arudsothy. 1995. "Economic Development, National Industrial Relations Policies, and Workplace IR Practices in Malaysia." In Anil Verma, Thomas A. Kochan, and Russel Lansbury, eds., *Employment Relations in the Growing Asian Economies.* London: Routledge.

Kuruvilla, Sarosh, and Christopher Erickson. 1994. "Critical Junctures in Industrial Relations System Transformation: A Study of Nine Countries." Paper Presented at the Fourth Bargaining Conference, University of Toronto, October 14–15.

Kuruvilla, Sarosh, and Adam Pagnucco. 1994. "NAFTA, AFTA, and Industrial Relations in Asia." In Harry C. Katz and Maria Cook, eds., *Regional Integration and Industrial Relations in North America.* Ithaca, N.Y.: Institute for Collective Bargaining.

Lansing, Paul, and Sarosh Kuruvilla. 1987. "Industrial Dispute Resolution in India: Theory and Practice." *Loyola of Los Angeles International and Comparative law Journal,* Vol. 9, No. 2, pp. 345–75.

Levin. David, and Sek Hong Ng. 1995. "Economic Development and Industrial Relations in Hongkong." In Anil Verma, Thomas A. Kochan, and Russel Lansbury, eds., *Employment Relations in the Growing Asian Economies.* London: Routledge.

Macaraya, Bach, and Rene Ofreneo. 1993. "Structural Adjustment and Industrial Relations: The Philippine Experience." Paper presented at the Conference on Industrial Relations in Asia and East Africa, Sydney, September 5–7.

Mathur, Ajeet. 1991. "The Experience of Consultation During Structural Adjustment in India (1990–1992)." *International Labour Review,* Vol. 132, No. 3, pp. 331–45.

———. 1994. "Labor and the Philippine Economy." Unpublished manuscript, University of the Philippines, School of Labor and Industrial Relations.

Onn, Fong Chan. 1989. "Wages and Labour Welfare in the Malaysian Electronics Industry." *Labour and Society,* Vol. 14 (Special Issue on High Tech and Labour), pp. 81–102.

———. "Singapore." 1981. In Albert Blum, ed., *International Handbook of Industrial Relations.* Westport, Conn.: Greenwood, pp. 481–98.

Park, Young-Bum, and Michael Byungnum Lee. 1995. "Economic Development, Globalization, and Practices in Industrial Relations and Human Resources

Management in Korea." In Anil Verma, Thomas A. Kochan, and Russel Lansbury, eds., *Employment Relations in the Growing Asian Economies*. London: Routledge.

PSDC (Penang Skills Development Center). 1993. *Training for Change: The Way to a Better Future*. Penang: PSDC.

Rajah, Rasiah. Forthcoming. "Changing Organization of Work in Malaysia's Electronics Industry." *International Labor Review*.

Ramaswamy, E. A. 1983. "Indian Management Dilemma: Economic Versus Political Unions." *Asian Survey*, Vol. 23, No. 8 (August), pp. 976–90.

Reddy, Y.R.K. 1978. "Determination of Collective Bargaining Agency: Search for a Procedure." *Indian Journal of Industrial Relations*, Vol. 14, No. 1 (July), pp. 73–86.

Rodan, Garry. 1989. *The Political Economy of Singapore's Industrialization: National State and International Capital*. New York: St. Martin's.

Roemer, Michael. 1981. "Dependence and Industrialization Strategies." *World Development*, Vol. 9, No. 5, pp. 429–34.

Salih, Kamal, Mei Ling Young, and Rajah Rasiah. 1988. *Transnational Capital and Local Conjuncture: The Semiconductor Industry in Penang*. Malaysian Institute of Economic Research.

Sarath, D. 1992. *Employment and Unionism in Indian Industry*. New Delhi: Frederick Ebert Foundation.

Sharma Basu. 1985. *Aspects of Industrial Relations in ASEAN*. Singapore: Institute for Asian Studies.

Sharma, Basu, Anil Verma, and Sarosh Kuruvilla. 1994. "Strategic Economic Co-operation and Growth Triangles in Southeast Asia." Paper presented at the Changing Employment Relations and Human Resource Management Conference in Asia, Taipei, Chung-Hua Institute for Economic Research, June.

Sheth, N. R. 1991. *Some Thoughts on Trade Unions*. Ahmedabad: Indian Institute of Management.

Sodhi. J. S. 1993. "New Economic Policies and Their Impact on Industrial Relations." *Indian Journal of Industrial Relations*, Vol. 29, No. 1 (July), pp. 31–54.

Spinanger, Dean. 1986. *Industrialization Policies and Regional Economic Development in Malaysia*. Singapore: Oxford University Press.

Straits Times. 1993. "SNEF to Workers, Don't Expect Too Much." Friday, November 19, p. 2.

Venkataratnam, C. 1993. "Impact of New Economic Policies on the Role of Trade Union." *Indian Journal of Industrial Relations*, Vol. 29, No. 1 (July), pp. 56–77.

Villegas, E. 1988. *The Political Economy of Philippine Labor Laws*. Quezon City, the Philippines: Foundation for Nationalist Studies, Inc., pp. 38–51.

Young, Mei Ling, and Kiat Ng Siew. 1992. *Balancing the Roles of Public and Private Sectors in Education and Training*. Kuala Lampur, Malaysia: Malaysian Institute for Economic Research.

Industrial Relations Law, Employment Security and Collective Bargaining in India: Myths, Realities and Hopes

Anil K. Sen Gupta and P.K. Sett

Economic liberalisation programme initiated by the Indian government in 1991 revived the debate over the need for comprehensive reforms in the industrial relations law of the country. While the issues central to the debate, namely, excessive state intervention in industrial disputes, the need for statutory union recognition and the role of employment security provisions in creating structural rigidities, remained unchanged over the years, the new economic context, with its inherent need for a market based labour system, lent an overriding urgency and salience to the last.

The Industrial Relations Law in India

Three important pieces of legislation have played a major role in shaping Indian industrial relations. They are: the Trade Unions Act, 1926 (TUA), the Industrial Employment (Standing Orders) Act, 1946 (IEA) and the Industrial Disputes Act, 1947 (IDA). These enactments are significant not merely in themselves, but also in the way they have interacted upon each other to produce a distinctly Indian system (Ramaswamy and Ramaswamy, 1981).

The most striking features of Indian industrial relations law are: absence of provisions on recognition of a trade union as a collective bargaining agent and the omnipresent role of the government in regulating the industrial relations. Mere registration of a union under the TUA does not entitle it to recognition by the employer as a legitimate representative of his workers, or to the bargaining relationship that would arise from such recognition. Under the IDA, the government enjoys full discretionary power whether or not, when, and how to intervene in an industrial dispute—actual or threatened. It may or may not decide to conciliate, it may refuse to send a dispute for adjudication or it may even decide not to implement the award of a Labour Court or Industrial Tribunal. While it may prohibit strikes or lock-outs, or it may refuse permission for a lay-off, retrenchment or closure, no court can take cognisance of an offence under the IDA, by way of an illegal strike/lock-out/lay-off/retrenchment/closure, unless the government formally notifies such an action as illegal and makes a complaint to the court. In total, in India, the government plays a vital role in shaping the industrial relations climate. Also, the adjudication system is so structured and manned that the state apparatus exercises substantial influence over its functioning.

The Legacy

State domination of industrial relations in India is a legacy of its colonial past. All the three relevant statutes mentioned above were enacted before Independence. IDA, which is the most important of the three, is a virtual replica of the Section 81A of the Defence of India Rules and was promulgated by the British government in 1942 in the wake of the Second World War. It intended to have complete state control over industrial relations, to ensure uninterrupted wartime production. After Independence, when initial attempts to reform IDA and TUA were shelved, state control was sought to be justified on the grounds of the need for industrial harmony in order to achieve speedy economic development. Intervention by the state was also required, it was argued, to ensure social and economic justice to the workers, who were perceived to be weaker. An ironic consequence of this line of reasoning, which could not later on be changed on populist political considerations, was that the emergency measures adopted by the British to fight the war, which bestowed upon the state an overwhelming interventionist role, continued to rule the industrial relations scene of an industrialising nation with a democratic political set-up.

A Broad Profile of the Debate

The debate on comprehensive reforms in industrial relations law in India has to be understood in the context of its colonial legacy. The current debate has three important themes: the need to encourage bipartism and strengthen collective bargaining as an institution, the need for relaxing the rigidities of employment security provisions, and the need for an independent empowered authority for promoting the settlement of industrial disputes without the intervention of the executive wing of the state.

(i) Bipartism and Collective Bargaining

The arguments on this issue revolve around the need for and alleged consequence of state intervention in industrial disputes. Those who argue against third party intervention claim that it has inhibited the growth of collective bargaining and trade union strength by providing a ready alternative leading to disinclination of the disputants to search for other options including bargaining. The widespread criticism of the functioning of the state conciliation machinery and the allegations of arbitrariness in referring disputes for adjudication are highlighted, in support. Instances are also cited to buttress their argument that the present system lends itself to subversion by unscrupulous politicians (Ramaswamy, 1984).

Those who favour retention of provisions relating to state intervention as a remedy, point out that it could not be reasonably argued that adjudication inhibited the growth of collective bargaining, as the parties were free to settle the disputes bilaterally and they could not go for adjudication directly. The fact that in a good many cases the government did not make a reference for adjudication itself had put enough pressures on the parties to settle their disputes bilaterally. They further contend that the employees have achieved better conditions of service through adjudication rather than through collective bargaining, given the endemic organisational weaknesses of the Indian trade unions (Government of India, 1969).

However, consensus appears to have emerged on three fundamental points. First, statutory union recognition is considered to be the most essential prerequisite for promoting long term industrial harmony, given

India's socio-political milieu. Lack of adequate pressure for union recognition prevented the emergence of strong trade unions and growth of collective bargaining—both being vital ingredients of sustained industrial peace. Secondly, a structural framework to support collective bargaining should be built into the present statute that lacks it. The framework envisaged is one of a *negotiating council* at corporate and industry levels, comprising representatives of the recognised trade unions—on a proportional representation basis. Lastly, third party intervention may be allowed, as a last resort, only by an autonomous agency like the proposed Industrial Relations Commission, and not by the state executive (Government of India, 1990).

(ii) Employment Security Provisions

The major points related to employment security being debated are the: need for obtaining prior permission of the government by the employer for lay-offs, retrenchment and closure and the level of compensation to be paid to the workers in such cases. These provisions are contained in the Chapter VB of the IDA that was incorporated into the statute in 1976.

The employers view the prior permission clauses, which did not exist in the statute before 1976, as unreasonable restrictions affecting the economic viability of an enterprise. They allege that the government invariably refuses permission on populist political grounds and point out that even the Supreme Court and some of the High Courts have struck down some of the related provisions of law as unconstitutional as they purported to confer arbitrary powers on the government to refuse permission.

The trade unions on the other hand hold the employers responsible for industrial sickness and point out that the employers in violation of the law have effected large-scale job loss. Cumbersome legal processes involved in prosecuting an erring employer and the meagre penalties that could be imposed even after conviction have helped the employers to break the law with impunity, they allege. The trade unions, therefore, insist that the employers must obtain the permission of the proposed negotiating council before resorting to any lay-offs, retrenchment or closure. If no agreement is reached within a stipulated period, then the matter could be raised as an industrial dispute to be adjudicated by the proposed Industrial Relations Commission. They demand that the rate of compensation has also to be raised substantially—at least twice or thrice the existing rate.

So, on the employment security provisions there is no apparent consensus, particularly on the need for prior permission—though many observers feel that trade unions might attenuate their stand on the prior permission clause if the employers could offer attractive severance compensation.

(iii) Industrial Relations Commission

The main criticism of the existing regulatory framework is that it is highly vulnerable to political misuse and hence lacks credibility. The conciliation process tends to be either powerless, when conducted by the lower functionaries, or highly discriminatory, when the ruling politicians take undue interest in it. The adjudication, apart from being time consuming and expensive as any other litigation process in India, is also charged to be discriminatory as the power to make reference rests with the government.

Because of the very structure of the present arrangements, the decisions of the government, though fair sometimes, have not appeared to be so to the affected party. On the other hand, in a democratic system the pressure on the government to actively intervene may be powerful. To resolve this essential tension, the National Labour Commission (1969) recommended setting up of an Industrial Relations Commission (IRC), independent of the state executive, entrusted with the functions of conciliation, adjudication and union recognition (Government of India, 1969). Appeal against an IRC award would lie only before the Supreme Court.

There exists a fair amount of unanimity on the desirability of formation of an independent empowered authority like the IRC to regulate the industrial relations system in India.

The Myths and the Realities

(i) Labour Restructuring at the Enterprise Level

Quite contrary to the commonly held perception that associate industrial restructuring with the economic liberalisation programme initiated in

1991, the process of labour adjustment at the enterprise level commenced in India roughly from the mid-seventies.

Two wars and successive droughts in the early sixties resulted in a severe economic crisis during the mid-sixties, which ultimately led to economic stagnation throughout the seventies. After 1965 the industrial growth rate slowed down considerably. This combined with the slower annual growth rates of food-grain and non-food grain production during the period caused the crisis (Sen Gupta, 1993). In the industrial sector it led to acute demand recession. The increased competition for the limited market, which did not achieve the anticipated growth, resulted in overcapacity.

Faced with the bleak economic prospects, the employers felt the urge to restructure their units. As a survival strategy the employers preferred risks in the labour market than in the product market. Their focus of attention was to use wage and employment related policies as a cutting edge for survival. Their main priority became introducing flexibility in labour processes and cutting down labour costs by reducing dependence on permanent labour force.

The main stumbling blocks, however, were not only the employment security related provisions of the IDA but also the provisions of the Contract Labour (Regulation and Abolition) Act, 1970 (CLA). Under the CLA the government had full powers to decide areas of work in an organisation where engagement of contract labour would be permitted and under what circumstances and, areas it would be prohibited. The government could decide, in its discretion, the sphere of prohibition and annex new areas, where contract labour may have been engaged traditionally in the past, under prohibition. For lawful engagement of contract labour, the contractor should possess a valid license issued by the government and the establishment that engages contract labour should obtain a certificate of registration under the CLA. Obtaining licence or permission of the government is a time-consuming and difficult task mired in a complex web of bureaucratic procedures. Moreover, the government quite often refused permission on the ground that the area of work applied for was of a 'perennial' nature, or was 'incidental' to the work of the establishment, for which permanent labour, rather than contract labour, could only be engaged. Under the statute the sole discretion for making such decisions lay with the government. Over the years, the governments in the states, yielding to the pressures created by growing levels of unemployment and also to keep promises made by them to provide more jobs, brought more areas under prohibition ostensibly to compel the employers to employ more permanent workers. That the result of such actions was just the opposite was another story. These prohibitions made company labour processes still more rigid and the employers even more desperate to break the shackles of the law in order to survive. To circumvent the provisions of the law, they contrived various ways and means; some common to what employers had adopted in other countries and some distinctively indigenous.

To reduce dependence on a permanent workforce the employers adopted predominantly two strategies. One was to escape the nexus and/or coverage of the law and the other was to farm out regular production to outside sources. To avoid the nexus, the employers increasingly hired labour through the intermediary of contractors, who undertook to supply labour in the guise of 'job contracts' or 'contracts for services'. Most of these were sham contracts, used merely to camouflage the real employment relationship within the firm. Some used still more blatant methods of forcing people to work without any written records of wage or attendance. In order to escape the coverage of law employers adopted several means, some demonstrating weird imagination and creativity of mind. Employment of persons on a casual basis, even for work of regular or permanent nature, became a wide practice. Since the Indian law prohibits such a practice, the employers devised ingenious ways to avoid the coverage of law. Designations such as 'learner', 'trainee', 'improver' were invented. Some employers even forced the workers to change their names or they shuffled the workers within their syndicated groups, several times during a year, so that the persons concerned could not earn the eligibility, in terms of required minimum length of continuous employment under one employer, to seek protection of the law. For white-collar workers descriptions of work or responsibilities and designations were so manipulated that they were projected as exempt categories of employees (Mathur, 1992). As a unionist in a pharmaceutical company, which redesignated telephone operator as 'communication officer' and accounts clerk as 'payroll executive', puts it (Davala, 1995): 'They were offered three things— an attractive designation, a visiting card and a tie'.

Several studies (Frensen, 1991; Goyal, 1984; Ramaswamy, 1988) point to a significant shift in employment from the organised to the unorganised sector through sub-contracting and emergence of a typical employment practice where those who work for an enterprise do not have direct employment relationship with it, even though they may be working within the firm's premises (Mathur, 1991). A study of six major industries also points to a rise in the incidence of casual and contract employment (Sarath, 1992).

The macro-level data amply support the above findings. During the period from 1971 to 1991 the percentage of casual workforce of the total organised labour increased from 23 to 35. Also, the unorganised sector employment has grown much faster than the organised sector employment in almost all non-agricultural sectors. Employment in organised manufacturing, for example, grew at an average annual rate of 1.44 per cent compared to 4.57 per cent growth in unorganised manufacturing, during the period from 1972–73 to 1987–88. In 1981 the employment in the 'middle sector' (comprising unorganised but non-household industries) constituted 45 per cent of the total manufacturing employment as against 27 per cent in 1961.

In the organised industry as a whole, the entire growth of about 8 per cent per annum during 1980s has been due to productivity growth as employment had a *negative* growth of about 0.5 per cent per annum while value added per worker grew, in real terms, at a rate over 9 per cent per annum. The employment elasticity of Gross Domestic Product (GDP) growth steadily declined during 1970s and 1980s. In 1980s the average employment elasticity in the manufacturing sector turned out to be as low as 0.2.

All the evidences indicate that permanent workers have lost their jobs not so much to machines as to cheap labour supplied by casual and contract labours. All kinds of industries, from the traditional and declining to the modern and buoyant were shifting work to such underpaid labour (Ramaswamy, 1992).

Interestingly, the measures to increase labour flexibility did not include retraining in new skill of any significance. Technological changes have generally not led to much reduction in employment within enterprises since enterprises upgrading technology were also the ones who expanded production and restructured their labour forces through recruitment (in new skills) and redeployment rather than shedding of manpower. Thus, employer strategy varied in response to context. For industries in a phase of growth and diversification, restructuring of labour processes were carried out painlessly without loss of employment or adverse impact on wages—as these firms followed a strategy of product innovation and could maintain an oligopolistic position in product market. Where the firms faced market competition or demand recession, the employers' approach was diametrically different.

To force rationalisation of labour forces in old plants with entrenched trade unions, high wages and inflexible work practices, the employers used several innovative tactical ploys to circumvent the rigidities imposed by the law. Without declaring 'closure', which required prior permission of the government, they stopped operations on the whole, or a part, of the establishment and forced the employees, or a group of them, to either accept transfer to a plant in a distant location, or take 'voluntary retirement'. Sometimes, closure of the business was brought about perfectly legally by deliberately defaulting on payments to the creditors and persuading some of them to file a petition in a civil court for winding-up of the company under the Companies Act. In a somewhat similar fashion, the arm of the law was twisted to allow the lay-off of workers due to continued non-availability of power where electricity supply was disconnected on account of persistent default in payment of electricity bills by the company! However, by far the most frequently used method was to resort to 'lock-outs'. Lock-outs, perceived as employers' counter-sanctions against workers' strikes, do not require any prior permission of the government and workers are not entitled to any compensation during a lock-out, unless it is declared as both unjustified and illegal by the government. From the employers' point of view, prolonged lock-outs were better than closures, as there were no liabilities of taking prior permission and making payment of any compensation to workers, as were required in formal closures. Depending upon the circumstances and employer objectives, declared or undeclared lock-outs have been used as an offensive to pressurise the workers in accepting either, tighter work-norms (as a precondition for wage negotiation) or, manpower rationalisation through 'voluntary retirements' (most popular with the MNCs operating in India). They have also been used to simply close down a business or, shift capital or employment from 'rigid' and 'high labour cost' to 'more flexible' and 'low labour cost' regions within the country (Mathur, 1991).

Thus in the absence of any means of dealing with the problem of redundancy under the existing statutes, the employers found their own ways, not always within the bounds of law, to tackle them. As they confronted the unions to alter balance of power and force through the restructuring on their own terms, the politically motivated and, often, pliant state machinery and dilatory adjudication process helped them to achieve their goals, as would be seen later.

(ii) Efforts to Weaken the Trade Unions

Trade unions as independent and countervailing power centres had been perceived by the employers in India as a serious impediment to restructuring, as anywhere else in the world. So, reducing union power had been high on their agenda. The emerging economic context greatly helped them to achieve their goals.

In the face of economic crises, particularly since the mid-eighties, the government's economic imperatives shifted, as it desperately needed to attract private investments to stimulate growth. There was concomitant change in the government labour policy that tended to become increasingly supportive of employers. Change in policy regime also seemed to influence the judicial interpretations of the statutes. They became increasingly aligned with the new policy. These congruent developments enabled the employers to emerge stronger and to snatch the initiative from the trade unions, which stood already weakened by the adverse economic circumstances. The balance of power in industry has decisively shifted in favour of the employers, especially since the mid-seventies (Sen Gupta, 1993). This is unambiguously reflected in the trends of strikes and lockouts (see Table 1). The average duration of lockouts—i.e., employer offensives—led to a steady increase in mandays lost from the early seventies until the end of the eighties—the period of largest relative increase being 1975–79. The severity of industrial action, as measured by the average number of mandays lost per year per worker involved, was far greater in case of lockouts than strikes, during this period.

Other evidence also corroborates the shift. The percentage of unsuccessful strikes steadily increased during this period, excepting during 1985–89 when it decreased compared to the previous five years. During 1990–94, 47.6 per cent of strikes proved to be unsuccessful as compared to 33.9 per cent during 1965–69. Conversely, the incidence of indefinite strikes, which reflect the workers' ability to engage the employers in a tough battle, declined consistently from 17.7 per cent in 1965–69 to 2.9 per cent in 1985–89 and thereafter it increased to 6.1 per cent during

1990–94. Similarly, the cases of voluntary resumption of work by the striking workers, which also reflect the breakdown of workers' resistance, steadily increased from 29.5 per cent in 1965–69 to 45 per cent in 1990–94 excepting during 1985–89 when it decreased compared to the previous five years. Union density in organised manufacturing, which was around 45 per cent in the late seventies, progressively declined through the eighties and stood around 25 per cent in early nineties. All evidence, therefore, consistently supports the hypothesis of the shift in the balance of power in favour of the employers, since the mid-seventies. Recent studies (Shrouti and Daur, 1995) suggest that this shift continues through the nineties.

(iii) Distinctively Indian Experience

The shift in the balance of power in favour of employers, in the face of economic adversity or product market competition, and associated crisis in unionism is not a uniquely Indian phenomenon. Several studies (Deyo, 1989; Frenkel, 1993; Frenkel and Harrod, 1995; Kuruvilla, 1996; Wilkinson, 1994) document this trend which appears to be common to both developed and developing countries. However, what is unique about the Indian experience is the way democratically elected governments used their enormous discretionary powers under the industrial statutes and subverted the functioning of dispute resolution machinery, to further their narrow political interests. In the process, growth of genuine trade union power base was stifled. Because, under such circumstances, power of a union was determined by its influence over the political party ruling the state; not by its ability to organise the workers.

Political interventions in industrial disputes took place through three sources: calculated use of police force, conciliation proceedings and discriminatory use of power of reference of the disputes for adjudication. The minister or the chief minister of the state entered the scene in the guise of a conciliator interested in finding an amicable settlement to the dispute. Then, taking advantage of the glaring weaknesses of the existing law (like absence of provisions for statutory union recognition or, foolproof method for union membership verification) and using their formidable political clout, they forced settlements which favoured trade unions, union leaders or employers of their choice. Under such dispensations, even the smallest union with only seven (minimum number required for registration under TUA) members but with right political patronage, could adroitly exploit conciliation and adjudication processes to carve out a role for itself and undermine the influence of an established union. The history of industrial disputes in India is replete with instances of abuse of political power and subversion of dispute settlement machinery to promote political interests (Government of India, 1968; Ramaswamy, 1984).

Table 1: Trends of Strikes and Lockouts during 1965–94

	1965–69	1970–74	1975–79	1980–84	1985–89	1990–94
* Average percentage of lockouts per year	10.6	11.9	13.4	16.4	29.6	31.1
** Average percentage of mandays lost per year due to lockouts	29.3	25.9	36.3	a 36.4	58.8	59.0
Average number of mandays lost per year per worker involved in:						
a) strikes	7.8	9.2	10.6	b 21.4	9.9	12.3
b) lockouts	29.0	30.4	50.0	63.1	84.9	45.2

*   As a percentage of average total number of industrial disputes per year.
** As a percentage of average total number of mandays lost per year due to industrial disputes
   a) During 1980–84 there have been two very large but localised strikes; one in public sector units in Bangalore in 1981 and another in textile mills in Bombay during 1982–83. If mandays lost in these two localised strikes are factored out, the percentage increases to 47.2 per cent.
   b) The sudden steep increase is attributed to the two very large but localised strikes mentioned earlier.
Source: *Pocket Book of Labour Statistics* of relevant years, published by the Labour Bureau, Government of India.

The time-consuming and cumbersome adjudication process, with in-built scope for multi-level appeals against the judgement of a lower court, could not provide any effective relief to the affected parties. Taking advantage of this dilatory and costly litigation process, the employers also could, with impunity, illegally terminate the services of the union activists to break the workers' resistance, even where the state did not act in a partisan manner.

A number of recent studies (Mathur, 1991) confirm that the earlier tradition continues unabated and reveal how the political executives of the state, aided and abetted the process of tilt in the balance of power in favour of the employers, as the restructuring process at the firm level went on. Apart from using the state apparatus in favour of the employers, the political party in power also used its affiliate trade union to facilitate restructuring. The political affiliations of the rival trade unions or the workers' groups did not help them in either deriving political strength or mobilising public support to fight their employers. Ironically, under such circumstances, agitation by the workers against restructuring only helped the employers to achieve their objectives faster by precipitating 'crises' and forcing the issues more vigorously.

(iv) Effect on Conditions of Labour

Conditions of labour varied greatly across industries and even regions. In traditional and mature industries gains of the permanent workforce, which was reducing in size, were achieved at the cost of new employment and worsening conditions of employment of the peripheral workforce. Even for the permanent workforce the economic gains were in exchange for intensification of work norms as reflected through data on productivity or value added per employee (Ahluwalia, 1991; Jose, 1992; Ramaswamy, 1988). With the balance of power shifting in their favour, the employers were able to impose a labour regime to meet their interests and requirements.

In new industries the essential nature of the power dynamics was the same; only some external manifestations were different. These firms, mostly enjoying oligopolistic product market conditions, offered larger increases in wages and benefits. But they ensured tight control over unit labour cost by pushing through improved labour standards as they up-graded their processes and technologies in tune with their changing product portfolios and diversifying businesses. There was no loss of employment as these businesses expanded and diversified. The pangs of change were made bearable by employing sophisticated human relations initiatives (Davala, 1995; Mathur, 1991).

The Hopes

By and large, the employers in India have been successful, particularly since the early seventies, in pushing through labour restructuring programmes at the enterprise level, in spite of the employment security provisions of the law. The trade unions have failed to stall them. The economic imperatives of the state to a large extent facilitated this course as the state machinery favoured the employers.

As the process of economic liberalisation in India advances further, the concomitant changes taking place in product market structure would have profound bearing upon the nature of employment and strength of trade union power base. By that logic, these would also determine the future prospects of collective bargaining, which is an important institutional edifice of the industrial democracy.

Given the supply characteristics of the Indian workforce, there is every likelihood that differentiation within the labour market will be heightened (Mukhopadhyay, 1992). Increasing product market differentiation and technological diversity between firms within the same industry would also differentiate the labour market. The tendency would be towards decentralised firm specific bargaining. Increasing geographical spread of firms in the same industry would also facilitate this emergent decentralised bargaining structure. Even in the same industry mutually exclusive market segments may emerge; one, oligolopistic, high technology firms catering for niche markets where competition is on brand equity and the other, price sensitive lower market segment. This market segmentation would not only have impact upon the collective bargaining structure but may also influence union-type at firm level (Bhattacherjee, 1989). Typically multiple-plant firms with decentralised bargaining structure put workers in their weakest position. So, if the present trend continues, the trade unions in India would continue to remain weak and to that extent the prospect of collective bargaining is not bright.

However, the only hope for a fundamental change in the industrial relations scene in India lies in the formation of the proposed Industrial Relations Commission (IRC) which is to be a high-power statutory body, independent of the state executive. It would be made responsible for conciliation and adjudication of industrial disputes as well as for granting statutory recognition of trade unions as bargaining agents.

Constitution of IRC at the central and state levels, along with the statutory recognition of trade unions as bargaining agents and formation of negotiating councils at plant and/or industry level, is likely to bring about fundamental change in the structure of industrial relations machinery. Impact of this change on consolidation of trade union power base and also on the process of collective bargaining would be important areas of future studies.

Formation of IRC is likely to make the settlement of industrial disputes faster, more effective and also less discriminatory, being insulated from political influence. A somewhat similar experiment with the disputes relating to the government employees in India has given encouraging results. It is likely to foster greater confidence among both employers and workers in institutional arrangements and thus help improving industrial relations. More effective conciliation by this high-powered body is likely to obviate the need for frequent adjudication. Similarly, a speedier adjudication process would make it less expensive. It would also result in better enforcement of the law as well as agreements and awards. Above all, IRC may possibly play the role of an effective bulwark against employer arbitrariness.

However, it may be prudent to put in a caveat here against any undue optimism. Efficient functioning of IRC as an effective dispute processing institution may well lead to some paradoxical consequences. It may encourage greater resort to the services of IRC by the disputants which, in turn, may lead to juridification of industrial relations. If this really happens, then that would greatly undermine the very process of collective bargaining, which is sought to be promoted. To avoid this adverse possibility, it is imperative that the IRC identifies an appropriate style of functioning from its inception.

Finally, the role of the state in India, particularly of its law and order enforcing agency, would always remain pivotal in determining the outcome of an industrial dispute that often involves open conflict.

References

Ahluwalia, I. J. (1991), *Productivity and Growth in Indian Manufacturing* (New Delhi: Oxford University Press).

Bhattacherjee, D. (1989), 'Evolution of Unionism and Labour Market Structure: Case of Bombay Textile Mills (1947–85)', *Economic and Political Weekly*, 24, May 27 Issue, M67–M76.

Davala, S. (1995), *Labour Strategies in Multinational Corporations in India* (Delhi: Friedrich Ebert Stiftung).

Deyo, F. C. (1989), *Beneath the Miracle: Labour Subordination in the New Asian Industrialism* (Los Angeles: University of California Press).

Frenkel, S. (ed) (1993), *Organised Labour in the Asia-Pacific Region: A Contemporary Study of Trade Unionism in Nine Countries* (New York: ILR Press).

Frenkel, S. and J. Harrod (1995), *Industrialisation and Labour Relations: Contemporary Research in Seven Countries* (New York: ILR Press).

Frensen, J. (1991), *Subcontracting and Inequality: The Case of Hindustan Lever in India* (Nijmegen: Third World Centre, Catholic University of Nijmegen).

Government of India (1968), *Sarkaria Commission of Inquiry—Final Report* (Delhi: Government of India).

Government of India (1969), *Report of the National Commission on Labour* (Delhi: Government of India).

Government of India (1990), *Report of the Bipartite Committee on New Industrial Relations Law* (Delhi: Government of India).

Goyal, S. K. (1984), *Small Scale Sector and Big Business* (New Delhi: Corporate Study Group, Indian Institute of Technology, Delhi).

Jose, A. V. (1992), 'Earnings, Employment and Productivity in Organized Industry in India', *The Indian Journal of Labour Economics*, 35, 3, 204–226.

Kuruvilla, S. (1996), 'Economic Development and Industrial Relations: The Case of South and SouthEast Asia', *Industrial Relations Journal*, 27, 1, 9–23.

Mathur, Ajeet N. (1991), *Industrial Restructuring and Union Power* (New Delhi: ILO-ARTEP).

——— (1992), 'Employment Security and Industrial Restructuring in India' (Calcutta: Paper presented in the National Seminar on *Restructuring Indian Economy*, January 17–18).

Mukhopadhyay, S. (1992), 'Casualisation of Labour in India: Concept, Incidence and Policy Options', *The Indian Journal of Labour Economics*, 35, 3, 262–265.

Ramaswamy, E. A. (1984), *Power and Justice: The State in Industrial Relations* (Calcutta: Oxford University Press).

——— (1988), *Worker Consciousness and Trade Union Response* (Delhi: Oxford University Press).

——— and Uma Ramaswamy (1981), *Industry and Labour: An Introduction* (Calcutta: Oxford University Press).

Sarath, D. (ed) (1992), *Employment and Unionisation in Indian Industries* (New Delhi: Friedrich Ebert Stiftung).

Sen Gupta, Anil K. (1993), *Trends in Industrial Conflict in India (1961–87)* (New Delhi: Friedrich Ebert Stiftung).

Shrouti, D. and A. Daur (1995), *Industrial Sickness and Its Impact on Workers* (New Delhi: Friedrich Ebert Stiftung).

Wilkinson, B. (1994), *Labour and Industry in the Asia-Pacific: Lessons from the New-Industrialised Countries* (Berlin: de Gruyter).

Section Five

MANAGERIAL ETHICS AND INDIAN VALUES

Global Imperatives and Indigenous Ethical Values in India

This section returns to the key question of ethical centrality for today's managers and leaders in India from two divergent perspectives. Domination of global economic logic as the central theme gives rise to organisational prioritisation away from the ethical core and it inevitably leads to serious consequences for people, institutions and society. In addition, the idea that managers have responsibilities extending beyond this economic logic needs to be a central theme of organisational sustainability. The societal, organisational and individual level ethics and social responsibilities are not easily distinguished in countries like India. The internal policies, procedures and administrative behaviour often reflect the values of the managerial elite.

Indian organisations have received widespread negative rankings in various global, regional and national surveys on corporate integrity and managerial probity in recent decades. In 2004, the Corruption Perception Index of Transparency International ranked India very low (90 out of 146 countries) with a score of 2.6 out of 10. This is quite a depressing picture given that China had been ranked a much cleaner ethical context with a ranking of 71.

This part highlights the 'ethical gap' common in Indian organisations. The two chapters here emphasise the need for 'ethical analysis' along with economic, technical, financial and other decision parameters as a very important managerial priority. One of the most prominent scholars on managerial ethics in India, S.K. Chakraborty (Chapter Ten), views the broad scene from a kaleidoscope of long tradition of Indian heritage. One of the key themes of his chapter is the distinction between 'intellectual' ethics and 'consciousness' ethics. He extends the meaning and content of a number of related issues including a range of practical ethical challenges. The second chapter by Chatterjee and Pearson, on the other hand, offers a field study of managerial perceptions of ethical views, social responsibilities and work-related values. The findings of this empirical exploration reveal the emergence of a 'hybrid' managerial approach to ethics which combines indigenous traditions and global parameters.

It is evident from the two chapters included in this section that increasing global linkages and professionalisation of managerial cadre is creating a new imperative of ethical imagination and deepening of managerial roots. While there has been extensive theoretical and practical debate and discussion on the role of corporate governance in East Asian societies, powerful indigenous doctrines of the Indian tradition have not been significantly featured in the literature on business ethics. Given the reality and perception of the managerial ethics in India, a great deal of progress is urgently needed in this area. Linking the modern corporate context to traditional Indian values and ethical roots is a blueprint that needs further attention. Higher social priorities of 'duty' as opposed to 'right', 'wisdom' as opposed to 'knowledge', 'character' as opposed to 'competency' are some of the indigenous values debated by Chakraborty. He touches on the need for organisations to move beyond economism and understand the deeper spiritual dimensions of those who work and grow with the organisation. The spiritual component of the managerial role can transform organisational 'motivation'. The responsibility of setting the strategic goals of an organisation gives a manager a 'dharmic' obligation in terms of a broad stakeholder commitment.

Editor's Note

For Information on the Transparency International Corruption Perceptions Index (2004), access: http://www.transparency.org/pressreleases_archive/2004/2004.1020.cpi.en.html.

10 Business Ethics in India

S. K. Chakraborty

1. A Macro Glance

A few initial, general points are worthwhile. Systematic empirical investigation in the field has yet to start in India. In fact, until the year 1992, ethics in business was hardly a topic of concerted engagement at any level—except in two or three business schools in the country. It was only the 2-billion dollar stock-exchange fiasco in 1992 which threw up the ethics issue at the macro-level. Since then, investigative journalism has been playing a key role in highlighting corrupt and fraudulent practices within the "business-politics-criminals" (BPC) triangle. Both the "legislature" and "executive" wings of nation-management seem to be losing their credibility. Presently the citizens are hopefully looking up to the assertive "judiciary" as the ultimate resort in these ethically troubled times. It has given rise to "judicial activism" triggered by public interest litigations instituted at the Supreme Court level by some citizens fora, e.g., Common Cause. The Chief Justice of India, however, believes that such activism will be a temporary phenomenon. Public feeling strongly supports this activism though (*Times of India*, February 27–29, 1996).

The elder generation often recalls that ethical decline in society had surfaced prominently during the Second World War when black-market was born, making contractors and traders wallow in riches overnight. But the "politics-bureaucracy" apparatus had not been dragged then into this black vortex of ill-gotten money. Since the 1950s however, with the launching of the era of state-planned and controlled economic development, things seem to have been going from bad to worse—though usually below the surface. This cumulative ethical depression began to break loose as an ethical cyclone with economic liberalization adopted by India in 1991. This storm has been exposing the supportive role of the "politics-bureaucracy" alliance in fostering and feeding upon economic terrorism of various kinds. The neutrality of bureaucracy has been tampered rather heavily since the mid-seventies by the political masters. Business thus got a readier opening into this caving citadel. Since increasingly expensive elections are not state-financed, the stimulus to politics-business corruption remains strong in an otherwise remarkably resilient democratic system.

However, business often complains, and perhaps rightly so, that they are more the victims than the perpetrators of economic crimes in a regime of government controls and bureaucratic stickiness. But for many of the big players this may not be true. They are able to feed the election process and allied aspects so sumptuously that often crucial government policies are perceived to be controlled by them. The "victim" syndrome is of course true for the vast majority of other enterprises.

One would have hoped that with the onset of "liberalization" from government controls since 1991, the scale and frequency of corrupt practices would lessen. Along the "business-bureaucracy-government" axis, this might be a growing reality, which is encouraging. But the accompanying "globalization" process has ushered some new dimensions into the field of business ethics. The competitive fray among global corporations to enter the Indian economy, and the eager overtures of Indian businesses to grow fast through collaborations with them, have begun to manifest fresh varieties of business non-ethics. The possibility of a two-way traffic is not imaginary: business veering towards criminals and criminals veering towards business. A perceptive analyst had foreseen this predicament as far back in 1982: "One comes across a wholesale condemnation of public regulation and controls . . . These views altogether forget the implications of an uncontrolled market-mechanism economy . . ." (Kabra, 1982, p. 150).

2. The Semantics of Business Ethics

The phrase "black market" rolled into circulation during the Second World War and has remained since that time. It denotes the process of clandestine sale of scarce, rationed, controlled commodities at inflated prices.

A cognate phrase "black money" seems to have gained currency during the 1960s. It covers the territory of business deals which entails money income and asset wealth not appearing in the books of accounts, thus evading taxes. Sometimes this sphere is described as the "parallel economy". According to one study, the percentage of black income to GDP rose from 42 in 1980–1981 to 51 in 1987–1988 (Gupta 1992, 146).

Expressions like "speed money", "palm greasing", "oiling the wheels" are also widely used to denote bribes. The indigenous words for bribe are "*ghoos*", "*rishwat*", etc. Words like "kickbacks" and "commissions" are also employed in this context.

Since 1992, the two words "scam" and "scandal" have become very common. They cover corrupt financial/economic practices of vast magnitude affecting large sections of the public. The B-P-C triangle has been prominently involved in these episodes.

Public perception does not condone such happenings. Yet, in the end, the scene is largely one of helpless condemnation. Newspaper columnists and editorials often come down heavily on the perpetrators of such economic terrorism, yet the general mood is one of resignation. Business enterprises themselves, with some highly honorable exceptions, often consider such practices to be part of the normal business process.

The intellectually articulate class usually chooses to ascribe these events to "systems" flaws and weaknesses. This was clearly evident in the stand taken regarding the 1992 stock-exchange scam. Perhaps this is one reason why no individuals are ultimately pinned down and held answerable. Some sensitive minds however feel that in the course of such elaborate system-directed explorations, the basic issues of personal character and integrity get side-tracked. Although terms like "accountability" and "transparency" are thrown in during public pronouncements, culpability on such scores is still dodged at all levels.

Whatever recent efforts the business community has been making seem all to be directed towards offering better deal to domestic consumers in respect of consumables and consumer durables (some illustrations will appear below). Consciousness of ethical imperatives in international business remains to be separately attended to—at least in terms of articulated norms and guidelines.

3. The Basis for Will-to-ethics in Business

A mute minority feels that a true long-term challenge for several major Indian business and financial sectors is: how far is it ethical to spread greed for goods and mercenariness for money in the name of business growth, economic development, and higher living standards? In fact, to make the point sharper, is it ethical to pronounce on "higher standard of living" when it is really "higher standard of consumption" which is being espoused?

Another general ethical problem relates to the social consequences of employment contraction in manpower-intensive basic industries. Modern, capital-intensive technology replacing older technologies is a process not without severe social-psychological fall-outs in a highly populated country like India. The ethical issue is: global economic competitiveness or local social-psychological stability? Is there really any objective method of rating one to be more desirable than the other?

The third general challenge appears to be one of abuse and misuse of sophisticated communication technology. Unless ethical-moral maturity keeps ahead of technological advancement, could we be moving towards a self-destructive society? Will it be more ethical to advocate decelerated technology for the sake of more natural and humane living?

Fourth, with increasing psychological drift and volatility in an artificially stimulated and exteriorized mind-set fueled by business, will society tend to lose mental health, replacing peace and harmony by conflict and violence? If business accepts the mantle of being the most important change-agent today, then is it required to confront this trans-commercial ethical dilemma? Is business the end or just a means? Means to what?

Fifth, how is "corruption-in-a-poor-society" to be dealt with on a footing different from "corruption-in-an-affluent-society"? Artificial cost escalation in tender bids, tax evasion, misappropriation of bank funds, cornerning of institutional finance, and diversion of funds from productive channels are common-place events in the formers. An opposition member of parliament of considerable integrity and courage has recently stated: "A country as poor as ours—judging by the quality of life—cannot afford to have such pervasive corruption. Crime has transcended moral barriers and is eating into the vitals of the economy." (Dasgupta, 1996)

Lastly, as touched upon earlier, the entry of big multinationals in certain key sectors of the economy, although welcome in general, is yet throwing up new challenges in business ethics. The capacity to corrupt and the willingness to be corrupted seem to be moving in alliance in several cases, e.g., the Enron contract for power generation in Maharashtra. Leaving aside other aspects, it has been reported that Rs. 650 million were ostensibly spent on "educating" the Indian counterparts involved in managing the project. This was a "suspect" outlay even according to an Enron official (*The Statesman*, August 10, 1995).

The reasons for vigorous engagement with such challenges would seem to be:

(a) Are we heading for a sick-and-cynical society? Will future generations be grateful for such a legacy, even if material prosperity were to increase?

(b) Are we going to prove the truth of the proverb "God and Mammon cannot both be served at the same time"?

(c) Or can we demonstrate that moderate and essential material prosperity is both the effect and cause of ethics in practice?

(d) Should we be sleepless that an unethical society, where every aspect of life being sucked into this vortex of competitive greed, is going to suffer from chronic mental ill-health, young children being the worst victims?

(e) Should we try to change gears and see that greater material equality across all layers and sectors of society and the globe is essentially more a matter of ethical values than of system skills? Are systems not themselves the products of varied ethical pre-dispositions? For example, was the joint family "system" not a concrete outcome of an ethical framework for cooperative living in society?

Of course, the "will-to-ethics" such as the above implies a complete circle—from the individual to the corporate to the national levels and thence back again through the same levels.

4. Will-to-ethics in the Practical Business World

In July 1956, The Forum of Free Enterprise had published a manifesto. It contained the following stern words: "Certain malpractices have crept into the system of company management. They are to be condemned and should be removed. Hoarding, black marketing and profiteering are anti-social and evil. Honest business practices can be promoted and encouraged by an honest and efficient administration in a democratic state." (Forum of Free Enterprise, 1956, p. 9)

During the forty years since the above declaration, neither the business community nor the administration seems to have come anywhere near such ardent hopes. A measure of this gulf can be obtained from the following scathing words of a Delhi High Court Judge, uttered while denying permission to a central minister, who had been arrested for sheltering notorious criminals, to attend Parliament in February 1996: "In ancient India kings and emperors thought it a privilege to sit at the feet of a man of learning. In today's India, MP's and ministers think it a privilege . . . to sit at the feet of underworld dons and base businessmen to get secret donations from them and to get their blessings." (*Sunday Telegraph*, February 27, 1992)

Yet during this period of down-slide, the positive side of will-to-ethics has also remained alive. To mention a notable instance, the Council of Fair Business Practices (CFBP) was established in 1966 by several leading private sector industrialists in Western India. It adopted the following code of fair business practices:

1. To charge only fair and reasonable prices and take every possible step to ensure that the prices to be charged to the consumer are brought to his notice.
2. To take every possible step to ensure that the agents or dealers . . . do not charge prices higher than fixed.
3. In times of scarcity, not to withhold or suppress stocks of goods with a view to hoarding or profiteering.
4. Not to produce or trade in spurious goods of standards lower than specified.
5. Not to adulterate goods supplied.
6. Not to publish misleading advertisements.
7. To invoice goods exported or imported at their correct prices.
8. To maintain accuracy in weights and measures of goods offered for sale.
9. Not to deal knowingly in smuggled goods.
10. Providing after-sales service where necessary or possible.
11. Honoring the fundamental rights of the consumers—Right of Safety, Right to Choose, Right to Information and Right to be Heard.
12. Discharging social responsibilities and the responsibility to protect the environment and nature's infrastructure.

13. Ensuring that the product-warranty is offered in simple, unambiguous and concise language, highlighting the rights of the consumer under it.

It is evident that the above recommendations constitute a primary-level, self-regulating charter for enlightened citizenship amongst business entities. The CFBP has instituted a set of prizes and awards called "Jamnalal Bajaj Uchit Vyavahar Puraskar" (or Jamnalal Bajaj Prize For Fair Business Practices) to promote exemplary application of the above norms. At a meeting with the current ex-officio President of the CFBP, we learnt that there is as yet no provision for deregistration of those members who are charged with violation of the above guidelines. The CFBP President claimed that sustained pressure from this Council had resulted in the creation of the Advertising Standards Council of India (ASOI) and in the promulgation of the Consumer Protection Act. We were also informed by him that at least 100 leading CFBP business-enterprise members had regular "Consumer Affairs Cells" operating in their offices. But Ethics Officers and Ethics Training are both beyond the pale of consideration for the time being.

The Federation of Indian Chambers of Commerce and Industry (which excludes the MNCs) has recently issued a declaration on "Norms of Business Ethics" consisting of ten points. The list is almost identical to that of the CFBP. The Punjab, Haryana and Delhi Chamber of Commerce has also lately formulated a "Code of Ethics" (*The Indian Journal of Public Administration*, July–September 1995, p. 638). Without going into specifics, this Code is intellectually deeper in content. It says:

- Business must maintain the highest standards of behavior . . . (for) the benefit of industry, employees, customers, shareholders, and society.
- Goods and services must conform to the commitment promised to customers. Business must be realistic and truthful in stating claims.
- Customers must be given best possible service and treated with respect and fairness.
- Business must understand and respect the needs, concerns, and welfare of the community and society. It should use knowledge and experience for upgrade of quality of life. All business endeavors must combine the qualities of private excellence for public good.

- The best way of promoting high standards of business practices is through self-regulation. The Code has been designed as an instrument of self-regulation to serve as a voluntary guideline towards better quality of life and higher standards of business practice.

The Advertising Standards Council of India expects, among other things, that there will be (Balachandra, 1996, p. 83):

(a) no offence to generally accepted norms of public decency;
(b) truthfulness and honesty in claims and representation; and
(c) no indiscriminate advertising of products which are hazardous to society or individuals.

In a recent "Times of India—MODE" opinion poll, "business" ranked fifth in a list of ten segments of society evaluated for corruption. Seventy-six percent of the respondents rated "business" as a corrupting force. "Politicians and Ministers" had the highest rank by virtue of receiving 98 percent score as being corrupt. "Teachers" fell in the ninth rank— 43 percent of the respondents ranking them as corrupt. "Liberalization" of the economy has not reduced corruption. "Ordinary people" were seen as corrupt by only 38 percent of the respondents, the lowest rank (*Times of India*, January 14, 1995).

HD Shourie of Common Cause put the proclamations of ethics and norms by business in its proper perspective: "A strange advertisement recently found prominent place in newspapers asking for quotations for the sales of 'damaged sugar' which has recently been imported . . . This is indicative of the present state of commitment of business to abide by the norms of conduct or code of ethics." (*Indian Journal of Public Administration*, July–September 1995, p. 639)

All this means is that will-to-ethics by business is hardly going to grow by means of resolutions, circulars, and conferences. The Steel Authority of India Ltd. offices have recently displayed prominently along its corridors and foyers a bare list of "Our Core Values": customer satisfaction, concern for people, consistent profitability, and commitment to excellence. Ethics finds no place in them despite several big and small revelations of internal and external ethical lapses in the last few years. A private sector outfit (Murugappa Group) has produced a more elaborate statement of "values and beliefs" consisting of seven items. The first item reads: "Adhere to ethical norms in all dealings with shareholders, employees, customers, suppliers, financial institutions and government."

This indicates more serious thought went into the formulation of this statement. But one does not know what company-wide educational efforts are made to sustain this ethical declaration in daily business practice at all levels.

In an interview with Dr. S. Ganguly, the Executive Vice-Chairman and Managing Director of one of the oldest and largest cement-making conglomerates, the status of the will-to-ethics appeared in a new light. This company was born with a strong dose of idealism when India was still being ruled by the British. An abiding sense of nationalism was the source of integrity, and the founders were both careful and lucky to secure an unbroken succession of CEOs imbued with an unflinching will-to-ethics. The result has been it does not enjoy the extent of market share or the quantum of profit as is rightfully its due. Yet, every hurdle is fought through available legal means, and never by cutting corners in a competitive commodity market. Patience, with an eye on the long-term, provides sustainability to corporate will-to-ethics. Clearly, there is the chain of successive individual CEOs behind such sustained corporate ethicality.

The above CEO also voiced two other profound concerns: the ethics of privatization and the flooding of India with multinational financial services companies. He questioned the ethical wisdom of privatizing the supply of basic needs like health and education in a poor country. This process of converting social goods into economic goods is going to push them beyond the bounds of the common citizen outside the orbit of metropolitan cities. The financial services whirlwind is also accentuating the great divide in respect to monetary remuneration in society. Management Graduates and their ilk in their twenties are being offered pay packages which can potentially subvert social harmony, even sanity. How can young managers remain ethical for long in such a heated atmosphere?, the CEO asked.

When we come to multinational or foreign corporations, two varieties of issues could be considered—"gross corruption" and "subtle unethicality". The much-publicized but yet-unresolved "Bofors deal" between India and the Swedish armaments company could be cited. This seems to be a major example of "gross corruption" on a massive scale. Driven by the intense desire to clinch Sweden's biggest export order, the Bofors company paid as much as 5 million USD in terms of "commissions" to various agents, politicians, and government functionaries, both legislative and executive (Subramaniam, 1993, p. 3). It is a classic case of the B-P-C triangle in action. The KFC (Kentucky Fried Chicken) controversy provides an illustration of "subtle unethicality". A spokesman of the Animal Welfare Society revealed some telling details about the use of harmful hormones and chemicals like mono sodium glutamate to fatten the chickens used by KFC (*Times of India*, letter to the Editor, February 29, 1996). Recently Glaxo (India) had announced an incredible 175 percent interim dividend. This is surmised to be a compensation for the U.K.-based parent company's investment of Rs. 340 million to raise its equity holding from 32 percent to 51 percent. The declaration had come too soon after this increase to rule out such a connection. Even if this dividend were largely paid out of the sales proceeds of one of the divisions, still the question remains: why repatriate large sums out of these proceeds instead of investing them for business growth in India? (*Business Today*, January 22, 1996, p. 51) Similarly, another U.S. company has recently patented an oil extracted from *neem* tree which grows in India. The medicinal properties of neem have been of household knowledge and use in India in numerous forms from time immemorial. The implication of the above patent secured by the U.S. company seems to be that henceforth neem oil cannot be used in India without paying royalty to this company. Is this a case of "intellectual property rights" versus "natural property rights"?

5. Will-to-ethics and Academia

Academic concern with applied ethics in business continues to be marginal, with a few honorable exceptions. The recent XLRI survey amongst 148 universities elicited only 7 institutions which claimed as having introduced ethics courses. The Xavier Labour Relations Institute (XLRI) at Jamshedpur has been the first business school in India to have introduced a compulsory course in Business Ethics since the early eighties. It is a Catholic institution and functions in the heart of the Tata business empire, the Tata Iron and Steel Co. Ltd. These two genetic factors seem to have synergized well to let an ethics course be born there. Fr. K. Cyriac is the Course instructor. But the leading management Institutes, established by the Government of India in academic collaboration with some leading U.S. business schools, have so far made no headway, except the Indian Institute of Management at Calcutta. It appears strange that the Indian Institute of Management (IIM) at Ahmedabad, set up in collaboration with the Harvard Business School, does not yet offer anything on this subject even as an option. The general attitude amongst academics in these places is one of avoidance of the normative dimension of management. It is better not to be involved in moralizing to business.

The IIM at Calcutta has started a new outfit called "Management Center for Human Values". It has crystallized the work being done by the author in the broader field of "human values for holistic effectiveness" since 1978. The Center takes the view that ethics-in-practice reflects the quality of the values corpus internalized by various role players, so, business ethics is seen a subset of human values. The Center has been financed entirely by grants and donations by Indian industry and financial institutions as many as 35 organizations at the time of this writing. The House of Tatas has been by far the largest contributor. The Center now offers two elective courses to second-year MBA students on ethics and human values (this course has been offered since 1983). It also offers 25 to 30 programs every year to various companies throughout India. An annual International Workshop on Management By Human Values in January each year is a major duty of the Center. Nearly 6000 managers have been through these programs since 1983.

The Xavier Institute of Management (a sister institution of XLRI) at Bhubaneswar also offers a course on business ethics. The course intends to "stimulate debate and discussion rather than to formulate principles". The course covers a very wide spectrum of issues ranging from ethical dilemmas in management, values clarification, company philosophies, social responsibility, advertising, market research, environmental issues, and social justice to job reservation, national problems, human world order, and ethics of MNCs.

Professor R. C. Sekhar of the TA Pai Institute of Management at Manipal is also seriously engaged with both the teaching of and research in business ethics. Like the XLRI, the TAPIM course also places substantial reliance upon case studies. He feels that ethical education cannot be delinked from ambiguous and contentious subjects like psychology, philosophy and religion (Sekhar, 1995, M-163). However, Sekhar is chary of "moral rhetoric" which, by implication, seems to endorse XLRI's eschewal of engagement with "moral principles". The empirical content of Sekhar's research (confined for the present to MBA students) indicates preference for exploring opinions and views, thereby enlarging the scope for dialogues and discussions. This again is akin to the XLRI approach.

The two courses at MCHV in IIM-C, however, attempt a more direct approach to ethico-moral upliftment by helping students to adopt a concrete process for cultivating recognized and universal noble emotions like gratitude, contentment, transparence, compassion, oneness, and honesty, all for their own sake. This is expected to establish the human values base on a healthy, virtuous footing. Ethics-in-practice would then gradually follow from this groundwork. Efforts are made through universally applicable psychological disciplines (as demonstrated by their ready acceptance amongst the participants of the International Workshop) to strengthen the will-to-ethics for personal character development. These mental exercises, derived from proven and enduring indigenous Indian spiritual traditions, convert theory into transformational experience. They pave the way for natural spill-over into the work context of management and business. The emphasis is more an "experiential ethics" than on "intellectual ethics", and more on personal "managerial/ entrepreneurial ethics" than on impersonal "business ethics". An important corollary of this is the greater emphasis on "direct ethics" compared to "dilemma ethics". Some small case studies are used, but with emphasis upon the finer nuances of individual values/ethics amongst various role players. The Jamnalal Bajaj Institute of Management Studies at Bombay University first introduced a course on Business Ethics in 1992. It was made a compulsory second year course in their Masters program in 1994. It is taught by a number of visiting faculty from industry. As such, it seems to be a more down-to-earth effort than the others mentioned above.

Giri provides us with the hitherto best and most comprehensive coverage of ethics education in Indian schools of management/business. At the end of his survey, he remarks: "In India teaching of ethics has still a long way to go. The barriers are far too many. Discussions with teachers in management schools suggest that the reason(s) for not teaching ethics to MBA students can work as a vicious circle." (Giri, 1995, p. 9)

A senior academic, Prof. N. R. Sheth, sharing the concern and diagnosis of Giri, asserts: "No, we cannot leave values alone. All the hurdles involved in capturing and dissecting values have not dampened public interest in them." (Sheth 1995, p. 85)

This, indeed, is true as demonstrated by the opening up of the *hawala* scam pandora's box (of clandestine foreign exchange deals). This was triggered by a "public interest litigation" (PIL) filed to the Supreme Court against administrative and legislative soft-pedaling (January–March, 1996).

Some of the reactions to ethics education efforts have been strange. In January 1994, the Government of India had selected five reputed educational institutions to impart spiritually-oriented values education. A sum of Rs. 2000 million was to be given to them. The National Council of Educational Research and Training criticized this plan by dubbing it as obscurantist, with the potential to erode the scientific temper in education. It observed sarcastically that the government should support the making of students, not monks! (*The Telegraph*, January 1995) Without going into the merits of the specific institutions chosen, the dissociation of spirituality from ethics and values amongst a section of educationists in India is intriguing.

Unlike the NCERT, later in the year the University Grants Commission mooted a detailed proposal for universities to engage in the dissemination of "essential sociocultural values" like love, sacrifice, compassion, nonviolence etc. The *Statesman* reacted soon by ridiculing the whole idea. Instead, it advised editorially: "Let us teach them physics, the beauty of literature and the science of logic properly, and they will do just fine" (*The Statesman*, December 12, 1995). Rather than sounding a helpful caution for the UGC efforts towards depth and purity and modeling for such values education, the idea itself was dismissed.

So far as publications on business ethics are concerned, there is hardly much to mention. The first book in this area, to our knowledge, was by Prof. Arun Monappa at the Institute of Management, Ahmedabad (Monappa, 1977). After a long interval, the hitherto most comprehensive volume has been a collection of readings and essays edited by Fr. T. A. Mathias (1994). In 1995, several other publications were released. *The Indian Journal of Public Administration's* special and comprehensive number appeared this year. This author's book also was published (Chakraborty, 1995). Mr. S. Balachandran's compact book appeared in 1996, and Prof. Sekhar's book should have also been published by the end of 1996. Broadly, Monappa's and Chakraborty's books emphasize ethics of managers as individuals, the former empirically on current status, the latter conceptually on what could be done to improve matters. The edited volume by Mathias takes a broad-spectrum look more at the corporate entity as an ethical unit rather than at the manager with an intense focus. Balachandran's book is a blend of Indian psycho-philosophical concepts and the current events in the sphere of ethics. The volume goes for "managing ethics" in its title.

Insofar as endowments for Professorships/Chairs in Ethics are concerned, they seem to be less than ten. XLRI Jamshedpur has a Chair endowed by the House of Tatas. JBIMS of Bombay University has one Chair in the name of the industrialist Jamnalal Bajaj. The TAPIM has a T. A. Pai Chair in Business Ethics. The Unit Trust of India has endowed three Professorships at the Indian institutes of Management at Ahmedabad, Bangalore, and Calcutta. Besides, IIM-Calcutta has two more permanent endowments for research in the areas of human values and business ethics offered by Orissa Cement Ltd. and the Associated Cement Companies Ltd. The tally thus is eight. In addition, the Sir Ratan Tata Trust has offered funds for two Visiting Professors per year for three academic years beginning with July 1996–June 1997 to the MCHV at IIM-Calcutta.

Research and consultancy by academia in the field of business ethics has not yet occurred. Even if some signs of research being undertaken are available now and then, no publication arising from such work has come to our notice except Monappa's book mentioned earlier, and this was long ago. So far as consultancy goes, it is perhaps for business to request it. Of this, there are no signs at all. Therefore, the common challenges before academia and business would now appear to be:

(a) An unflinching grasp that since "business" is being acclaimed as the most significant change agent, it must, as an aspect of human endeavor, work for an ethico-moral foundation for itself, otherwise, it may be discredited as unbridled mammonism.

(b) "Experiential ethics" should undergird "legislative ethics". Academia has a special responsibility to engage in the former and attract people in business towards it.

(c) The richer and more powerful businesses have greater accountability for ethics-in-practice.

(d) Recruitment, selection, and evaluation processes should begin to incorporate ethico-moral criteria.

(e) Academia and business should both realize that ethics can be learnt and assimilated by means of reasoning and experiencing.

6. Conclusion

What could be the nature or characteristics of a paradigm that might generate useful responses to these challenges? Fr. Bogaert has suggested a fruitful, simple two-axis model for the Indian context: "sustainability of natural environment" plus "doing good for the poor". (D'Bogaert, 1994, pp. 60–61) This indeed is a good starting point. The MCHV at IIM-C is attempting to go a little deeper—why is it that most of us are irresponsible towards the poor despite intellectual lip-service?—and a little wider—why is it that the feeling of harmonious relationships across all components and elements of the universe is conspicuous by its absence despite the declarations of new science? In response to these two fundamental challenges, the MCHV is trying to work out a paradigm of the following kind:

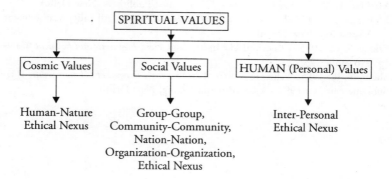

We are aware that it is not easy or common as yet to bring ethics and values to their base in the holistic spirit-foundation in our discourses on business/management. Thus, the admirable collection edited by Fr. Mathias (285 pages) contains no entry in the long index on "spirit/spirituality". Yet, responsible academic engagement in business ethics has to create this foundation for the ultimate survival of human society through business. The "social responsibility" thrust of business ethics is necessary, but it must be anchored to its source: "spiritual responsibility."

The latter is the real justification of the former. Because of her rich and living spiritual heritage, India has perhaps a bigger share of duty in this respect. While India ought to learn "analytical ethics" from the western approach to business ethics, she ought to offer "intuitive" or "being" or "consciousness" ethics in her turn.

References

Balachandran, S.: 1996, *Managing Ethics* (Sangeeta Associates, Bombay).

Chakraborty, S. K.: 1995. *Ethics in Management — Vedantic Perspectives* (Oxford University Press, New Delhi).

d'Bogaert, M. V. Fr.: 1994, 'Managerial Decisions in a Developing Economy', in Mathias (1994), pp. 52–64.

Dasgupta, G.: 1996, 'Beyond Salvage', *The Statesman* (February 26).

Forum of Free Enterprise: 1956, *Basic Document.*

Giri, A. K.: 1995. 'Management Education and Teaching of Ethics', Working Paper 137, *Madras Institute of Development Studies.*

Gupta, S. B.: 1992, *Black Income in India* (Sage, New Delhi).

Kabra, K. N.: 1982, *The Black Economy in India* (Chanakya Publishing, New Delhi).

Mathias, T. A., Fr.: 1994. *Corporate Ethics* (Allied Publishers, New Delhi).

Monappa, A.: 1977, *Ethical Attitudes of Indian Managers* (All India Management Association, New Delhi).

Sekhar, R. C.: 1995. 'Ethics and The Indian Manager', *Economic and Political Weekly* (November 25).

Sheth, N. R.: 1995. 'Values in Search of an Identity', *Journal of Human Values* 1(1).

Subramaniam, C: 1993, *Bofors* (Penguin Viking, New Delhi).

11 Indian Managers in Transition: Orientations, Work Goals, Values and Ethics[1]

Samir R. Chatterjee and Cecil A. L. Pearson

Introduction

The ideal society envisioned in ancient India is often referred to as "Ramraj" (benevolent social order of the great King Ram). The key principle guiding this ancient ideal was the idea of 'dharma' or the source of values guiding action. This traditional social ethos was, however, not well enshrined in the corporate values that emerged during the British rule of India since the eighteenth century. In the contemporary context, multiple layers of values have emerged where, societal values remained very much rooted to the ancient traditions while institutional and corporate values reflected values of the colonial era. The recent large scale economic reforms and the imperatives of globalisation have impacted on managerial mindsets with a set of new values and world views creating further tensions at the individual level (Kao Sinha/Ng 1995).

Five decades after gaining independence, a new managerial generation has come into its own. The world view of this generation has been linked less to the tradition of the ancient land or the guiding ideologies of the colonial era, but is more influenced by the market culture and reform of the past decades. Among the most important factors creating the sea change of Indian management are the homogenisation of social structure (*People of India Report* 1992), technological education, consumerism, electronic mass media, trade union culture, foreign investment, changing infrastructure and urbanisation of values.

The dilemma faced by the managers of Indian organisations with the widespread impacts of economic reform and global imperatives is in the search for a fine balance of tradition and change. Transforming Indian organisations into efficient, productive, humane and dynamic institutions that could match in quality and reputations to other countries is a major challenge. The lesson of the Asian tiger economics may have some relevance to India in so far as their search for a balance in aligning the Confucian values with modern managerialism. It is not the temptation of 'adopting' managerial techniques by 'adapting' values and cultures that underlines the economic reform process. The core beliefs and values of an ancient and complex society with a massive rural population (unlike the east Asian tiger economies) need to be sharpened to make them context relevant rather than be replaced by wholesale imported values (Chakraborty 1998, Garg/Parikh 1995, Sinha/Sinha 1995, Tripathy 1995).

In terms of the Indian corporations, a striking feature is evident in the differences of managerial values espoused by large tradition bound organisations and born global new generation organisations. It is often contended that an unique set of values have been one of the driving forces for successful emergence of computer software technology industry in India in the recent decade. There is a distinct divergence of work culture and it is contended that the older and more traditional organisations are not economically dynamic because of their work culture being out of alignment to the reform process. England (1978) suggested that it was the better understanding of the value orientations that facilitated the design of organisations and their motivational dynamics. The perspectives of senior managers are the key parameters in translating these values and linking the organisations to their external environment.

Tradition and modernity have combined to transform the Indian managerial mindset in an unique way and this has created dualities of value that is often difficult for others to understand (Chatterjee 1991, Garg/Parikh 1995). In one of the landmark studies of managerial values in India it was suggested that the Indian managers gave much more importance to organisational stability than in other countries (England/ Lee 1974). Many commentators (Athreya 1995, Chakraborty 1991) have suggested that Indian managers feel comfortable with the traditional system of hierarchy in all spheres of life and a sense of discomfort with the managerial culture of instant feedback, performance and empowerment. For most Indian mangers, a modern technological and globalised world view does not extend beyond the boundaries of their professional role. It has been contended that, "The incidence of this fundamental contradiction in India's top leadership may very well be an important factor in numerous failures of implementation in the country's development programme. There is almost certainly a causal link between ambivalent attitudes towards modernity and an unconscious reservation as to the ultimate value of modernisation". (Lannoy 1971, p. 416). A study of this complexity of balancing tradition, culture and the imperatives of global economic reform is, therefore, of considerable relevance at this time in India.

The study reported in this paper examines the value orientations of senior level managers in Indian organisations at a time of economic liberalisation and globalisation of corporate ideologies. Indian society as a whole is in a complex process of change, and there are multiple cross-impacts of educational, economic, political, technological and managerial reforms. A close examination of value orientations of senior managers when widespread reforms are being implemented will lead to a better understanding of the social and organisational priorities. The purpose of this study is to develop a profile of work-related values among senior Indian managers at a time when most of them are engaged in large scale reform programmes.

Economic Reform and Value Reorientations of Managers

Values by nature, are relatively stable standards at the societal level. Personal work values or ethical yardsticks, therefore, are usually influenced by these relatively permanent frameworks. The literature has tended to indicate this symbiosis only through mono-dimensional directionality (Westwood/Posner 1997). Value reorientation due to changes in macro-level or micro-level economic ideology and practices has only recently been discussed in the management literature. Allport, Vernon and Lindsey (1970), England (1967), Hofstede (1980), and Rokeach (1973) were criticised by Becker and Connor (1986) to have created a disjointed literature in value studies. Harpaz (1990) introduced the concept of work values in measuring the degree of convergence amongst nations.

Two deficiencies emerge out of the approaches in the previous literature. Firstly, the work values are usually considered as a generalised national aggregate; and secondly, they are viewed to be static in nature. The study reported here is highly context specific to India at a time of dynamic reform at macro and micro levels. A country bound by strong traditions of religious, cultural and organisational imperatives may not have one set of work values across managerial levels, gender and organisational type. The degree to which tradition and economic pressures of reform are combined to form these values may vary from region to region and from organisation to organisation in a country as large as India. Ralston et al. (1997) termed such values as crossvergent values and defined the condition as, "crossvergence occurs where an individual incorporates both national culture influences and economic ideology influences synergistically to form an unique value system that is different from the value system set supported by either national culture or economic ideology" (Ralston et al. 1997, p. 183). This emphasises the synergy approach. However, in a country like India, managers may not synergise divergent values in a terminal sense, but may rearrange their work goals and other work related values in different layers at different points of time. As Westwood and Posner contend, "Personal value systems begin to be formed early in life as individuals encounter the socialising mechanisms of their society. Inevitably, individuals' values are shaped by the social milieu in which they develop, and in this way the cultural values prevalent in the society strongly inform and become part of their personal value system" (Westwood/Posner 1997, p. 34). The argument here is that, in spite of deriving personal values from the embedded culture and tradition, managerial values at the individual level, are strongly influenced by the crossvergent influences of organisational and social forces. The evidence of this study attempts to highlight this feature.

India had pursued a policy of self-sufficiency until the economic reform movement of recent years. This has in effect created a work culture of internal focus and widespread lack of autonomy. With the increases in autonomy for all types of enterprises created through the process of economic reform, the areas of individual discretion has enlarged widely, particularly in the ethical domain of managerial endeavours. The interaction levels of competing values may be conceptualised in three layers as is shown in Figure 1.

Figure 1. Layers of Managerial Values

Layer One	*Core Traditional Values*: deeply held robust and widely shared values.
Layer Two	*Individual Managerial Values*: work values, ethical values and other such values anchored to the core tradition but also in the process of transition.
Layer Three	*Situational Values*: role dependent values contingent upon situational elements of macro-environmental policies and corporate culture.

Leading Indian Scholars (Athreya 1995, Chakraborty 1991, Gupta 1996) suggest that the economic reform or market culture only affects the layers two and three of Figure 1. They contend that the overwhelming force of core traditional values still dominates the Indian managerial cadre at a latent level. The cultural factors have been widely researched in relation to their effects on work related values by scholars (Hofstede 1991). However, Hofstede (1991) contended that the cultural dimensions specific to a national population is not moderated by organisational type, size and strategy. He argued that cultural values and management practices need to be consistently matched with one another. Over a long period of time this may be true, but the current research suggests that matching culture and management practices may not be possible from time to time during a period of rapid change. Successful management practices not only differ from country to country, as suggested by Hofstede, they also vary within a national group based on the diversity of member demography, industry culture, technology orientation and degree of internationalisation.

Methodology

Site and Respondents

The study was conducted under the auspice of the Centre for Human Values Indian Institute of Management, Calcutta. Each of the study respondents was a participant either of a week long residential programme at this most prestigious centre for value studies, or they attended similar courses that were conducted by programme directors, from the Institute, at other Indian capital cities. A total of 421 completed questionnaires were received. The questionnaire was administered to most of the study managers by the first author, at the Institute, where he was the Sir Ratan Tata Fellow for six months. In most cases the participants were briefed by him, and this ensured the very high response rate of 85%. Generally, the participants completed the questionnaire on the first day of their seminar.

A feature of the respondents was the manner of their selection. Almost all the study participants were from companies that had approached the Indian Institute of Management to provide appropriate training for Indian human values. The need for integration of the human values paradigm in Indian business is increasingly being recognised by powerful and socially conscious business leaders. There is a growing belief that senior managerial cadre need to reimmerse themselves in traditional Indian values. Therefore, the sample had an element of self selection in terms of the respondents being predispositioned to incorporating ethical considerations in their business practices. This was a deliberately chosen research strategy as otherwise a cross sectional sample of respondents with diverse assumptions would have been obtained, and then it would have been difficult to generalise for a society as large and as complex as India.

Measures

A questionnaire was administered to obtain demographic and perceptual data. The demographic data, which included facets of gender, age, and details about childhood upbringing, were used to develop a profile of the study managers. Demographic detail about the company ownership, main business activity and organisational size were also obtained.

Perceptions about work goals, societal values and views about the relevance of ethics in decision making were provided by the respondents. Eleven facets of work goals were assessed with an instrument that was employed by Harpaz (1990) in an extensive international study. The managers were required to rank each work goal from most important (1) to least important (11).

To evaluate the manager's societal values a 12 item instrument was designed. These items, that tapped concerns fundamental to the Indian world view, were established after considerable consultation with respectable Indian academics. To complete the societal value scale managers were required to rank each item for importance, from the most important (1) to the least important (12).

Consensus or divergence in decision making, in terms of ethical business perspectives, was assessed. Respondents were asked to assess 24 statements with a seven point Likert scale (1 = strongly disagree to 7 = strongly agree). Each item was established by the same procedure that was employed to generate the societal values statements. This scale assessed the extent of convergence on four ethical domains. These four subscales were 1) global, 2) societal, 3) organisational, and 4) personal (Chatterjee 1995). There were six statements for each ethical domain, and a mean score was computed for each domain. Also, the extent of convergence or divergence was computed for each one of the 24 items. It was determined that managers had an ethical dilemma (for the item) if the mean score was in the range of 3 to 5. For scores greater than 5 it was deemed levels of violations were low and there was a higher degree of consensus and a low ethical dilemma.

Analysis

Frequency tables were constructed to establish the range of responses for the 421 study mangers. Means and their standard deviations were computed for each item, for the three main scales, and the four subscales of ethical domains. The differences of the ranked items, for the work goals and the societal values, were assessed for their level of significance. These analyses were undertaken with Statistical Analysis System (SAS) subroutines.

Results

Table 1 details the demographic profile of the study business managers. These data show that the sample was dominated by senior men who were mainly employed in large organisations. The gender/organisational size correlation was 0.13, significant at $p < 0.01$. An unique feature of the sample is that 70.1% of the managers were employed in senior managerial positions. A striking feature of the sample was that 94% of the managers held senior level university qualifications (56% PhD and Masters degrees. 38% Bachelors degrees). Age and managerial level was significantly correlated ($r = 0.55$, $p < 0.0001$). Nearly one half of the managers worked in government and local government institutions, most of which were involved in financial activities (e.g., banking, accounting). Almost two thirds of the study managers lived in eastern and northern India for the first 25 years of their life and there was a strong relationship between the region of their birth and their vocation ($r = 0.22$, $p < 0.0001$). A great deal of the participants were from joint families. From the profile of the managers (as given by Table 1) it could be predicted that the respondents would be anchored to traditional values that would encourage the maintenance of the status quo. However, the data of Tables 2 and 3 indicate significant shifts from conventional foundations.

Table 1: Demographic Data % for the Indian Managers (N = 421)

Gender:	Male	93.1		Female	6.9
Age: years	<30	4.7	Company Size:	<100	8.6
	31–39	16.9		100–499	11.9
	40–49	34.2		500–1000	8.8
	>49	44.2		>1000	70.7
Organisation:	Government	46.6	Business:	Finance/Banking	41.1
(Ownership)	National	17.3	(Activity)	Manufacturing	26.4
	Corporate	10.9		Government	11.2
	International	9.5		Professional	10.8
	Private	7.8		Other	10.3
Residence:	Eastern	34.0	Childhood:	Joint	61.8
(First 25 years)	Northern	30.6	(Family)	Nuclear	31.8
	Western	17.3		Hostel/boarding	5.7
	Southern	16.4		Other	0.7

In Table 2 is presented the respondent's work goals mean scores and standard deviations. The study managers nominated the opportunity to learn new things as their most important work goal. The next three important work goals, that were identified by the managers, were strongly associated with elements of enrichment, and the matching of their skills and competencies with the work place dimensional requirements. Interestingly, the work goal of good social interpersonal relations was the fifth most important work goal, yet Indian society is considered to be a collective community (Hofstede 1991). The study managers regarded physical work conditions and convenient work hours as the least important of their work goals. Also of low importance was salary and job security.

Table 2: Means and Standard Deviations of Work Goals (N = 421)

Variable Description	Mean	Std
Opportunity to learn new things	3.81	2.52
Work that is liked and interesting	4.09	2.74
Job with a variety of tasks and roles	4.33	2.37
Job that is matched with abilities/experience	4.75	2.64
Social inter-relationships colleagues/supervisors	5.24	2.65
Opportunity to improve and be promoted	5.62	2.59
Autonomy in decision making	6.00	3.25
Good job security	7.16	3.00
A good salary	7.60	2.78
Good physical working conditions	8.69	2.12
Convenient work hours	8.69	2.52

Note: The lower the mean the higher the perceived level of importance.

Table 3: Means and Standard Deviations of Societal Values (N = 421)

Variable Description	Mean	Std
Work quality	3.61	2.40
Personal integrity	3.86	3.10
Team work	4.37	2.33
Customer service	4.90	2.98
Social responsibility	5.13	3.00
Workplace harmony	6.57	2.59
Organisational learning	7.16	2.45
Respect for seniority	7.17	2.75
Innovation and creativity	7.29	3.56
Value tradition	8.94	2.83
Wealth and material possession	10.21	2.31

Note: The lower the mean the higher the perceived level of importance.

Not only is this observation at considerable variance with other international studies (Harpaz 1990, Lawler 1971), where salary has always been highly ranked, but in Indian society the possession of a job and the associated income is vital. Overall, the findings of Table 2 indicate that the managers realise that their society is in transition and their focus is more on the attributes needed to be successful in a market economy, and considerably less importance is attached to the work goals that had greater relevance prior to the Indian economic reform (England/Dhingra/Agarwal 1974).

The means and standard deviations of societal values of the study managers, which is shown in Table 3, may be partitioned into two distinct sections. The first section, including work quality, personal integrity, team work, customer service and social responsibility can be ascribed to be associated with features of a market orientated society. The second section including, workplace harmony, organisational learning, respect for seniority, innovation and creativity, value tradition, and wealth and material possession may arguably be linked to a society's concept of organisational configuration. In the context of India, the data surprisingly places work quality ahead of all of the other items which are commonly stereotyped to have greater priority in the Indian context. In addition, the low ranking of tradition may also be misconstrued to mean a displacement of tradition in preference to the higher ranked items. In fact, Table 3 shows a realistic contradiction amongst Indian managers in balancing these two sections of societal values. For example, personal integrity could have been linked to the second section, whereas organisational learning, and innovation and creativity could have been associated with the first section. Such ambivalence points to a definite shift and confirms a transition in the perceptions of societal values amongst senior managers.

Table 4: Decision Making Means Across Ethical Domains

Ethical Domain	Mean	Std
Global	5.20	0.72
Societal	4.93	0.68
Organisational	5.20	0.68
Personal	4.88	0.79

Table 4 details the decision making means and their standard deviations for the four examined ethical domains. The respondent managers expressed the highest states of convergence in ethical decision making was accommodated in the global, societal and organisational domains. In contrast, the study mangers reported that the greatest level of ethical violations or the highest intensity of ethical dilemmas occurred in the personal domain. Two inferences may be drawn from these observations. First, as a consequence of the shift in the importance of work goals and societal values away from traditional orientations, the application of ethical ideas in the contemporary context needs much deeper level of understanding and should be given greater emphasis. Second, this calls for a broadening of management education and development to incorporate value based inputs and processes.

Table 5: Extent of Divergence for Levels of Ethical Domains

Ethical Domain	Extent of Respondent Divergence		
	Mean	# Items	Ratio
Global	3.96 to 4.14	2	0.32
Societal	4.80	1	0.16
Organisational	4.10 to 4.75	2	0.32
Personal	3.41 to 4.78	5	0.82

Notes: a. Ratio = $\dfrac{\text{\# questionnaire items with divergence}}{\text{\# questionnaire items}}$

b. Divergence = 3 < item mean < 5, else convergence

Table 5 outlines the extent of decision making divergence for the four levels of ethical domain. For the global, societal and organisational domains the means of the questionnaire items revealed only one or two of the six items (for each domain) was considered by the managers to be an ethical dilemma. For the remaining questionnaire items a strong convergence was recorded. However, for the personal domain five of the six questionnaire items were reported as ethical dilemmas. The evidence presented in Table 5 is that in the emerging competitive Indian market place managers are being increasingly confronted by ethical dilemmas. This finding suggests the need for both guiding frameworks as well as managerial education to reduce the gap between standards and normative societal conceptualisation of ethical codes.

In Table 6 is presented the degree of consensus or divergence in decision making across four levels of ethical domain. Shown for each domain is a questionnaire item that is representative of the six items that were used to measure the ethical domain. As presented previously, higher degrees of consensus were shown for the global, societal and organisational domains. The greatest level of violations occurred in the personal domain.

Table 6: Degree of Convergence for Levels Of Ethical Domains

Domain	Mean	Questionnaire item description	Divergence extent
Global	5.96	The building of a modern global economy should be underpinned by the adherence to a set of universally accepted values	Convergence
Societal	5.66	Civilised societies guide and control citizen behaviours by embracing legal codes and conventions that are derived from their respective cultures	Convergence
Organisational	5.69	Organisations are guided by strong values and cultures and these are reflected by the way customers are treated, employees are valued, and quality issues are addressed	Convergence
Personal	4.41	The role of an individual in an Indian organisation is shaped more by the conceptualisation and interpretation of personal dharma, rather than the controls exercised in legal codes	Dilemma

Notes: a. Subject N = 421.
   b. Divergence = 3 < item mean < 5, else convergence.

Conclusion and Discussion

This paper attempts to contribute to the growing field of International management in three distinct ways. Firstly, by being able to collect an unique set of empirical data from a population of very senior Indian managers who are well known for their reluctance for participation in this type of research. The credibility of the sample was enhanced as the participants came from a wide range of industry sectors, regions and educational backgrounds. Secondly, the study captures the work goal measures and social value prioritisations at a time in India when the macro level economic reform agenda of that country has been one of the key social debates impacting all levels of society. Thirdly, the results of the study demonstrate an interesting transition in the managerial conceptualisation of work goals, societal values and ethics. Undoubtedly, the traditional values still dominate the consciousness of the Indian society and institutions, but surprisingly managers were able to work with global values at their individual levels of work ideology by successfully building and relying upon 'meso' level work value sets.

The Confucian—plus explanation linking the economic success and managerial value in East Asia has been widely discussed (Bond/Hofstede 1989, Chen 1995, Kao et al. 1995, Redding 1990). This explanation of economic and managerial success in East Asia being enriched by the common Confucian heritage has led to a new hybrid notion of Asian management. The importance of these managerial perspectives, which enrich the micro-level synergies in East Asia, may not have direct relevance to India. But like the East Asian case, the role of indigenous tradition and the localisation of professional practices still remains a challenge. No aspect of the managerial values in India appears simple, self-evident or certain across industries, demographics and regional diversities. But the ability of Indians, and specifically the Indian managerial elite to reconcile such complexities with a distinct degree of uniqueness may become a model from which to draw lessons. This is a striking contrast to the less optimistic view espoused by Huntington who contended that the post-modern world would necessarily create a irreconcilable conflict between economic ideologies and cultural values (Huntington 1996).

The traditional roots of ancient values in India have been deeply universal in nature. The core problematics addressed through the age old human values paradigms reflected the richness of human experiences. But the modern technological market ideology based societies need managers who are able to add extra dimensions to the classical problematics. Several management scholars have recently developed models linking broad cultural value dimensions with micro-level managerial issues (Anderson 1997, Hampden-Turner/Trompenaars 1993, Kabanoff/Waldersee/Cohen 1995, McCoy 1985, Trompenaars 1993). However, these frameworks neither take into account the dynamics of culture nor the imperatives of economic reform agenda. This paper argues that although the influence of deep-seated and all pervasive tradition may remain at, the core level, the imperatives of economic experimentation and learning continues to dominate other levels. Managers' responses and priorities with respect to their work related assumptions tend to be significantly shaped also by other personal weightings such as their upbringing, life experience, organisational culture and worldview of value frameworks.

Tables presented earlier in this paper suggest that the contemporary environment of discontinuity is confronting traditional managerial mindsets. The evidence suggests that managers need to deepen their understanding of values as they acquire and reprioritise their competencies. Interestingly, in Table 2 the opportunity to learn and undertake challenging tasks are work goals that align strongly with attributes of major importance in today's organisational climates of rapid change and aggressive competition, which are features that encourage companies to embrace the philosophy of organisational learning (Black/Synan 1997, Kloot 1996). It is interesting to note that with the growing importance if non-financial work goals in terms of quality, learning, teamwork and customer service there has been a displacement of the traditional goals of pay and working condition. This suggests a transition in values away from the old paradigm to a paradigm more in tune with contemporary managerial approaches elsewhere. For instance, Harpaz's (1990) study employed data that were obtained from 1981 to 1983. This was a period when corporations exercised economic priorities in terms of production costs, efficiency and profit, a time before the emergence of new business ideas (eg. TQM, reengineering) and the rejuvenation of US and UK business for operation in the global market place. Table 3 provides evidence to suggest a perceived distinction between contemporary societal values and those that were relevant in earlier periods. The respondents held the strongest preferences for a set of societal values that are consistent with attributes of a market driven economy, where some of the more well known attributes were displaced by new features affecting managerial mindsets.

The ethical values, reported by the study managers in Tables 4, 5, and 6 indicate that on the one hand there was a general degree of consensus among the managers in terms of global, societal and organisational ethics, but on the other hand it is suggested by the evidence that there was a very high degree of ambivalence at the individual level with respect to their commitment to actions. A strong inference of these results is that the study managers perceived successful organisations are held together by transcendental values that overarch the corporate activity in such domains as learning skills, customer service and the pursuit of ethical excellence. Nevertheless, the evidence reveals that the senior managers of the examined Indian organisations have difficulty in reconciling their value paradigms with frameworks of action at least in the ethical domain.

With the increasing dominance of market ideology in all spheres of economic life in the country, there is considerable demand on managers to come to terms with new ways of conceptualising their work, organisational processes and approaches. Some well known scholars of Indian management strongly advocate that this paradigm shift in managerial values and assumptions can only be possible by adhering to the traditional wisdom of the country (Chakraborty 1998). These scholars suggest that like the Japanese, Indian managerial values and goals need to arise out of the deeply rooted tradition. While tradition is unmistakably observable in the daily lives of the country, the work organisations appear to be at the crossroads. There is an emergence of global value paradigms at least amongst the senior level Indian managers. The study findings presented here suggest that Indian managerial work goals tend to be in line with attributes needed in a market dominated business culture.

Indian organisations have generally favoured the Webberian model for designing their management approach over the present century. This model had totally ignored the indigenous social forces of caste, tradition or regional ethos, and, generally, created work cultures of apathy and negatism. A reconceptualisation of work organisations needs to begin by profiling the contemporary imperatives and this paper aims to contribute to that process.

Note

1. The authors wish to acknowledge their gratitude to the Indian Institute of Management, Culcutta for the support of the research and thank the reviewers for insightful comments on the earlier submissions.

References

Allport, G. W./Vernon. P. E./Lindsey, G., *Study of Values*, New York: Houghton Mifflin 1970.

Anderson, C, Values-Based Management, *Academy of Management Executive*, 11, 4, 1997, pp. 25–46.

Athreya, M. B., Ancient Wisdom for National Human Resource Management, in *Selected Papers from the National Conference on HRM in Darsanas Ahmedabad Management Association*, Ahmedabad 1995.

Becker, B. W./Connor, P. E., On the Status and Promise of Value Research, *Management Bibliographies and Reviews*, 12, 1986, pp. 3–17.

Black, D. H./Synan. C. D., The Learning Organisation: The Sixth Dimension, *Management Accounting—London*, 75, 10, 1997, pp. 70–72.

Bond, M. H./Hofstede, G., The Cash Value of Confucian Values, *Human Systems Management*, 8, 1989. pp. 199–200.

Chakraborty, S. K., *Management by Values: Towards Cultural Congruence*, Delhi: Oxford University Press 1991.

Chakraborty, S. K., *Values and Ethics for Organisations: Theory and Practice*, Delhi: Oxford University Press 1998.

Chatterjee. S. R., *Business Culture in India: An Analysis of Trends and Transitions*, Perth International Business Unit: Curtin University 1991.

Chatterjee, S. R., Business Ethics in a Global Context: Practices and Perspectives, *Proceedings of the Academy of International Business, South East Regional Conference*, Perth, 1995. pp. 257–260.

Chen, M., *Asian Management Systems*, London: Routledge 1995.

England, G. W., Personal Value Systems of American Managers, *Academy of Management Journal*, 10, 1967. pp. 53–68.

England, G. W., Managers and their Value Systems: A Five Country Comparative Study. *Columbia Journal of World Business* 13, 1978, pp. 33–34.

England, G. W./Dhingra, O. P./Agarwal, N. C: *The Manager and the Man: A Cross-Cultural Study of Personal Values*, Kent, Ohio: The Kent State University Press 1974

England, G. W./Lee, R., The Relationship between Managerial Values and Managerial Success in the United States, Japan, India and Australia, *Journal of Applied Psychology*, 59, 1974, pp. 411–419.

Garg, P. K./Parikh. I., Crossroads of Culture: A Study in the Culture of Transience, New Delhi: Sage 1995.

Gupta, G. P., (ed.) *Management by Consciousness: A Spirito-Technical Approach*, Sri Aurobindo Society: Pondicherry 1996.

Hampden-Turner, C./Trompenaars, F., *The Seven Cultures of Capitalism*, New York: Doubleday 1993.

Harpaz, I., The Importance of Work Goals: An International Perspective, *Journal of International Business Studies*, 21,1, 1990, pp. 75–93.

Hofstede, G., *Culture's Consequences: International Differences in Work Related Values*, London: Sage 1980.

Hofstede, G., *Cultures Consequences: Software of the Mind*, London: McGraw Hill 1991.

Huntington. S. P., *The Clash of Civilisations and the Remarking of World Order*, New York: Simon & Schuster 1996.

Kabanoff, B./Waldersee, R./Cohen, M., Espoused Values and Organisational Change Themes, *Academy of Management Journal*, 38, 4, 1995, pp. 1075–1104.

Kao, H. S. R./Sinha. D./Ng, S. H., (Eds.) *Effective Organisations and Social Values*, London: Sage 1995.

Kloot, L., Looping the Loop: New Directions for the Learning Organisation, *Australian Accountant*, 66, 6, 1996, pp. 26–27.

Lannoy, R., *The Speaking Tree: A Study of Indian Culture and Society*, London: Oxford University Press 1971.

Lawler, E. E., *Pay and Organizational Effectiveness: A Psychological View*, New York: McGraw Hill 1971.

McCoy, C., *Management of Values: The Ethical Difference in Corporate Policy and Performance*, Pitman: Marchfield, MA, 1985.

People of India Report, Anthropological Survey of India, New Delhi 1992.

Ralston, D. A./Holt, D. H./Terpestra, R. H./Yu, K. C., The Impact of National Culture and Economic Ideology on Managerial Work Values : A Study of the United States, Russia, Japan and China, *Journal of International Business Studies*, 28, 1, 1997, pp. 177–207.

Redding, S. G., *The Spirit of Chinese Capitalism*, Berlin: Walter de Gruyter 1990.

Rokeach, M., *The Nature of Human Values*, New York: Free Press 1973.

Sinha, J. B. P./Sinha, D., Role of Social Values in Indian Organisations, in Kao, H. S. R./Sinha, D./Ng, S. H. (eds.), *Effective Organisations and Social Values*, London: Sage 1995.

Tripathy R. C. Interplay of Values in the Functioning of Indian Organisations, in Kao H. S. R./Sinha, D./Ng, S. H. (eds.), *Effective Organisations and Social Values*, London: Sage 1995.

Trompenaars, F., *Riding the Waves of Culture*, London: Nicholas Brearly 1993.

Westwood, R. I./Posner. B. Z., Managerial Values Across Cultures: Australia, Hong Kong and the United States, *Asia Pacific Journal of Management*, 14, 1997, pp. 31–66.

SOME SPECIAL MANAGERIAL CONCERNS IN CONTEMPORARY INDIA

Contemporary Issues and Challenges

This section provides three illustrations of the current *shifts in managerial transitions* taking place in India. The first chapter here highlights the emergence of the service sector as a competitive niche for India in the recent years in addition to its overall implication for managers. Chapter Thirteen explores the slow but steady dilution of male domination of the senior managerial levels in India. Chapter Fourteen turns its attention to the special challenges facing the management of international joint ventures in India. These three examples of managerial challenges demonstrate three distinct areas where Indian management has recorded impressive transformations from very humble beginnings to global consolidation.

The chapter by Kapur and Ramamurti is an in-depth analysis of the knowledge intensive service sector. Not only is the back office service provision through outsourcing in sectors like software, biotechnology, pharmaceuticals or financial services, catapulting India into a high-tech nation, but so are some other emerging sectors. The authors also provide an interesting comparison with China. They highlight how the establishment of large R&D bases in India by a number of Chinese companies attest to the sophistication of the service sector in India and it is perhaps this area where urgent managerial inputs is required.

The chapter by Gupta et al. provides an empirical argument on the new opportunities of enriching the national managerial talent pool. The authors make a set of recommendations for enriching the gender diversity in large and dynamic Indian organisations. It is interesting to note the shift in gender diversity across Asia, particularly China where about 28 per cent of the entrepreneurial cadre consists of women. In contrast, Indian women managers are more highly trained and professionally oriented. As Lithgow observed,

> many Indian industrialists say that India, in many ways a functioning matriarchy, should capitalise on and invest in the special skills of its women. Ambani says in the Indian workplace, women bring patience, perseverance, the ability to work in a team and the much valued emotional intelligence (Lithgow, 2000, p. 116).

The chapter by Thakur and Srivastava reports a study of 22 US and 26 Indian organisations operating as alliance partners in India. Numerous gaps in the concepts and practices of joint venture management are raised for closer attention and research. The discussion presented in this chapter is an excellent platform for future researchers as the challenge of managing joint ventures is bound to become critical to India's emergence as a global power. The authors highlight the need for a greater understanding of the nature and scope of alliances from positioning, resource-pooling, competency-leveraging to learning alliances. Obviously, the value extraction of the partners is a dependent variable of the value created by the alliance. The value creation of international joint ventures on the other hand depends on the respective contributions, 'fit' in the areas of culture, capability and organisational dimensions. 'Capability fit' explores the complementarity, redundancies, gaps and opportunities. 'Culture fit' evaluates the divergences in national cultures of the partners, industry cultures and specific divergences of the administrative culture of the joint ventures. It is evident that Indian managers will be increasingly involved in cross-border alliances and therefore shedding of the old 'hierarchical mindset' and development of 'network mindset' is an unavoidable imperative.

Reference

Lithgow, L. (2000). *Special Blend: Fusion Management from Asia and the West*, Singapore, John Wiley and Sons, p. 116.

12 | India's Emerging Competitive Advantage in Services

Devesh Kapur and Ravi Ramamurti

The real treasure of India is its intellectual capital. The real opportunity of India is its incredibly skilled work force. Raw talent here is like nowhere else in the world.

—Jack Welch, CEO, General Electric[1]

India has not yet caught the fancy of foreign investors—even though its population exceeds one billion and its gross domestic product (GDP) of half a trillion dollars ranks it as the 11th largest economy in the world. In purchasing-power parity, India is the fourth largest economy, behind only the United States, China, and Japan. Yet India's integration into the world economy has been limited, as measured by such indicators as exports and foreign direct investment (FDI). (See Table 1.) But all this is about to change—not overnight, but through a slow revolution that will probably take another decade to run its full course.

Meanwhile, what can one glean from the changes under way about the sectors in which India is likely to be internationally competitive? And how can foreign firms take advantage of the emerging opportunities? Our conclusion is that India's competitiveness does not lie in the same fields as other low-income developing countries. Rather than enjoying competitiveness in natural resource industries or low-skill, labor-intensive manufacturing, India is revealing surprising strength in skill-intensive tradable services, including software development, information technology (IT)-enabled services, product/project engineering and design, biotechnology, Pharmaceuticals, media, entertainment, and healthcare.

New clusters are emerging in these activities in cities like Bangalore and Hyderabad, where vibrant Indian firms are being joined by well-known multinationals. One interesting example is General Electric (GE), which is investing $100 million in Bangalore to build its largest R&D lab in the world, employing 2,600 scientists, including more than 300 with Ph.D. degrees. It was while inaugurating this lab that GE's CEO Jack Welch made the remark quoted above.

Similar investments have been made in research and development centers by dozens of other well-known firms, including Lucent, Hewlett-Packard, IBM, Microsoft, Cisco, and Eli Lilly. Indian manufacturing is not showing similar dynamism, although in the medium run it may do so as India's physical infrastructure improves. However, in the short run, services will be the engine of India's export growth. In that regard, India's international competitiveness—and the corresponding opportunities for multinational corporations—will differ from those in high-performing Asian economies that have emerged as manufacturing powerhouses.

Table 1: India vs. Brazil and China

Indicator	India	Brazil	China
Population (millions)	998.0	168.0	1,250.0
GNP (US$ B) (rank), 1999	442.0 (11)	743.0 (8)	980.0 (7)
GNP at purchasing power parity (US$ B) (rank)	2,144.0 (4)	1,062.0 (9)	4,112.0 (2)
Exports, 1998 (US$ B)	44.7	58.2	207.8
FDI inflows, 1998 (US$ B)	2.6	31.9	43.7
Share of FDI flows to developing countries (%)	1.5	18.6	25.6
GDP growth rate, 1990–99 (%)	6.1	2.9	10.4
World competitiveness Scoreboard ranking, out of 47 countries, May 2000	43.0	34.0	31.0
Per capita income (US$)	450.0	4,420.0	780.0

Sources: World Bank 2001. *World Development Report,* New York: Oxford University Press; International Institute for Management Development (IMD), 2000. *The world competitiveness Scoreboard,* Lausanne, Switzerland: IMD.

We begin this article with a brief overview of the changing economic and political landscape of India and its implications for the business climate. Then, using Porter's "diamond of international competitiveness," we explain why clusters have begun to emerge in India in such tradable services as software. However, we relax Porter's requirement that all elements of the diamond be physically co-located. Instead, we argue that social networks, connecting India-based participants with U.S.-based customers, have created a virtual diamond, with some of the same advantages that co-location would have bestowed. We highlight the role of overseas Indians in building and sustaining the virtual diamond. We conclude by arguing that India's success in software services will spill over into other IT-based services, and, more generally, into knowledge-based services, such as design, engineering, and research in diverse industries and in education and healthcare. India is likely to emerge as the back office of global corporations in the short to medium term and as a leading provider of tradable services in the medium to long term.

India is likely to emerge as the back office of global corporations in the short to medium term and as a leading provider of tradable services in the medium to long term.

These conclusions have important implications for managers. Within this decade, India will probably figure in the global portfolio of leading multinationals, but firms that enter now will be in a better position to profit from the emerging opportunities than firms that wait longer. In manufacturing, the main opportunity for MNCs will be that of serving the large and growing domestic market, because in the near term India is unlikely to become an attractive platform for exports. But for service sector firms, and for the service activities of manufacturing firms, India is already emerging as an attractive location for global operations.

India's Role in the World Economy

From 1950 to the 1980s, India pursued import-substituting industrialization aimed at achieving economic self-reliance. In these decades, India's international trade shrank to as little as 8.5 percent of GDP. The economy grew at only 3.5 percent annually for three decades, and foreign direct investment was an anemic $300 million annually. Economic growth accelerated in the 1980s, following the onset of gradual economic reforms. Major reforms followed the balance of payments crisis of 1991. Since then, international trade has more than doubled in importance, FDI inflows increased 10-fold by 1998, to $3 billion annually, and the economic growth rate has been a robust 6.1 percent annually. Commenting on India's macroeconomic performance, the IMF in a 2001 report has argued that, "since the 1990s, India has been among the fastest growing economies in the world, inflation has been relatively well contained and the balance of payments has been maintained at comfortable levels."[2]

Nonetheless, despite these improvements, India's exports are only three-fourths those of Brazil and barely a fifth those of China. India's share of world trade is less than one-third of China's. And both Brazil and China receive FDI that is an order of magnitude greater than India's. Both countries also fare better than India in rankings such as IMD's World Competitiveness Scoreboard or A.T. Kearney's FDI Confidence Index, which is based on a survey of one thousand global companies.

Making too much of the backward-looking statistics in Table 1 is a mistake, however, because the economic and political changes underway in India are capable of changing those indicators significantly. Even surveys of senior managers of MNCs can be misleading to the extent that they might reflect a herd mentality rather than independent assessments. Looking more carefully at the circumstances in India reveals an improving climate for FDI and exports, especially in the field of services.

Political Environment: Complexity and Bright Spots

Indian politics is cacophonous and fractious, playing itself out in one of the most socially heterogeneous societies in the world, with sharp social inequities, a corrupt and inefficient bureaucracy, and poor accountability of political actors. India's material resources are relatively modest and its poverty levels are quite high, although income inequalities are much lower than Latin America or even China.

Accentuating these problems is political instability in New Delhi, resulting from the multiplicity of regional parties and the necessity of forming coalition governments to cobble together a majority in parliament. As a result, there have been four general elections and six prime ministers in the last decade. In such an environment, economic reforms have been predictably slow and uneven. Although the Vajpayee government that came to power in 1999 was more stable than the three before it, it was still a coalition government of 24 disparate parties with differing agendas, and was considerably weakened by an arms scandal in March 2001.

But the headline-grabbing manifestations of political instability mask a deeper systemic stability, anchored by deep-rooted, democratic institutions. An array of powerful and independent institutions, ranging from the judiciary, the election commission, and the media, have all ensured that the Indian system has multiple veto points that slow decision making but underpin its systemic resilience. Multiparty coalitions at the center have resulted in unstable governments at the central level, but have also contributed to strengthening India's federalism. Another stabilizing factor has been that, unlike many other low-income countries, India's military has been apolitical and very much under the thumb of its civilian leadership. Finally, India's relations with Western nations, particularly the United States, have become much warmer, despite the strains cast by India's 1998 nuclear tests. U.S.-India relations were bolstered by reciprocal visits by the leaders of the two countries in 2000. An important lubricant greasing this relationship is the growing economic clout of the people of Indian origin in the United States.

Multiparty coalitions at the center have resulted in unstable governments at the central level, but have also contributed to strengthening India's federalism.

Economic Environment: Achievements and Challenges Ahead

On the economic front, the good news is that in the last decade India has opened up greatly to private participation and global competition. Tariffs have come down from an average of 100 percent or more to 30 percent, with commitments to the World Trade Organization (WTO) for further reductions. Most forms of import or industrial licensing have gone. FDI is automatic, and 100-percent foreign ownership is permitted in many sectors, including software. The rupee has been made freely convertible on the current account. Corporate income taxes have been reduced to 45 percent. Foreign portfolio investment and venture-capital financing have been encouraged. Many other structural reforms, requiring new legislation, were underway in 2001. As Finance Minister Sinha notes in his interview in this issue, these second-generation reforms are harder to push through than those undertaken in the 1990s. Implementation is slowed by the need to work in a democratic framework, by coalition politics in Delhi, and rivalries between parties in power at the center and in the states.

Yet in both Delhi and the state capitals, economic growth and effective governance are becoming more important concerns of politicians in power. The country's 10th five-year plan aims for 9-percent annual growth, which, if achieved, would see India growing faster than China. We believe that sustained annual growth of 7 to 8 percent by the end of this decade is quite realistic, with still faster growth possible thereafter—if painful reforms, such as privatization, cuts in public spending, and re-direction of government expenditures towards developing human and physical capital, are implemented. To be sure, even with these reforms, India's poor physical infrastructure—from ports and internal transportation to power and water—and its bureaucracy will continue to pose challenges for business. However, with current growth projections, India's GDP should double by 2010 to about $900 billion, and growth itself is likely to ease some of these bottlenecks.

Expect Gradual Reforms

These features of the Indian situation have several implications for investors. First, periodic short-term governmental instability will remain, but like Italy of the not-so-distant past, this will affect the pace of policy reform rather than the trend. A silver lining has been that the different parties rotating through power in Delhi have all signed off on opening up India to greater internal and external competition. Consequently, political rhetoric notwithstanding, economic reforms had more broad-based support in 2001 than at any time in the past.

Second, India's growth has been one of the least volatile among developing countries. Because India's external accounts have been managed cautiously and prudently, its foreign-debt-to-GDP ratio and debt-service ratios have been low and declining, and it has escaped damage from international events like the Asian financial crisis.

Third, a more robust federalism has meant there is increasing variance in strategies and policies at the subnational level, with states increasingly competing with one other to attract investment. With the central government having considerably liberalized its policies towards foreign investment, an understanding of the considerable differences in business environments among Indian states is becoming more important for private investors. As in China, coastal states have been the locomotive of India's expanding economy.

India's Success in Software

India has received much attention recently on the prowess of its software industry, prompting Bill Gates to proclaim that "India is likely to be the next software superpower." How has a country whose economic achievements were otherwise modest, managed to develop a reputation for excellence in this rapidly growing high-tech sector? Before answering that question, India's accomplishments in software need highlighting.[3]

For the better part of a decade, India's software industry has been growing at 50 percent annually. By 2000, the software sector's output had grown to $8 billion and exports had risen to $6.2 billion. More than 800 firms, located in cities like Bangalore, Hyderabad, Pune, Chennai, and New Delhi, provided a range of software services, mostly targeted at foreign customers. The United States accounted for nearly 60 percent of Indian software exports, followed by Europe with 23.5 percent, and Japan with just 3.5 percent.

> For the better part of a decade, India's software industry has been growing at 50 percent annually.

India's software industry grew out of the pioneering efforts of companies like Tata Consultancy Services (TCS), in the aftermath of IBM's departure from India in 1977 over policy differences with the government. These firms undertook small projects overseas for multinational firms, and slowly climbed up the value chain as their reputations were established. Although low-end work, such as maintenance of legacy systems or projects associated with the Y2K millennium bug and euro conversion, accounted for about 20 percent of export revenues in 2000, the Indian industry has moved up the technology ladder over time. One indicator of that shift is that more than half of the software development centers in the world with Carnegie Mellon University's CMM Level-5 rating are located in India. The first company in the world to obtain this distinction was an Indian company, Wipro, and companies like Citicorp, GE, Honeywell, IBM, and Motorola had their only CMM-certified operations in India rather than the U.S.[5] By 2000, more than 200 of the *Fortune* 1000 companies were outsourcing their software requirements to Indian software houses,[6] and in software services "made in India" was becoming a sign of quality, according to an MIT expert.[7] By 1999, 41 percent of software services were provided in India rather than on-site at the client's location, compared with only five percent in 1990, indicating a growing confidence in India-based service provision. Indian software companies also became the darlings of the stock market, accounting for seven of Asia's top-20 growth stocks, according to *Asiaweek*.[8]

Two recent analyses of India's IT industry underline the country's potential. A study by Goldman Sachs in 2000 projected that India would capture five percent, or $30 billion, of the $585 billion of the IT services market by 2004, up from just 1.6 percent in 1999. Another study by McKinsey & Company projects the Indian software and services industry's output to rise to $87 billion in 2008, of which $50 billion would be exported.[9] Two-thirds of the increase is projected to come from new growth opportunities in IT-enabled services, such as call-center operations, transcription, and design and engineering services. The number of Indian software companies listed on the stock exchange in 2008 is projected to quadruple to 400, with a combined market capitalization of $225 billion. By then, software and IT-related services are expected to employ 2.2 million people. However, as in the past, McKinsey expects Indian firms to account for most of the future growth: only $5 billion in FDI is anticipated to achieve the 2008 projections for IT-sector output and exports. Fueling new-business formation in 2000 were more than 50 venture-capital firms, compared with only half a dozen in 1998. The dot-com bust in the U.S. will not affect the Indian IT sector's growth, which relies mostly on the outsourcing of existing activities rather than on future growth of e-commerce. Even if McKinsey's growth projections for 2008 are met, India's share of the U.S. software market will be only 4.1 percent, although Field observes that "India enjoys first-to-market advantage and owns anywhere from 80 percent to 95 percent of the U.S. offshore market [for software services]."[10]

Why is India Competitive in Software?

India has done well in software because that industry makes intensive use of resources in which India enjoys international competitive advantage, while making less intensive use of resources in which India is at a comparative disadvantage. Figure 1, drawing on Porter, depicts India's diamond of competitive advantage in this sector.[11]

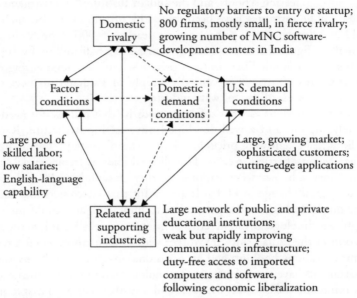

Figure 1: India's Virtual Diamond in Software

Domestic rivalry — No regulatory barriers to entry or startup; 800 firms, mostly small, in fierce rivalry; growing number of MNC software-development centers in India

Factor conditions

Domestic demand conditions

U.S. demand conditions

Large pool of skilled labor; low salaries; English-language capability

Large, growing market; sophisticated customers; cutting-edge applications

Related and supporting industries — Large network of public and private educational institutions; weak but rapidly improving communications infrastructure; duty-free access to imported computers and software, following economic liberalization

Note: Dashed lines represent weaker interactions.

Software makes intensive use of human capital, and India has several advantages in this regard. India produces the second largest annual output of scientists and engineers in the world, behind only the United States. This labor pool is relatively cheap. Even with the rapid growth of the last few years, an Indian software engineer costs one-half to one-fourth that of an American software engineer. The English-language capability of Indian graduates facilitates interaction and collaboration with programmers in the United States or Europe. In this respect, Indian graduates enjoy a decisive advantage over their Chinese counterparts, who are otherwise nearly as numerous and cost competitive as Indian programmers.

A large and sophisticated network of educational institutes supplies the human capital required by the software industry. The Indian Institutes of Technology, which admit one student for every 100 applicants, churn out first-rate graduates, who today are sought out by firms from all over the world. Many of its graduates migrated to the United States for higher education and jobs and form part of the social network that nurtures the Indian software industry. Other institutions include the Indian Institutes of Information Technology, the Indian Institute of Science, a network of regional engineering schools, and the Indian Institutes of Management. These public institutes have been joined by private institutes, such as NIIT and Aptech, that together produce nearly 100,000 IT professionals annually, a figure that is projected to increase to a half-million by 2006. Thanks to economic liberalization, private schools are augmenting the government's efforts to expand the supply of students to meet the anticipated needs of the software industry.

Just as important as what software needs is what is does not need— namely capital, and a well-developed physical infrastructure. Rapid declines in IT hardware prices and import tariffs in the 1990s sharply lowered capital barriers to entry. This allowed a new entrepreneurial class to commence bootstrap operations and then to rapidly scale up. Rapid technological change in IT hardware meant that latecomers like India were not locked into older-generation technologies, and could instead leapfrog technologies. And in terms of infrastructure, all that is necessary to connect the Indian software worker with foreign customers is a tele-communications hook-up and an occasional overseas trip. Many state governments have created software technology parks in which the necessary infrastructure is readily available and is vastly superior to that found elsewhere in the country. Notable examples include Bangalore's Electronic City and Hyderabad's HITEC City, which offer not only office space and communications links, but housing and other social amenities, as well.

Rapid technological change in IT hardware meant that latecomers like India were not locked into older-generation technologies, and could instead leapfrog technologies.

Improving telecommunications links and airtransport services has been much easier than upgrading India's roads, ports, power supply, and rail transportation—all of which are necessary to boost Indian manufactured exports. Ghemawat and Patibandla note that Indian garment exports are hampered by the lack of high quality local suppliers, and the inability to respond quickly to foreign customers.[12] The other leading goods export sector, gems and jewelry, seems also to have hit a plateau, with limited prospects for rapid growth. The Indian government has begun only recently to create special economic zones, similar to those in China, that lie outside the country's customs territory and enjoy full flexibility of operations. That is why we expect tradable services like software, rather than manufactured goods, to be the engine of India's export growth in the coming decade.

The third node of Porter's diamond—rivalry— has been strong in the Indian software industry, possibly because the industry was not subject to industrial licensing by the central government, and by and large the India government's policies have been facilitative, at least relative to other sectors. Although firms like TCS, Infosys, and Wipro have become large, they were quite small only five years ago, and aspiring to catch up with them are dozens of small and mid-sized companies. New venture formation is fueled by overseas Indians, who return to start new companies, supply venture capital, or act as angel investors. It is also fueled by the many state governments that have attempted to replicate Bangalore and Hyderabad's success in software by creating their own software-technology parks. Recognizing the possibility that more Indian firms will want to list on foreign stock exchanges, Nasdaq has opened only its third foreign office, in Bangalore.

However, Porter's diamond model does not readily explain India's software success in terms of demand conditions—if one takes that to mean domestic demand, which is not nearly as large or sophisticated as overseas demand.[13] Although many Indian software firms cut their teeth in the domestic market after IBM left India, their success today comes from serving foreign customers, especially in the U.S. To understand how the Indian software could become internationally competitive despite being 12,000 miles away from Silicon Valley, one must recognize the unique features of software that make co-connection a good enough alternative to co-location, and the many bridging mechanisms that link supply and demand.[14]

The Virtual Diamond: Linking Indian Supply with U.S. Demand[15]

One key difference between software and the industries that Porter studied is that software can be digitized and therefore moved back and forth between different locations instantaneously through telecommunication links.

In manufacturing industries, on the other hand, physical co-location is necessary for similar hand-offs between firms in the value chain. Given the ease of moving software work-in-process, physical distance has turned into a time-zone advantage for Indian firms, allowing for 24-hour development by teams in India and the U.S.—an advantage unavailable with co-location.

> Given the ease of moving software work-in-process, physical distance has turned into a time-zone advantage for Indian firms, allowing for 24-hour development by teams in India and the U.S.—an advantage unavailable with co-location.

But physical co-location also promises other advantages, such as face-to-face interaction between firms, suppliers, and customers that can spur innovation. How can India-based organizations be competitive if they don't enjoy those advantages? The answer is that some of the work done in India is not at the cutting edge and can therefore be uncoupled from U.S. activities; examples include software maintenance or the upgrading of legacy systems. In such cases, occasional visits by Indian programmers to the United States and by U.S. customers to India may suffice. As Azim Premji, chairman of Wipro, explains in his interview in this issue, Indian software firms internationalized by initially seeking low-skill work in the United States. Indian programmers visited the U.S. for several weeks or months to carry out these assignments at the customers' premises—what is known in the industry as body shopping. This strategy was then mimicked by other Indian firms and by overseas Indians, who started their own body-shopping outfits in the U.S., staffed with Indian programmers. An important benefit was that this led to rapid skill upgrading through learning-by-doing in the most sophisticated IT market in the world.

As the reputation of these software service organizations grew, more and more of the actual work was done in India, to take advantage of lower costs there. Simultaneously, as Indian firms gained experience and software salaries rose in India, they moved up the value chain to more technically complex assignments. Several mechanisms emerged to bridge the physical distance between Indian suppliers and U.S. customers, so that the necessary supplier-customer interactions could take place.

One important mechanism was the social network connecting people of Indian origin in the U.S., often working in Silicon Valley, with engineers and managers in India. Indian technology professionals working in the U.S., who had upgraded their skills through learning-by-doing, sometimes returned to India, while others circulated between the two countries, thereby diffusing technology and skills. More than 40 percent of the HI-B visa petitions approved recently in the U.S. have been for nationals from India, with China and Canada a distant second and third, respectively. This is enhancing both the network effects of the Indian IT sector and the human capital of this segment of the workforce. Just as Korea climbed up the technological ladder by importing capital equipment of recent vintage, which embodied frontier technologies, India has moved up the software ladder by importing human capital, in the form of U.S.-trained Indians. Another bridging mechanism was American companies that opened software centers in India to strengthen interaction between their organizations and Indian suppliers or to do development work in wholly owned R&D subsidiaries. By 2001, that list included Cisco, Hewlett-Packard, IBM, Lucent, Microsoft, Motorola, Oracle, and Sun Microsystems. At the same time, Indian software firms like Infosys and Wipro opened offices in the U.S., or acquired U.S. companies, to better serve their clients on high-end projects and to have listening posts in Silicon Valley. To facilitate this process, the government made it easier for Indian firms to raise capital abroad and to make foreign acquisitions. Thus physical distance was bridged by the strengthening of cross-national, intrafirm networks and by interfirm social networks among Indians and overseas Indians. The head of the U.S. firm's software development center in India was often an American of Indian origin, as was the head of the U.S. subsidiary of an Indian software company. Overseas Indians helped enrich and cement the ties between India-based supply and U.S.-based demand.

Geographic Spillover

Even as India's software industry migrated upwards to higher value-adding activities, its target markets broadened beyond the United States and its success spilled over into other knowledge-based services. (See Figure 2)

Figure 2: Competitiveness Building: From Low-End to High-End Software, to Other Knowledge-Based Services

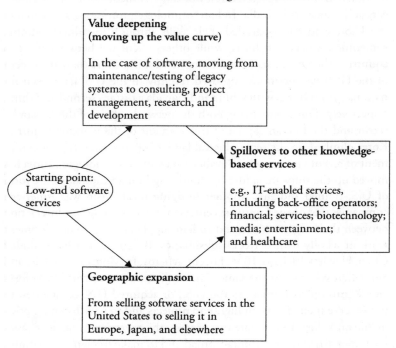

Value deepening (moving up the value curve)

In the case of software, moving from maintenance/testing of legacy systems to consulting, project management, research, and development

Starting point: Low-end software services

Spillovers to other knowledge-based services

e.g., IT-enabled services, including back-office operators; financial; services; biotechnology; media; entertainment; and healthcare

Geographic expansion

From selling software services in the United States to selling it in Europe, Japan, and elsewhere

The geographic spillover occurred because of positive brand-name externalities—that is, because "made in India" became a signal of quality in software, just as "made in Japan" is a signal of quality in consumer electronics. As a result, more countries began to court Indian IT talent and outsource software development to Indian firms. Among these are countries like the United Kingdom, where Indian emigration had slowed to a trickle, and countries like Finland, France, Germany, Ireland, Japan, New Zealand, and South Korea, where Indian emigration was small to begin with. Indian IT experts accounted for 20 percent of the green cards issued by Germany for non-EU computer specialists in 2000.[16] Singapore has set a goal of attracting 250,000 Indian IT professionals over a five-year period.[17] Leaders of these countries, as well as of Britain, France, Japan, and China, made official trips to India in 2000 that invariably included a half-day visit to a software cluster and initiatives to strengthen ties with India in the IT sector. Within software and IT-based services, a virtuous cycle has been set in motion, with success in the U.S. leading to a global expansion of demand for Indian IT experts and a corresponding expansion of the social network of overseas Indians.

Spillover into Other Knowledge-Based Services

India's success in software is spilling over into success in other knowledge-based services for several reasons. Software success has enhanced India's reputation and credibility as a provider of skilled services, given that software is seen as a sunrise, high-technology sector rather than a mature, low-technology sector. It is no longer improbable for MNCs to consider India a location for such services.

Other knowledge-based services leverage many of the same strengths India enjoys in software—namely, access to a large pool of skilled, inexpensive, English-speaking talent, except that these sectors require doctors, scientists, chartered accountants, consultants, or mathematicians, rather than programmers. As in the case of software, public educational and research institutes nurture talent in these fields too, and increasingly they will be supplemented by private institutions as demand grows.

Software and IT are general-purpose technologies with economy-wide applications: capabilities built up in software can be leveraged in other high-technology fields such as bioinformatics, Pharmaceuticals, media, and entertainment.[18]

Indian professionals are well represented in the United States, not just in software and Silicon Valley but also in other high value-added services, such as education, management consulting, technical consulting, medicine, and finance. Some of them have also reached the upper rungs of management in *Fortune* 500 companies, such as Arthur Andersen, Citigroup, Computer Associates, McKinsey, PepsiCo, United Airlines, and US Airways. These factors may increase the propensity of these companies to do business in, and with, India.

Finally, Indian-Americans have also become more active in promoting startups in the U.S. and elsewhere. The IndUS Entrepreneur (TIE), founded in 1992, is a network of Indian entrepreneurs and professionals with 25 chapters, including five in India, several in the U.S., and one each in countries like Singapore, Switzerland, and the United Kingdom.[19] At TIE's core is a group of angel investors, who got rich by starting companies in the U.S., and have been recycling their wealth as venture capitalists in the U.S. and in India. While most of their wealth goes to U.S. companies, they are also funneling funds into a new generation of start-ups in India, as well as into hybrid companies and investment funds that operate in both India and the U.S.[20]

For all these reasons, India has begun to attract foreign contracts and investments in other knowledge-based industries, which, while modest in FDI terms, have significant economic effects in the long term. In a sign of things to come, between 1990–91 and 1998–99, India's foreign exchange earnings from inward remittances and service exports grew more than twice as fast as the exports of manufactured goods.[21] By 2000, India's exports of services exceeded the total exports of her two leading manufactured goods—textiles/garments and gems/jewelry.

Emerging Services

One set of emerging activities leverages the IT revolution to provide such lower-skill services as call-center operations and medical transcription. An example is GE Capital's call-center operation, which grew from two employees in 1997 to a $30 million business in 2000, employing 2,500 people who examined medical claims, car-loan applications, and credit-card debt.[22] Another example is accounting services, whose exports are projected to grow rapidly within a few years. Towards that goal, the association of Indian public accountants is negotiating mutual recognition agreements that would allow Indian accountants to provide bookkeeping services for companies in the European Union and the United States. The first such agreement was signed with Italy in March 2001.[23]

A more advanced knowledge-based service is doing design and engineering work for industrial and construction projects. The Indian firm, Satyam Computer, has formed a strategic alliance with TRW to provide a range of IT-related and engineering services for automotive applications. Even more advanced work is planned in GE's R&D lab in such areas as basic chemistry, polymer science, mechanical engineering, ceramics, and metallurgy. Other foreign investors with similar aims include Ford, AOL Time Warner, and Advanced Micro Devices.

Another area holding enormous potential is biotechnology and pharmaceuticals. Indian firms, such as Dr. Reddy's Lab, Ranbaxy, and Shanta Biotech, have developed new molecules and drugs, sometimes funded by MNCs like Bayer, Unilever, and Pfizer. Hoping to replicate the success in software, the Karnataka government is setting up a Biotech City and an Institute of Bioinformatics and Applied Biotechnology. Not surprisingly, the government's strategy replicates many elements of the strategy that worked in software services. A neighboring state, Tamil Nadu, announced in January 2001 plans to set up its own biotechnology research center in collaboration with Cornell University, well-known for life-science, agricultural, veterinarian, and healthcare research. For its part, the central government has extended a 10-year tax holiday for research and development companies on their royalty income and fees, and has created a new Department of Biotechnology.

India is also becoming an attractive site for conducting clinical trials of new drugs—a procedure that makes up one-third of the cost of introducing a new drug. Not only are Indian technicians cheap, but the country's large and heterogeneous population is an advantage, as is the sad fact that its people suffer from numerous ailments. With improvements in the institutional and regulatory infrastructure for trials and pharmaceutical research, India's exports of services in this sector should grow.[24] In a sign of things to come, by 2001, Quintiles Transnational and Covance, two leading U.S. contract-research organizations, had started operations in India. Eli Lilly and AstraZeneca had bought out their Indian joint venture partners, and the latter was planning a "super-duper research center," according to one of its executives.[25] Pfizer was doing biometrics in its Indian facility, Novo Nordisk was testing two new diabetes drugs, and GlaxoSmithKline was sourcing components for its ulcer, hepatitis B, asthma, and AIDS drugs in India. To encourage knowledge-based investments of this sort, the Indian government is rapidly becoming much more receptive to the idea of protecting intellectual property (IP). Leading the crusade for tougher IP laws and enforcement is Nasscom, the Indian association of software and service companies.

India is also becoming an attractive site for conducting clinical trials of new drugs—a procedure that makes up one-third of the cost of introducing a new drug.

Finally, India has vast potential in media and entertainment as well. Apart from the technical synergy between software and media—for instance, in producing animation—India enjoys a home-market advantage in this sector, as the world's largest producer of movies (ahead of Hollywood, with 800 titles annually). It also has a very large installed base of subscribers to cable TV, through which 60 channels of entertainment are available, a lot of it local fare. Given the large population of overseas Indians, foreign distribution rights alone have become sufficient to cover the cost of making movies. Recognizing this potential, Sony Entertainment recently announced plans to invest $250 million in India over the next three years, developing two new TV channels, and getting into film production and distribution. To leverage India's resources in export markets, the Andhra Pradesh government has created Film City, a studio complex with advanced filming and editing facilities.[26] Arthur Andersen predicts that by 2006, Indian exports of movies will reach $3 billion annually.

Spillover Effects on Indian Business Climate

India's success in IT has had positive spillover effects on the general business climate in India. For one thing, it has helped unleash entrepreneurship in a country whose cultural and bureaucratic ethos was long regarded as inimical to capitalism. It has boosted the confidence of the younger generation that they could make good money in India, and ethically too. Success in software and IT has blunted domestic political opposition to India's integration with the world economy. Equally important, the IT sector has affected Indian capitalism, because the corporate culture and business practices of India's IT firms are vastly superior to those of India's traditional business houses, which honed their business practices in a closed, state-dominated system. Indian IT firms have been at the forefront of improving corporate governance.[27] India's high-technology firms have also been at the forefront of corporate philanthropy, particularly in education and civic improvement, through innovative public-private partnerships. Furthermore, the IT revolution has substantially enlarged India's entrepreneurial pool, bringing new social groups, particularly from South India, into the business mainstream.

India vs. China

We conclude with comparisons between India and the other large Asian country, China, whose GDP growth, exports, and inward FDI have all been much higher than India's. Economic reforms began in earnest in India about a decade after they did in China. Therefore, India's perform-ance improvement can be expected to lag China's by at least a decade. The surge in China's inward FDI occurred several years after the surge in the 1980s in China's annual growth rate to 10 percent. The implication is that in India, too, the surge in FDI is likely to occur after her growth rate rises to 8 to 10 percent in this decade. The institutional foundations of India's capitalism—be it the legal system, accounting practices, working language (English), or the democratic context—are more compatible with those in the United States than are China's foundations, because of the common British legacy in India and the U.S. Nonetheless, the annual FDI inflow into India is unlikely to exceed $10 billion, compared with $40–50 billion in China. To understand why, one must recognize another important difference between the two countries, namely, the differing contributions of overseas Chinese and overseas Indians to their respective home country's development.[28] (See Table 2.)

Overseas Chinese—the so-called Chinese diaspora—are about 50 mil-lion, but concentrated in countries close to China, with Hong Kong and Taiwan accounting for more than half.[29] The Indian diaspora is smaller, at 15–20 million, and more widely dispersed in far-flung regions, such as the Middle East, the U.K., and North America. More importantly, the Chinese diaspora is wealthier than the Indian diaspora, and accounted for up to 80 percent of China's FDI inflows in the 1980s.[30] Overseas Indians have not been as affluent: in places like the Middle East, they hold relatively low-skilled jobs and hence have modest incomes; and even though in North America they hold high-skilled and professional jobs, only a few have achieved high net-worth positions, and that only recently. In contrast, the Chinese diaspora is entrepreneurial and quite affluent everywhere. For these reasons, FDI into China by the affluent Chinese diaspora has been 20-fold that by overseas Indians into India. In contrast, remittances by the Indian diaspora have been seven times that of the Chinese diaspora ($49.8 billion and $7.6 billion, respectively, between 1991–1998). Furthermore, Indians in the U.S. are mostly profes-sionals, while overseas Chinese are manufacturers, traders, and exporters. Therefore, overseas Chinese have helped China boost its exports of manu-factured goods, especially labor-intensive products, while overseas Indians have helped India boost its exports of knowledge-based services. In both cases, though, overseas nationals have played key roles in information, reputation building, technology transfer, and capital supply.

Table 2: Overseas Chinese vs. Overseas Indians

Characteristic	Overseas Chinese	Overseas Indians
Number and location	50 million (including Hong Kong), concentrated in countries close to China, such as Taiwan, Singapore, Indonesia, Thailand, Malaysia	15–20 million, dispersed across Southeast Asia, Middle East, North America, United Kingdom, Australia
Assets	High net-worth individuals Manufacturing and distribution networks in Asia Contacts and reputation in rich-country export markets	Low-skill guest workers with modest incomes and savings, partly remitted home (e.g. in the Middle East) Salaried professionals in North America, positioned in high-tech companies, universities, consulting, and financial services—the "knowledge diaspora" Senior positions in *Fortune* 500 companies Only a few high net-worth individuals, but with more likely in the future
Competencies	Entrepreneurship Light manufacturing Trading Export marketing	Technical know-how Knowledge-based services High-tech startups Venture financing

Implications for Managers

India is undergoing a slow but steady revolution whose significance may not yet be readily apparent to foreign investors. Statistics on India's exports or inward FDI are still unimpressive compared to other large Asian countries like China. But significant changes are underway beneath the surface that have reduced political risk for investors, by strengthening democratic processes and institutions, and by creating a multiparty consensus on economic liberalization. They have resulted in greater decentralization to the states and fostered competition among them for private investment. And they have begun to lift the heavy hand of government in economic matters, boosting the growth rate to 6 to 7 percent annually, with 8 to 10 percent growth likely within a decade. Other promising trends include the growth of software exports through the 1990s at 50 percent or more annually and signs that this boom will not only continue in the 2000s but spread to other knowledge-based industries. Aiding this transformation process at critical stages has been the overseas Indian community.

Recruit Indian Talent

How should foreign firms and managers take advantage of these developments in India? In the short run, a few safe opportunities present themselves. For starters, foreign firms can tap into India's well-educated, inexpensive, English-speaking manpower, as consulting companies like BCG and McKinsey or financial services firms like Citigroup have done. In the past, Indian manpower went abroad searching for jobs or training; today foreign companies go to India to recruit talent, be it at the Indian Institutes of Management, the Indian Institutes of Technology, or from their Indian subsidiaries (e.g., Citibank, Proctor & Gamble, and Unilever).

Outsource Back-office Services

Another relatively low-risk option is to move less critical steps of the value chain to India, such as back-office services like accounting, payroll, or benefits administration. Potential cost savings are estimated at more than 50 percent of the cost of providing these same services in the U.S. Firms can set up their own operations in India, as GE Capital has done, or outsource the work to Indian companies. Similarly, customer interaction services, such as call-center operations, can and are being relocated to India.

Relocate High-skill Services

Although moving higher value-added services to India, such as design and engineering services, education services, or R&D (as many well-known software companies have already done) may appear riskier, we believe that India has a comparative advantage in all such activities that make intensive use of human rather than physical capital. Similar opportunities wait to be exploited in biotechnology, financial services, media, and entertainment. The FDI associated with these ventures is low—which means the financial risks are low—but the potential payoff to the foreign investor are substantial, as are the gains to India by way of high-paying jobs and foreign exchange earnings. It is becoming easier by the day to create such operations in India, because of the incentives and help that state governments are extending to foreign investors. Overseas Indians, who now number nearly two million in the U.S. alone, can help launch such operations or help locate reliable Indian suppliers.

Proceed Cautiously with Manufacturing

We have focused on opportunities to move service stages of the value chain to India because India is much less attractive as a location for manufacturing operations. That may change, once Special Economic Zones become functional or the bottlenecks in India's physical infra-structure are removed. Until then, manufacturing FDI should mostly be targeted at serving the Indian market. However, we think it ill-advised for firms to wait until India's economic growth rate rises high enough to catch the attention of the average manager. Because of the complexity of doing business in India, and the fierce nature of local competitors, there will be several bumps along the way for foreign investors.[31] It is also im-portant that foreign investors make those investments in the states that are most business-friendly, such as Andhra Pradesh, Gujarat, Karnataka, Maharashtra, or Tamil Nadu. Having thus established a toehold in India, larger manufacturing investments may merit consideration. In the short run, though, the most promising opportunities for foreign investors will lie in knowledge-based services.

Endnotes

1. GE research lab in Bangalore will be our largest soon—Jack Welch. *The Financial Express*, 17 September 2000, *www.financialexpress.com/fe/daily/20000917/feo17037.html.*
2. Callen, T., Reynolds, P., & Christopher, T. (Eds.), 2001. *India at the crossroads—Sustaining growth and reducing poverty.* Washington, DC: International Monetary Fund, February.
3. For one overview, see Moitra, D. 2001. Country report: India's software industry. *IEEE Software,* February 27, 2001, as seen at *http://computer.org/software/homepage/2001/moitra.htm.*

4. Kennedy, R. E. 2000. *Tata Consultancy Services: High technology in* a low-income country. Boston: Harvard Business School Publishing, Case No. 9-700-092.
5. Ghemawat, P. 1999. *The Indian software industry at the millennium.* Boston: Harvard Business School Publishing, Case No. 9700036.
6. According to Web site of the National Association of Software and Services Companies (NASSCOM), February 2001, *www.nasscom.org.*
7. Cusumano, M. "Made in India" a new sign of software quality. *Computerworld,* March 2000.
8. Ghemawat, op. cit., 7.
9. McKinsey & Company. 1999. *NASSCOM McKinsey study: Indian IT. strategies.* New Delhi: NASSCOM.
10. Field, T. India unbound. *CIO: The magazine for information executives.* Special field report on India. 1 December 2000, 176.
11. Porter, M. E. 1990. *The competitive advantage of nations.* New York: The Free Press; and Porter, M. E. 1998. Clusters and the new economics of competition. *Harvard Business Review,* November–December 1998: 77–90.
12. Ghemawat, P. & Patibandla, M. 1999. India's exports since the reforms: Three analytical industry studies. In J. Sachs, A. Varshney, & N. Bajpai, (Eds.), *India in the era of economic reforms.* New Delhi: Oxford University Press, 185–221.
13. Ibid.
14. The term "co-connection" was suggested by K. R. Paramesvar.
15. We borrow the term "virtual diamond" from Don Lessard of MIT, who, to the best of our knowledge, first used this term in his informal teaching notes to explain the success of Acer Computers in the personal computer business.
16. Indian IT experts account for 20 percent in Germany. *The Economic Times (Bombay),* 22 March 2001, as reported in *www.economictimes.com/today/in08.htm.*
17. Singapore to outsource 250,000 IT professionals from India. *BroadcastIndia.* 1 November 2000, as reported in *www.broadcastindia.com/techpart/showstory.asp?strid=4329.*
18. Helpman, E., (Ed.), 1998. *General purpose technologies and economic growth.* Cambridge, MA: MIT Press.
19. In May 2000, Fortune magazine estimated that the combined market value of Indian-run firms in Silicon Valley was $235 billion. See The Indians of Silicon Valley. *Fortune,* 15 May 2000.
20. Clark, D. South Asian "angels" reap riches, spread wealth in Silicon Valley. *Wall Street Journal,* 2 May 2000, B1.
21. In this period, manufactured exports grew at 8.0 percent annually, compared with 11.5 percent in the two-decade period before that. On the other hand, remittances and export of "other services" grew at 17.5 percent annually. Details in Kapur, D. & Ramamurti, R. 2001. The Indian economy in transition. Working paper, March 2001, 25.
22. Field, op. cit.

23. ICAI in talks with A/C bodies of Italy, Turkey, Israel. *Economic Times.* 21 March 2001. *http://216.34.146.167.8000/servlet/form.*
24. Clinical trials in India: Patient capital. *The Economist*, 29 January 2000, 77–78.
25. India braces for brave new drug world. *Wall Street Journal*, 7 March 2001, A17.
26. India's film industry: Growing up. *The Economist*, 12 August 2000, 57–58.
27. They are also becoming more focused—corporate M&A in India totaled more than $9 billion in 2000.
28. See Kapur, D. 2001. Diasporas and technology transfer. Background paper prepared for Human Development Report.
29. Weidenbaum, M. & Hughes, S. 1996. *The bamboo network: How expatriate Chinese entrepreneurs are creating a new economic superpower in Asia.* New York: The Free Press.
30. Based on data in Guha, A. & Ray, A. S. 2000. Multinational versus expatriate FDI: A comparative analysis of the Chinese and Indian experience. New Delhi: Indian Council for Research on International Economic Relations, Working Paper No. 58.
31. United States Foreign Commercial Service and U.S. Department of State. 2000. *Country commercial guide: India 2000.* Washington D.C.: National Trade Data Bank.

13 Women Managers in India: Challenges and Opportunities

Ashok Gupta, Manjulika Koshal and Rajindar K. Koshal

Introduction and Purpose

A plethora of popular books on women managers have flooded the academic market. However, it was not until 1970's that a few corporations and legislatures started addressing the issues of women managers seriously. Since then, a gender revolution has been sweeping the corporate organizational structure and women have joined the workforce in unprecedented numbers. Women represent more than 40 percent of the world's labor force and half the world's population (40, p. 6). Governments, enterprises and organizations have over years committed themselves to policies and programs to advance women (40, p. 7). Women make up 31 percent of the official labor force in developing countries and 46.7 percent worldwide (37). Also, rural women produce more than 55 percent of all food grown in developing countries (36). History shows that women have also proved to be successful managers and owners of businesses. In 1996, women held 35.1 percent of professional posts in the United Nations Secretariat including 17.9 percent in the senior management.

In the U.S.A., between 1987 to 1996, there was a 78 percent increase in companies owned by women (8). In fact, American women now own one-third of all U.S. Businesses that employ about 26 percent of the nation's workforce (39). Also sales in these businesses jumped 236 percent in nine years (1988–1996). According to another study, women-owned businesses in America continue to create more jobs than the Fortune

500 U.S. firms worldwide. This is a tremendous achievement (39). This data strongly document that women-owned businesses are an increasing potent economic force. The success stories of professional and business-women are not only concentrated to U.S.A., it is a world trend. In India, there is a new group of self-employed women who own and run their business very profitably and with remarkable elegance. The Self-employed Women's Association (SEWA) Bank of India makes loans to "questionable risks" and it has ninety-six percent repayment rate. In Malaysia, the new generation of businesswomen is very much a reality.

There is no question that compared to the earlier decade, women today are better educated and hold more jobs worldwide. Companies and enterprises have started to recognize the unique characteristics, attitudes, behaviors, and management style, that women bring to the professional world and which is different than that of men. Few companies have started debates on more, "flexible managerial styles approaches with a view to maximizing human resource utilization." The catch phrase of modern management gurus is "why can't a man be more like a woman?" (40). In a new book just out from the Penn State University Press, management gurus claim to be revaluing feminine "soft skills" as qualities necessary for corporate success (40). Part of the reason for this change in the attitude is the movement of global competitiveness. The growing interdependence of national economies has created a demand for sophisticated managers who are skilled in working with people of other cultures and who understand international business.

Experts (15, 19, 26, 27) believe in greater numbers now than ever before that women possess a unique "interactive management" skill that needs to be utilized fully in the organizations of the future if the economies of tomorrow want to be prepared for competing in the 21st century. Aburdene and Naisbitt in their book entitled "Megatrends for Women" predicted that 1990's would be "the decade of women as leaders in revitalizing business and inspiring competition in the new global economy" (1). Burnside and Guthrie believe (1992) that the so-called minorities-women and Hispanics are becoming large majorities and therefore they no longer can be denied access to leadership (18). According to Kuhn (1996, p.261), "the number of women leaders in the next century will eventually reach a critical mass" (18). The data from the U.S. Labor Department of Statistics, estimates that American women will account for 62 percent of all net civilian workforce between 1990–2005.

The United Nations' data also predicts that by the year 2000 there will be as many women employees in the world as men in many industrialized Nations (34, 35, 33).

While these predictions may be true, the current trend does not paint a promising future for senior women managers. It is now the end of the nineties (1998) and women still feel worldwide that their advancement into upper echelons of senior management needs to be improved. A new ILO (International Labor Organization) report states that, "while substantial progress has been made in closing the gender gap in managerial and professional jobs for women in management, it is still lonely at the top" (40, p.7).

Statistics reveal that the higher the position, the more glaring is the gender gap. The ILO report questions if the "glass ceiling," a term coined in the United States in the seventies to describe the "invisible artificial barriers created by attitudinal and organizational prejudices barring women to executives jobs," will ever be broken. According to this report, the glass ceiling is still very much in tact (42). There are other revealing statistics that support the statement of the ILO Report.

Globally speaking, women hold less than 5 percent of the top jobs in corporations all over the world. In the most powerful organizations, the proportion to top positions going to women is generally two to three percent. "One of the troubles is that old rules about women's role are gone and there are no new ones to replace them." (37) Karin Klenke in her book "Women & Leadership" (18) states that even though, it is no longer politically correct to be avertly gender biased, subtle forms of discrimination continue to exist. According to a report based on the tripartite meeting on, "Breaking through the Glass Ceiling," at the ILO headquarters in December 1997, it was found that, the major underlining factors for discriminating against women and holding them back from attaining higher level jobs, were social attitudes, cultural biases and male prejudices (42).

A survey of top women executives also revealed that many women feel that the "glass ceiling" is not simply a barrier for an individual, based on the person's inability to handle a higher level job. Rather, the "glass ceiling" applies to "women as a group"; who are kept from advancing higher because they are women (29). Karin Klenke and others (29) report that the nature of discrimination against women has changed from "avert" to more "subtle."

There are some interesting and additional striking statistics on women around the globe that support the above statements. According to the United Nations publications on "women challenges of year 2000," "women constitute half the world's population, perform two-thirds of the world's work, but receive only one tenth of its income and own less than one-hundredth of its property" (37). "In the largest and most powerful organizations, the proportion of top positions going to women is generally 2 to 3 percent (35)." A survey of 70,000 German companies, in 1995, reported that only 1 or 2 percent of board members and top executives were women." In the U.S., women in 1996 held just over 2 percent of the higher-ranking corporate positions of the 500 largest companies (of Fortune 500)." Number of women managers all over the world have increased at the lower and middle level positions, in non-strategic sectors such as human resources, personnel and administrative fields (39). It is the nature of these positions that do not allow women to reach to the top because in these sectors, the positions become dead-end after sometime. ILO report confirms that the nature of women's career paths block their progress to the top positions (41).

According to ILO, the classification of "administrative and managerial" jobs is deceptive as it includes legislative officials, administrative officials, and managers that are concentrated mainly in the lower and middle level of management. In other countries and especially Asian countries, the situation is worse. For example, in Sri Lanka 48 percent of women are in the total labor force but only 17 percent are holding managerial level jobs. In Japan, 41 percent of women are in the labor force and 9 percent are holding administrative positions. In India the number of females holding administrative and managerial jobs is two per one hundred economically active men.

The U.S. Labor Department reports that in 1994, American women held only 5 percent of senior management level jobs in the 1000 largest companies and less than one percent of women were CEO's of these 1000 companies. The report further forecast that if things move at this rate, it would take several generations for women to achieve proportional representation at the top of American businesses. The period may be much longer for other nations. Studies on surveys of American women managers indicate that 91 percent of women believe that barriers exist to women's advancement, 88 percent agreed that existence of glass ceiling is a barrier and 86–88 percent indicated that exclusion from informal network due to male prejudices against women act as barriers (41).

From the above discussions it is clear that for tomorrow's women executives the question is not to find the reasons for the existing barriers to women advancement or to analyze if the barriers are really there. Rather the challenge is to find solutions, ways and means to break the barriers and improve the situation. Although the literature is full on the "barriers" the "glass walls," the "glass ceilings" and "male stereotypes," not much research is done on the solutions to remove the barriers.

The ILO report aptly sets the directions for future women mangers. According to this report "a watershed change from within the corporations is needed" that requires a change in the structure of the organizations and the attitudes and cultural biases of the male and female managers. The "watershed change" implies, "creation of workplaces which are more dynamic, flexible, value-diverse, people oriented and family-friendly" (42). Already new management structures and work roles involving restructuring, downsizing, decentralization and delayering in the bid to be more globally competitive have started. However, one of the greatest challenges that remain to be faced is, "how to make the structures and dynamics within organizations more conducive and sensitive to gender equality concepts and practice" (42). One can create organizational structures on paper but it is impossible to transform the hearts, the "mind set" attitudes, the prejudices and cultural biases, that are ingrained for centuries in many of the autocratic, aggressive and stereotyped males. Without such a transformation of human minds, a "watershed change" within firms and enterprises is not possible. The organizational delayered structures on paper will not work and women executives will, in the years to come, continue to experience "glass ceilings" to attain top executives and "glass walls" to reach to the top (42. p.8).

Important Issues

This study attempts to focus on one region of South Asia—India. The attempt here is to find out to what degree the glass ceiling exists in the largest democracy of the world and how women managers function? Other issues that this study intends to analyze are as follows: To what extent the male and female managers feel comfortable taking orders and working under a female as subordinate? To what extent or if at all the "watershed change" (as referred above by the ILO) has been introduced in the business circles of India? What kind of cultural barriers if any are existing for women executives in India that prevent them from advancing to corporate leadership positions? Is it possible that a land that was ruled by woman as the political head for at least ten years could be infested with prejudices and cultural biases against women managers? Other additional questions that we intend to answer in our study are:

(1) How is the work environment for women managers in India with respect to recruitment, retention, pay and advancement?
(2) What are the managerial competencies and societal expectations of women managers in India?
(3) Against the gender biased organizations, what kind of coping strategy/strategies, women managers in India use?
(4) What special talents, traits, and perspective women bring to work with them just because they are women?
(5) How do men feel working with women at different levels of administration?
(6) What prevents Indian women from advancing to corporate leadership positions?
(7) What initiatives companies in India could take to assist women advance in the corporate ladder?

We have selected India for our study due to various reasons. India is the largest democracy of the world with a population of 900 million, the seventh industrial nation in the World and is getting global attention for investment due to liberalization of its economy. It has a great potential for future economic expansion and growth. Women in India have played significant roles in politics, social organizations and administration and therefore there is a need to study the status of the female executives in the corporations. During the last few years, India is showing strength not only to become economically independent but also to prepare itself for global competition.

Since 1975, India's per capita income has risen from $250 a year to $1,150. At 1980–1981 prices the per capita income in India has been steadily rising since 1990 i.e. from Rupees 4,983 in 1990–1991 to Rupees 9,321.4 in 1995–1996. The rate of growth of the gross domestic product (GDP) is also steady (from Rupees 4,778 Billion to Rupees 8,541 Billion in 1994–1995). In foreign trade the percentage increase in both exports and imports has been tremendous. Exports increased from Rupees 67 Billion to Rupees 325 Billion, an increase of 385 percent in ten years. For imports the percentage growth was 242.8 percent; from Rupees 126 Billion in 1980–81 to Rupees 432 Billion in 1990–91 (34).

The data for labor force participation rate indicates that between 1970 to 1990, the average annual growth rate of economically active women population in India was 1.2 percent. For men it was 2.3 percent. Women constituted 25 percent of total economically active population in 1990 in India. However, their contribution in the world of business has been limited. The number of female administrators and managers per one hundred economically active males in India was only two. This figure was the lowest when compared to all other countries in Asia and Pacific. However for 1992–2005, the projections for the annual growth of women in the labor force by race or Hispanic origin is fastest for "Asians and others." "Asians and others" are expected to grow at a rate of 4.9 percent per year as against 4.3 percent for Hispanics, two percent for blacks and 1.5 percent for white women (35). Also, by the year 2000, there will be as many women employees as men in many industrial countries. There-fore, the need to improve the status of women mangers is more now in the 21st century than ever before. For India, such studies are particularly beneficial because large number of students graduating from business and engineering schools today are women but most corporate top pos-itions are still held by men. When the data for the proportion on female mangers to male mangers is compared for the countries in Asia and the Pacific regions, India seems to be at the lowest on the ladder.

Method and Sample Design

In this study, we present the key issues facing the women managers in corporate India. This study reflects the perspectives of both the male and female managers. Our sample consists of a total of 162 managers that includes 63 percent male and 37 percent female. Fifty five percent of the respondents are between 30 to 49 years of age. The average years of work experience of the respondent are 21 years. Sixty seven percent of the respondents had a master's degree and twenty two percent had an undergraduate degree. Fifty four percent of the spouses of the respondents were working. From the perspective of the levels of administration 64 percent of the respondents were working as senior level managers, 27 percent were at the middle level and 9 percent were lower level managers. The sample therefore is quite mixed and has a good representation of all demographic and human resource management (HRM) characteristics. Speaking from the "business area" perspectives, 27 percent were working in general management, 32 percent in human resource management (HRM), 9 percent in sales and marketing, 6 percent in finance/accounting and the rest 26 percent in related fields.

A profile of the participating organizations indicates that 42 percent of the companies were in the service sector and 33 percent in manufacturing. The average workforce of these companies was around 15,000 employees with on average annual sales of Rupees 270 million. Fifty five percent of the participating organizations were private, 24 percent were public and only 8 percent were government operated. The rest 13 percent were mixed. It is interesting to note that in sixty percent of the companies participating in this study, the number of senior and middle level women managers was less than five percent. In 17 percent of the participating companies, the percentage of senior and middle level women managers fluctuated between 5 to 10 percent. Seventy three percent of these companies did not provide any child care services.

The method of survey for this study was based on mail questionnaires. Questionnaire was first tested on a limited number of participants. Based on their feedback, the questionnaire was later revised and finalized.

How The Study Was Conducted

Mailing lists of Executives who have attended programs conducted by Eicher Consultancy Services and members of All India Management Association were prepared. Personalized letters with a questionnaire and an offer to provide an Executive Summary were mailed to those on the mailing lists. We received 162 completed questionnaires.

Results

Our results focus on seven key issues. These are (1) hiring practices, promotion and advancement, (2) equity in pay and reward, (3) organizational perceptions of gender issues, (4) the management and leadership skills of women and how useful they are, (5) how men feel working with women, (6) coping strategies against gender bias in organizations and what prevents women from advancing, (7) and what initiatives companies could take. Each of these issues are discussed in the subsequent sections.

Hiring Practices

Perceptions of male and female managers with respect to hiring practices of corporate India are very similar. To a great extent, both perceive that employment in their companies is based on merit and not gender. Both also believe that pregnancy makes women a less desirable employee to recruit. However, merit is the most important criteria for recruitment. Only a small group (less than 5%) thought that women are hired to stay away from legal troubles, or to appear to be a good corporate citizen.

Encouragement for the Advancement of Women

Perceptions of male and female managers regarding encouragement/advancement of women in corporate India differ on the basis of promotions/advancements. More men (91%) than women (72%) agree that the promotions are based on merit and not on gender. In other areas both male and female managers agreed. For example, we found that about 60% men and women managers perceive that their organizations encourage women to assume leadership roles, about 62% men and women managers agree that there are few barriers for women to advance in the organization. However, only about third of the male or female managers perceive that their organizations are trying to increase the number of women executives in senior management positions. The chart presented on the next page shows percentage of male and female managers who agree/strongly agree with each statement regarding encouragement to women to advance in the organization.

Equity in Work & Reward

Even though, both male and female managers perceive that employees are hired based on their qualifications, merit, and accomplishments, but gender becomes an important consideration during salary raises, promotions or advancement decisions. More women believe that they must work harder than men, are paid less than men for the same qualification, are forced to prove their competence all the time, and to succeed in the corporate world, must develop management style which is comfortable to men. Even at senior level, her status as women does not become irrelevant; she continues to be perceived as "women" who needs to "prove" her worth while men are assumed competent till proven otherwise. Fewer women (71% vs. 81% men) perceive that competence, not gender is an issue in organizations. We noticed an interesting difference between male and female managers on performance expectations. More men (48%) than women (38%) believe that to be successful, women managers need to consistently exceed performance expectations more often than men. We were expecting these percentages to be reversed. The way these percentages came out in our study suggest that men expect more from women while women are underestimating these expectations—which may not be good for their careers.

Organizational Perception of Importance of Gender Issues

Table 1, provides the result of the perceptual gap between male and female managers on key gender issues. While 93% women feel that they are as committed to their jobs as men, only 78% men feel so. In fact, about 20% men perceive that women are less capable than men in contributing to achieving organizational goals. Only about 38% women (and 65% men) indicated that their organizations help women managers 'fit' in the male culture. Few organizations realize that addressing gender issues are important to them. While more men than women appear to think that competence not gender is an issue, only 52% of the women feel that their organizations are committed to using the talents of women and only about 20% see that business community is ready to accept women in key managerial positions. In fact, we found that 22% women perceive that men do not even consider them as professional colleagues, half feel that they must sacrifice their femininity to succeed in the business world and should act more like men, and 74% consider them as less desirable employees due to the possibility of becoming pregnant. There appears to be a lack of sensitivity to gender issues and appreciation for women's capabilities and talents in corporations.

Table 1: Organizational Perception of Importance of Gender Issues
(Percentage of Managers Agreeing with these Statements)

	Male	Female
In this organization, women are as committed to their jobs as men	78%	93%
Competence, not gender, is an issue in this organization	81%	71%
Pregnancy makes women less desirable employees	80%	74%
This organization helps women managers 'fit' into male culture	65%	38%
This organization is committed to utilizing talents of women	62%	52%
To be successful, a woman has to sacrifice some of her femininity	56%	57%
Addressing gender issues are important for this organization	30%	28%
Business community accepts women in key managerial positions	21%	19%
Women are less capable of contributing to org. goals than men	20%	7%
Men consider women as women, not professional colleagues	18%	22%

What Women Bring To Work?

In this section we will discuss three issues:

(a) Management skills of women managers.
(b) Perspectives that woman brings to work because of their gender.
(c) How important these perspectives are?

(a) Management Skills of Women Managers

Significant differences were observed between male and female managers regarding the management skills of women. Although, about 97% of both men and women agree that women have the capability to acquire necessary skills to be successful managers, fewer male managers believe so. It seems that 58% men vs. 74% women believe that women have the *objectivity* required for evaluating business situation properly and that they possess the self-confidence required of a good business leader (74% men vs. 91% women). In fact, our study revealed that 60% male managers and 36% female managers feel that women managers would let their emotions influence their managerial behavior. A greater proportion of men also perceives that women are not *ambitious* enough to be successful in the business world (23% men and 12% women). Also, 19% men vs. 12% women think that women cannot be *assertive* enough in business situations that demand it. Twenty three percent men and fifteen percent women believe that women are not *competitive* enough to be successful in the business world and 21% men vs. 14% women are of the opinion that women cannot be *aggressive* enough in business situations. On the positive note, we found that about 26% of men as well as women perceive that female managers are more comfortable with ambiguity than male managers.

(b) What Women Bring To Work?

Do female managers bring different perspective to solving business problems because of their gender? We found significant differences in the perceptions of male and female managers regarding what women bring to workplace? Chart 1 indicates that more female than male managers believe that women bring sensitivity to human relations in solving business problems (43% women vs. 25% men). Also, women have greater compassion or care in making business decisions (27% vs. 16%) and greater initiative and willingness to go an extra mile to solve a business problem (34% women vs. 11% men). Women pay greater attention to details in decision-making (34% women vs. 17% men). When solving business problems, more women seem to focus on process and not just the outcome (33% women vs. 9% men). Overall, 29% women and only 8% men perceive that women bring different perspective to business problem.

(c) How Important Is What Women Bring To Work?

We asked both male and female managers their opinions on the importance of traits women bring to workplace or decision making. Details are in Chart 2. Even though, men and women agreed on the relative importance of these traits, there are significant differences on their importance ratings. For example, while 53% women agree that being sensitive to human relations issues in decision making and willingness to go an extra mile are important traits in a business executive, only about

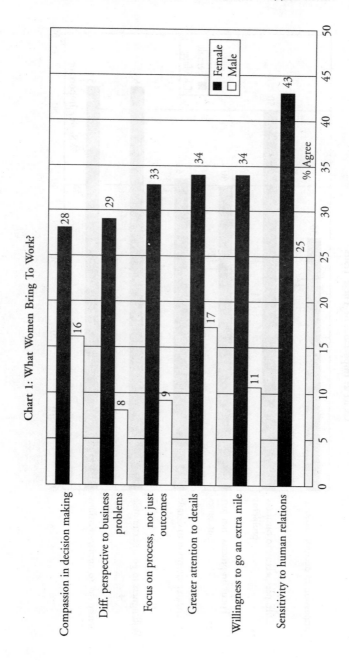

Chart 1: What Women Bring To Work?

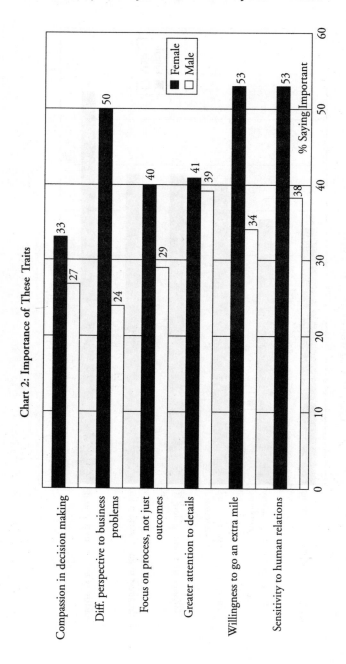

Chart 2: Importance of These Traits

1/3rd of the male managers thought so. Similarly, for 40% of female managers focusing on decision making process and not just outcomes is very important, only 29% male managers agreed to this.

We were surprised to learn that only 24% male managers (vs. 50% female managers) think that it is important that women bring different perspective to solving business problems.

Leadership Style of Women Managers

A review of Chart 3 and 4 indicates that majority of both male and female managers believe that they differ in the ways they think and approach business problems. However, in Chart 4, more women (86%) than men (67%) agree that they have similar leadership traits such as vision, intelligence, charisma, commitment, and drive. Nevertheless, more women seem to adopt different leadership styles than men. For example, in Chart 3, we found that women are more relationship oriented, pay more attention to processes and how tasks are done while focusing on results and outcomes, support innovation and change more than men, emphasize collaboration more than men, and like to build consensus to a greater degree than men. On the other hand, more men perceive women to see power as a symbol of prestige and "personal goal fulfillment" rather than as a tool for getting things done. Men also perceive that women do not empower subordinates as much as they do, and treat them poorly. There seem to be some discrepancy between men's perception of women's use of power in the organization and women's management style. Our study suggests that more women exhibit/prefer interactive leadership style while men prefer/exhibit command and control leadership style. Eighty-two percent male managers (vs. 8% female managers) believe that women cannot lead in command and control style. Only 14% women and 33% men perceive that command and control style is more effective for men. The literature suggests that in dynamic environments command and control style is neither effective for men nor for women. While 78% women and 58% men believe that interactive style is the preferred choice of women, it is interesting to note that, to succeed in business, more men want women to act like men. Although women do not feel the need to act more like men, they realize that they need to de-velop a management style that is comfortable for men.

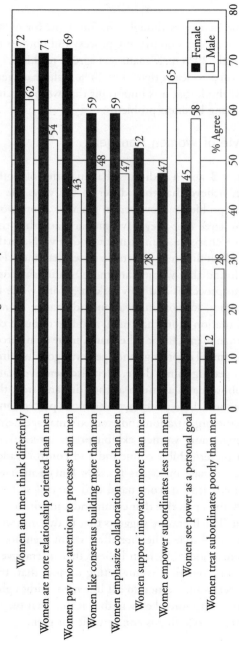

Chart 3: Thinking Differently

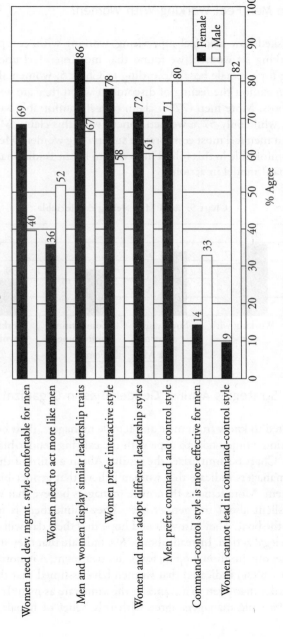

Chart 4: Leading Differently

% Agree

How Do Men Feel Working With Women?

When asked how men feel supervising, working with, competing with, and working *for* women, we found that most men feel uncomfortable working for a female boss. According to Chart 5, women also perceive that men exhibit the feeling of discomfort when they are working for a female boss. More men (77%) claim to feel comfortable working with women, while only 57% women concur with this claim. Most women agree that men feel most comfortable supervising women. Men also seem quite comfortable in this role. This seems to be the traditional "organizational man" model in action.

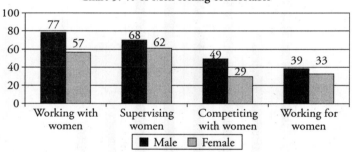

Chart 5: % of Men feeling comfortable

Coping Strategies Against Gender-Bias in Organizations

We wanted to know from male and female managers, their beliefs about what action women take to cope with the existing gender-bias in organizations. Chart 6 summarizes the results. About a third of the male and female managers indicate that women believe that gender-bias does not affect them. More females than male managers believe that woman just remain silent about the gender bias. They think there is no point in rocking the boat. They just wait and hope that their day will come. Very few take legal action. Instead, about 26% indicate that they simply move to another organization, hoping for better treatment. A majority of female managers (59%) indicated that women have assumed that they need to work harder than men to advance at the same rate as men. Interestingly, only 28% male managers agree with this belief of female managers.

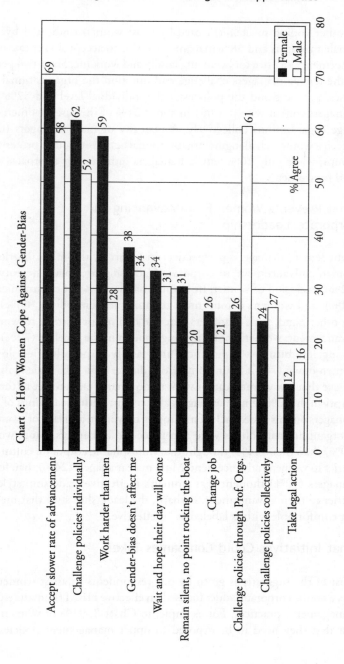

Chart 6: How Women Cope Against Gender-Bias

% Agree

Female
Male

Accept slower rate of advancement — 69, 58
Challenge policies individually — 62, 52
Work harder than men — 59, 28
Gender-bias doesn't affect me — 38, 34
Wait and hope their day will come — 34, 31
Remain silent, no point rocking the boat — 31, 20
Change job — 26, 21
Challenge policies through Prof. Orgs. — 26, 61
Challenge policies collectively — 24, 27
Take legal action — 12, 16

Another coping mechanism used by most women (indicated by 69% female managers and 58% male managers) is to accept slower rate of advancement as a price for balancing family and work life. Sixty-two percent of the female managers challenge and question the organizational processes, practices and the policies at the individual level and 52% male managers concur with it. Only in about 24% of the cases, women challenge organizations collectively. A majority of male managers (61%) perceive women challenging organizational actions through professional groups; while only 26% female managers indicate this approach being used by women.

What Prevents Women From Advancing to Corporate Leadership

From female managers' perspective, in Chart 7, the major barriers to women's advancement to corporate leadership are: male stereotyping (72%), exclusion of women from informal networks of communication (71%), and women's commitment to family responsibilities (65%). On the other hand, male managers perceive two major barriers to women's advancement: women not being long enough in the pipeline (72%) thus having less business experience, and family responsibilities slowing women down (70%). Our study also indicates that 59% male managers believe that few women can or want to do what it takes to get to the top. Surprisingly 52% female managers also concur with the feelings of male managers on this issue. Lack of mentoring of women and lack of awareness of organizational politics were also perceived as barriers. More women (50%) than men (34%) thought that inhospitable corporate culture is a barrier to women's advancement. More male managers (24%) than female managers (10%) thought that woman's ineffective leadership style is a barrier to their advancement. Perhaps, the leadership style that men are not comfortable with is labeled as "ineffective."

What Initiatives Could Companies Take?

Most of the suggestions given by our respondents to assist women advance on the corporate ladder focused on effective HRM (human resource management) practices. For example, in Chart 8, 91% of women suggest that they need to be exposed to upper management policies and

Chart 7: What Prevents Women From Advancing to Corporate Leadership

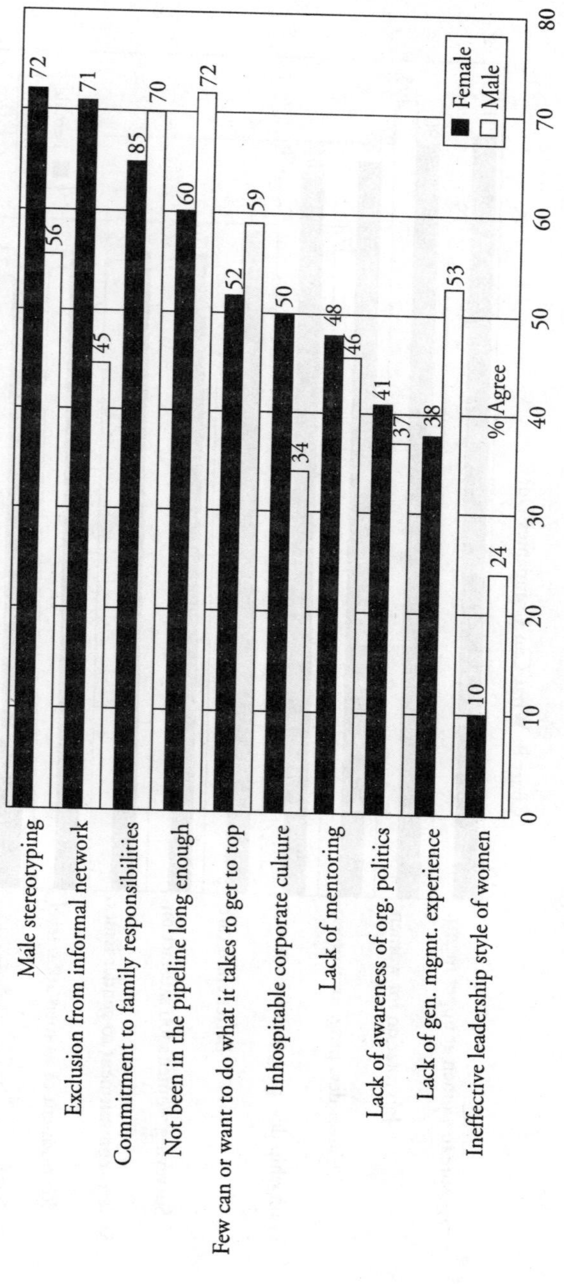

Category	Female	Male
Male stereotyping	72	56
Exclusion from informal network	71	45
Commitment to family responsibilities	85	70
Not been in the pipeline long enough	60	72
Few can or want to do what it takes to get to top	52	59
Inhospitable corporate culture	50	34
Lack of mentoring	48	46
Lack of awareness of org. politics	41	37
Lack of gen. mgmt. experience	38	53
Ineffective leadership style of women	10	24

% Agree

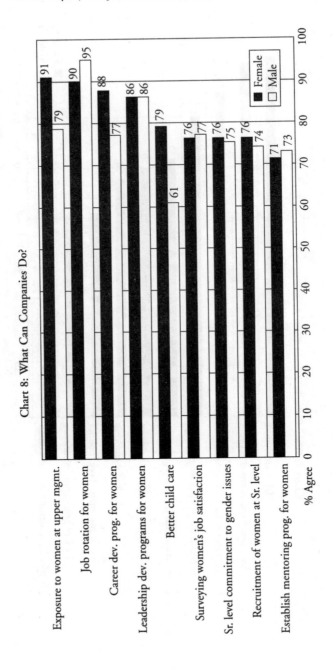

Chart 8: What Can Companies Do?

procedures. Their work and accomplishments need to be showcased to the top management. They need to know how top management thinks and makes decisions. A large number of female executives also emphasized the need for job rotation (90%), career and leadership development programs (88%), and good child care facility at work (86 & 88%).

Male managers agree with most of the suggestions made by female managers, however, fewer men are as enthusiastic as female with respect to the need for: exposure of women to top management, career development programs, and better child-care facility at work. More men actually thought that job rotation for women is a good idea to help them learn about the company and develop leadership skills. Almost, 3/4th of our respondents, both male and female, thought that surveying women employees every year about issues of concern to them, showing senior management commitment to gender issues, launching a formal recruitment program to recruit women at senior level positions and establishing mentoring programs for women will be beneficial to achieving gender equity in corporations.

Summary and Conclusions

Gender is an important issue in corporate India. While there are some similarities, there are significant differences in the perceptions of male and female managers in several key areas. Our study found that

- 79% women and 90% men believe that in their organizations, employment is based on merit and not on gender. However, 74% women and 80% men perceive that pregnancy makes women less desirable employees than men.
- 72% women and 91% men believe that promotion and advancement is based on merit and not genders. More than 40% men and women believe that there are significant barriers to women's advancement in their organizations and organizations do not encourage women enough to assume leadership positions. In fact, only about a third perceive that organizations are seeking ways to increase the numbers of women at senior management positions. In our survey, 60% companies had less than 5% of their senior and middle managers as females.

Among our respondents, 82% of men indicated that they were at senior level as compared to 33% women.

- There appears to be some inequity in pay in corporate India. While 77% women agreed that they are paid equal to men for the same qualification, 89% men thought that women are paid equal to men. Gender and not competence, is an issue in the minds of 30% women and 20% men. Even at senior level positions, female managers continue to be perceived as "women" first. Women need to work harder than men and need to prove their competence more often than men. Men perceive women as less committed to their jobs and less capable of contributing to organizational goals. Almost half the women think that their organizations are committed to utilizing their talents and only about 38% think that organizations help women fit into "male" culture. In fact, to succeed, 57% women think that they need to sacrifice some of their femininity and 36% indicate that they need to act more like men. We found that job satisfaction among women managers was significantly lower than men.

- Significant differences were observed between male and female managers regarding the management skills of women. Men perceive women less self-confident, more emotional, and less objective in evaluating business situations. Also, more men think women are not aggressive enough, competitive enough, ambitious enough and assertive enough in the situations that demand such traits. Male managers also do not seem to appreciate the perspectives or approach women bring to work. For example, a significantly lower percent of men believe that in decision making women focus on process and not just outcomes, that they pay a great deal of attention to details, exhibit sensitivity to human relations, and are willing to go an extra mile. More women than men believe that these are important traits for a successful executive.

- Women and men think differently and lead differently. More female managers than male managers think that women are more relationship oriented, consensus builder, process oriented, supportive of innovation and change and emphasize collaboration. On the other hand, more male managers think that women are power hungry, do not empower subordinates and treat them poorly. Women realize that to succeed in the business world, they need to develop a management style, which is comfortable for men. In fact, more men want women to act like men. Women prefer interactive style vs. men preferring command and control style of management. Few men feel comfortable working for women. Most like either to be colleagues or supervise women.

- Most women cope with gender-bias by accepting slower rate of advancement, challenging organizational policies or decisions on an individual basis, work harder to get what men have, and simply believing that gender-bias doesn't affect them. Men seem to think that women also exert pressure against gender-bias through professional organizations.

- Male stereotyping, exclusion of women from informal communication network, commitment to family responsibilities, lack of business experience, and not being in the pipeline long enough are some of the barriers to women's advancement. About half the women and 60% men think that few women can or want to do what it takes to get to the top.

- To assist women advance on corporate ladder, both men and women agree that HRM practices need to be changed. Women need to get greater exposure to top management, they should be encouraged to engage in job rotation within the company, and should participate in career development programs. Companies also need to provide better child-care facilities, survey women more often, establish mentoring programs for women and actively recruit women at senior level positions.

Recommendations

People are an organization's most important assets. Both men and women need to be effectively managed and nurtured to utilize their special talents. We found that there are significant differences in perceptions between male and female managers on key gender issues in corporate India. To develop a healthy, creative and learning community within a corporation, such perceptual differences need to be addressed aggressively. We recommend:

- Open dialogue between men and women in organizations to learn about gender differences that exist on important issues affecting the work environment.

- Offer educational and training programs for men and women to learn how to effectively manage the gender diversity in organization.
- Re-engineer HRM practices and implement other suggestions offered by our respondents to make organizations more "women friendly." Such suggestions include:

  - Exposure of women to top management
  - Job rotation for women
  - Career development programs for women
  - Leadership development programs for women
  - Better child care facilities at work
  - Surveying women regularly to assess their job satisfaction
  - Senior level commitment to gender issues
  - Recruitment of women at senior level positions
  - Establishing mentoring program for women

- Although, a few women organizations have emerged in India, we are not aware if there is an *Association of Women Managers*. We recommend establishing such a professional body to organize educational, training, development and research on gender issues in corporations.

The greatest limitation of our study is the small sample size of women managers. We would also like to collect some qualitative data by interviewing both male and female managers to capture what is missing from our paper and pencil survey.

References

Aburdene, P. and J. Naisbitt, (1992). *Megatrends for Women* New York: Villard Publishers.

Adler, N., & and Izraeli, D., (1994). *Competitive Frontiers: Women Managers in A Global Economy.* Cambridge: MA: Blackwell Publishers, p. 10.

Anon J., (1992). "Corporate Women," *Business Week* pp. 74–83.

Bass, B.M., Krusell, J. & Alexander, R. H., (1971). "Male Manager's Attitudes toward Working Women." *American Behavioral Scientist* V. (15), pp. 221–23.

Benda, Nancy., (1995). "Why are girls still getting short changed? Confirming the Backlash." A hand-out from the keynote speaker at the American Association of University Women (AAUW) Annual Conference, Disneyland, Florida,

Thursday June 22, pp. 1–6. (Nancy Benda is the Director of the Equal Educational Opportunity Program at Florida Department of Education Office).

Bennis, Warren., (1990). *Why Leaders Can't Lead? The Unconscious Conspiracy Continues* San Francisco, CA: Jossey-Bass Publishers, p. 161.

Boneman, G.W., Worthy, N.B. & Greyser, S.A., (1965). "Are Women Executive People?" *Harvard Business Review*, pp. 14–28 and 164–178.

Brown, D. Donald., & Hisrich, Robert D. "The Female Entreprenuers: A Career Development Perspective". *Academy of Management Review*, V, (11), p. 393.

Broverman, L. K., Vogal, S. R. and Boverman, D.M., et. al, (1972). "Sex-Role Stereotypes: A Current Appraisal." *Journal of Social Issues* V. (28), pp. 59–78.

Bryman, A., (1992). *Charisma and Leadership in Business Organizations.* London: Sage Publications.

Bryman, A., (1993). "Charismatic Leadership in Business Organization: Some Neglected Issues," *Leadership Quarterly* 3 & 4, V, (4), pp. 289–304.

Chaudhri, P. C., (1998). "Indian Women in Vedic Age." *SANSKRITI.* (I), V, (5), A Publication Bhartiya Hindu Temple, Powell-Ohio. (This article is reproduced partially from Kalyan Kalpatguru).

Culverhouse, G., President, Notre Dame College, South Euclid, Ohio, (1996). "A Profile". *Women In Higher Education*, p. 7.

Gilmer, B. Von H., (1996). "Women in Industry," *Industrial Psychology* 2nd ed., London: McGraw Hill: Publishers, pp. 455–475.

Helgesen, S., (1990). *The Female Advantage: Women's Ways of Leadership*, New York: Doubleday.

Jelinek, M. and Adler N., (1998). "Women World-Class Managers for Global Competition." *Academy of Management Executive*, V. (2), pp. 11–19.

Kelly, Rita Mae, (1992). *The Gendered Economy.* London: Sage, p. 125.

Klenke, Karin, (1996). *Women and Leadership- A Contextual Perspective* New York: Springer Publishing Company, pp. 187, 227, 217, 257, 261–264, total pages 337.

Loden, M., (1985). "Feminine Leadership: or how to succeed in business without being one of the Boys", *Times* New York.

Maier, N. R. F., (1970). "Male Versus Female Discussion Leaders." *Personal Psychology* V. (23), pp. 455–461.

Megargee, E. L., (1969). "Influence of Sex Roles on the Manifestation of Leadership." *Journal of Applied Psychology* V. (53), pp. 377–382.

Morrisom M. Ann., Randall P. White & Velsor, E.V., (1987). *Breaking the Glass Ceiling-Can Women Reach the Top of America's Largest Corporation?* New York: Addison Wesley Inc., p. 225.

National Association for Women in Education *(NAWE).*, (1995). *About Women on Campus.* V. (4), (2), (spring), pp. 2–18.

Osborn, N. Richard & Vicars William M., (1976). "Sex Stereotypes: An Artifact in Leader Behavior and Subordinate Satisfaction Analysis?" *Academy of Management Journal*, V, (19). (3), pp. 439–449.

Powell, Gary N., (1994). "Investigating the Glass Ceiling Phenomenon: An Empirical Study of Actual Promotions to Top Management." *Academy of Management Journal*, V, (37), (1), pp. 68–86.

Rosener, J., (1990). "Ways Women Lead". *Harvard Business Review* V. (68), pp. 119–125.

Roddick, A., (1991). *Body and Soul* New York: Crown.

Schein, V. E., (1973). "The Relationship Between Sex Role Stereotypes and Requisite Management Characteristics." *Journal of Applied Psychology.* V. (57), pp. 95–100.

Smith, Vivian., (1998). "The Old Rules About Women's Roles Are Gone And There Are No New Ones To Replace Them." *Women in Management.* IVEY School of Business, University of Western Ontario, CANADA, V. (8), (3), pp. 4–5.

Statistical Record of Women Worldwide, 2nd edition, (1990). Sections on "Labor Employment" and "Occupations", Tables 542, 558, 561, 562, and 567, pages 519, 533, 536, and 543, Geneva: United Nations.

Swarup, H. & Sinha N., "Women in Public Administration in India." *Women and Politics.* V, (11), (4).

The New York Times (1996). "Gaps and Barriers and Women's Careers." February 21, p. C-2.

United Nations Publications, (1993). ISBN# 93-1-100U58-6, *Women Challenges to the Year 2000* United Nations Sales # E.91.1.21., p. 96.

United Nation's homepage at World Wide Web at http://www.un.org.

United Nations., (1996). *Special Report on Women.* Department of Public Information, Development and Human Rights Section, Room S-1040, New York: United Nations, (DPI/1862/REV.l -December, 1996).

United Nations Report., *The World's Women - Trends and Statistics.* (1995), prepared by the Statistical Division of the United Nations Secretariat based on various sources such as the Women's and Statistics Database, Statistical Yearbook of United Nations etc.

United Nations Publications., (1991). *The Worlds' Women 1970–1990: Trends and Statistics,* New York, p. 131.

U.S. Department of Labor Women's Bureau., (1995). *Facts on Working Women.* NO. 95-1, (May 1995).

U.S. Census Bureau Report., (1996). *Facts on Women's Owned Businesses.*

Wajcman, Judy., (1998). *Managing Like a Man* Penn State University Press.

Women at Work- a Special Report On The Status and Satisfaction Of Working women and Initiative For Their Advancement (1996). *Fortune,* 3, V, ( ), Prepared by Fortune Marketing Research for Deloitte and Touch LLP.

World of Work: The Magazine of the ILO. (1998) "Will the Glass Ceiling Ever Be Broken? Women in Management Still Lonely At The Top", (24), V. (2), (February), pp. 6–7.

Young, G., Samarasinghe, Vidyamali and Kusterer, K., (1993). *Women at the Center: Development Issues and Practices for 1990s,* West Hartford, Connecticut: Kumarian Press, p. 211.

14 Managing Alliance Intricacies: An Exploratory Study of U.S. and Indian Alliance Partners

Manab Thakur and B.N. Srivastava

1. Introduction

The study of alliances, as a strategic choice, has posited management of competitive-collaborative nexus as a critical challenge for the coming decade. Managing this nexus has provided a renewed understanding that competition is not analogous to destruction of one's enemies, and co-operation assures no smooth sailing for a higher market share and better margin. It is this delicate tightrope between competition and cooperation that has attracted many scholars to study the intricacies of alliance management (Bartlett and Ghoshal 1992; Bresser 1988; Buckley and Casson 1988; Hamel and Prahalad 1994; Harrigan 1988; Rumelt *et al.* 1994; Teece, 1992).

Walking the tightrope is hazardous at any time but having a safety net before starting helps to cushion the effect of the fall. In this research study, we aimed to minimize the hazard by (a) generating a set of transaction-specific variables, and (b) integrating the content and the process issues of an alliance. Data was collected, using quantitative and qualitative techniques, from U.S. and Indian firms engaged in alliance arrangements since 1988.

This paper is published as a tribute to Dr. Thakur, who passed away after submission of this paper to the *APJM*.

2. Study Perspectives

In the 1960s, the entry mode of many multinational companies (MNCs) to less developed countries (LDCs) constituted a mixed bag of *ad hoc* transactions. Very little strategic thought, if any, went into forming such arrangements. In the 1990s, as numerous LDCs embraced the concept of economic liberalization the opportunities for long-term collaborative ventures mushroomed. The new economic ethos, complemented by the explosive growth in information technology, has elevated alliance as a much sought-after strategic choice for many U.S. firms. Intriguing no doubt that while alliances are expected to grow by 25% per year, over half of them are expected to fail (Harrigan 1988; Kogut 1989; Porter 1987). Bleeke and Ernst's study (1991) found a failure rate of over 70% and predicted a rough ride for many alliances in the future. Replete with multiple theories and research designs, Osborn and Hagedoorn (1997) called it 'a chaotic research field.' More aptly, the field looks like a patient hemorrhaging internally while having a blood transfusion.

While the growth of alliances with the LDCs appears to be irreversible, cultural incompatibility has been posited as a problem in terms of communication, coordination, and interpretation of and responses to strategic issues (Barkema *et al.* 1986; Kogut and Singh 1988; Lane and Beamish 1990). However, the thrust of the argument is seemingly based on the inelastic or static assumption of compatibility which ignores the impact of discontinuity in industry structure and the global search for new strategic paradigm (Hamel 1997; Prahalad and Hamel 1994). Given the strength of the argument, a gradual convergence of management practices between culturally distant partners is highly desirable, and to an extent, achievable (see Park and Ungson 1997; Saxton 1997). To illustrate how such a convergence might come about, consider the alliance between Tata of India and IBM where the former had to adopt a set of structures and strategies understandable to IBM in order to enter the PC market with a brand name product. IBM, on the other hand, had to be cognizant of the prevailing regional structures, strategies, industry norms, and organization memories. The role of IBM, in this example, is not that of an enforcer but more of a synthesizer of discordant practices of its partner. Tata's role is not to emulate IBM's practices but to address the perceived discordance between the partnering organizations and work through it to come to mutually agreed governance structures and strategies.

The probability of opportunistic behavior is another dimension of the cultural compatibility debate. Opportunism is decried primarily when one party gains at the cost of and often without the prior knowledge of the other partner. In order to ensure that neither partner behaves opportunistically, transaction cost economists suggest erecting contractual safeguards (e.g. Williamson 1985, 1991). However, the more stringent and inclusive the contractual safeguards are, the more the cost of writing such a contractual arrangement and maintaining it. Nooteboom *et al.* (1997) argue that 'habitualization' increases the propensity of trust and becomes a 'significant source of cooperation.' Parkhe (1993) contends that the more the frequency of interactions, the more careful the partners will be in examining their mutual benefits and payoff. Oliver (1990) suggests that the ability of one partner to reciprocate reduces the propensity of the other to cheat or take a free ride. Inkpen and Beamish, summarizing the essence of the resource dependency theory, conclude that 'the possession or control of key resources by one entity may make other organizations dependent on that entity' (1997: 182–183).

3. Study Design

As a non-hierarchical and a hybrid form of organizational arrangement, alliances should be viewed in a symbiotic context when all future contingencies will not be anticipated at a given point in time. The symbiosis will give rise to piecemeal disclosure of information and this may be irritating, to say the least. In the context of LDCs, managers are commonly advised to be 'flexible,' 'accommodative,' and 'sensitive to cultural differences.' 'These are hallowed phrases when it comes to direction setting,' responded an American manager operating a US$200 million alliance in India. Referring to asymmetries, a senior executive in India, echoing many of his counterparts in both countries, argued that 'as our resource mix changes, so does our expectations from the alliance . . . . And this is why we should think seriously about how to mesh the differences in the ways tasks are designed without reacting endlessly to recurring problems.'

The process of meshing the differences does not mean that one partner needs to accept a subservient role or one party has to sacrifice its bargaining leverage. The central premise of co-dependency is to create structural *similarities* between the partnering firms on a variety of institutional rules, 'in a desire to achieve a fit, or become isomorphic with their normative environments' (Dacin 1997: 48). Isomorphism warrants a contextual framework which, we postulate, originates from clear standards of performance and behavior, a shared vision, fairness and equity, and by lending assistance and countenance to the other partner (Deephouse 1996). Aspiring a fit on these dimensions is a struggle in a headquarters-subsidiary relationship but it should not be any more or any less of a struggle in an alliance when the transacting partners realize that a similar strategic template, cognition, and a common language system need to be developed to manage the asymmetries so that the alliance is not saddled with 'procedurities' and legalism.

The Conceptual Quandary

We explored this conceptual quandary with five management consultants experienced in advising joint venture arrangements in the U.S. and India. Two of them worked earlier as senior executives for U.S.-based multinational companies in Asia and Europe. Three of the consultants were from India and each of them held senior managerial positions before they became independent agents. All of them had post-graduate education either in the United States or England and the Indian nationals had visited Western nations several times. Our request to these professionals was to translate and evaluate cultural compatibility in the context of this study. We exchanged our thoughts with the consultants over a period of six months by fax, e-mail, telephones, and personal meetings. The salient points of their deliberations are summarized below:

(a) the need for modernization of industries and technology development were forcing isomorphic effects in organization design in culturally divergent countries (the proliferation of MBAs in Indian universities following curriculum identical to American universities, investments by non-resident Indians, and the impact of British rule for two centuries were cited as factors leading to isomorphism);

(b) indigenous businesses realized that they could not insulate themselves from international competition, and the new economic ethos did not support the old 'bailing out' policies for failed businesses by the government. In a new competitive environment, they realized that a new form of organization design was emerging and this design might not be strikingly different from the design in Western nations.

(c) realization by executives that the destabilizing forces of the alliances could not be sheltered under the 'Indian or American way of doing things,' and strategic and structural differences had to be managed;

(d) Indian alliance partners were able to learn about creating and allocating resources in a competitive environment as much as their American counterparts did, and

(e) The factors leading to isomorphism should be examined by the partners ex ante.

We translated these points into the study design by developing and testing the predictive strengths of the variables specific to the transaction, and by generating a sequential model integrating the content and process issues of alliance management which lead to strategic isomorphism. See Figure 1 for study design.

Figure 1: The Study Design

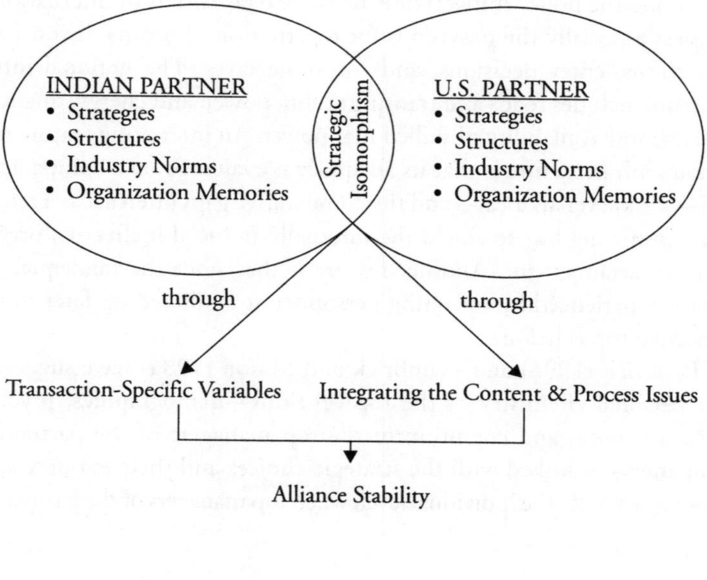

INDIAN PARTNER
• Strategies
• Structures
• Industry Norms
• Organization Memories

Strategic Isomorphism

U.S. PARTNER
• Strategies
• Structures
• Industry Norms
• Organization Memories

through   through

Transaction-Specific Variables   Integrating the Content & Process Issues

Alliance Stability

Transaction-Specific Variables

Chakravarthy and Lorange define strategic intent as 'a concise description of the direction in which an organizational unit should head in order to survive and prosper,' and they argue, that this intent should 'reconfigure the available resources to yield distinctive competencies' (1991: 98). Hamel and Prahalad (1989) conceptualize strategic intent as an active management process which leverages the firm's internal resources into capabilities, and then to core competencies. Sharing of intent reveals the extent to which the alliance decision has been strategically driven, and the degree to which each partner is willing to commit resources for the return they expect from the alliance. For this to happen, the role of each partner spelling out 'who provides what input when by how much' helps to maintain an equilibrium between the respective partner's input and output. Any distortion of the equilibrium can elevate a tactical issue into a strategic impasse leading to unintended dissolution of the alliance. As one U.S. executive commented that the 'impasse can perforate the rules of engagement and brings the venture to a halt without knowing why and how it is perceived this way.'

Alliances with corporations from developing economies warrant a careful examination of the economic policy and its national infrastructure. The economic policy impacts directly on several aspects of international business especially the provisions for repatriation of profits, investment restrictions, entry decisions, and corporate taxes. The national infrastructure includes roads and transportation, power, and energy, financial services, and availability of skilled manpower. An interesting feature of a nation's infrastructure is that its adequacy is evaluated on a comparative basis—home versus local—and the comparative gaps often act as a refuge and a punching bag to shield the internally-induced ineffectual organizational arrangement. Another feature is that since the inadequacy is mostly experienced by operating personnel, it is filtered up later to the respective top echelons.

Hambrick (1994) and Hambrick and Mason (1984) have suggested that personal chemistry of the top echelons—demographics, psychosocial attributes and cognition of the top managers of the partnering companies—is linked with the strategic choices and their resource allocation process. At the individual level, when top managers of the partnering firms 'like each other,' it radiates far enough in smoothing out the rough patches and works like glue in holding together the alliance arrangement. An important dimension of this personal likeability transcends into the top echelons' willingness to involve their mid-level managers in alliance management. Involvement of middle managers not only helps them to sell issues to top management but it also epitomizes the self-development needs of attention and recognition from their bosses. The role of middle managers, as summarized by Dutton and Ashford (1993), includes: (a) providing or concealing information about issues (b) framing an issue in a particular manner (c) directing top management attention to certain issues by mobilizing appropriate resources, and (d) linking actions and ideas between the technical and the institutional levels in the organizations. This unheeded power could be effectively used by cross-training these managers in framing alliance arrangements. In many companies, cross-training is limited to site visits by a selected few managers 'to get acquainted' with their counterparts. There is nothing wrong with being acquainted but unless the training is planned to initiate conversations, it is unlikely to trigger new norms of performance and behavior (Westley 1990). The purpose of cross-training is for the managers to learn how the other partner creates resources, allocates them, and prepares the cognitive maps that guides its organizational behavior (Senge 1990).

Having a designated group of managers responsible for concurrent exploration of the administrative heritage of the respective partners and working through the labyrinth helps in providing both strategic and operational focus (Geringer and Herbert 1989). Such a group should ideally comprise managers from both transacting firms whose primary job is to reflexively monitor the on-going events. Chesley and Huff define reflexive monitoring as 'the capacity of humans to routinely observe and understand what they are doing both while they are doing it and after retrospection' (1994: 8). Thus, their task is not just limited to minimize operational hitches but also to provide a retrospective focus for the venture.

The Sequential Model

Several authors suggest that strategy research has begun to focus towards an integration of the content and the process issues (Fahey and Christensen 1986; Huff and Reger 1987; Robinson and Pearce 1988) but they have hardly suggested ways to achieve it. In building a sequence, one has to note that complementing each other's need is a built-in feature of an alliance, not dominance. A high global stature of one partner should neither prevent the other from learning nor should it be a pretext for one to squeeze out from the other its bargaining leverage. The exacting responsibility of the partners is to energize their strategic conversation about 'what we agreed to do (content) and how do we make it happen (process).' Content defines the legally enforceable boundary of the agreement whereas the process spells out the arrangements by which the content is to be realized. In order to have the conversation strategically poised, an ideal sequence needs to be constructed using the stages of alliance negotiation as the theoretical backdrop. The stages, suggested by various authors, are: placing the option of alliance against other strategic choices, selecting the alliance partner, negotiating the resources and return, operationalizing the alliance, and evaluating the alliance performance (Beamish 1988; Das and Teng 1996; Devlin and Bleackley 1988). Against this ideal sequence, the actual sequence has to be examined and reasoned.

4. Method

Sample

Selection of Firms
A total of 43 U.S. and 44 Indian alliance partners were identified from several business publications in both countries. For the U.S., we identified alliance partners from the Department of Commerce publication, *Directory of Firms Operating in Foreign countries, Fortune, Business Week*, and the *Wall Street Journal*. For India, the following publications were used: *Economic Times, Business World, Business India*, and *India Today*. The process of identification of alliance partners also included active support of several prominent individuals and institutions in both countries. We targeted only the alliances that were formed between 1988–95, excluded those who signed only the memorandum of understanding (MOU) and were yet to set up their operations. The participating companies were guaranteed no cross-funneling of information between the partnering organizations.[1]

The Respondents

A cover letter explaining the purpose of the study was sent to the offices of the chief executive officer of all 87 partnering firms requesting details of the alliances formed, and names and mailing addresses of six of their key managers (top and middle) involved in the management of the alliance. Restricting it to six managers was for our administrative convenience. For the purpose of the study, a mid-level manager was defined as below the vice-president and two levels up from the first-line supervisor. Consistent with the literature, 'involvement' of managers was defined as those who spent time visiting the location, attended meetings at the formulation and implementation stages, and continued to provide inputs (see Woolridge and Floyd 1990).

Out of 43 U.S. and 44 Indian organizations, 22 U.S. and 26 Indian organizations responded providing 123 and 141 names of managers, respectively. The most commonly cited reason for companies at both ends for not responding to the questionnaire was because they were in the middle of restructuring their alliance arrangements, and therefore participation at this point was difficult. A total of 109 and 114 managers from the U.S. and India, respectively, responded to the questionnaire. A high response rate of above 80% and 90% for Indian and U.S. managers suggests absence of non-respondent bias in the sample.

Procedures

The data was collected in two phases: (a) quantitative data collection and (b) qualitative data collection. In the first phase, the questionnaire on transaction-specific variables was addressed to the managers, the questionnaire contained 43 statements incorporating the independent variables as discussed in the study design. The statements were presented on a 5-point scale of (5)—most definitely to (1)—not at all. A factor analysis of the questionnaire revealed seven orthogonal factors with eigenvalues greater than 1 accounting for 64.4% and 61% of the total variance for the U.S. and Indian data, respectively. The relatively similar factor loadings suggests that each factor was equally important in explaining the variance.[2] These factors were: (a) strategic intent, (b) partners role, (c) designated group, (d) mid-managers (MM) involvement, (e) infrastructure adequacy, (f) personal chemistry, (g) macro-policy of the nation.

Stability, as a measure of dependent variable, was defined as the absence of 'unplanned or premature events from the perspective of either one or both partners' (Inkpen and Beamish 1997: 182) necessitating a joint deliberation on the respective scope, resource deployments and synergy. We preferred stability over 'success' as the former denotes a continuation of the engagement whereas the latter denotes finality. Furthermore, stability in managing the quasi-lateral relationships includes both financial return and learning dimension in forming the alliance (Ring and Van de Ven 1994). We measured stability as a composite of: (a) Did the alliance meet the expressed demand of each other? (b) Did the alliance help to spread the fixed costs? (c) Were the managers of both partners involved willing to address the alliance problems on time? and (d) Did the transacting parties envisage continuing with the current alliance arrangement? This composite was measured by averaging the total score of the four questions (a through d) with a cut-off point of 12 from a scale of 1 (low) to 5 (high). In addition, we collected a wide range of information on demographics of the managers and their partnering firms.

The second phase of qualitative data collection focused on the development of a schematic diagram integrating the content and process. For this purpose, we selected a small group of U.S. (n = 43) and Indian (n = 39) managers representing nine and seven alliance partners, respectively. The selection of managers was based on our assessment of their (a) understanding of the intricacies of alliance management including their formal education and experience, (b) openness in sharing alliance experiences without being defensive, and (c) willingness to spend time for the study. We identified these attributes in the managers during the first phase of quantitative data collection. The meetings, in groups of three to five managers were conducted in three stages at the respective company's location. The meetings at each stage lasted about four hours. At the first stage, we asked the participants to recall the 'story' of his/her company's alliance efforts from the beginning to the end—how and why was this alliance formed, who said what, when, with whom, and where. From these accounts, we wrote three different versions of each story. Each version was different but not the substance. We disguised the names or the nationalities of the partnering organizations. A total of 16 stories (9 + 7) were collected and 48 (16 × 3) versions were mailed to the participating managers requesting them to read up before the meetings.

At the second stage of the meetings, they were asked to sketch out the sequences followed by the partnering firms, and then to note the actual sequential order followed by their respective firms. After a gap of two months, at the third stage, we asked the same group of managers (lost seven of them out of 82) to concentrate on the stages of alliance bargaining suggested by the authors (each of them was provided with a summary of stages from the literature), and to delineate the ideal sequential order from the writings but within the confines of alliances of the study.

5. Results

Demographic Differences

The organizations in India ranged in size from 570 to 1530 employees. The U.S. partners consisted of multinational companies or a division of an MNC, most of them being ten to a hundred times larger. Eighty-seven percent of the partners in the U.S. viewed their choice of alliance as furthering their related businesses whereas 77% of their Indian counterparts saw alliance as strengthening their unrelated businesses. Almost all participating firms in India had at least 10% to 15% higher retained earnings than their industry average, and 62% of them had been active in domestic acquisitions, not domestic alliances, in recent years. Only 11% of the alliances were reported to be time-certain (three to five years duration).

The nature of alliance partnership in the U.S. and India, respectively, was: technical collaborations—46% and 42%; manufacturing arrangements—22% and 26%; marketing arrangements—19% and 21%, and R&D Sharing 11% and 14%. Six American partners reported having equity sharing arrangements. The industries represented were: electronics, computer software, financial services, publishing and printing, textiles, and agricultural products. The number of businesses represented in each industry category was about the same in the U.S. and India. The market values (share price on December 1, 1995 multiplied by the latest available common shares outstanding), return on invested capital (profits plus minority interest and interest expense adjusted by tax rate as a percentage of debt and equity funds), and profits (as a percentage of sales) were computed for each partner at the corporate level. In each measure, 67%

of the American partners performed above their respective industry averages, and 31% of them averaged their industry ratios. Seventy-three percent of the Indian partners performed above the industry average and 19% averaged the industry norms. These figures, in all, indicate that companies aspiring for formulating alliances do so from a position of financial strength, which we took as a proxy measure for firm reputation. The actual return from the alliance arrangements was not determined as the participating firms were unwilling to provide or determine their actual return from the ventures.

The median age of managers (U.S. = 109, India = 114) was 34 and 44 years, respectively. While 28% of the U.S. managers had MBAs or equivalent degrees, the corresponding figure for India was 43%. On average, the U.S. managers had six years of experience in dealing with alliance management. The modal experience of Indian managers was only one year. The average tenure of the Indian managers in the current job was 11 years, the U.S. was 4.5 years.

Sixty-two percent of the managers in the U.S. categorized themselves as middle managers whereas 41% of the responding managers in India did so. Others claimed to be in top management positions. Irrespective of their experience in dealing with alliances, over 87% and 79% of the U.S. and Indian managers, respectively, did not think management of alliances to be 'any more difficult than other ventures.' Several of them commented that cultural distance 'was a novelty at the outset and it then changed from curiosity to learning.' It confirms Saxton's argument that 'a certain degree of similarity may be necessary and desirable, (but) too much similarity could limit the benefits because nothing novel is being brought to the relationship (1997: 456).'

Predictive Strengths of Transaction-Specific Variables

Table 1 provides the means, standard deviations, *t*-values, and correlation matrix of the variables.

The U.S. partners associated involvement of mid-level management and the designated group of managers in explaining stability. They were not significant for the Indian respondents. Strategic intent, for the Indian respondents, was only moderately correlated with the role of partners, national infrastructures, personal chemistry and macro-policy. These variables, for the U.S., were strongly correlated with other variables except

Table 1: Means, Standard Deviations, *t*-values, and Correlations

Variable	Mean	s.d.	t-value	1	2	3	4	5	6
1. Strategic Intent	4.1 (4.2)	0.61 (1.01)	0.86						
2. Partners' Role	4.6 (4.31)	1.26 (0.93)	2.07*	.41* (.47)*					
3. Designated Group of Managers	4.9 (2.12)	0.74 (2.87)	34.88**	.61** (.14)	.43* (.11)				
4. MM Involvement	4.35 (2.09)	1.11 (2.87)	8.69***	.38* (.16)	.44* (.21)	.18 (.09)			
5. Infrastructure	3.12 (2.76)	1.85 (1.95)	1.52	.31* (.44)*	.19 (.34)*	.11 (.08)	.17 (.14)		
6. Chemistry	1.19 (4.46)	2.76 (.55)	13.08***	.47* (.49)**	.39 (.55)***	.53*** (.43)*	.31* (.25)	.12 (.46)**	
7. Macro Policy	4.19 (2.66)	.82 (1.05)	13.42***	.16 (.41)*	.19 (.38)*	.12 (-.18)	.22 (-.14)	.55*** (.39)*	.49** (.21)

Figures in parentheses represent Indian data. Scale: Strongly agree (5) to Strongly Disagree (1).
*$p < .05$, **$p < .01$, ***$p < .001$

macro-economic policy. In sum, the U.S. data appears to emphasize the strategic components in managing alliances whereas their Indian counterparts are seemingly manifesting their reverence to top management and holding the coat tails of externalities such as the inadequacy of national infrastructure and macro-economic policy. The *t*-values confirm that there were significant differences between the U.S. and Indian respondents on four variables—involvement of middle management, designated group of managers, personal chemistry, and macro-economic policy ($p < .001$).

Multiple regression results are presented in Table 2. The predictor variables accounted for the variation in the outcome variable by 67% and 62% for the U.S. and Indian data, respectively. The beta values for the U.S. are highly significant for all variables except personal chemistry. On the other hand, personal chemistry and economic policy were found to be highly significant for the Indian respondents. The beta values for the Indian data, however, failed to show any significant effect of strategic intent and designated group on alliance stability.

Table 2: Multiple Regression Results

		U.S.		*India*
Independent Variables	Beta	F-Value	Beta	F-Value
Strategic Intent	.83	192.28***	.09	9.52
Partners' Role	.32	112.27***	.31	67.18*
Designated Group	.68	131.28***	.06	2.18
MM Involvement	.35	157.19***	.10	61.34*
Infrastructure	.72	169.27***	.10	64.23*
Personal chemistry	.23	87.59*	.24	122.38***
Macro Policy	.32	112.67***	.34	102.61***
R^2		0.67		0.62

*$p<.05$, **$p<.01$, ***$p<.001$

In order to measure the independent contributions of the predictor variables, a stepwise regression analysis was performed. Table 3 provides the stepwise regression results. The first equation (A), strategic intent, explained 18% of the variance for the U.S., and the role of partners (B) added another 14%, closely followed by the need to have a designated group of managers (C) adding a further 12%. Consistent with earlier results, the predictive strengths of the four variables—strategic intent, role of partners, designated group of managers, and middle managers' involvement explained a total of 52% of variance for the U.S. data. Forty-nine percent of the variations of Indian respondents were explained by personal chemistry (13%), economic policy (12%), designated group of managers (10%) and national infrastructure (9%). Strategic intent for the Indian respondents explained only 5% of the variance.

Table 3: Stepwise Regression

U.S. equation:	Variable	R^2
A	Strategic Intent	.18
B	SI + Partners Role	.32
C	SI + PR + Designated Group	.44
D	SI + PR + Designated Group + MM Involvement	.52
E & F	Infrastructure and personal chemistry added .06 and .05, respectively	

India equation:	Variable	R^2
A	Personal Chemistry	.13
B	PC + Macro Policy	.25
C	PC + MP + Designated Group	.35
D	PC + MP + Designated Group + Infrastructure	.44
E	PC + MP + Designated Group + Infrastructure + Strategic Intent	.49

The Sequential Model

There was a great deal of congruence among the managers in the development of an ideal sequential order. The congruence was striking irrespective of the types of alliance, industry effect, equity or non-equity alliance participation and nationality. The participants envisaged the ideal sequential order as a continuum of annulment and acculturation (in our terms). Acculturation was viewed as reformation and readjustment of the alliance operation to minimize appeasement. Appeasement signifies correction of a position, not necessarily understanding. However, appeasement might lead to annulment, and not acculturation, if not managed effectively. The steps drawn from the stories helped sequencing the order progressing from aspiration—assimilation—attenuation—association, and back to aspiration. The explicit assumption here was that termination of an alliance should not be equated with failure as long as it was planned in advance. The recantation of the stories, as described below, provides a unique insight about the ways the alliance partners at both ends went about forming their venture arrangements.

Step 1

A small group of key managers planted the seed of alliance by identifying the target firms in response to a felt need expressed in earlier meetings by the members of the top echelons. Sustained competitive advantage was the primary concern at this step and the economic exchange models were the guiding principles. (Aspiration)

Step 2

After some initial soundings with a restricted group of the dominant coalition members, the managers instrumental in the earlier step gathered hard and soft data about the target firms. The country data came mainly from published sources. With a larger group of coalition members, the managers hammered out the content of the prospective alliance arrangements. This was followed by euphoria for some, but a handful of managers kept on insisting for more information without necessarily explaining reasons for it. Formal contacts with the target partner and the country officials were established. (Assimilation)

Step 3

The partner tuned in to the possibility of alliance. The key stockholders were briefed with cost-benefit analysis and the possible effects of the alliance on the company's global operation were discussed. The top echelons visited each other's facility followed by visits of the technically qualified managers and human resource personnel. (Attenuation)

Step 4

Each partner's strategic disposition was debated within and between the partners. Contractual obligations for each partner were spelt out and the contract was formally drawn. (Association)

The insight to the steps actually followed by the partners assisted the respondents' group to develop an ideal sequence. Having read the stories of how the partners went about forming their alliances and then moving to the theoretical steps of alliance bargaining provided contextual grounding for the schematic model. Figure 2 provides the ideal sequence.

Figure 2: The Sequential Order of the Content-process Issues

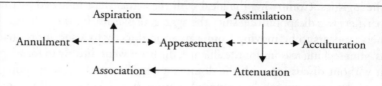

Consider the Basic Effects

Aspiration: Why alliance? Why, when and how does this alliance add value? How will it help our margin? When? What are we asking from our partner? Why? How long do we wish to continue this alliance?

Discuss with Dominant Coalition Members

Assimilation: Why this country? How does the host government view alliances? What are the restrictions for future investment, corporate taxes, and convertibility of currency into dollar? Why this partner? How reputable is the partner? How similar or different are its structures and strategies from us? How much of our earlier experiences are of value here? Does the target company have any prior experiences in managing alliances? Does it have alliances with others at this time? With whom and why? Could we draw a profile of its existing top- and mid-level managers?

Tuning in to the Possibility

Attenuation: Do we have enough information to draw a T-account of the alliance? Which managers visited the location? What do they say? How does our alliance help or hinder the partnering company? What does it expect from alliance? Who are the most 'capable' managers we have to manage the alliance? How is our information system like?

Make the Final Decision

Association: How does our partner view the world compared to us? Are the goals sufficiently clear for both parties? Should this alliance be time-certain? What are the costs of exit? What will be the signposts for exit? Have we interacted with all of our stakeholders that matter? Are we enthused about the alliance? Are all the internal logistics in place?

The ideal sequence based on the stories and against the theoretical backdrop suggests that, at the outset, alliance is placed in the corporate context examining the value-added component of the proposed alliance. The final decision is made after elaborate discussions with the firm's dominant coalition and preparation of a thorough capital budget and the logistics. Comparing the ideal with the actual steps followed by the partners was disappointing since the aggregate picture, for the U.S. partners, appears to be moving from aspiration directly to association, that is, after seeking reasons for the alliance, the firms went directly to forming it without discussing with the dominant coalition and without tuning in to the company for the proposed venture. Just the opposite direction appeared to be followed by the Indian partners, i.e. 'let us get the 'business' first and we will then think strategically and put the logistics in place.' Figure 3 provides a summary of both the U.S. and the Indian responses.

Figure 3: The Sequential Order (Ideal and Actual)

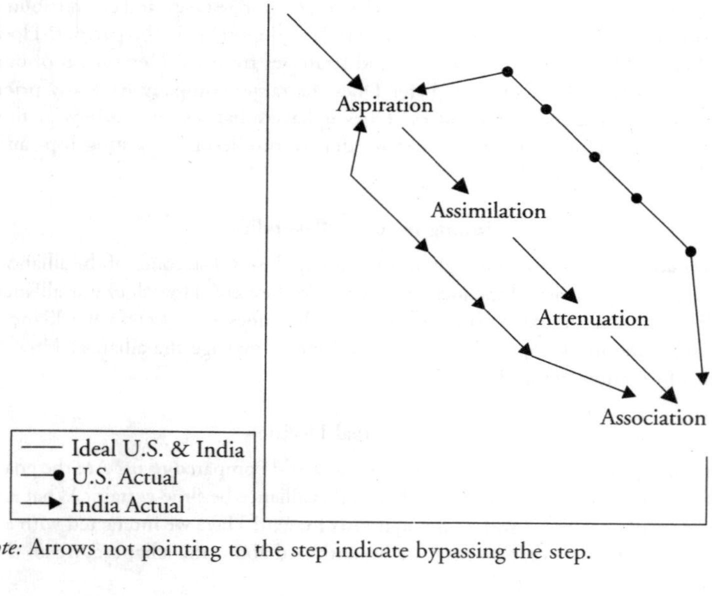

Aspiration

Assimilation

Attenuation

Association

—— Ideal U.S. & India
—●→ U.S. Actual
—→ India Actual

Note: Arrows not pointing to the step indicate bypassing the step.

Was it the rush 'to get going' that produced the gap between the ideal and the actual sequence? We do not know. What we do know is that alliances with developing nations are perceived largely as 'a bundle of opportunity' and opportunism is still the mantra. The cases where the alliances became strategic were those with high investment volume. In this sense, *ad hocism* may have lost some of its luster but it is far from being dead. 'Expediency is truly stateless,' retorted an experienced Indian executive and added, 'we started thinking strategically when we found our American partner was serious about managing the venture.' An American consultant advising companies on alliances summed up the issue thus, 'An unstable alliance in India might not have serious impact on most American corporations' future EPS or P/E ratio but will certainly damage their reputations in this part of the world and instability has a great multiplier effect.'

Implications for International Management

This research is the first attempt to explore the intricacies of alliance management in the context of U.S. and Indian partners. Using both quantitative and qualitative approaches, the study generates a set of variables that are specific to the transaction and provides a sequential order to integrate the content and process. The high predictive strength of variables has the theoretical support but the strengths of the variables are found to be quite different in two countries. Results of the study reinforce our contention that cultural compatibility is not an intractable barrier for stability. Examining the transaction-specific variables and framing a sequential order before the alliance is formed are not just finding room for co-existence; they are about setting the direction of the alliance in a stable environment, and doing it before the alliance is signed and sealed. Stability, in itself, does not assure growth but it provides the time to focus on the strategic issues which might otherwise be diluted in the noise and hoopla of managing the venture.

Accepting each alliance as unique benefits the arrangement in several ways. The effort to identify the transaction-specific variables signals a level of seriousness which reduces the propensity to behave opportunistically. Another benefit is that seriousness of one partner surreptitiously transforms the expected outcome of the alliance from short-term to long-term financial returns and from mercantilism to professionalism. According to our U.S. respondents, stability is greatly dependent on the understanding of the strategic intent of each other, though it is not clear whether they appreciate that a formal clarification of the intent is not enough. As the alliance proceeds, the original intents are often supplemented by a new set of intents as the partners continue to configure their norms of engagement. For the Indian partners, reverence to top management, macro-economic policy and a designated group of managers addressing the alliance issues were critical for alliance stability but not strategic intent. The managerial inputs, by involving middle managers in the formulation and implementation of the alliance arrangement, cross-training them, and having a designated group of managers seem to have high predictive strengths for the U.S. partners. The importance of the role of each partner, both in strategic and operational terms, also explained stability. Personal chemistry between the top managers was important, and more so in India, but this chemistry, according to the American partners, had to be reinforced by maintaining a linearity between 'saying' and 'doing'—by allocating resources in proportion to what was agreed upon and intended. The exogenous factors—economic policy and national infrastructure—were not seen to be significant by the U.S. partners. The Indian partners thought differently.

The attempt to develop a sequential model integrating the content and process issues demanded from the participating managers a great deal of time and energy. Not only did they have to read 16 stories, they were also forced to think of a contextually appropriate sequence. That most of the alliance partners shortchanged the ideal sequential order raises the question of whether the order was sufficiently grounded or the rush 'to get going' obfuscates the discipline we thought they required. Yet, the participating managers in this phase of the study voiced the necessity of adhering to the ideal sequence for alliance stability. And the same group of managers in recalling the actual sequence pointed out the gaps from the ideal sequence. Instability, as one senior executive summarized, echoing many of his counterparts, led to 'fiat, fiefdom and fiasco which inevitably leads to cost escalation and narrowing margin ... at that point you don't care much about the future, you just want to get hell out of here.' It was interesting to find that 89% of the alliances did not have any stipulated dissolution dates, and that a motley number of managers in both countries did not see alliances any more difficult to manage than other types of ventures which, we believe, was largely contributed by the fact that the partnering organizations did not view themselves as direct competitors in the foreseeable future.

One of the important limitations was confining the study to dyadic alliances—the alliances of the U.S. corporations with Indian firms ignoring other existing parallel venturing arrangements. For example, a large consumer electronics manufacturer in India was found to have alliances with companies from Japan, Holland, Britain as well as the U.S. Similarly, many of the American partners had alliances with companies in Europe, the newly industrialized nations as well as with Indian firms. Isolating the experience with the U.S. from other on-going alliances was difficult, and to this end, this study remains incomplete.

We scratched the surface in deciphering the role of middle managers in alliance management, which in itself is a subject of study. Our experience is that middle managers will play a critical role in alliances with LDCs for two main reasons: (a) since most of the alliances are at the low level of investments, these managers are increasingly bestowed with strategic and operating responsibilities, and (b) through repeated ineractions, they are most likely to be able to cut through the double-layered acculturation of both national and corporate cultures and make things happen.

Future research should account for the fact that institutional environment is not always a 'result of connectedness with other organizations... it can result from pressures exerted by societal expectations as well as from organization–organization interdependencies' (Dacin 1997: 50). Managing the intricacies of alliances provides legitimacy of the ventures and we did not explore the issues related to isomorphism–legitimacy linkage. It is more than a theoretical interest to examine how the MNCs legitimize their presence in a developing country and how they change the contextual role of their Asian partners from mere outsourcing agents to agents of transformation. One cannot ignore the overarching impact of 'nationalism' which forms the subtexts of alliance management in a developing country. For instance, corporations like Enron, KFC, Coke and Pepsi have in recent years experienced the earnestness of nationalism in India. Our aim was not to delve into the realm of public policy though we recognize the nature of interdependency. Until free market concept is entrenched and monetary discipline takes root, it would be wise for MNCs to concentrate on garnering internal stability of their alliances and empower their local partners to think strategically from which the regulatory and public endorsements of their existence will ensue.

Notes

1. Oster defines the central features of an alliance as an arrangement in which the partners agree to operate 'for a period of time and for a defined set of operations,' and 'agree not to operate through the marketplace' (1994: 229). Buckley, in the

similar vein, defines it as 'inter-firm collaboration over a given economic space and time for the attainment of mutually defined goals' (1992: 91). He excludes buyer-seller relationships, sub-contracting agreements, licensing and franchising but includes joint ventures. Glaister and Buckley suggest that an alliance becomes strategic when it has 'inputs from all parties and are defined in terms of goals over a well-defined economic space' (1996: 302). We accepted this definition for the study and excluded separate entity joint ventures since the number of 'children' are too small in the present context of the U.S. and the Indian alliances.
2. Factor analysis results are separately available from the authors.

References

Barkema, H.G., Bell, J.H. and Pennings, J.M. 1996. Foreign entry, cultural barriers, and learning. *Strategic Management Journal*, 17: 151–161.

Bartlett, C.A. and Ghoshal, S. 1992. *Transnational Management*. Homewood, IL: Irwin.

Beamish, P.W. 1988. *Multinational Joint Ventures in Developing Countries*. London: Routledge.

Bleeke, J. and Ernst, D. 1991. The way to win in cross-border alliances. *Harvard Business Review*, 69: 127–135.

Bresser, R.K.F. 1988. Matching collective and competitive strategies. *Strategic Management Journal*, 9: 375–385.

Buckley, P.J. 1992. Alliances, technology and markets: A coutionary tale. In P.J. Buckley's *Studies in International Business*. London: Macmillan.

Buckley, P.J. and Casson, M. 1988. A theory of cooperation in international business. In F.J. Contractor and P. Lorange (eds) *Co-operative Strategies in International Business*, pp. 31–54. Lexington, MA: Lexington Books.

Chakravarthy, B.S. and Lorange, P. 1991. *Managing the Strategy Process*. Englewood Cliffs, New Jersey: Prentice Hall.

Chesley, J.A. and Huff, A.S. 1994. A broader, more contextually oriented agenda for upper echelon research. *Academy of Management Meeting*. Dallas, TX.

Dacin, M.T. 1997. Isomorphism in context: The power and prescription of institutional norms. *Academy of Management Journal*, 40: 46–81.

Das, T.K. and Teng, B. 1996. Strategic alliance structuring: A risk perception model. *Academy of Management Meeting*, Cincinnati, Ohio.

Deephouse, D.L. 1996. Does isomorphism legitimate? *Academy of Management Journal*, 39: 1024–1030.

Devlin, G. and Bleackley, M. 1988. Strategic alliances — Guidelines for success, *Long Range Planning*, 21: 18–23.

Dutton, J.E. and Ashford, S.J. 1993. Selling issues to top management. *Academy of Management Review*, 18: 397–428.

Fahey, L. and Christensen, H.K. 1986. Evaluating the research on strategy content. *Journal of Management*, 12: 167–183.

Geringer, J.M. and Herbert, L. 1989. Control and performance of international joint ventures. *Journal of International Business Studies*, 20: 425–435.

Glaister, K.W. and Buckley, P.J. 1996. Strategic motives for international alliance formation, *Journal of Management Studies*, 33: 31–332.

Hambrick, D.C. 1994. Top management groups. A conceptual integration and reconsideration of the 'team' label. In B.M. Staw & L.L. Cummings (eds) *Research in Organizational Behavior*. Vol. 16, pp. 171–213. Greenwich CT: JAI Press.

Hambrick, D.C. and Mason, P.A. 1984. Upper echelons: the organization as a reflection of its top managers. *Academy of Management Review*, 9: 193–206.

Hamel, G. 1997. Killer strategies that make shareholders rich. *Fortune*, June 23, 1997: 70–84.

Hamel, G. and Prahalad, C.K. 1989. Collaborate with your competitors and win. *Harvard Business Review*, 67: 63–76.

Hamel, G. and Prahalad, C.K. 1994. *Competing for the Future*. Boston: Harvard Business Review Press.

Harrigan, K.R. 1988. Joint ventures and competitive strategy. *Strategic Management Journal*, 12: 105–124.

Huff, A.S. and Reger, R.K. 1987. A review of strategy process research. *Journal of Management*, 13: 211–236.

Inkpen, A.C. and Beamish, P.W. 1997. Knowledge, bargaining power, and the instability of international joint ventures. *Academy of Management Review*, 22: 177–202.

Kogut, B. 1989. The stability of joint ventures: Reciprocity and competitive rivalry. *The Journal of Industrial Economics*, 38: 183–198.

Kogut, B. and Singh, H. 1988. The effect of national culture on the choice of entry model. *Journal of International Business Studies*, 19: 411–432.

Lane, H.W. and Beamish, P.W. 1990. Cross-cultural cooperative behavior in joint ventures in LDCs. *Management International Review*, 30 (special issue): 87–102.

Nooteboom, B., Berger, H. and Noorderhave, N.G. 1997. Effects of trust and governance on relational risk. *Academy of Management Journal*, 40: 308–338.

Oliver, C. 1990. Determinants of inter-organizational relationships: integration and future directions. *Academy of Management Review*, 15: 241–265.

Osborn, R.N. and Hagedoorn, J. 1997. The institutionalization and evolutionary dynamics of inter-organizational alliances and networks. *Academy of Management Journal*, 40: 261–278.

Oster, S.M. 1994. *Modern Competitive Analysis*. NY: Oxford University Press.

Park, S.H. and Ungson, G.R. 1997. The effect of national culture, organizational complementarity, and economic motivation on joint venture dissolution. *Academy of Management Journal*, 40: 279–307.

Parkhe, A. 1993. 'Messy' research, methodological predisposition and theory development in international joint ventures. *Academy of Management Review*, 18: 227–268.

Porter, M.E. 1987. From competitive strategy to cooperative strategy. *Harvard Business Review*, 65(3): 43–59.

Prahalad, C.K. and Hamel, G. 1994. Strategy as a field of study: Why search for a new paradigm? *Strategic Management Journal* (special issue), 15: 5–16.

Ring, P.S. and Van de Ven, A.H. 1994. Structuring cooperative relationships between organizations. *Strategic Management Journal*, 13: 483–498.

Robinson, R.B. and Pearce, J.A. 1988. Planned patterns of strategic behavior and their relationship to business-unit performance. *Strategic Management Journal*, 9: 43–60.

Rumelt, Schendel, D.P. and Teece, D.J. (eds) 1994. *Fundamental Issues in Strategy.* Boston: Harvard Business School Press.

Saxton, T. 1997. The effects of partner and relationship characteristics on alliance outcome. *Academy of Management Journal*, 40: 443–461.

Senge, P.M. 1990. The leader's new work: Building learning organizations. *Sloan Management Review*, 32(1): 7–23.

Teece, D.J. 1992. Competition, cooperation, and innovation: Organizational arrangements or regimes of rapid technological progress. *Journal of Economic Behavior and Organization*, 18: 1–25.

Westley, F.R. 1990. Middle managers and strategy: Microdynamics of inclusion. *Strategic Management Journal*, 11: 337–351.

Williamson, O.E. 1985. *The Economic Institutions of Capitalism.* New York: Free Press.

Williamson, O.E. 1991. Comparative economic organization: the analysis of discrete structural alternatives. *Administrative Science Quarterly*, 26: 269–296.

Woolridge, B. and Floyd, S.W. 1990. The strategy process, middle management involvement, and organizational performance. *Strategic Management Journal*, 11: 231–241.

INDIAN MANAGEMENT IN TRANSITION AND IMPLICATIONS FOR GLOBAL MANAGEMENT PRACTICES

Future Directions in Indian Management

This section returns to the analysis of the micro-level responses to the macro-level imperatives of the strongly contested frames of globality. As we arrive at a world in which consumer tastes and preferences are homogenised and responded to through the design and delivery of standardised global products and services, the intervention of global corporations with less than desirable commitment to the forces of locality becomes critical. The pace and intensity of managerial change necessary to sustain the global linkages may often overlook the slow 'domestication' of many of these forces. The active role that managers play in the Indian corporate context in shaping the global managerial imperatives needs to be given more prominence to produce a more 'grounded' understanding of the absorption and adaptation of a range of managerial philosophies and practices.

The two chapters here analyse the cultural limits of globalisation in the context of the Indian managerial outlook. In the chapter by respected managerial scholar P.N. Khandwalla we get a synoptic and aerial view of the recent economic environment before proceeding to clinically evaluate three corporate cases to arrive at a generalised view of corporate responses to globalisation. The discussion in this chapter is centred around a model and an empirical exploration of 139 Indian businesses. The study design allows the author to report on the correlation with an index of relative excellence in areas like entrepreneurial management policies, organic management policies, professional management-oriented policies, participatory employee-oriented management policies, differentiation-related practices. The findings are immensely relevant in assessing the impact of the waning influence of regulatory regimes and the new vigour by which the corporate sector may be able to respond to the world of global competitiveness.

The chapter by Gopalan and Stahl examines the transferability of a number of culture-specific management ideas from the American context to the Indian context. The importation of concepts and ideas on human nature orientation, time orientation, approaches to work and relationships in society are compared with a speculation that Indian managers are demonstrating a strong 'cross-vergence' in terms of accepting some American ideas while keeping their divergent ideas at the forefront of others.

The two chapters presented here challenge the simplistic notion of Westernisation of the Indian managerial world view. They instead demonstrate the emergence of 'multiple responses' rather than a single global gradient of assumption that modern management resided exclusively in the West. Little more than a decade ago, it was commonplace to write about the dearth of research in the area of local responses to global imperatives, but these two chapters demonstrate the breaking down of the hegemonic domination of the field. The radical and cutting-edge quality of Khandwalla's propositions may prove to be attractive to new researchers in India in extending the ideas further by adopting new methodologies and empirical foci. Reassuringly, some of the stories of world-class companies in India attest to the view that the achievement of sophistication may not be widely known, but it is real (Ghoshal et al., 2001).

Reference

Ghoshal, S., G. Piramal and S. Budhiraja (2001), *World Class in India: A Casebook of Companies in Transformation*. New Delhi: Penguin Books.

15 Effective Organisational Response by Corporates to India's Liberalisation and Globalisation

Pradip N. Khandwalla

Introduction

The 20th century saw major societal changes: the Great Depression; the Russian and Chinese revolutions; independence for many former colonies; democratisation and planned socio-economic development in many poor countries; and relatively more recently, the liberalisation and globalisation of most economies. Studies of organisational adaptations to such major societal changes are relatively infrequent. But they can be rich in insights (Stinchcombe, 1965; Barley and Kunda, 1992; Clark and Soulsby, 1995; Wilkinson, 1996; Suhomlinova, 1999). They can provide insights into the general organization adaptation to a major societal change, alternative adaptations that are or can be utilised, and what may be the more effective among these adaptations in performance terms. The attempt in this paper is to examine how the liberalisation and globalisation of the Indian economy after 1990 have influenced corporate organisations in a country that was earlier quite statist, and what sort of organisational adaptation may be relatively more effective in the new context. After presenting the model of effective adaptation, the paper presents evidence from four different sources: published information on how Indian corporates have been coping with liberalisation and globalisation; two corporate case studies of what appear to be effective adaptations and one of ineffective adaptation; data from a post-liberalisation study of 139 Indian corporate organisations; and the major findings from a recent study of 54 Indian organisations.

The Indian Economy

India is a country with an immense economic potential. It has a billion customers; and one of the world's largest pools of entrepreneurial, managerial, scientific, and technical manpower. It is one of the world's leaders in IT, nuclear, space satellite, and rocket technologies. It has among the ten largest industrial economies and among the five largest agricultural economies. It has been growing for the past 20 years at just about 6% per annum (World Bank, 2001, Table 1, pp. 274–275), nearly twice the rate of the US economy. In purchasing power parity terms, the World Bank has estimated the size of its economy in 1999 at US $2144 b (World Bank, 2001, Table 1, pp. 274–275), the fourth largest economy in the world. And yet it has miles to go. It was ranked 52 in an international competitiveness assessment (World Economic Forum, 1999). By way of comparison, China was ranked 32, Malaysia 16, Thailand 30, and Indonesia 37 respectively. IMD's 1999 world competitiveness rankings indicated that on customer orientation, entrepreneurship, social responsibility of managers, and shareholder value creation, India ranked well below China and Malaysia (Sharma, Nair and Suny, 2000). Its overall manufacturing productivity is perhaps a tenth of the world average (Sharma, Nair and Suny, 2000, Table 6). Its cement and steel plants, again on an average, consume twice the fuel per ton as do the Japanese plants (Sharma, Nair and Suny, Table 12). Its exports at around US $45 b are quite small for the size of the economy. Indian goods have yet to establish a reputation for quality. Indian infrastructure has significantly improved, but yet lags far behind that of even China. There are huge intra-industry variations in productivity and efficiency, suggesting highly variable management competence. For instance, in a study of ten Indian machine tools producers, value added per employee varied by a factor of seven, and order delivery times by a factor of six (Nandi, 1995). The liberalisation and the globalisation of the economy was attempted in a major way beginning in 1991 to modernise the country's economy and actualise India's economic potential through a competitive market economy.

Liberalization of the Indian Economy

India began to decontrol its statist, centrally planned economy in the 1980s. But substantial liberalisation of the economy began in earnest in 1991. In that year, following a serious balance of payments crisis when foreign exchange reserves were down to a billion dollars, India resorted to a bailout by IMF, and accepted the structural adjustment of its economy broadly as per IMF and World Bank conditionalities.

Indian structural adjustment so far has had several components that have made the economy far more competitive and turbulent than before 1991 (Ahluwalia, 1996). These include graduated deregulation of industry through substantial but phased elimination of licensing for setting up industries and for expanding capacity, abolition of the office of Controller of Capital Issues, drastic reduction in the number of industries reserved for the public sector, liberalization of corporate access to foreign technology, phased elimination of import and export controls, and phased reduction in import duties (from an average of around 100 per cent in 1991 to about a third of this by 2000–2001). The economy has been opened up to foreign private investment. At the same time the government has also taken several business friendly initiatives. Overseas investments by Indian firms have been liberalised. There has been rationalisation of taxes, substantial reductions in income tax, wealth tax, and corporate tax on profits, selective and phased lowering of excise duties, the setting up of a national stock exchange with electronic operations, the enforcement of new accounting norms to bring reporting of income by corporates and banks to international standards, increase in the functioning autonomy of public enterprises (but also greater risk to them of closure, if they malfunction). The government has also stepped up investment in infrastructure and human resource development. Public policy after 1990 has considerably increased the exposure of corporates to competitive pressures and at the same time also raised opportunities for relatively unfettered growth and diversification. A recently concluded study of 54 Indian corporates reveals that out of eight items of rated change in the business environment over the past five years, the four largest perceived changes were: greater turbulence in the product market environment characterised by many unexpected changes, more intense competition, greater buoyancy and growth potential, and greater requirements for technological sophistication (Som, 2002).

Economy's Response to Liberalization

The economy's response to liberalisation and structural adjustment appears, by and large, to have been effective (Business Today, 1995b; Jain, 1996; Raghavan, 1996). After a stall in 1991, the economy resumed its growth path, with the GDP growth rate of about 6 percent per annum during 1992–2000. After China, India has been the fastest growing of the world's major economies in the 1990s. Inflation is sharply down from 1991, and by 2000, exports have increased by 150% in dollar terms. Private foreign direct investment, about US $ 160 m in 1991, has risen to about US 2 billion dollars a year. A large number of MNCs have set up shop in several manufacturing industries like automobile, white goods, foods, cosmetics, and IT hardware, and service industries like IT software, banking, management consultancy, and merchandising. Foreign collaboration approvals were around 1600 during 1991–1995, compared to around 700 in 1980–1990 (Subrahmaniam et al., 1996). Thousands of indigenous enterprises have also got set up. Industrial production doubled during 1991–2000 (Reserve Bank of India, 2002:56–57), and the services sector has emerged as a dynamic growth sector. These changes are in stark contrast to the post-liberalisation performance of several other countries, notably the constituents of the former Soviet block, several African countries, and several South American countries as well (World Bank, 2001, Table 1, pp. 274–275). For instance, Russia began its liberalisation and structural adjustment also in 1991. The performance of the Russian economy up until the late 1990s has been disastrous (World Bank, 2001, Table 1, pp. 274–275), with sharp declines in GDP and industrial output.

Model of Effective Corporate Response to Economic Liberalisation

Economic liberalization and globalization have two major implications for the corporate world (Khandwalla, 1996). They intensify competition by lowering barriers to entry. They also open up many opportunities for growth through the removal of regulations and artificial barriers on pricing and output decisions, investments, plant scales, mergers, acquisitions, joint ventures, technology imports, import of foreign capital, etc. They enable corporations to expand, diversify, integrate, and globalize more freely. Both these implications may have profound consequences for the effective management of corporations in a liberalizing economy.

Corporate organisational designs represent strategic choices (Child, 1972; Peters and Waterman, 1980; Khandwalla, 1977, 1992; Bobbitt and Ford, 1980; Miller and Friesen, 1984) and they are likely to vary from enterprise to enterprise, industry to industry, and economy to economy. And yet there may be some core adaptations to liberalisation suggested by contingency theory (Thompson, 1967; Lawrence and Lorsch, 1967; Child and Kieser, 1981; Donaldson, 1996). These cover systemic and strategic organisational responses. Systemic responses encompass organisational structural, process, functional, and cultural responses, while strategic responses relate to the formulation of goals, priorities, business strategy, etc. (Khandwalla, 1996).

Greater competition, especially when competition is multi-dimensional, poses a serious problem to the organisation's decision makers of coping with uncertainty (Khandawlla, 1981). This uncertainty stems from competitive moves by domestic, and with globalisation, by foreign rivals vis-à-vis price cutting, introduction of new or differentiated products, promotion campaigns, acquisition of distribution channels and advantageous locations, etc. Each competitive move triggers chains of reactions, which in turn trigger further reactions, rendering the environment turbulent (Thompson, 1967). Uncertainty makes planning of operations difficult (March and Simon, 1958; Thompson, 1967), and organisations therefore need to consider various uncertainty control measures.

Where there are a lot of local uncertainties, regional decentralisation of operations may be required. Where parts of the external environment are particularly ambiguous, specialised units to monitor them may be needed. More and more mechanisms and more and more powerful uncertainty control mechanisms may be required by the corporation as an economy moves towards a full liberalisation and globalisation. To remain viable, the organisation increasingly needs to become a strong information acquiring, information processing, and quickly learning and adapting organism (Burns and Stalker, 1961; Nilakant and Ramnarayan, 1998).

Multi-sided competition has another systemic consequence. It tends to differentiate the decision structure of the organisation (Lawrence and Lorsch, 1967). A wide range of expertise is needed to cope with the numerous contingencies created by a competitive environment, and a wide range of organisational mechanisms needs to be considered to cope with these contingencies, such as sophisticated quality control, MIS, planning, formal market research, and functional and role specialisation. These may imply the setting up of specialised staff units. A structure differentiated by numerous specialised units would imply the existence of correspondingly numerous operating subcultures (Katz and Kahn, 1966; Lawrence and Lorsch, 1967; Van de Ven and Delbecq, 1974), each with its distinctive mode of conducting its operations. Under liberalisation induced competition, therefore, to remain viable the corporate organisation may need to get much more differentiated as compared to that in a regulated, protected economy. In turn, such differentiation may need to be offset by the greater use of integrative mechanisms (Lawrence and Lorsch, 1967), such as core values (Peters and Waterman, 1982), professionalism, and participatory, consensus seeking decision making (Likert, 1961). Thus, competition, especially multi-faceted competition, may require the organisation to deploy extensively uncertainty reduction, differentiation, and integration mechanisms for remaining viable. There is evidence that synchronised deployment of uncertainty reduction, differentiation, and integration mechanisms as a response to high levels of environmental uncertainty is associated with organizational performance (Lawrence and Lorsch, 1967; Khandwalla, 1973; Miller and Friesen, 1984). There is also evidence of positive synergy in competitive environments between professional and participative modes of management (Khandwalla, 1977, ch. 11).

Indian economic liberalisation has opened up many entrepreneurial opportunities, such as for relatively unfettered expansion and diversification, joint ventures, mergers and acquisitions, and internationalisation of operations. Such opportunities can be seized by a "prospector" organisation, and an "entrepreneurial" mode of strategic management (Mintzberg, 1973; Miles and Snow, 1978; Manimala, 1992) that is flexible and organic (Burns and Stalker, 1961). Research on entrepreneurial management suggests a strong synergy between entrepreneurial management and the organic style of management (Khandwalla, 1977, ch. 11; Covin and Slevin, 1988; Naman and Slevin, 1993).

Diagram 1 summarises the model of an effective corporate management response to liberalisation and globalisation.

Diagram 1: Economic liberalisation and effective corporate response

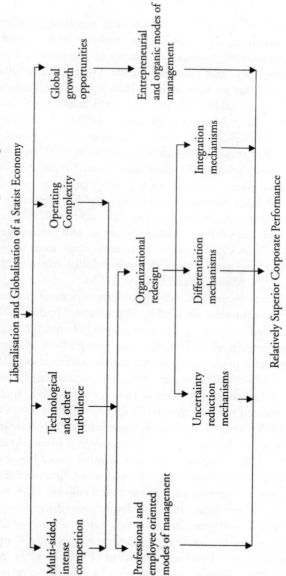

Reported Corporate Response to Indian Liberalization

A national policy of stepping up domestic and foreign competition through deregulation and globalisation seems to have elicited greater corporate attention to productivity, quality of processes and products, operating efficiency, and customer needs. During the 1990s, many corporations appear to have utilized business process reengineering, quality circles, computerisation, and ISO certification (Abraham, 1995a, 1995b; Joseph, 1995; Mukerjea and George, 1995). There were barely a dozen ISO certifications in 1990; the number in 2000 may be over 2000. In a poll of corporate executives reported in 1995, over half rated quality as extremely important (Business Today, 1995a). Service to the customer as an essential adjunct to marketing products, called morph marketing, has been picking up (Chatterjee, 1995). Marketing expenditure as a percentage of sales has gone up. In a survey of 200 large corporations, the increase was from marketing cost to sales percentage of 5.07 in 1990 to 5.65 in 1993; however, marketing flops seem to be on the increase, suggesting greater corporate vulnerability due to competition (Mukerjea, 1995; Mukerjea and George, 1995).

The corporate sector has also apparently responded proactively to the growth opportunities afforded by liberalisation. Earlier, Indian corporations tended to opt for plant sizes keeping in mind the size of the protected domestic market. They have increasingly been opting for sizes that can cater also to the international market and thus avail of greater economies of scale. For instance, by 1995 there were at least fifteen Indian private sector companies that were already one of the five largest in the world (or expected to be so shortly) in specific product lines (Vora and Assomull, 1995). There were virtually none before 1991. As of end 1993 there were at least a hundred private sector projects involving an investment of 200 million dollars or more, a number vastly larger than the number before liberalisation (Ghani, 1994). Earlier, "internationalisation" amounted mostly to getting a foreign technical collaboration with a firm from a developed economy, and a modest export effort. Not only have foreign technical collaborations gone up, but in a study of 200 large Indian corporations, corporate exports appear to have risen sharply, from 4.5 percent of sales in 1990 to 6.4 percent of sales in 1993 (Mukerjea and George, 1995). True globalization may have begun in earnest in the form of Indian companies buying foreign firms and plants, large joint ventures with MNCs, global marketing, raising of finance overseas, etc. (Kawatra, 1995; Mukerjea and George, 1995; Ramachandran, 1995; Vora and Assomull, 1995). Several business houses have been re-examining their strategies in the new economic environment. Some seem to be seeking aggressive diversification in their areas of competence to build up competitive strength, while the more entrepreneurial ones appear to be actively seeking opportunistic diversification to take advantage of opportunities afforded by liberalisation and globalisation (Khanna, 1994). Mergers and acquisitions have sharply increased, from 2 in 1992 to 97 in 1997 (Rao and Das, 1998). A recently concluded study of 54 Indian corporates indicates that over the past five years 74% reported change in their business focus, 69% reported a new product/market strategy, 61% reported significant outsourcing, and 54% reported engaging in joint ventures (Som, 2002).

Liberalization also seems to be inducing significant cultural and management systems related changes in the corporate sector in the expected direction. The new rhetoric of corporate India seems to be "change is the only constant," "only quality ensures survival," "people, not products, are paramount," and "information is everything"; and the main challenges before their chief executives are seen to be to create flexible systems, to develop a culture of excellence, to facilitate teamwork and empower employees, and to speed up and decentralize data flows (Business Today, 1994). There may still be a gap between rhetoric and reality. But the change in corporate culture and management seems to be increasingly compatible with a competitive market environment.

Organizational structures, too, seem to be changing to cope with greater competition and to avail of growth opportunities afforded by liberalization and globalization (Business Today, 1994; Roy, 1995). Corporate restructurings, many involving the services of international management consultants (Som, 2002), have become far more frequent (National Management Forum, 1995; Monga, 1997; Khandwalla, 2001). The major reason for restructuring appears to be unsatisfactory corporate structure and business processes in a much more competitive and technologically turbulent operating environment (National Management Forum, 1995; Monga, 1997). Intensive scanning of the national and the international environment for growth opportunities is on the rise, and so is comprehensive strategy-making that is integrated with a human resource management strategy (Som, 2002). By the mid-1990s, some business houses, such as the Duncan Goenka Group, were regrouping their varied product lines spread over diverse companies into synergistic product clusters for sharper focus; some, such as Godrej, were graduating product divisions into "strategic business units" with more freedom to make financial and investment decisions and for entering into alliances; some, such as Modi Xerox, were converting functional departments into profit centres via the transfer pricing mechanism for greater bottom line consciousness in management (Roy, 1995; Mukerjea and George, 1995; National Management Forum, 1995; Monga, 1997). Some multi-product companies, such as Chloride India, were transiting to a division-alized set up for greater market responsiveness; while some, such as the public sector Balmer Lawrie, were spinning off joint ventures with foreign partners into companies, each with equity stakes by the parent organizations, in order to escape organizational limits to growth. A few, such as Tata Consultancy Services and Wipro Infotech, in the business of executing projects, were resorting to the matrix structure in which staff members were grouped both by areas of core competencies and by principal markets or industries served. Divisionalization, resort to stra-tegic business units, spin offs, matrix structure, etc., often create problems of corporate-wide coordination, economizing, synergy, integration, etc. To tackle this problem some businesses, such as the Lloyds Group, were setting up a central monitoring group to coordinate strategies formulated by the chief executives of its different businesses, and also to serve as a nodal agency for technical and financial alliances. Some others, such as Asea Brown Boveri India, were setting up a holding company to propagate corporate vision and core values in the subsidiaries. The preferences seem to be to try and increase organizational differentiation through decentral-ization (Som, 2002), and through setting up self-contained, autonomous units with bottom line responsibility, and try and increase integration through a system of apex coordination, use of coordinating committees and cross functional teams, internal communications, participative deci-sion making, shared vision, and institutionalisation of core values (Som, 2002). There seems also a sharply rising resort to establishing a compre-hensive, computer-based MIS (Som, 2002). Greater focus on businesses in which the corporation has "core competence" (Prahalad and Hamel, 1994), attempts to realise synergies between the businesses of the diversi-fied corporation or business group, and some divestment of peripheral or unprofitable businesses also appears to be growing (Monga, 1997). Two emerging priorities appears to be becoming "world class" and managing business professionally to expand overseas (Monga, 1997). Downsizing through voluntary retirement schemes, and human resource development also seems to be on the rise (Monga, 1997; Som, 2002). The human resource management systems of the corporates seem characterised by rising emphasis on professionalism, skills development, incentives, accountability, flexibility and openness, and rightsizing (Som, 2002).

The foregoing suggests that many of the post-liberalisation changes in corporate organisations in India are along the lines predicted by the model. Greater emphasis on scanning, MIS, internal communications on corporation-related developments, and the services of consultants for diagnosis and restructuring purposes indicates increased resort to uncertainty reduction mechanisms. Increased recourse to decentralisation, divisionalisation, spin offs, etc. indicates increased differentiation. Increased recourse to visioning and core values, apex coordination, and core competence indicates greater attempt at integration. Greater emphasis on mergers, acquisitions, joint ventures, collaborative ventures, and internationalisation of operations indicates a step up in the entrepreneurial mode of management. There seems also to be greater emphasis on operating flexibility and responsiveness to environmental change (organic management); on marketing, profit centres, matrix structure, more focused and comprehensive business strategies (professional management); and on better human resource management, HRD, and more consultative, participative decision making (participative management).

Aggregate corporate performance has improved, indicating that the reported organisational strategic, structural, cultural, and operating changes have been effective overall. Corporate private sector sales and profits have practically doubled in real terms. There has also been sizeable growth in the sales and profits of central government-oriented public enterprises (Rekhi, 1995). Between 1990 and 1997 their aggregate sales tripled in nominal terms and profits increased six times (Department of Public Enterprises, 1997–98). Since the reported organizational changes during liberalisation have broadly been along the lines indicated by Diagram 1, the improved performance of the corporate sector may constitute a broad support for the model of effective corporate response to liberalisation.

Performance Variability during Liberalization

Although the overall corporate response in India to liberalization seems to have been compatible with the model outlined earlier, an interesting development has been high intra-industry and intra-sector variability. Practically in every industry, some companies have done very well while a number have floundered. For instance, several corporate stars of the 1980s, including companies of big business groups like the Birlas, the Tatas, the Mafatlals, the Thapars and so forth, have lost their lustre in the era of liberalization. On the other hand, several companies have also held their own, and some have grown drammatically, such as Reliance Industries, L&T, East India Hotels, Grasim, and Hero Honda. While the well-established subsidiaries of such MNCs as Unilever, Pfizer, Novartis, Glaxo, British Tobacco, Britannia, Cadbury, Castrol, Nestle, etc. have tended to continue to prosper, there are also MNC subsidiaries whose performance has declined, or is unsatisfactory, such as Siemens, German Remedies, BOC, Thermax, Pepsi, Coca Cola, Kelloggs, GM, Ford, and Daewoo. In the public sector, while the majority of the 250-odd enterprises owned by the central government have held their own, several that were sickly before liberalization have floundered further. With a few exceptions, the performance of the 800-odd enterprises owned by the various state governments in India, generally with a politician as the board chairperson and a bureaucrat as the chief executive, has declined disastrously.

Across a broad swathe of Indian industries, operating margins have been varying wildly in the same industry. Operating profit as a percentage of sales in the financial year 2000–2001 varied in the computer software industry from 0.9% to 65.7%; in the entertainment industry from –27.1% to 90.9%; among financial services companies from 0.5% to 96.5%; among hotels from 7.7% to 46.1%, among 2 and 3 wheeler producers from 2% to 17.5%; among cement producers, from 3.5% to 37.2%; among petrochemicals companies, from 1.0% to 25.4%; among pharmaceutical companies, from 2.5% to 34.2%; among electronics firms, from 0.9% to 14.7%, and so forth (Fortune India, 2002:25–38).

There can be many reasons for the considerable variability in the performance of Indian corporates in the post-liberalization era in each industry. For instance, some companies may be occupying highly profitable niches while others may be occupying far less lucrative niches. But this may not explain sustained variability because in a liberalised economy no niche is likely to remain highly profitable for long without inviting the entry of competitors. Variation in management and organisational capabilities may be a surer reason for persistently large intra-industry variability in profitability (Peters and Waterman, 1980; Collins and Porras, 1994). Adequate development of the uncertainty reduction, differentiation, and integration mechanisms needed to cope with much greater market turbulence after liberalization, and appropriate policy frameworks and modes of management may have been responsible in part for the relative successes, while inadequate adaptation may have been responsible for the relative failures. Three case studies illustrate what may be appropriate and inappropriate restructuring responses to liberalisation.

Case Studies of Corporate Response to Indian Liberalisation

Clariant India

Clariant India came into existence as a result of the global divestiture by Sandoz, an MNC, of its chemicals business in 1995. These businesses went to Clariant, and its Indian subsidiary came to be known as Clariant (India) Limited. The subsidiary's shares were listed on the Indian stock exchanges. The company had then a staff strength of 1500. The new CEO, Mr. Prakash Rastogi, an insider with a marketing background, set about the process of transforming a relatively sleepy operation with substantial management deficiencies into a dynamic, customer focussed organisation (Khandwalla, 2001).

Several steps were taken to reduce operating uncertainty. Early on, all 170 executives met to grapple with a tough question: how did they want the company to be known 3 years later by its customers, owners, employees, and vendors? Out of the intense deliberations emerged a clarity: a shared vision of being a customer-driven company with a mission of providing high quality products. A powerful communications effort was launched. Boards went up at each plant to keep employees informed about targets and achievements. Executives were enabled to access any report prepared by any department. Members of the Board interacted with the shopfloor staff. Every manager set four monthly priorities for himself/herself, and these were shared with the others. Under a new system, service departments entered into an agreement with their internal "customers" for specified services and greater accountability. To get to know the customers better, and for them to get to know the organisation better, the customers were invited to the company's manufacturing facilities to interact with the staff. They communicated their concerns about the quality of Clariant's products and services directly to the staff. Cross-functional staff teams were formed and sent to the premises of the major customers to understand their needs better. They also sought to understand more fully the complexities of competition in Clariant's markets, including the importance of speed and service.

From the differentiation angle, the autonomy of SBUs was strengthened, and their missions were clarified. Managers, too, got to enjoy a lot more autonomy. Several management functions were professionalised further.

Several integrative mechanisms were initiated/strengthened. The new vision statement was widely discussed and internalised by the staff. A core value that was strengthened was transparency in operations. Any manager could access the reports to management of any other manager. The successes and failures of the organisation were shared even with the lower staff. Efforts were strengthened to inspire the staff with corporate vision and challenges, and to involve them in the corporation's decision making processes. A quarterly system of performance review was framed through the participation of all the managers. Targets were set or reset participatively, and most policy decisions were also taken participatively.

In terms of the style of management, the company was already highly professionlised. But now the management became a lot more participative. The company also veered towards an entrepreneurial mode of management. It mounted a strong exports thrust by seeking a greater integration with the parent company's global operations. Market development was given priority. In 1997–1998 alone 30 new products were introduced. The company began exiting from high volume/low margin commodity markets, and into speciality chemicals and fashion related and eco-friendly products. In terms of organic management policies, the company stepped up interactive decision making, innovations in processes, solutions, and products, and customization.

Possibly because of these initiatives, the company turned into an attractive "bluechip" company, and its share price rose smartly. Its sales and profits grew from Rs. 1450 m and Rs. 70 m in 1995 to Rs. 2350 m and Rs. 150 m in 1998.

Bharat Petroleum Corporation (BPCL)

The former subsidiary of Burmah Shell was nationalised by the Government of India several decades back. Up until the early 1990s, this petroleum refining and petroleum products company, as other government-owned oil companies, operated in an administered prices regime (APR). After the mid-1990s, the APR began to be dismantled, and was scheduled to be completely dismantled by 2002. Anticipating the onrush of competition, the giant company (annual sales of about US $8 billions) began its restructuring in earnest in 1997 with the help of an international management consultant, who, unlike many others operating in India, strongly emphasised innovation and highly participative change (Khandwalla, 2001; Som, 2002).

Uncertainty reduction was sought in an imaginative fashion. Like Clariant, the top management first sought clarity in its vision for the company. At the suggestion of the consultant, this exercise was extended to all 3000 managers of the company. When the vision statements were compared there was a lot of commonality, and a vision statement acceptable to all was developed. Six internal teams were formed to scrutinise refining, logistics, LPG (cooking gas cylinders), lubricants, marketing of other products, and support services and management processes. The outcome was a change plan that ran into 1600 pages. It included an assessment of current reality, definition of organisational values, the long term vision for each of the critical activities of the organisation, and specification of what was needed to be done to turn the vision into reality. Further, linkages across opportunities for more effective operations were sought. The change plan was widely distributed throughout the organisations at all levels, including to the unions. It articulated not only what needed to be done, but also how to develop/modify business strategy, brand creation, and better human relations. The management information system was strengthened through computerisation.

Differentiation was attempted by creating a new decentralised structure that enabled better customer satisfaction. The old functional structure was dismantled. It was replaced by several strategic business units, notably for the refining, petroleum retailing, lubricants, aviation fuel, bottling gas cylinders (LPG), and the industrial customers businesses. In addition, corporate-wide support service departments were formed under the board level directors of finance, personnel, and marketing. These had a policy making role and also the role of general supervision of the corporate-wide functions. They provided policy guidance to relevant functional specialists located in the SBUs. Considerable authority was delegated to the SBUs and down the line. Shared services teams were also set up for non-business specific support tasks like brand building and IT.

Besides the elaborate corporate visioning exercise, integration was provided by the corporate centre and various councils. The corporate centre consisted of the committee of functional directors, the governance council consisting of the top executives, and the integrative council. The governance council itself consisted of an apex council, an executive council, and a management council of a large number of managers whose role was advisory. Each major function, such as human resource management or IT, had its own across-the-SBUs policy making and learning oriented council. The board inducted several independent directors, and played an overall guidance role. Integration was also strengthened through the human resource development route. The consultant coached an internal inter-disciplinary team to play the change agent and coaching role. The coaches have been working with various business teams to enable each team to develop its collective vision and enhance its capabilities. All these teams participate in the Foundations Learning Training Programme and Visionary Leadership and Planning Workshops. For each territory, an integrator and mentor role has been created to provide guidance to territory managers. The company's operations have been integrated through computerisation and SAP-designed enterprise resources planning.

Compared to the conservative and bureaucratic management style upto 1995, the management has become notably more entrepreneurial, organic, professionalist, and participative. A number of entrepreneurial initiatives have been taken. These include the acquisition of a couple of refineries and expansion of the existing refinery, and the launch of a retail business in which several of the company's petrol stations also site general provisions stores. An R&D centre is in the process of being set up. Several joint ventures have been set up or are in the pipeline. The organisation has become notably more flexible and resilient, and innovation and experimentation in all the technical as well as management areas have been stressed. The company bagged several innovation awards in a recent petroleum sector competition. Participative management at all levels is being stressed, primarily through councils, committees, and teams. Professionalism and the tools and techniques of professional management are also being stressed—two recent mechanisms are a sophisticated "balanced scorecard" performance management system tied to the company's vision and priorities, and ERP.

The company has thrived despite increasing competition. Sales have more than doubled between 1996 and 1999, and profits have increased from Rs. 4.3 billions to Rs. 7.2 billions. The company's shares have been quoting at a very healthy premium (as of February 2002 they were quoting at 30 times their par value, substantially higher than those of the other major petroleum products companies in India).

Mahut

A case study of a corporate that substantially failed to respond to the policy and structural implications of economic liberalisation indicates the costs of such a failure (Som, 2002, Appendix A). The Mahut group (name disguised) is a business group that operates two cement companies in the state of Gujarat in western India. As of 1999, each had a production capacity of 1.2 million tons of cement a year. Prior to 1998 both used to compete with one another, as also with other cement players operating in the region.

In terms of uncertainty reduction, an American consultant was hired in 1998 to restructure the two companies and integrate their marketing operations. Based on the consultant's recommendations, competency exercises were carried out for the redefined positions in the new structure. As per the practice before the restructuring, market information was collected by the combined sales force of the two companies; forecasting continued to be done by the forecasting and planning unit. Some initiatives, like masons' meets, were organised to meet important stakeholders like engineers, architects, house builders, masons, etc., both to seek their views and concerns and to inform these stakeholders about corporate developments. However, this sort of interaction appeared to be done less professionally compared to major competitors. One persistent area of weakness was low interaction with industry associations and bureaucrats, politicians, traders, and dealers—often very important sources of market and public policy information. Some other weaknesses were the absence of a formal management information system and the absence of teams and task forces to probe areas of weakness.

As far as differentiation is concerned, some new roles were created pertaining to technical, industry, and market research functions, and suitable personnel were recruited. But a critical weakness was a relative lack of decentralisation. All powers appeared to be concentrated in the hands of the managing director of the cement operations. Equally serious was erosion of differentiation through attrition: several specialists like geologists, engineers, quality control persons left the organisation during the past 3–4 years. Another problem was that the organisation continued to be riven by casteism and regionalism.

As far as integrative mechanisms are concerned, the style of the owners appeared to be benevolently paternalistic. But it was not a strong integrative factor because this sort of paternalism did not percolate downwards. The top management was autocratic, and since the owners had pretty much left the functioning to the top management, the kind of loyalty benevolent paternalism generates in India was largely eroded. The style of the top management appears to have been a factor in the exit of a large number of specialists. Very few management committees were in operation, and control systems were weak. Nor were corporate communications utilised to knit the company together through vision, core values, challenges, and stretch goals.

The management style appeared to be reactive (Miles and Snow, 1978). Despite being in a cyclical industry, with margins under pressure due to excess capacity, there were no significant attempts at product mix changes, diversification, or joint ventures. The management was neither entrepreneurial nor organic nor participative nor professional. Instead, there was much autocracy, adhocism, and stasis.

The performance of the company seems to reflect the many unaddressed management deficiencies relating to the management style as well as to the uncertainty reduction, differentiation, and integration mechanisms. Sales have been falling, and so, too, the market share. Both the cement operations have been making losses. The net worth of one of the two cement units has got completely eroded; that of the other is nearing the bottom.

The three cases indicate differential corporate responses to Indian economic liberalisation and the much more intense competition it has generated. Clariant and BPCL have restructured aggressively and imaginatively; Mahut has appeared so far to be a far more sleepy organization. Both Clariant and BPCL have resorted to many more uncertainty reduction, differentiation and integration mechanisms than Mahut, and have turned much more entrepreneurial, organic, professionalist, and participative. Mahut has remained autocratic and conservative. A strategic choice in both Clariant and BPCL was the cooptation of several significant stakeholders in their respective restructurings. Lower level managers and employees were coopted in the decision making process in both the companies. In addition, in Clariant the customers, too, were coopted, while in BPCL independent professionals on the company's board of directors were coopted. In Mahut, the cooptation of managers and employees appeared to be non-existent, though there was a relatively feeble effort at coopting customers like engineers, architects, and builders.

As a result, Mahut management missed out on the suggestions for change that the internal stakeholders may have made, thus depleting its restructuring choices. Such differential responses to major new contingencies may reflect differences in the personalities of top level managers, their cognitive functioning, their differential interpretation of contingencies, the ingrained culture of the organization, and past commitments (Child, 1972; Bobbitt and Ford, 1980; Miller and Friesen, 1984; Carroll, 1993; Ginsberg, 1994).

From anecdotal evidence we turn to a fairly large sample study of the systemic and management style response of Indian corporates to liberalisation.

A Post-liberalisation Study of Indian Corporate Management

Reported below are the findings of a study on the policies and practices of 139 corporates during the post-liberalisation period in India. Policies are more strategic in nature than practices. They have organisation-wide implications, and they are more guides to management actions than actions themselves (Simon, 1965). That is, there is usually greater discretionary action component in policies than in practices, although practices, too, need to be interpreted in the various situations that arise in an organisation's functioning. The study reports the performance-related correlations of certain policies thought to represent an effective response to the uncertainties, competitive pressures, complexities, and opportunities created by liberalisation. These policies reflect four styles of management, namely, the entrepreneurial, the organic, the professionalist, and the participative styles. The study also reports the performance correlates of uncertainty reduction, differentiation, and integration-related practices in the sample of 139 Indian businesses.

The data were gathered in the context of a programme on the management of excellence by chief executives conducted at the Indian Institute of Management Ahmedabad and coordinated by the author. The participants were chief executives or their direct reports. An important part of the programme was the feedback to the participants on the policies and practices of their respective organisations, and the benchmarking of these with the scores of a sample of high performance Indian organisations. The data were gathered anonymously from an average of about five top level respondents from each organisation, who provided ratings on Likert-type 6-point scales. Their responses were averaged to derive the organisation's score. Table 1 shows some sample characteristics.

Table 1: Sample Profile (*N* = 139)

A. *Sector-wise distribution*	
Indian private sector organisations	69%
Indian public sector organisations	18%
MNC subsidiaries operating in India	13%
B. *Annual sales* (in millions of rupees)	
Small (up to Rs. 500 m)	33%
Medium (Rs. 501 m to Rs. 2000 m)	29%
Large (Rs. 2001 m to 10000 m)	25%
Very large (Rs. 10001 m to Rs. 100000 m)	10%
Giant (over Rs. 100 b.)	3%
C. *Number of employees*	
Small (up to 500 employees)	45%
Medium (501 to 5000 employees)	42%
Large (over 5000 employees)	13%
D. *Industries represented*	
Consumer durable goods	5%
Consumer non-durable goods	13%
Industrial and producer goods	39%
Capital goods	13%
Services	27%
Miscellaneous	3%

The corporate performance measure was called the index of relative performance. It consisted of ten indicators of performance, namely profitability, growth rate, financial strength, performance stability, operating efficiency, staff morale, corporate public image, impact (through e.g. pioneering of new products in India), adaptability, and innovativeness. These indicators were rated anonymously by the associates of the participants, and each rating was done in relation to the perceived performance on the indicator of the best-performing organisation(s) in the industry. The ratings on all the indicators were aggregated and averaged across the respondents from the organisation to derive the organization's score on the index of relative performance. The use of numerous indicators obviated over-reliance on just one or two indicators, and yielded a score compatible with a multiple stakeholders' perspective on organizational effectiveness (Price, 1968; Kanter and Brinkerhoff, 1981; Khandwalla, 1988). The index had a very satisfactory reliability of .89. For a sample of 45 Indian companies, the index was correlated .40 with the ratio of cash profit to sales (Verma, 2002). Table 2 shows the basic statistics of the aggregates of the policies comprising, respectively, the entrepreneurial, organic, professional, and participative styles of management, as well as the aggregates of respectively, uncertainty reduction, differentiation, and integration mechanisms. It also shows their rehabilities (Cronbach's alpha), which range from .70 to .94, satisfactory for an exploratory study (Nunnally, 1967:193).

The aggregated variables seem to have reasonable construct validity. In prior Canadian research, risk taking, conceptually and operationally similar to entrepreneurial style, and flexibility, conceptually and operationally similar to organic management style were significantly positively correlated, as were technocracy (resembling professional management style) and participation (resembling participative management style) (Khandwalla, 1977, Table A-3). In the present study, too, entrepreneurial and organic management styles are significantly positively correlated, as are professional management and participative management styles (see Table 2). In prior US research, uncertainty reduction, differentiation, and integration mechanisms were positively correlated, especially for high performance firms (Khandwalla, 1973). In the present study uncertainty reduction, differentiation, and integration aggregates are significantly positively correlated and also with the measure of performance (see Table 2). In a study of Australian, Canadian, and published data samples, too, measures of uncertainty reduction, differentiation, and integration variables were positively correlated, especially for the "successful" samples (Miller and Friesen, 1984, Table A 9-1). In their study (Miller and Friesen,

Table 2: Intercorrelations of Policies and Practices Aggregates and
their Correlations with Index of Relative Performance (N = 139 Indian Corporates)

"Best" policies and practices aggregates	*Mean (Std. Dev.)*	*Reliability*	*Correlations*						*Index of relative performance*
			2	*3*	*4*	*5*	*6*	*7*	
1. Entrepreneurial management policies aggregate[a]	18.2 (4.1)	.70	.42	.75	.47	.33	.41	.41	.48
2. Organic management policies aggregate[a]	15.1 (2.8)	.72		.59	.66	.70	.66	.65	.36
3. Professional management policies aggregate[a]	18.7 (3.6)	.73			.53	.51	.51	.57	.49
4. Participative management policies aggregate[a]	19.7 (3.3)	.74				.63	.69	.66	.45
5. Uncertainty reduction practices aggregate[b]	33.8 (6.1)	.92					.84	.90	.55
6. Differentiation practices aggregate[b]	34.0 (5.7)	.89						.88	.56
7. Integration practices aggregate[b]	35.7 (6.1)	.94							.63

Note: all the correlations are statistically significant at the 1 % level (2 tails).
[a] Aggregate of 5 scales.
[b] Aggregate of 9 scales.

1984, Appendix 7-A), "entrepreneurship" and "technocratization" were significantly positively correlated as are entrepreneurial management and professional management in the present study, and "entrepreneurship" was significantly correlated with "scanning", a form of uncertainty reduction, and with "differentiation, as are entrepreneurial management with uncertainty reduction and differentiation in the present study—see Table 2.

The eight aggregated variables in this study could be correlated simply because of set effects induced by subjective ratings by the same group of respondents. The maximum likelihood factor analysis (Bobko, 1998: 666–669) of the eight aggregated variables yielded three factors explaining 79% of the variance, explaining respectively 43%, 23%, and 13% of the total variance. The results indicate that set effects may not be a predominant factor explaining the structure of observed correlations. Discriminant validity is also indicated by the variability in the inter-correlations (see Table 2). The correlations among the seven organisational variables range from .33 to .90, the difference being significant at well beyond the .01 level. The correlations between the organizational variables and the index of relative performance also vary substantially, although less drammatically, ranging from .36 to .63, the difference being significant at the 1% level.

Table 3 shows the product moment correlations of the items of entrepreneurial, organic, professional and participative policies and their respective aggregates with the index of relative performance. Table 4 shows the correlations of the items of uncertainty reduction, differentiation, and integration related practices as well as their respective aggregates with this index.

Fit between Model and Practices

Economic liberalisation, as argued earlier, renders the corporate operating environment much more turbulent and uncertain, competitive, complex, and opportunity-rich. In such an environment the model of effective corporate response described earlier (Diagram 1) indicates the need for relatively high deployment of uncertainty reduction, differentiation, and integration mechanisms, and the use of policy frameworks that embody entrepreneurial, organic, professional, and participatory styles of management.

Table 3: Correlations of Entrepreneurial, Organic,
Professional, and Participative Management Policies with
Index of Relative Excellence *(N* = 139 Indian Corporates)

	Correlation with index of relative excellence
Entrepreneurial management policies	
1. Emphasis on pioneering into one's industry technologically sophisticated products/services	.38**
2. Emphasis on exploring all growth avenues including risky ones	.15
3. Emphasis on growing into a truly multinational corporation	.35**
4. Strong export orientation	.36**
5. Emphasis on cultivation of informative contacts for intelligence on future developments	.41**
Aggregate of 1 through 5 above	.48**
Organic management policies	
1. Emphasis on sharing all important business-related information with the staff and other stakeholders	.22*
2. Emphasis on setting up task forces to examine complex issues to find innovative solutions	.24*
3. Emphasis on experimentation and innovation in all the operations of the organization	.43**
4. Preference for periodic reorganization studies (to respond flexibly to the emerging context)	.33**
5. Emphasis on managers settling their disputes directly without the boss's intervention	.24*
Aggregate of 1 through 5 above	.36**
Professional management oriented policies	
1. Emphasis on long range planning and forecasting	.49**
2. Emphasis on detailed annual planning and operations scheduling	.49**
3. Emphasis on benchmarking with globally best management practices	.28**
4. Emphasis on locating plants or operations at globally most advantageous places	.25**
5. Emphasis on shopping globally for optimal know-how and technology	.27**
Aggregate of 1 through 5 above	.49**

(*Table 3 contd.*)

(*Table 3 contd.*)

	Correlation with index of relative excellence
Participatory, employee oriented management policies	
1. Emphasis on participative, consensus based decision making	.29**
2. Emphasis on group brainstorming to generate consensus-based novel solutions	.26**
3. Emphasis on empowerment through training	.35**
4. Emphasis on family like relations at work	.34**
5. Provision of benefits and amenities to staff above the industry norm	.34**
Aggregate of 1 through 5 above	.45**

*correlation significant at 5% (2 tails).
**correlation significant at 1% (2 tails).

Table 4: Correlations of Uncertainty Reduction, Differentiation, and Integration Related Practices with Relative Performance Excellence (*N* = 139 Indian Corporates)

	Correlation with relative performance index
Uncertainty reduction related practices	
1. Openness, frankness, and participative brainstorming for options	.47**
2. Systematic research, forecasts, data-based analysis for formulating goals and strategy	.52**
3. Quantitative assessment of costs and benefits of options	.51**
4. Information on challenges, goals, etc. shared with all managers and staff on a systematic basis	.38**
5. Management periodically disseminates information to staff on significant external developments	.40**
6. Sharing of targets, budgets, performance by departments with one another on a regular basis	.44**
7. Periodic performance review meetings of top management	.35**
8. Strong emphasis on research and data-based decision making	.56**
9. Use of a comprehensive management information system	.36**
Aggregate of 1 to 9 above	.55**

(*Table 4 contd.*)

(*Table 4 contd.*)

	Correlation with relative performance index
Differentiation-related practices	

1. Departmental/divisional goals and strategy evolved by departmental committees (decentralisation of departmental goals and strategies) — .43**
2. Conflicts resolved as low down in the hierarchy as possible, and without intervention by top bosses (decentralised conflict resolution) — .40**
3. Use of inter-functional tasks forces for designing innovations/changes (decentralised designing of innovations/changes) — .33**
4. Use of peer group pressure for staff excellence in performance (decentralised control device) — .46**
5. Use of responsibility centres for decision making (form of decentralisation) — .33**
6. Practice of making new employees members of committees (decentralised induction) — .31**
7. Rewards to staff for innovations and successful experimentation (decentralised initiative taking) — .45**
8. Emphasis on building up expertise at all levels and in all areas and on technical training — .49**
9. Strong emphasis on professionalism and professional pride — .48**

Aggregate of 1 to 9 above — .56**

Integration-related practices

1. Emphasis on developing strong staff identification with the organisation's core values, vision, mission (through training, various communications, corporate functions) — .65**
2. Corporate goals and strategy evolved by top level committees — .38**
3. Emphasis on teamwork and cooperation at and between all levels of the organisation — .51**
4. Emphasis on interdepartmental cooperation and teamwork — .49**
5. Management looks after all the stakeholders (to ensure collaborative relations) — .48**
6. Emphasis on comprehensive, integrated strategy — .56**
7. Long term planning and goal setting — .54**

(*Table 4 contd.*)

(*Table 4 contd.*)

	Correlation with relative performance index
8. Advance planning of activities and initiatives (to anticipate coordination problems)	.53**
9. Managers and supervisors rewarded for practising participative leadership	.53**
Aggregate of 1 to 9 above	.63**

** Correlation significant at the 1% level (2 tails).

All but one of the 54 correlations reported in Tables 3 and 4 were statistically significant at the 5% level (2 tails), and of these, all but three were significant at the 1 % level (2 tails). All the aggregated policies and practices variables were correlated with the relative index of performance at the 1% level, and ranged from .36 to .63. This constitutes a substantial support for the model shown in Diagram 1. Interestingly, the practices aggregates had higher correlations with the index of relative performance than the policies aggregates. This suggests that policy prescriptions are not enough; appropriate practices may matter even more. A regression of the index of relative index on these seven aggregated variables yielded a multiple correlation coefficient of .68, R^2 of 47%, and adjusted R^2 of 44%. Thus, the model of effective corporate response to liberalisation seems well-supported, although over 50% of the variance in the performance index remains to be explained.

Additional support for part of the model has come from another recent study of 54 Indian corporates (Som, 2002). Som's model was change in environment (liberalisation) causes corporate strategy changes, which in turn lead to changes in the "redesign" variables of uncertainty reduction, differentiation, and integration, and these changes in redesign variables, in association with changes in human relations management, produce change in corporate performance (index of relative performance). For the purposes of his study, Som calculated "now" minus scores 5 years earlier. The correlations of the first differences of strategy, redesign, and human relations variables with change in corporate performance indicated that changes in uncertainty reduction, differentiation, and integration were most strongly and positively correlated with change in the relative index of performance. These averaged .58 versus .06 for the strategic changes and .28 for the changes in human relations management variables.

Discussion

Published work on corporate restructuring during the liberalisation of the Indian economy after 1991, three case studies of corporate restructuring, the study of 139 Indian corporates, and Som's study of 54 Indian corporates all seem to converge broadly in their support for the model shown in Diagram 1.

Since the model in Diagram 1 was based on Western research, the support for it in the Indian setting extends the generalisability of the contingency theory models of organisational adaptation to environmental competition (Khandwalla, 1981) and to uncertainty (Burns and Stalker, 1961; Lawrence and Lorsch, 1967; Khandwalla, 1973; Miller and Friesen, 1984; Miller, 1986).

The support for the model also extends the generalisability of strategic choice models (Child, 1972; Montanari, 1979; Hrebiniak and Joyce, 1985). Not all organisations in India have responded to liberaisation identically. The three cases described earlier show large differences in the response to liberalisation. The data for 139 Indian corporates indicate fair variation in each of the organisational variables (see the standard deviations in Table 2). What is more, the correlations in Table 2 indicate that some organisations conformed to the model far more than others. The former chose to enlarge the armoury of their uncertainty reduction, differentiation, and integration mechanisms and to adopt more professional, participative, entrepreneurial, and organic modes of management; the latter chose not to do so, even though the change in their task environments required a proactive response along the lines shown in Diagram 1. If contingency theory explains most of the variation in organisational strategies, structure, systems, and functioning (Donaldson, 1996), the intercorrelations in Table 2 should be much smaller, since there is a large amount of shared task uncertainty, competitive pressure, turbulence, etc. due to the liberalisation of the Indian economy. The fact that they are sizeable suggests that the adaptation variables in Diagram 1 are also strategic choice variables. Thus, strategic choices are not restricted only to business growth or competitive strategies but extend also to such other organisation design variabₗes as management style and uncertainty reduction, differentiation, and integration mechanisms.

The model in Diagram 1 is intended to be both a descriptive model and a normative model. It is descriptive to the extent that it says that liberalisation tends to produce certain kinds of changes in corporate organisations affected by liberalisation. It is normative to the extent that it says that such changes are desirable for superior corporate performance. The support for the model, therefore, reinforces both its descriptive and normative dimensions.

There have been studies of the organisational response to the de-regulation of specific industries like the savings and loan association industry in the US and the electronics industry in China (Haveman, 1992; Jennings and Seaman, 1994; Tan and Litschert, 1994). Studies of the organisational adaptation to the de-regulation and globalisation of an entire economy, especially in a Third World context, seem much rarer. Thus this study fills a void. The organisational studies of industry-level deregulation indicate a frequent "defender" (Miles and Snow, 1978) organisational response (Haveman, 1992; Jennings and Seaman, 1994; Tan and Litschert, 1994). But Jennings and Seaman (1994) also found an interesting variation in their study of de-regulated US savings and loan associations. Some of these stuck close to their original domain of activities, that is, stuck to the knitting (Peters and Waterman, 1982), and they worked well with a "defender" organisational response with a mechanistic structure. The others broadened their legitimate domains, and thrived with a "prospector" (Miles and Snow, 1978) organisational response and an organic, flexible structure (Burns and Stalker, 1961). Thus, both the defender as well as the prospector response are possible in a liberalising environment, and indeed, as the case studies of BPCL and Clariant indicate, their combinations are also possible. BPCL has not only been adding refining capacity and diversifying its existing product portfolio, along with many efficiency enhancing initiatives such as SAP, balanced performance scorecard, more professional and participative management ("defender"—"analyser" response), but it has also sought to diversify into consumer goods retailing and has entered into a number of entrepreneurial joint ventures ("prospector" response). Clariant, too, has been demonstrating a similar "defender," "analyser," and "propsector" response. The study of 139 Indian corporates reported in this paper suggests that a proactive response to liberalisation may make it possible for the organisation to adopt a "prospector" (entrepreneurial and organic management style), "analyser" (professional management style, uncertainty reduction mechanisms), and "defender" (participative management, differentiation and integrative mechanisms) responses.

The support for the model makes it possible to argue that the policies and practices in Tables 3 and 4 constitute "metacapabilities." Liedtka defines metacapabilities to be those that "allow organisations to adapt to change on a continuous basis by contributing the kinds of skills and knowledge that underlie the process of capability building itself" (Liedtka, 1999; 5). Since the policies and practices studied in this paper are not a random collection, but stem from the functionally logical corporate adaptation to a hypercompetitive, complex, but opportunity-rich environment, it should be possible to call them a community of adaptive "best" policies and practices that yields performance excellence in such an environment.

How universal is this community of adaptive policies and practices? They or their close versions seem to have applicability both in the economically developed West (Khandwalla, 1973, 1977, ch. 11; Child, 1974, 1975; Miller and Friesen, 1984; Covin and Slevin, 1988; Naman and Slevin, 1993) and in an emergent market economy like India, and therefore may be relevant to most sectors and industries anywhere in the world wherever there is a competitive market economy or a movement towards it. "Cultural relativity" (Hofstede, 1983) does not seem to impede seriously the widespread applicability of this model. Obviously, a lot more research needs to be done to test out this generalisation, but there are fairly strong logical reasons why these practices may have wide relevance in the globally emerging market economy.

Taken together, this community of adaptive policies and practices incorporates many strengths. In a world of flux, the first mover advantage is critically important. The entrepreneurial policies cluster may provide this. But entrepreneurial moves can be quite risky, since they often represent bold excursions in relatively unfamiliar areas (Mintzberg, 1973; Miles and Snow, 1978). The organisation must have the capacity to be flexible, to learn quickly, to improvise and innovate (Burns and Stalker, 1961). The organic policies cluster may provide these capabilities. Effective implementation of entrepreneurial initiatives may be buttressed by appropriate systems of forecasting, planning, research-based assessment of options, optimisation in the context of multiple constraints, contingencies, and objectives. These may help initial risks to be drastically reduced by the time implementation begins. These capabilities are provided by the professional management cluster of policies. In a time of flux and cut-throat competition, effective inter-departmental collaboration, staff motivation, and commitment and so forth assume great importance. These capabilities are provided by the cluster of progressive human resources management related policies. Thus, these four policies clusters provide to a beleaguered organisation the capacities of seizing new opportunities and implementing them effectively. The uncertainty reduction, differentiation, and integration mechanisms not only enlarge the capacities to take risks and implement them effectively, they keep the organisation finely tuned to the environment by reducing uncertainties associated with initiatives, issues, and options. They provide to the decision makers the depth of expertise required for making and implementing sound decisions. They reduce drastically the overload of relatively routine decisions and functions from the shoulders of decision makers. Despite the multiplicity and diversity of management initiatives needed to respond to a complex and turbulent environment, they keep the organisation cohesive and focused on its priorities. As a community of adaptive policies and practices, they may well obviate many of the incompatibilities between internal and external "fit" reported by Miller (1992).

There is a difference between the universal applicability of "best" practices and policies and their acceptability. Even when "best" practices are demonstrated to be good for performance, many organisational barriers can impede their adoption (Pfeffer, 1996). Pfeffer has described several best practices that failed to diffuse much. He has listed several impediments to such diffusion, such as preoccupation of top management with fancy strategy and finance models, the over-hyped role of visionary, "big picture" leadership, organisational vested interests in the status quo, hierarchical barriers, etc.

There is, however, considerable evidence that many "best" practices are able to migrate across countries, cultures, and industries (Mueller, 1994; Lillrank, 1995). Mueller indicates that many MNCs from the First World have been able to transport their best practices into their Third World subsidiaries or joint ventures. Most contemporary societies offer a wide variety of niches, and these include niches in which MNC "best" practices evolved in the "home" country can flourish in societies across the world. Indeed, many Japanese management practices have been transplanted even into such fiercely individualistic societies as the US. Globalisation has been proceeding apace for several decades now, and this has not only linked economies but also management systems. Thus, many of the practices and policies identified in this paper may

have not only wide applicability in the industries of most market economies, they may also have wide acceptability.

A point of importance concerning the diffusion of "best" policies and
practices is their form. If a policy or practice is too specific, it is unlikely
to diffuse much, for there may be too few organisational situations where
it could fit. Some years ago an MNC subsidiary operating in India and
marketing personal care products decided to improve customer orientation by getting all 300 employees (including the CEO) to hit the road
for at least 3 days in a year and meet the company's customers. It worked
like a charm in changing the mindset. Another company with ten times
the number of employees tried it out, but soon gave up. Its customers
were spread out all over India, and they were industrial customers. Neither
the customers appreciated the hordes of "sight seers", nor could the
company afford the high costs of travel, hotel stay, and absence from
work. Thus, "best" policies and practices are likely to diffuse much more
when they are not too context specific, but broad enough to be contextually adaptable. In other words, diffusion is likely to depend upon whether
local variants of the "best" policy or practice are feasible. The "best" policies and practices identified in the present study are mostly of this
interpretable and contextualisable form.

There is a further issue concerning the institutionalisation of the
policies and practices identified in this study. Any change in policy or
practice needs to be buttressed in certain ways (Pfeffer, 1996). It needs
to be participatively emplaced so that it is more appropriately context-
ualised, and there is reasonably enthusiastic commitment to it of those
who are its stakeholders. It needs to be publicised internally so that every-
one is aware that a change is being implemented. Progress of emplacement
or modification has to be monitored. An incentive system needs to be
enacted that rewards those falling in line and punishes those that do not.
To improve execution, training needs to be provided to those who operate the new policy or practice. Without this sort of buttressing, "best"
practices and policies may yield little.

Finally, how best can "best" policies and practices remain when they
get widely diffused? Many business strategies and management tools and
techniques no longer provide a sustainable competitive advantage when
they diffuse so much as to get institutionalised in industry (Collis, 1994).
Business strategies like price leadership or product differentiation are too
highly visible and imitable to sustain for long any competitive advantage

(Barney, 1991; Peteraf, 1993; Ginsberg, 1994). This has also been the fate of such widely imitable tools and techniques as budgeting, annual planning, market research, internal audit, inventory control, and so forth. However, this sort of erosion of competitive advantage may not take place when the practices and policies form a whole cluster of interpretable rather than imitable, functionally inter-related, aligned (Powell, 1992) policies and practices. Thus, although some of the policies and practices identified in this study may lose their sustainable competitive advantage, given their number (47), the synergies they incorporate as a group, and their capacity to be contextually modified, it is unlikely that as a system they would lose their sustainable competitive advantage for a fairly long period (Khandwalla, 1998). And even if all these polices and practices do get diffused, they may still be able to provide a sustainable competitive advantage depending upon how creatively and effectively they are interpreted and executed.

References

Abraham, S. (1995a). "Shopfloors of Change." *Business India* March 13–26, 173–177.

Abraham, S. (1995b). "Workplace 1995." *Business India* April 24–May 7, 64–70.

Ahluwalia, M.S. (1996). "India's Economic Reforms." Ch. 2 in R. Cassen and V. Joshi (eds.), *India: The Future of Economic Reforms.* Delhi: Oxford University Press.

Barley, S.R. and G. Kunda. (1992). "Design and Devotion: Surges of Rational and Normative Ideologies of Control in Managerial Discourse." *Administrative Science Quarterly* 37, 363–399.

Barney, J.B. (1991). "Firm Resources and Sustained Competitive Advantage." *Journal of Management* 17, 99–120.

Bobbitt, H.R. Jr. and J.D. Ford. (1980). "Decision Maker Choice as a Determinant of Organizational Structure." *Academy of Management Review* 5(1), 13–23.

Bobko, P. (1998). "Multivariate Analysis." In M.D. Dunnette and M.H. Heather (eds.), *Handbook of Industrial and Organizational Psychology.* Vol.1 Indian edition, Mumbai: Jaico, pp. 637–686.

Burns, T. and G.M. Stalker. (1961). *The Management of Innovation.* London: Tavistock.

Business Today. (1994). 'The New CEO: To Survive, CEOs Must Transform Themselves into Post-Liberalisation Leaders." *Business Today* April 7–21, 48–69.

Business Today. (1995a). "Perceptions of Quality." *Business Today* January 7–21, 40–42.

Business Today. (1995b). 'The Economy 1995: Charting Out the Reforms." *Business Today* March 22–April 6, 142–147.

Carroll, G.R. (1993). "A Sociological View on Why Firms Differ." *Strategic Management Journal* 14, 237–249.

Chatterjee, A. (1995). "Morph Marketing." *Business Today* April 22–May 6, 70–83.

Child, J. (1972). "Organizational Structure Environment and Performance: The Role of Strategic Choice." *Sociology* 6, 1–22.

Child, J. (1974/1975). "Managerial and Organizational Factors Associated with Company Performance, Parts I and II." *Journal of Management Studies* 11(3), 175–189; and 12(1), 12–27.

Child, J. and A. Kieser. (1981). "Development of Organizations Over Time." In P.C. Nystrom and W.H. Starbuck (eds.), *Handbook of Organizational Design,* Vol. 1. New York: Oxford University Press, pp. 28-64.

Clark, E. and A. Soulsby. (1995). "Transforming Former State Enterprises in the Czech Republic." *Organization Studies* 16(2), 215–242.

Collins, J. and J. Porras. (1994). *Built to Last: Successful Habits of Visionary Companies.* New York: Harper and Row.

Collis, D. (1994). "Research Note: How Valuable are Organizational Capabilities." *Strategic Management Journal* 15, 143–152.

Covin, J. and D. Slevin. (1988). "The Influence of Organization Structure on the Utility of an Entrepreneurial Top Management Style." *Journal of Management Studies* 25(3), 217–234.

Donaldson, L. (1996). *For Positivist Organization Theory.* London: Sage.

Department of Public Enterprises. (1997–98). *Public Enterprises Survey,* Vol. 1 New Delhi: Department of Public Enterprises, Ministry of Industry, Government of India.

Fortune India. (2002). "Fortune India Score Board." *Fortune India* Jan. 31, 2002, 25–38.

Ghani, A. (1994). "Managing Mega Projects." *Business Today* Aug. 22–Sept. 6, 64–73.

Ginsberg, A. (1994). "Minding the Competition: From Mapping to Mastery." *Strategic Management Journal* 15, 153–174.

Haveman, H. (1992). "Between a Rock and a Hard Face: Organizational Change and Performance Under Conditions of Fundamental Environmental Transformation." *Administrative Science Quarterly* 37, 48–75.

Hofstede, G. (1983). "The Cultural Relativity of Organizational Practices and Theories." *Journal of International Business Studies* Fall, pp. 75–89.

Hrebeniak, L. and W. Joyce. (1985). "Organizational Adaptation: Strategic Choice and Environmental Determinism." *Administrative Science Quarterly* 30, 336–349.

Jain, S. (1996). "Cripling Cash Crunch." *India Today* Jan. 31, 51–56.

Jennings, D. and S. Seaman. (1994). "High and Low Levels of Organizational Adaptation: An Empirical Analysis of Strategy, Structure, and Performance." *Strategic Management Journal* 15, 459–475.

Joseph, T. (1995). "Remaking the Factory." *The Strategist Quarterly* 1(1), 7–13.

Kanter, R. and D. Brinkerhoff. (1981). "Organizational Performance: Recent Developments in Measurement." *Annual Review of Sociology* 7, 321–349.

Katz, D. and R. Kahn. (1966). The Social Psychology of Organizations. New York: Wiley.

Kawatra, P. (1995). "Globalisation: The New Entrepreneurs." *Business Today* June 7–21, 70–77.

Khandwalla, P. (1973). "Viable and Effective Organizational Designs of Firms." *Academy of Management Journal* 16, 481–495.

Khandwalla, P. (1977). *The Design of Organizations*, New York: Harcourt Brace Jovanovich.

Khandwalla, P. (1981). "Properties of Competing Organizations." In P.C. Nystrom and W.H. Starbuck (eds.), *Handbook of Organization Design*, Vol. 1. New York: Oxford University Press, pp. 409–432.

Khandwalla, P. (1988). "Organizational Effectiveness." In J. Pandey (ed.), *Psychology in India.* Vol. 3, New Delhi: Sage, pp. 97–215.

Khandwalla, P. (1992). *Organizational Designs for Excellence*, New Delhi: Tata McGraw-Hill.

Khandwalla, P. (1995). "Effective Management Styles: An Indian Study." *Journal of Euro-Asian Management* 1(1), 39–64.

Khandwalla, P. (1996). "Effective Corporate Response to Liberalization: The Indian Case." *The Social Engineer* 5(2), 5–33.

Khandwalla, P. (1998). "Thorny Glory: Toward Organizational Greatness." In S. Srivastava and D.L. Cooperrider (eds.), *Organizational Wisdom and Executive Courage.* San Francisco: Lexington Press, pp. 157–204.

Khandwalla, P. (2001). "Creative Restructuring." *Vikalpa* 26(1), 3–18.

Khanna, S. (1994). "Core vs. Anti-Core: Why is Corporate India Defying the Logic of the Theory of Core Competence." *Business Today* Aug. 7–21, 68–77.

Lawrence, R. and J.W. Lorsch. (1967). *Organizational and Environment: Managing Differentiation and Integration.* Boston: Division of Research, Graduate School of Business Administration, Harvard University.

Liedtka. (1999). "Linking Competitive Advantage with Communities of Practice." *Journal of Management Enquiry* 8(1), 5–16.

Likert, R. (1961). *New Patterns of Management.* New York: McGraw-Hill.

Lillrank, P. (1995). 'The Transfer of Management Innovations from Japan." *Organization Studies* 16(6), 971–989.

Manimala, M. (1992). "Entrepreneurial Heuristics." *Journal of Business Ventures* 7, 477–504.

March, J.G. and H.A. Simon. (1958). *Organizations.* New York: Wiley.

Miles, R.E. and C. Snow. (1978). *Organizational Strategy, Structure, and Process.* New York: McGraw-Hill.

Miller, D. (1986). "Configurations of Strategy and Structure: Towards a Synthesis." *Strategic Management Journal* 7, 233–249.

Miller, D. (1992). "Environmental Fit Versus Internal Fit." *Organizational Science* 3(2), 159–178.

Miller, D. and P. Friesen. (1984). "Organizations: A Quantum View." Englewood Cliffs, N.J.: Prentice-Hall.

Mintzberg, H. (1973). "Strategy Making in Three Modes." *California Management Review* 16, 44–58.

Monga, M.L. (1997). "Corporate Restructuring: The Search for a Fit by Indian Organizations." *South Asian Journal of Management* 4(1), 27–32.

Montanari, J.R. (1979). "Strategic Choice: A Theoretical Analysis." *Journal of Management Studies* 16(2), 202–221.

Mueller, F. (1994). "Societal Effect, Organization Effect and Globalization." *Organization Studies* 15(3), 407–428.

Mukerjea, D. (1995). "Marketing Flops." *Business World* Nov. 15–28, 34–37.

Mukerjea, D. and P. George. (1995). "Corporate India in the Age of Reform." *Business World* Sept. 6–19.

Naman, J. and D. Slevin. (1993). "Entrepreneurship and the Concept of Fit: A Model and Empirical Tests." *Strategic Management Journal* 14, 137–153.

Nandi, S.N. (1995). "Benchmarking: Principles, Typology and Applications in India." *Productivity* 36(3), 359–370.

National Management Forum. (1995). Corporate Restructuring (a Survey Report). New Delhi: All India Management Association.

Nilakant, V. and S. Ramanarayan. (1998). *Managing Organizational Change.* New Delhi: Response Books of Sage.

Nunnally, J.C. (1967). *Psychometric Theory.* New York: McGraw-Hill.

Peteraf, M.A. (1993). "The Cornerstones of Competitive Advantage: A Resource-Based View." *Strategic Management Journal* 14(3), 179–191.

Peters, T. and R. Waterman. (1982). *In Search of Excellence: Lessons from America's Best Run Companies.* New York: Harper and Row.

Pfeffer, J. (1996). "When it Comes to "Best Practices"—Why Do Smart Organizations Occasionally Do Dumb Things? *Organizational Dynamics* 25(1), 33–44.

Powell, T. (1992). "Organizational Alignment as Competitive Advantage." *Strategic Management Journal* 13, 119–134.

Prahalad, C. and G. Hamel. (1994). *Competing for the future.* Boston: Harvard Business School Press.

Price, J.L. (1968). *Organizational Effectiveness: An Inventory of Propositions.* Homewood, Ill.: Richard D. Irwin.

Raghavan, P. (1996). "The Outlook is Uncertain." *Business World* Jan. 10–23, 40–41.

Ramachandran, R. (1995). "The Truth About Technology Imports." *The Economic Times* Oct. 12, 8.

Ramnarayan, S. and J. Bhatnagar. (1993). "How Do Indian Organizations Meet Learning Challenges." *Vikalpa* 18(1), 39–48.

Rao, N. and R.P. Das. (1998). "Restrategising Mergers and Acquisitions for Global-isation: Some Hidden Agenda." *Prestige Journal of Management* 2(2), 42–50.

Rekhi, S. (1995). "Public Sector Enterprises: Warming to Competition." *India Today* July 15, 92–93.

Reserve Bank of India. (2002). Reserve Bank of India Bulletin Jan. 2002, 56–57.

Roy, A. (1995). "Forms for the Future." *Business Today* Aug. 7–21, 68–79.

Senge, P. (1990). *The Fifth Discipline: The Art and Practice of the Learning Organization.* New York: Double-day/Currency.

Sharma, S.S., N.K. Nair, and K.P. Suny. (2000). "Productivity and Competitiveness. Theme Paper." *Convention of National Productivity Policy*, New Delhi.

Simon, H.A. (1965). *Administrative Behavior: A Study of Decision-Making Processes on Administrative Organization.* 2nd edn. New York: Free Press.

Singh, P. and A. Bhandarkar. (1990). *Corporate Success and Transformational Leadership*, New Delhi: Wiley Eastern.

Som, A. (2002). "Role of Human Resource Management in Organizational Design." Unpublished doctoral dissertation. Ahmedabad: Indian Institute of Management.

Stinchcombe, A. (1965). "Social Structure and Organizations." In J.G. March (ed.), *Handbook of Organizations*, Chicago: Rand McNally, pp. 142–193.

Subrahmanian, K.K., D.V.S. Sastry, S. Pattanaik, and S. Hajra. (1996). "Foreign Collaboration Under Liberalisation Policy." Mumbai: Department of Economic Analysis and Policy, Reserve Bank of India, Study 14.

Suhomlinova, O.O. (1999). "Constructive Destruction: Transformation of Russian State-Owned Construction Enterprises During Market Transition." *Organization Studies* 20(3), 451–484.

Tan, J. and R. Litschert. (1994). "Environment-Strategy Relationship and its Performance Implications: An Empirical Study of the Chinese Electronics Industry." *Strategic Management Journal* 15, 1–20.

Thompson, J.D. (1967). *Organizations in Actions*, New York: McGraw-Hill.

Van de Ven, A. and A. Delbecq. (1974). "A Task Contingent Model of Work Unit Structure." *Administrative Science Quarterly* 19(2), 183–197.

Verma, S. (2002). "Freedom Related Practices and Corporate Effectiveness." Unpublished doctoral dissertation. Ahmedabad: Indian Institute of Management.

Vora, S. and S. Assomull. (1995). "Taking on the World." *Business India* Jan. 16–29, 165–167.

Wilkinson, B. (1996). "Culture, Institutions and Business in East-Asia." *Organization Studies* 17(3), 421–447.

World Bank. (2001). *World Development Report 2000–2001: Attacking Poverty.* New York: Oxford University Press.

World Economic Forum. (1999). *The Global Competitiveness Report 1999.* New York: Oxford University Press.

16 Application of American Management Theories and Practices to the Indian Business Environment: Understanding the Impact of National Culture

Suresh Gopalan and Angie Stahl

Introduction

Falling trade and economic barriers have increased global trade. Increasingly, South Asian countries like India which have embraced free market reforms are facing increased exposure to not only Western (particularly American) products and services, but also to their management philosophies, ideologies, and practices. According to Gopalan and Dixon (1996), the United States has emerged as a significant investor in India accounting for over seventeen percent of all actual foreign direct investment from 1991 until 1994. Additionally, the Clinton Administration has designated India as one of the world's "ten big emerging markets." Future projections indicate an increased U.S. presence and involvement in diverse areas ranging from telecommunications, consumer goods, power generation, financial services, software, and automobile manu-facturing (Phillips, 1992).

While some management ideas (especially those of a technical nature) are easily transferred across countries (i.e, they are culture free), a large number of American management ideas and practices are "culture-specific" (Hofstede, 1980b; Kanungo and Jaeger, 1990). They cannot and should not be blindly imported to developing countries such as India where the cultural, social, political, economic, and judicial environments are vastly different than that of the United States. Unfortunately, this has not been the case—as the American business model is considered to be the paradigm for success, American management ideas and practices have been largely replicated with little or no modification in several developing countries including India (Jaeger, 1990).

American and Indian managers would benefit a great deal if they gained a better understanding of the *cultural context* in which American management theories originated. Such knowledge would enhance their ability to better discriminate and differentiate between management ideas that are culturally compatible against others that are incompatible (Davis and Rasool, 1988). Additionally, cultural awareness will enable managers from both countries to make suitable modifications and revisions to American management ideas and approaches in their application to the Indian business environment.

Can Behavioral Models and Management Theories be Universally Transplanted? The Debate within the Management Community

The majority of organizational behavioral theories (a) originate from the United States, and (b) are for the most part based on samples consisting of Anglo-Saxon male managers who have been socialized in cultural, political, and economic environments that are vastly different from Asian and African cultures (Kanungo and Jaeger, 1990; Kanungo, 1983). Consequently, a question arises whether these management models can be transplanted universally. In other words, would such management theories be effective in countries where the socio-cultural environments are vastly different from that of the United States?

There are three schools of thought that address the above mentioned question. Management scholars such as Weber (1958), Negandhi (1975), and Pascale and Maguire (1980) who advocate the *"convergence perspective"* (which is the first school of thought) contend that as countries across the world achieve similar levels of industrialization and standards of living, business behavior and thinking would become similar and come together (hence the term convergence). Under such circumstances, the effects of national culture would vastly diminish as managers will be thinking, speaking, and acting with common global business values, beliefs, and behaviors. In such situations, behavioral models and management theories may have universal application and relevance even if their origins are rooted in American culture.

Scholars who believe in the *"Divergence perspective"* propose that national culture is (and will continue to be) the primary force in shaping the values, beliefs, and attitudes of managers within a country (Ottoway, Bhatnagar, & Korol, 1989; Hofstede, 1980a, Laurent, 1983). They reject the arguments of convergence and maintain that as long as countries have dissimilar values, management ideas and practices cannot be universally transplanted. These scholars maintain that while organizational structures and work processes may tend to converge with increasing levels of industrialization, the behavior of people within organizations will be largely influenced by the national culture.

More recently, the *"cross-vergence"* perspective has gained increasing attention from the management community (Bond & King, 1985; Ralston, Gustafson, Cheung, & Terspstra, 1993; Gopalan and Dixon, 1996). Management researchers have found that in many developing countries, a new management ideology has emerged over the last 10 years. The new management ideology appears to be a hybrid—one which combines both domestic and "imported" ideas. As managers in many developing countries have come into increased contact with international counterparts, they have learned to adapt by creating a management approach that blends the best elements of both their native and foreign cultures.

The Primary Focus of this Paper

Regardless of which school of thought one belongs to, it is important that *both* American and Indian managers develop a basic understanding of the national culture-management relationship. Therefore, this paper has two objectives. The first is to offer a comprehensive explanation of the cultural context and origins of American management practices and the second is to examine the degree of their relevance and effectiveness with respect to the Indian business environment. Although a brief explanation of the Indian national culture is offered to facilitate comparison with that of American national culture, it is not the intent of this paper to focus on Indian national culture.

Description of American National Culture and Ensuing Management Practices

Developing a cultural profile of any country is difficult because culture is a multi-dimensional and multi-layered concept (Nahavandi and Malekzadeh, 1988, Schein, 1984). Additionally, culture is hard to define due to multiple definitions from several fields (Rousseau, 1990). Despite such difficulties, management scholars (Adler and Jelinek, 1986; Adler, 1997) are increasingly using five value orientations developed by two anthropologists, Kluckhohn and Strodtbeck (1961) to develop cultural profiles of countries. The basic assumption behind this framework is that in any country, there are fundamental assumptions and choices regarding the following:

- Human nature (Is human nature *evil?* Is it *good?* Is it a *combination of good and evil?*) A separate but related issue is whether human nature can be fundamentally changed in this lifetime.
- Natural and supernatural elements (Is man *dominant* over nature? Does man live in *harmony* with nature? Does he *subjugate* himself to nature?)
- Time (Do we look to the Past? Do we focus on the *Present?* Is a *Future* orientation the most important way to approach life?)
- Work (Does man derive his identity from Work and is it a calling from God? [*Doing* orientation]; Should we work just for meeting short term needs necessary to enjoy life? [*Being* orientation]; Should work be considered as a means for fulfilling one's duty after which one should seek salvation as the ultimate goal? [*Being-in-becoming* orientation])
- Relationships (Should *individualism* and individual rights be the foundation for a society? Or should it be based on a *lineal* collective group-oriented approach? Or should it be based on an organized *hierarchical* structure with an elaborate definition of roles, duties, and responsi bilities?)

By identifying the *preferred choice* by the *majority of the population* for each of these five value orientations, it is possible to develop a cultural profile for any country. The Kluckhohn and Strodtbeck framework is used to describe value orientations that are typical of American national culture. This cultural profile may not represent the values of sub-cultural groups within the country whose cultural preferences may be markedly different than that of mainstream culture.

Human Nature Orientation

Americans tend to believe that humans have a combination of both good and evil qualities and that they are capable of evolving into better persons.

The majority of Americans believe that by appealing to the good nature within individuals, change and improvement is possible and desirable. Fundamental changes in human nature can be accomplished through a combination of right training, education, and exposure (Adler, 1997; Samovar, Porter and Jain, 1981). The origin of such a belief can be traced to the Christian theological belief that "no matter how sinful you have been, you can be saved if you seek redemption by being born again."

Such beliefs affect business thinking considerably. Organizations spend millions of dollars annually in training seminars and other human resource development activities (Adler and Jelinek, 1986). Such seminars include a wide range of topics from sexual harassment, diversity sensitivity, discrimination in the workplace, team work and development, employee empowerment, leadership skills, improving speaking and other communication skills, positive thinking, and so forth.

The underlying principle behind such investments is that employees can "change," and that will result in a "better" and "improved" workforce. Alcoholism, for example, is considered to be a disease and many organizations have Employee Assistance Programs to help them kick the habit. Alcoholism is not considered a "moral lapse" or a "character flaw" in an organizational context. The focus is on helping the individual change his/her behavior instead of making moral judgements about his/her habits.

Companies large and small are actively involved in helping and interacting with the local community through organizations such as the UNITED WAY which supports an umbrella of local agencies that help the sick, the young, the elderly, and the indigent. Executives volunteer time, effort, and other resources to help with many of the civic organizations in their city (Romano, 1994). More recently, several organizations have been in the forefront of promoting their employees' health by having "smoke free" work environments. Smoking or use of tobacco items are prohibited inside office buildings—smokers have to go outside the building in order to smoke. A growing number are experimenting with policies that would ban smoking on company premises and property including the parking lot. Smokers have to go outside the company's property if they have to light up! (McShulskis, 1996; Lang, 1992) While there are those who may consider such measures an intrusion on freedom and individual choice, the underlying assumption behind such actions is that "intervention can result in an improved society" and that by extension, a healthier society is an improved society. From an organizational viewpoint, such interventionist measures translate into a healthier and more productive workforce—leading to higher job satisfaction in the long run (Sorohan, 1994; Wolfe and Johnson, 1993; Lau, 1990).

Most (not all) Indians believe that an individual's situation in this present life is largely a consequence of actions committed in previous birth or births (in other words life is predetermined) and that change is relatively difficult to accomplish (Saha, 1992; Kuppuswamy, 1994). While a sizeable number of Indians may not subscribe to such a view, there is nevertheless a widespread sense of fatalism found in the Indian psyche that has been documented by Indian scholars (Srinivas, 1972; Kuppuswamy, 1994). For example, poverty in India is tolerated to a greater extent than other cultures. It is endured without widespread protest both by the observer and the person experiencing it. Does such a sense of resignation result as a consequence of fatalism or apathy or a combination of both factors?

If the mind set stated earlier is true for the most part (i.e., life is predetermined), would Indian organizations be committed to investing in human resource development programs at a high level? Would senior managers believe that their junior managers can fundamentally change their belief systems and become beacons of change and progress after receiving the right training and education? Do hiring practices focus more on hiring the "right type" of people because once hired it may not be possible to "change" the individual to suit the organizational mold? Would a "Theory X" type of management approach be more suitable than a "Theory Y" type approach in the Indian environment?

Obviously, additional research is needed to answer these and other questions. But clearly one has to better understand the inherent differences underlying American and Indian value orientations about human nature before transferring American management ideas to India. It is possible that the contemporary Indian manager has moved away from traditional ideas such as the theory of *karma* and has evolved a more Western (Americanized) approach to the idea of human nature. This issue is worthy of further exploration.

Relationship to Nature and Supernatural Elements

The traditional American relationship to nature has been one of Dominance although there is an increasing emphasis on conservation and ecological awareness suggesting a trend towards living in Harmony with nature.

The traditional view towards nature has been one of Dominance— exploiting natural resources is one of the primary reasons for the economic progress achieved by the United States (Kluckhohn and Stodtbeck, 1961; Stewart, 1972; Turner, 1920). The majority of Americans believe that natural resources and elements can and should be utilized for the benefit of mankind (Tersptra and David, 1991). Science and technology are considered allies used to minimize or mitigate the effects of disease, pestilence, drought, floods, earthquakes, and other natural catastrophes that have been the bane of mankind.

Only in recent years have Americans been concerned with issues of ecological preservation, conservation of resources, and the harmful effects of pollution. These concerns have influenced a somewhat paradoxical approach to the manipulation of nature. Advanced technology is developed to further maximize progress towards a higher future standard of living. Yet advancing technology is also expected to minimize depletion or destruction of ecological, environmental, or scarce natural resources requisitioned for use in past progress efforts (White, 1996; Barnett, Weathersby & Aram, 1995; Gold-smith, 1993).

Dominance over nature and other elements has resulted in most Americans having an internal locus of control (Stewart, 1972). In other words, they believe that they are in control of most if not all of life's events and that their individual actions and effort will make a difference in their personal lives. Responsibility and accountability lie with the individual and outcomes, whether successful or unsuccessful, cannot be shifted to an unknown supernatural force.

Such a fundamental assumption is reflected in the goal-setting and motivational practices that have originated in the United States (Locke, Latham, and Erez, 1988; Locke and Latham, 1990). Central to the idea of any goal-setting theory is that if an individual expends the right type and degree of behavior, he/she can control and reasonably predict the outcome of his/her output. While several factors can affect the effectiveness of goal-setting practices in organizations, one critical factor is an individual's internal locus of control. Individuals with a strong internal locus of control are more likely to actively pursue, and thus achieve their goals than are those with an external locus of control.

Traditional cultures such as those found in India socialize people to have a predisposition towards an external locus of control. Individuals with an external locus of control believe that man is basically helpless in affecting life's events which are largely controlled by fate and/or by supernatural forces that are largely beyond human control (Husain, 1961, Tripathi, 1988). Even if individuals in the Indian corporate environment can intellectually relate to and understand the basic premise behind goal-setting practices, to what extent will they be effective in implementing such practices over the long run if it is not positively reinforced by societal values? Can advanced education neutralize and overcome the notion of fatalism? Will exposure to international management practices neutralize the effects of national culture allowing Indian employees to develop a stronger internal locus of control?

Although India has one of the largest pool of well qualified and talented scientists, technicians, and other professionals in the world, it lags behind several countries in both basic and cutting edge research in many areas. While some may attribute this phenomenon to lack of resources and other structural issues, an alternative explanation may be that it could be due to a lack of adequate positive reinforcement from society (McClelland, 1961). It is reasonable to hypothesize that Indian scientists and other professionals working in the United States and other Western countries are able to have a high level of achievement not only because of access to superior resources but also because of the prevailing mind set found in both organizational and societal atmosphere that encourages and nurtures an internal locus of control.

Time Orientation

Americans are oriented towards the Future with respect to both personal and business time orientations. The American notion of Future is relatively short term oriented extending at best from four months to a year.

The Future time orientation results in several assumptions, two of which are discussed in this paragraph. These assumptions are true for most Americans in both their professional and personal lives (Hall and Hall, 1989; Weber, 1958). First, time is viewed as an asset with a perishable value and secondly as a linear entity which when utilized improperly or inefficiently is wasted. Time is compartmentalized wherein meeting deadlines, schedules, and appointments are emphasized. People are socialized to value punctuality and promptness and express strong disapproval towards late-coming, tardiness, and excessive delays. Lateness may be considered a reflection of rudeness and/ or slothfulness.

The two key assumptions mentioned earlier are building blocks for strategic management practices found in American organizations (Collins & Montgomery, 1997; Thompson & Strickland, 1997). Strategic management includes the development of (a) a vision and mission statement, (b) long-term goals and objectives spanning five or more years, (c) annual goals and objectives up to a year, (d) monthly and weekly goals and objectives. The entire planning process is based on the assumptions that (a) "management is time-bound" and (b) unless critical targets and outcomes are achieved by a specified time period organizational success will be severely compromised. Many seminars and workshops on time management are offered to American managers. These training sessions reinforce and strengthen the presuppositions of time management (Sunoo, 1996; Oshagbemi, 1995). Utility is gained and maximized by efficient use of time. As quantity of time is considered to be a limited and fixed resource, Americans tend to view time utilization as a zero sum game— time not efficiently used to gain maximum productivity is time wasted. Since most American employees profess the same time orientation in their personal and professional lives, they tend to exhibit required behaviors that conform to meeting organizational goals based on preestablished time tables (Adler, 1997; Hall and Hall, 1989).

Future time orientation also results in the belief that the future will be "bigger," "brighter," and "better" than either the present or the past. Consequently, not much emphasis is given in the United States to maintaining or upholding traditional customs or beliefs—the focus is not on maintaining the status quo—change is valued and embraced (Tocqueville, 1945). One of the class assignments given by the first author to students over the past few years is the "Circle Test" developed by Tom Cottle (1967). This assignment requires students to draw three circles, each representing the past, present, and the future. Students are asked to draw these circles in any manner (including size and arrangement) as they see fit. A trend emerged. The majority of the American students tend to draw the circle representing future as biggest in size and mostly unconnected with either the present or the past circles. Most students from Asian countries tend to assign a bigger size to the circle representing the past relative to Americans and to draw all three circles intersecting one another. Although this study is unscientific in nature, such pictorial representations of time reflect cultural patterns that are unconsciously embedded in the minds of young people from different backgrounds. Americans value the future and think that eventual outcomes are unconnected to either the present or the past. Asians tend to attach more importance to the past and believe that events are influenced and interconnected through the three time orientations (Trompenaars, 1993).

Despite the rhetoric of strategic management with long term plans, in reality the focus of corporate America is on achieving short term goals based on quarterly targets (Cavanagh, 1990). Companies that fail to declare dividends on a quarterly basis have seen their stock price plummet in Wall Street and other capital markets. High-level management and CEO compensation plans including bonuses, pay raises and stock options are often based on their firm's quarterly performance and stock price (Frazee, 1996; Dimma, 1996). Consequently, "making the numbers" is of paramount importance to American managers. This environment tends to promote a more impatient short-term orientation that focuses on "here-and-now" results than patient long-term thinking (Adler, 1997). This may be one of the many reasons why Americans have not been as effective as the Japanese in their approach to world markets. While the Japanese are willing to wait for five or more years to see the results of an investment, Americans tend to get impatient if no tangible returns are seen within a year.

Indian time orientation appears to be significantly different than that of the United States. Time is not viewed in a linear fashion, nor is it viewed as a commodity with perishable value (Sinha, 1990; Saha, 1992). Time is viewed as an infinite loop—one which has always been there and which will continue to exist. Consequently, Indian society has evolved with a more relaxed and reflective attitude towards time—one which is quite different from and at odds with the Indian corporate/business environment which tends to be more similar to the American corporate environment. Additionally, Indians attach pride and importance to maintaining their heritage by following practices that are handed down from the past by tradition. Such past time orientation places tremendous pressure to conform to time-honored practices and beliefs. Therefore, the focus may be maintaining status quo through perpetuation of the past, and not change. The preference for planning, compartmentalizing, scheduling time, and a sense of urgency—key factors that enable the successful implementation of strategic planning and compensation practices characteristic of future-oriented societies such as the U.S. may have to be extensively modified in India due to a different time orientation.

Approach to Work

A combination of historical and religious factors have led Americans to link individual identity with his/her occupation/career. Additionally, work is considered as an end to itself and not as the means to an end.

Traditional American ideas of work are derived from a Protestant belief which considered work to be a calling from God and to pursued for its own sake (Cavanagh, 1990). Individuals who became wealthy were considered to have been blessed or rewarded for their hard work, effort, dedication, and perseverance. Although the biblical origins of work are seldom consciously considered in contemporary living, the centrality of work to one's life is widely prevalent in the United States (Weber, 1958; Ferraro, 1990). Individuals derive their identity from work and will continue to work even after they have "retired." If you ask an American individual who he/she is they will identify themselves by their occupation or profession (Adler, 1997).

Able-bodied individuals who remain poor over their lifetime are looked at with disdain as they are perceived to be lazy—poverty in such situations is attributed to indolence and a lack of effort, not fate or chance. Social loafing is discouraged. Most Americans believe that all individuals regardless of their background or origin can become materially successful if they "work hard." Social welfare policies, though widespread, are increasingly coming under attack and are being scaled back because they are thought to perpetuate poverty instead of relieving it (Friedlander & Hamilton, 1996; Ulhman, 1996).

The strong work ethic in the United States favors objectivity, competitiveness, and a need for achievement (Ferraro, 1990; McLelland, 1961). Consequently, the laws pertaining to hiring new employees are structured with the idea that the most qualified candidate should be hired for the job—not the owner's son or son-in-law. Individuals are respected for the quality of their work and contribution they make to the organization—not for the status ascribed to them by caste membership or family connections. Such sentiments of anti-nepotism are reflected in human resource policies that prohibit family members such as husband and wife or father and son from working for the same organization (Reed & Cohen, 1989; Young, 1995). While discrimination and favoritism do exist in corporate America to some extent, the nation's laws and popular sentiment are against such practices.

A flip side to the American approach to work is that loyalty from the employee to the organization or from the organization to the employee tends to be based on self-interest, and therefore is short-lived at best and nonexistent in most instances (Friedman and Friedman, 1980). Employees are loyal to their profession—not to their organization. Job hopping is fairly common and layoffs are even more common. In most situations, employees work at the "will" and "pleasure" of the employer. If the employer no longer requires the services of any employee the employer can "let them go." A two weeks notice of termination from the employee's side is standard industry practice. Work relationships are relatively impersonal, legal, and contractual—nothing is implied or assumed—it has to be in the form of a contract in a written form (Trompenaars, 1993). This type of atmosphere results in low trust and a "us" versus "them" mentality. Management operates from the assumption that the organization exists to provide a return to the stockholders and that is their primary goal. If profits are at stake, management may resort to restructuring and downsizing (typically resulting in hundreds of employees losing their jobs) to strengthen the bottom line. With managerial performance linked to financial performance of the firm (i.e. share valuation), it is reasonable to conclude that the primary focus is on meeting the shareholder needs and not on providing employees long term employment. Employees likewise are under no obligation to stay with the organization even after receiving advanced technical or management training at the organization's expense. They are not required to sign a bond or compensate the organization and are free to leave anytime without any restraint or constraint. Freedom is a two-way street in the United States.

Motivational theories originating from the United States advocate that "job enrichment" is the primary way to motivate employees (Herzberg, 1968). In other words, the assumption is that individuals derive more satisfaction from job content such as increased autonomy, responsibility, and recognition and less fulfillment from contextual factors such as pay raises, bonuses, and relationships with bosses and co-workers. Managers exhort are encouraged to enhance intrinsic factors at work to sustain worker motivation (Staw, 1976, 1977; Deci, 1975; Petty, McGee & Cavender, 1984).

Space not does not permit a comprehensive assessment to examine the relevance of all American work related practices. But suffice to say, the widespread practice of layoffs and terminations will be highly unpopular in India for a variety of reasons (Bedi, 1995). Indian employers and employees are more inclined to exhibit feelings of loyalty and desire to have a long term relationship relative to the United States although job hopping has become increasingly common among the younger generation. Employment in India is also considered to be an extension of social justice (Khandwalla, 1990). For example, most (not all) Indian public sector organizations India have been "running in the red" for several years. They continue to exist solely due to massive government subsidies which are an indirect form of taxation paid by Indian citizens. Yet it is unthinkable to shut these organizations down or streamline their operations as hundreds and thousands of workers will be laid off. Keeping people employed appears to be more important than achieving profitability in the Indian context.

While Indian multinationals may be similar to their Western counterparts in hiring practices (reflecting impartiality and hiring someone with the best credentials), it may not be reflected in family-owned organizations and public sector companies where caste and family considerations along with political pressures may favor less qualified candidates (Khandwalla, 1990). Sinha (1990) noted that Indians have a strong distinction between "insiders" and "outsiders" and prefer loyalty and dependability over efficiency and independence. These preferences will certainly continue to make the hiring and promotion practices more "personal" than "impersonal." While motivational theories that focus on enhancing job content may have relevance in materially advanced and comparably wealthy countries such as the United States, their widespread application may have to be examined with caution in developing countries such as India where satisfaction of economic needs may be more important to many employees. So focusing on contextual factors such as pay and bonus may be more relevant than increasing autonomy or independence at work. Additionally, most Indians value relationships that have been built over a lifetime and tend to display increased spiritualism and less emphasis on material goods as they get older. Therefore, work in an Indian context is a means to an end (for most if not all Indians).

People may approach work primarily for satisfying their family's needs; or for finding work for their relatives and friends; or because they like their superior and want to show their affection and regard for him/her (Sinha and Sinha, 1994). Once the primary needs are satisfied, for example, all the children are educated and married, a house has been constructed and fully paid for, and grandchildren are born, it is reasonable to expect the average Indian to shift his/her focus in life away from work towards other pursuits.

Relationships in Society

Americans tend to be highly individualistic, autonomous, and egalitarian (non-hierarchical) in nature. Socialization practices stress independence over dependence and ascendancy of individual rights over group goals and aspirations.

It would not be an exaggeration to state that Americans exhibit the highest individualism of any country in the world (Hofstede, 1980a; Adler, 1997). The focus is on maintaining and enhancing individual rights, liberties, goals, and aspirations. Parents encourage their children from a very young age to become "independent" and it is common practice for teens over 18 years to "leave" their parent's home and live by themselves. From their infancy, most children have their own room in their parent's homes which is considered their private space. It is customary for parents to knock and obtain permission before entering their childrens' rooms. Babies that are a few months old learn to sleep by themselves in a separate room—the practice of children sleeping with their parents either in the same bed or room is atypical and uncommon. Elderly Americans often choose to live by themselves or in a retirement home rather than stay with their children—the preference is for independence and individuality over dependence and collectivism. Social relationships in the United States tend to be relatively transient and ephemeral resulting in high divorce rates and large numbers of single parents.

Educational practices in schools and colleges encourage students to ask a lot of questions and express personal opinions. It is acceptable for students to disagree with their teachers as long as it is done in a polite manner. University-bound students do not have to choose a major area of specialization until the end of their second year (a bachelors degree is typically obtained over four years). Once a major area of specialization is chosen, students are not "locked in" that particular choice for the rest of their lives. They have the option of changing their minds as many times as they want—while they will certainly take a longer time to graduate in such situations, the choice of "who they want to be" is in their own hands. Interpersonal relationships between teachers and students tend to be relatively informal and casual. For example, students do not stand and greet the professor when he/she walks into the classroom nor do they display a highly deferential manner of communication. In relating to one another, Americans display a strong streak of egalitarianism wherein social equality is desired and hierarchy downplayed (Cox, 1993).

Similarly, in workplace environments, there is a sizeable and growing movment towards a form of egalitarianism in the workplace. Many employers encourage an "open door" policy which encourages employers to discuss issues or concerns with any member of management—not simply the employee's immediate supervisor. Additionally, American employers are generally more supportive of a participative management style which allows employees from all organizational levels to engage in managerial decisions and practices through direct input (Cox, 1993).

Socialization practices emphasize competitiveness over cooperation (Cox, 1993). Two assumptions prevail here. First, an individual's achievement must be measured by standards external to that individual (not by their family connections or money) and second, an individual maximizes his/her talents and abilities to the fullest extent only in a competitive atmosphere. Notice that the emphasis is on developing the individual to the fullest extent—not the group or another collective entity. Athletic programs glorify the spirit of competitiveness . There are "little league" soccer teams where children as young as 4–5 years old compete with other teams. Even in team-oriented sports such as basketball and football, individuals are singled out for their proficiency and skill over their team mates.

These cultural practices have given rise to certain management practices, such as Management by Objectives (MBO), which have their origins in the United States. Implicit assumptions that serve as a foundation for MBO are that (a) subordinates can sit down with their superiors and have meaningful negotiations on future job performance (i.e., low power distance is present), (b) the superior welcomes and invites subordinates to participate in a joint-management process, and (c) hierarchy is best when minimized. In such an organizational situation both the supervisor and the employee are psychologically comfortable in coming together to initiate the MBO process (Drucker, 1954; McGregor, 1960; McClelland, 1961).

Human resource development (HRD) practices in the United States are driven by law with a strong emphasis on protecting individual rights and welfare. Two examples illustrate this point. The Americans with Disabilities Act considers employees infected with HIV and those with full blown AIDS as "protected" workers who cannot be discriminated in organizational recruitment, transfer, promotional, or termination practices (Gopalan and Summers, 1994). Organizations cannot require a blood test for HIV or AIDS as a condition of employment (for new employees) nor can they fire someone if they are HIV positive (for current employees). If requested, reasonable accommodation must be made for such employees such as a transfer from a field to a desk job. Managers are required not to discuss or disclose the medical conditions of these employees with anyone including their immediate superiors, unless the employee has authorized them to do so.

An increasing number of American organizations do not discriminate between heterosexual and homosexual lifestyles and extend health care, dental, and life insurance benefits to the gay and lesbian partners of their employees (Gopalan and Summers, 1994). Some communities in which these companies were located, initially expressed their objections to such HRD practices which, in the minds of some community members, contributed to encouraging "sinful" and "undesirable" lifestyles. Most organizations contended that their response was consistent in meeting their employees changing needs and wants. In all such HRD practices, the reader will note that the focus is on meeting and enhancing individual (and not a group's) needs.

Indians are socialized in a culture where an individual derives his/her identity based on family and caste membership. The group is considered to be more important than the individual (Prakash, 1994; Tripathi, 1994). Additionally, age and seniority is given great respect in Indian tradition. Children are raised to obey their elders and teachers who are considered to be the "experts" having answers to all questions. In India, relationships are long lasting, organized on a hierarchical basis, and status oriented— husband over wife, elder brother over younger brothers and sisters, patriarchical side over matriarchical side, etc (Sinha, 1988). It is not uncommon to see Indians sacrifice and/or defer their individual goals and desires for the collective goals and welfare of their family or a larger collective entity. The degree of psychological distance and social interactions between different groups in society is impacted by a variety of factors including but not limited to age, seniority, socio-economic class, caste affiliation, religion, and so forth. It should be noted that there are subcultures within India whose relationship norms may deviate substantially from the description given here.

Nevertheless, it is obvious that socialization practices in Indian are vastly different than that of the United States. Given this situation, it is interesting to examine the degree of relevance of general management practices such as MBO and other American HRD practices mentioned earlier. Given the large power distance between superiors and subordinates in most social and organizational settings, would MBO or variations of MBO and participative management be truly effective in India? Would Indian managers and employees put aside feelings of hierarchy and status and relate to one another as equals? Would age and seniority take backseat to knowledge and competence (even if coming from a younger person) in an organizational setting? Alternatively, would a benevolent and nurturing patriarchical style be more suitable for an Indian setting as it may be more compatible with Indian culture where people do not relate as equals? A related but separate issue is the impact of regional cultures. Are there regional differences in the values emphasized in India? For example, is Western India more aggressive and risk embracing? Is Southern India more conservative and risk aversive? What part (or parts) of the country would be more inclined to be neutral to organizational policies that recognize gay and lesbian lifestyles? What part (or parts) of India would be more inclined to oppose such lifestyles? More importantly, would Indian society even tolerate such policies that deviate from "traditional" notions of family? Obviously, there are no easy answers to such questions but they are raised to demonstrate the vacuity of replicating American management practices.

Conclusions and Suggestions for Further Research

The primary objective of this paper is to trace the cultural origins of some of the behavioral theories and practices commonly found in American management approaches and to discuss their applicability to the Indian business environment. A profile of American cultural values are presented through the Kluckhohn and Strodbeck (1961) cultural profile and are juxtaposed with brief glimpses of Indian cultural values. The close relationship between American cultural values and management styles and practices are illustrated through several examples. A number of questions are offered to initiate discussion and offer suggestions for future research regarding relevancy and transferability of American management practices to India.

Globalization of business will have a tremendous impact on lifestyles and role relationships especially in developing countries such as India. For example, as multinational companies (MNCs) establish operations in what are previously "closed economies", they will begin to affect tradition and culture. Compared to domestic companies, MNCs may be more inclined to hire women, pay high salaries, and promote them to managerial positions. Under such conditions, economic disparities and earning capabilities between women and men are likely to disappear allowing women to achieve a status equal to men. Increasing financial independence will enable Indian women to remove externally imposed constraints and become more assertive. This in turn will eventually cause women to reexamine traditional male-female role relationships which historically placed Indian males at the focus of power and control within the family. Therefore we theorize that, as we head into the 21st century, business institutions will continue to become more powerful in India and international influences will be felt to a greater degree than ever before.

We speculate that along with the factors mentioned above, the widespread usage of English language, familiarity with Western modes of education especially in urban areas in India, and the influence of the INTERNET may lead Indian management thinking to a state where some ideologies and approaches will reflect national culture while others will become more similar to Western practices and ideas (i.e., they will reject Indian national cultural values). Indian managers would develop and follow a hybrid, or cross-vergence approach in the future, which will reflect a combination of indigenous and imported approaches to managing people at work. For example, Loyalty, which is an integral Indian value, may still be retained in Indian organizations as it maintains and fosters and environment of trust necessary to maintain build effective business relationships. On the other hand, exposure to equal employment opportunity practices may create a desire to hire the most qualified person for a job, as opposed to preferential hiring of family members or relatives. These issues are worthy of further exploration for cross-cultural researchers.

References

Adler, N.J., & Jelinek, M. (1986). Is 'organization culture' culture bound? *Human Resource Management*, 25 (1): 73–90.

Adler, N. J. (1997). *International Dimensions of Organizational Behavior*. Cincinnati, OH: South-Western Publishing Company.

Barnett, J. H., Weathersby, R., and Aram, J. D. (1995-Winter/Spring). American cultural values: Shedding cowboy ways for global thinking. *Business Forum*. 20 (1, 2): 9–13.

Bedi, H. (1995-June). From blue chip to blue skies. *Asian Business*. 31(6): 45–47.

Bond, M., and King, A. (1985). Coping with the threat of Westernization in Hong Kong. *International Journal of Intercultural Relations*, 9, 351–364.

Collins, D. J., and Montgomery, C. A. (1997). *Corporate Strategy: Resources and the Scope of the Firm*. Chicago, IL: McGraw-Hill.

Cavanagh, G. F. (1990). *American Business Values*. Englewood Cliffs, NJ: Prentice-Hall.

Cottle, T. (1967). The circles test; an investigation of perception of temporal relatedness and dominance. *Journal of Projective Technique and Personality Assessments*, 31, 58–71.

Cox, T. (1993). *Cultural Diversity in Organizations: Theory, Research, & Practice*. San Francisco, CA: Berrett-Koehler Publishers, Inc.

Davis, H. J., and Rasool, S. A. (1988). Values research and managerial behavior: Implications for devising culturally consistent managerial styles. *Management International Review*, 28,11–20.

Deci, E. L. (1975). *Intrinsic Motivation*. New York, NY: Plenum Press.

Dimma, W. A. (1996-Autumn). Executive compensation gets its share. *Business Quarterly*, 61 (1): 77–80.

Drucker, P. (1954). *The Practice of Management*. New York, NY: Harper & Row.

Ferraro, G. P. (1990). *The Cultural Dimensions of International Business*. Englewood Cliffs, NJ: Prentice-Hall.

Frazee, V. (1996). Pay-for-performance bonuses are on the rise. *Personnel Journal*, 75 (10): 22–23.

Friedlander, D., & Hamilton, G. (1996). The impact of a continuous participation obligation in a welfare employment program. *Journal of Human Resources*, 31 (4): 734–756.

Friedman, M. and Friedman, R. (1980). *Free to Choose: A Personal Statement*. New York, NY: Harcourt Brace Jovanovich.

Goldsmith, E. (1993). *The Way: An Ecological World-view*. Boston, MA: Shambhala.

Gopalan, S., and Summers, D. (1994-Autumn). AIDS and the American manager; An assessment of management's response. *SAM Advanced Management Journal*, 59 (4): 15–26.

Gopalan, S., and Dixon, R. (1996). An exploratory investigation of organizational values in the United States and India. *Journal of Transnational Management Development*, 2 (2): 87–111.

Hall, E. T., & Hall, M. R. (1989). *Understanding cultural differences*. Yarmoth, ME: Intercultural Press.

Herzberg, F. (1966). *Work and the Nature of Man*. Cleveland, OH: World.

Herzberg, F. (1968, January/February). One more time: How do you motivate employees? *Harvard Business Review*, 53–62.

Hofstede, G. (1980a). *Culture's consequences*. New York: Sage Publications.

Hofstede, G. (1980b-Summer). Motivation, leadership, and organization: Do American theories apply abroad? *Organization Dynamics*.

Husain, A. S. (1961). *The National Culture of India*. Bombay: Asia Publishing House.

Kanungo, R. N. (1983). Work alienation: A pancultural perspective. *International Studies of Management and Organization*, 13 (1–2): 119–138.

Jaeger, A. M. (1990). The applicability of Western management techniques in developing countries: A cultural perspective. In A.M. Jaeger and R.N. Kanungo, Eds., *Management in Developing Countries*. New York: Routledge.

Khandwalla, P. N. (1990). Strategic developmental organizations: Some behavioral properties. In A.M. Jaeger and R.N. Kanungo, Eds., *Management in Developing Countries*. New York: Routledge.

Kluckhohn, C. L., & Strodtbeck, F. L. (1961). *Variations in Value Orientations*. Evanston, Illinois: Row, Peterson and Company.

Kuppuswamy, B. (1994). *Social Change in India*. New Delhi: Konark Publishers.

Lang, N. (1992). The last gasp: Workplace smokers near extinction. *Management Review*, 81 (2): 33–36.

Lau, B. (1990-Fall). Four key ways to protect your employees' health and productivity. *Management Quarterly*, 31 (3): 51–53.

Laurent, A. (1983). The cultural diversity of western conceptions of management. *International Studies of Management and Organization*, 13 (1–2): 75–96.

Locke, E. A., Latham, G. P., and Erez, M. (1988). The determinants of goal commitment. *Academy of Management Review*, 13 (1): 23–39.

Locke, E. A. & Latham, G. P. (1990). *A Theory of Goal Setting and Task Performance*. Englewood Cliffs: NJ: Prentice-Hall.

Mariotti, J. (1994, October 17). There's a sickness sweeping the land. *Industry Week*, 243 (19): 14.

McClelland, D. C. (1961). *The Achieving Society*. New York, NY: Van Nostrand Reinhold.

McGregor, D. (1960). *The Human Side of Enterprise*, New York, NY: McGraw-Hill.

McShulskis, E. (1996). Smoke-free workplaces prevalent. *HRMagazine*, 41 (6): 18.

Nahavandi, A. and Malekzadeh, A. R. (1988). Acculturation in mergers and acquisitions. *Academy of Management Review*, 13 (1), 79–90.

Negandhi, A. R. (1975). Comparative management and organization theory: A marriage needed. *Academy of Management Journal*, 18, 334–344.

Oshagbemi, T. (1995). Management development and managers' use of their time. *Journal of Management Development*, 14 (8), 19–34.

Ottoway, R., Bhatnagar, D., and Korol,T. (1989). A cross-cultural study of work related beliefs held by MBA students. In William A. Ward and Eugene G. Gomolka, (eds.), *Proceedings of the 26th. Annual Meeting of the Eastern Academy of Management*, 155–157.

Pascale, R. T., and Maguire, M. A. (1980). Comparison of selected work factors in Japan and the United States. *Human Relations*, 33, 433–455.

Petty, M. M., McGee, G. W, and Cavender, J. W. (1984). A meta-analysis of the relationships between individual job satisfaction and individual performance. *Academy of Management Review*, 9, 712–721.

Prakash, A. (1994). Organizational functioning and values in the Indian context. In Henry S. R. Kao, Durganand Sinha, and Ng Sek-Hong (eds.), *Effective Organizations and Social Values*. New Delhi: Sage Publications, 193–201.

Phillips, E. J. (1992). India—The next manufacturing frontier. *Manufacturing Systems*, 10 (7) 91–98.

Ralston, D. A., Gustafson, D. J., Cheung, F. M., and Terpstra, R. H. (1993-second quarter). Differences in managerial values: A study of U.S., Hong Kong and PRC managers. *Journal of International Business Studies*, 249–275.

Reed, C. M, and Cohen, L. J. (1989). Anti-nepotism rules: The legal rights of married co-workers. *Public Personnel Management*, 18 (1): 37–44.

Romano, C. (1994). Pressed to service. *Management Review*, 83 (6): 37–39.

Rousseau, D. (1990). Assessing organizational culture: The case for multiple methods. In Benjamin Schneider (ed.). *Organizational Climate and Culture*. San Francisco, CA: Jossey-Bass. 153–192.

Saha, A. (1992). Basic human nature in India tradition and its economic consequences. *International Journal of Sociology and Social Policy*, 12 (1–2), 1–50.

Samover, L., Porter, R., and Jain, N. (1981). *Understanding Intercultural Communication.* Belmont, California: Wadsworth Publishing Company.

Schein, E. H. (1984-Winter). Coming to a new awareness of organizational culture. *Sloan Management Review,* 3–15.

Sinha, J. B. P. and Sinha, D. (1994). Role of social values in Indian organizations. In Henry S. R. Kao, Durganand Sinha, and Ng Sek-Hong (eds.), *Effective Organizations and Social Values.* New Delhi: Sage Publications, 164–173.

Sinha, D. (1988). Basic Indian values and behaviour dispositions in the context of national development: An appraisal. In D. Sinha and H.S.R. Kao (eds.), *Social values and development: An Asian Perspective.* New Delhi: Sage.

Sinha, J.B.P. (1990a). *Work Culture in an Indian Context.* New Delhi: Sage.

Sorohan, E. G. (1994). Healthy companies. *Training & Development,* 48 (3): 9–10.

Srinivas, M. N. (1971). *Social Changes in Modern India.* University of California Press.

Staw, B. M. (1976). *Intrinsic and Extrinsic Motivation.* Morristown, NJ: General Learning Press.

Staw, B. M. (1977). Motivation in organizations: Toward synthesis and redirection. In B. M. Staw & G. R. Salancik (eds.), *New Directions in Organizational Behavior.* Chicago, IL: St. Clair Press.

Stewart, E. (1972). *American Cultural Patterns: A Cross-Cultural Perspective.* Pittsburgh, PA: Intercultural Communications Network.

Sunoo, B. P. (1996). This employee may be loafing: Can you tell? Should you care? *Personnel Journal,* 75 (12), 54–62.

Terpstra, V, and David, K. (1991). *The Cultural Environment of International Business.* Cincinnati, Ohio: South-Western Publishing Company.

Thompson, A., and Strickland, A. J. (1996). *Strategic Management: Concepts and Cases.* Chicago, IL: Irwin.

Tocqueville, A. (1945). *Democracy in America.* New York, NY: Alfred A. Knoph.

Tripathi, R. C. (1988). Aligning development to values in India. In D. Sinha and H.S.R. Kao, (Eds.), *Social Values and Development: Asian Perspectives.* New Delhi: Sage Publications.

Tripathi, R. C. (1994). Interplay of values in the functioning of Indian organizations. In Henry S. R. Kao, Durganand Sinha, and Ng Sek-Hong (eds.), *Effective Organizations and Social Values.* New Delhi: Sage Publications, 174–192.

Trompenaars, F. (1993). *Riding the Waves of Culture: Understanding Cultural Diversity in Business.* London: Nicholas Publishing Company.

Turner, F. J. (1920). *The Frontier in American History.* New York, NY: Holt.

Ullman, O. (1996-Sept. 23). Good politics, bad policy: Tapping big business to fix welfare. *Business Week,* (3494), 49.

Weber, M. (1958). *The Protestant Ethic and the Spirit of Capitalism.* New York: Scribner.

White, M. A. (1996). Valuing unique natural resources: Endangered species. *The Appraisal Journal*, 64 (3): 295–303.

Wolfe, R., and Johnson, T. (1993). Work, health, and productivity. *Academy of Management Review*, 18 (1): 160–165.

Young, B. S. (1995). Family matters. *HRMagazine*, 40 (11), 31–31.

Section Eight

GLOBAL MANAGERS IN INDIA

17 Managing in a Changing Environment: Implications and Suggestions for Expatriate Managers in India

Samir R. Chatterjee, Herbert J. Davis and Mark Heuer

Introduction

India's gradual integration into a global trading system and its growing appeal as an investment and production location, particularly in 'knowledge' industries, means that the question of the place of expatriates in the Indian management system is more crucial than ever. In particular, there has been the significant growth of the information technology (IT) and knowledge-related industries in a number of key development 'clusters' that are often located adjacent to major Indian cities. Thus, in key knowledge industry 'clusters' such as New Delhi-Noida, Chennai, Bangalore, and Hyderabad, there have been major investments on the part of several leading multinational corporations who have established their regional headquarters in these areas and there has been the mushrooming of associated small- to medium-sized IT consultancy firms. The increasingly global nature of Indian industry in both the 'old' and the 'new' economy therefore requires greater inputs in terms of globally-oriented managers and technical competencies.

Expatriate management is nothing new in Indian business culture. In fact, the development of the modern Indian business system occurred under British colonial rule with expatriate British managers filling executive positions in the emerging local enterprises of the 19th and early 20th centuries. The legacy of expatriate management from this period was mixed. On the one hand, British managers were influential in setting organizational norms, values and systems of corporate administration and governance. On the other, local Indian managers became resentful and frustrated with the inherent inequities of the colonial context and demanded greater control and executive authority within these enterprises. In the post-Independence (1947) era there was a decisive culmination to this trend as British expatriates largely left the Indian business scene and local managers and entrepreneurs assumed full control of local enterprises and industries.

By the dawn of the 21st century, the wheel had again turned and the arrival of expatriate managers and employees in India was being welcomed as a sign of India's emergence within the global economy. From an expatriate viewpoint, however, working and living in India poses a series of very considerable challenges. These challenges range from learning to work successfully with local colleagues, to dealing with 'culture shock' and the everyday difficulties of relocating home and family to India—a nation that is often complex and confusing for newly arrived expatriates but which is also characterized by economic potential and astounding cultural and geographic diversity. This chapter will consider some of the general challenges confronting expatriate managers in the workplace before moving on to briefly note some of the more practical aspects of successfully adjusting to life in India.

Working in India: An Overview

Expatriate Managers and Employees in India: A Rare Commodity?

In the past, because of a more inwardly focused national strategy that focused on import substitution and government 'command' over economic development, expatriate management in India was limited in terms of both size and scope. To a certain extent the limited involvement of expatriate managers in Indian business culture has also continued during the 'liberalization' (post 1991) era. In many ways, this is not surprising. India has a solid pool of local managerial talent and technical expertise, with the most prominent and skilled individuals often drawn from the internationally renowned Indian Institutes of Management (IIMs) and Indian Institutes of Technology (IITs). Aside from local companies, a wide range of multinational corporations and foreign-owned enterprises operating in India continue to draw on these resources. In fact, given the complexity of the operational business environment in India and the importance of 'local knowledge', relying primarily on the recruitment of local managers has been one strategy for managing risk and pursuing competitive advantage.

A defining feature of the Indian business environment in the liberalization era has been the perceived influence of Non Resident Indians (NRIs). The term NRI is often used to refer to both 'first generation' overseas-based Indians as well as individuals who are ethnically of Indian origin but who have been raised in nations such as the US or the UK. Although no statistical evidence is available, anecdotal evidence suggests that a number of NRIs have returned to India to establish 'start-up' companies and consultancies and to provide managerial leadership in foreign-owned subsidiaries (Sharma, 2003). The advantages of 'returning' NRI's include their comparative familiarity with the local culture and business environment. Their presence in many of India's emerging knowledge industry clusters is causing observers to switch from lamenting 'brain drain' to discussing the new phenomenon of 'brain circulation' as these skilled professionals and managers re-engage with India (Patel, 2002). According to one report on returned Indians in the information technology sector:

> The returnees are often familiar with the latest trends and standards in America. They have networks of friends and contacts in Silicon Valley and other tech hot spots. Since many return for personal reasons, they are less likely than their Indian counterparts to be lured by the glamour and fat salaries of the West—giving companies the chance to acquire the solid middle- and senior-level backbone many lack. They also bring other, less tangible skills (Dhume, 2000).

As the aggregate size of international business activity in India is set for long-term growth, non-Indian expatriate managers are also likely to become increasingly evident in Indian business culture. In this sense the days where 'foreign' managers and employees were a rare commodity appear to be numbered. In fact, there have been some notable recent developments in terms of the growth in the number of expatriate managers and employees working in India. In previous years, there was a clear expectation that expatriates were brought to India to fill senior managerial positions in multinational enterprises. According to a recent report (Basu, 2003) a remarkable shift is beginning to occur as expatriates begin to fill middle-ranking positions in process management or to provide specialist skills across a wide range of industries including telecommunications and media, pharmaceuticals, IT services and the retail sector, biotechnology and tourism.

Rather than merely being restricted to 'global' companies operating in India, domestic companies are now leading this drive for international talent. Indian companies are now seeking to lift their competitiveness and quality in order to be successful in the international product and service markets and thus the experiences of international managers and skilled employees are even more essential. By 2003, recruitment agencies estimated that there were 20,000 expatriate employees and managers in India drawn from North America, Asia and a wide range of Western European nations (Prayag, 2002; Basu, 2003). The vast majority of these expatriates have been hired by local Indian companies to provide specialist competencies, prominent examples include the garment manufacturing company S. Kumars, Ranbaxy Labs, Reliance Infocom and Bharti Televentures (Basu, 2003). Thus, ingrained perceptions of the prevalence and the organizational role of expatriates are giving way to a new dynamic within the Indian business culture. As one senior Indian executive stated 'expatriate induction into India has become more a rule than an exception. If Indian companies have to stay in the business, they have to identify the right talent' (Basu, 2003).

Business Regulations and Procedures

As specified by the Companies Act, foreign companies in India are those that have been incorporated outside India while conducting business in India. These companies are required to comply with a set of special legal requirements. All companies are required to maintain a very high standard of records and accounts. These records and accounts are also required to be audited periodically as per the provisions of the Act. Indian companies may recruit foreign nationals for short-term assignments without prior regulatory approval. Business visas may be issued for up to five years with the provision for multiple entries. Foreign passport holders wishing to work in India need to obtain a 'Residential Permit' from the Foreigners Regional Registration Offices (FRRO). These offices are located in major cities and, in the case of a foreigner living in a smaller city, approval may be obtained from the area police station. However, such registration is normally not required for stays not exceeding 180 days by a foreign passport holder.

Foreign executives arriving in India for stays of reasonably long duration may find the 'Transfer of Residence' scheme to be a very helpful method. This scheme allows foreign nationals to import personal effects without having to pay customs duties. A foreign national is allowed to repatriate two-thirds of the *net after tax income* once his/her employment is approved by the government and the exchange control authorities. A foreign national working under government approval is allowed to open bank accounts in India and receive funds from abroad. India has recently signed treaties with many countries where foreigners working in India are not liable for double taxation. The double taxation relief is normally available to persons employed by foreign companies to work in India. Such managers can stay in India for not more than 180 days during a financial year. The individual remuneration for such employees is not allowed to be claimed as a tax deduction in India by the foreign company.

India is a member of the International Labour Organization (ILO) and is a signatory to many global conventions on labour relations. Trained managerial, professional and technical staff is available in India, and employment in foreign companies is considered highly prestigious in the society. The quality of graduates from the premier national institutions like IIM and IIT is well known.

Managing the Expectations and Perceptions of Local Managers and Employees

As indicated, an increasing number of foreign businesses and MNCs are now establishing major operations in India. Their entry has introduced a new 'global' dynamic within Indian management culture as employees and local managers learn to operate within the broader context of the unique corporate cultures of these transnational business corporations. Nonetheless, very often there is also an equivalent need for these corporations to adapt their management strategies to the local Indian context.

Perhaps one of the most difficult challenges confronting an expatriate manager is managing preconceived expectations. First, the expatriate manager should be aware of his/her own expectations. For example, is he/she beginning placement with an unjustifiably negative perception of the challenges of living in India and the nature of the local workforce?

Is he/she expecting instant results or is he/she prepared to invest time in learning about the local culture and in forging relationships? Is the expatriate manager expecting that his/her established individual style of managerial leadership will be wholly relevant to the Indian context?

Second, the expatriate manager should be aware that local managers and employees might have preconceived ideas (both negative and positive) about the priorities, motivation, skills and general leadership styles of foreign managers. The period in which foreign managers were viewed with suspicion or distrust is no doubt over. In certain circumstances, however, especially where managers are perceived to have gained a position through their expatriate status rather than through demonstrable competencies, resentment could surface among local colleagues. The case of Hyundai Motors in India (see Box 1) demonstrates that language and cultural barriers can also lead to perceptual differences between local and expatriate managers.

Nonetheless, there are also indications that the new global focus of Indian industry is beginning to break down some of these barriers as the competitive advantage afforded by expatriate knowledge and experience becomes recognized and more highly valued. According to the director of human resources for the RPG Group (Goenka), one of India's oldest and largest traditional family-based business 'houses', resentment on the part of local managers was 'definitely an issue at one point of time, but Indian managers have come around to accepting expatriate managers as people bringing specialized skills to the table' (Basu, 2003). However, the same manager also suggested that such attitudes could resurface when an expatriate is unable to demonstrate core competencies or is a highly unsuitable 'hire' for the needs of the local Indian organization (Basu, 2003).

Managing Working Relationships

Developing the most appropriate type of managerial leadership in India is often context dependent. Some 'global' managerial leadership styles are well suited to certain industries but inappropriate for others. While it is very difficult to generalize, a number of observers have suggested that senior managers need to adopt a more 'familial' approach to building relationships in the Indian workplace. Gopalan and Rivera (1997) suggest 'leadership styles accentuating an impersonal distant and contractual relationship may be ineffective in an Indian work environment.' Instead,

---

Box 1: Hyundai Motor Company in India: Managing Perceptions

In 1996, the Korean automotive giant Hyundai Motor Company (HMC) began construction of a new manufacturing plant in Chennai (South India) to produce vehicles suited to the unique demands of urban life in India. The plant manufactured two vehicles, the *Santro* and the *Accent*, which quickly became extraordinarily popular with Indian consumers. This required a rapid increase in production and employment in the Chennai plant. By 2001, the Chennai plant had 3000 employees.

Expatriate Korean managers made most key strategic and operational decisions at the plant. This generated some tension between local and expatriate managers. Some local managers observed that expatriates adopted a management style that was unsympathetic to prevailing customs and practices in India and complained that the expatriates communicated with each other in Korean, which excluded Indian managers from the decision making process. Alternately, the study found that expatriates displayed a negative impression of the local 'work ethic' and complained that the caste system interfered with the efficient operation of the plant, as some Indian managers were appointed to positions based on their caste position rather than on the basis of merit.

HMC is now employing a greater number of Indian managers, particularly in production related activities, and is working to dissolve some of these perceptual differences. This case illustrates the common problem of dealing with preconceived expectations on both sides of the local-expatriate management divide.

Source: Lansbury et al., 2003.

---

they argue that expatriates could participate in the social dimensions of the workplace community (weddings and other important community events) and should look, where possible, to develop a 'personalized and nurturing relationship with their subordinates' in order to foster 'a sense of mutual obligation and loyalty'. Similarly, an overly participative leadership style could be open to misinterpretation by some local employees who expect a more assertive personal style and directive process of strategy formation.

The caste system, which originates from the social structures of ancient India, is now officially outlawed; however, the system remains a significant element in Indian national culture. Analysts of expatriate management in India often discuss the importance of the caste system. These discussions often address the inappropriate utilization of 'team'-based HRM approaches in a cultural environment where the acknowledgement of hierarchy and social status are crucial (Gopalan and Rivera, 1997; Frazee, 1998). The caste system is an extremely difficult issue for expatriate managers to fully understand. While the caste system in India has not been removed through official measures, the caste system is certainly *dynamic* rather than *static*. Also, there are significant differences between various regions, as well as rural and urban areas, in terms of its relevance. It is, therefore, advisable for an expatriate not to overestimate, or make simplistic assumptions about, the significance of caste in Indian society and local workplaces.

There are four main castes in which most Hindus can be categorized:

1. Brahmins: originating in the religious roles as priests, teachers and idea leaders.
2. Khatriyas: the warriors, administrators and *keepers of faith*.
3. Vaidyas: traders and commercial workers.
4. Shudras: *skilled labourers and farmers*.

Caste categories, such as the 'untouchables,' are not included in the four main categories.

On the general issue of working relationships, Frazee (1998) has suggested that there are two major differences between expatriate Americans and local employees and managers. First, American managers are likely to have a different conception of the idea of control, believing that through sheer persistence, all variables can be brought under control and all problems definitively resolved. In contrast, Indians are more likely to accept ambiguity and their inability to achieve full control or final closure over all aspects of a project or a business strategy decision. Second, there is a strong cultural preference in India for criticism to be subtly implied rather than directly stated. American expatriates often fail to understand the true state of their working relationships with Indian colleagues. Accordingly, developing a more accurate assessment of the current state of working relationships and the effectiveness of management practice may require a considerably greater investment of *time* than the expatriate would otherwise be accustomed to in their ordinary 'home' environment.

Gopalan and Rivera (1997) also advise expatriate managers to understand differing sources of employee motivation in India (extrinsic–collectivist rather than intrinsic–individual) and to beware of reacting negatively to local cultural practices such as bestowing small 'favours' and gifts on superiors. However, while these observations are generally useful, it is again wise to sound a note of caution. Management practice is changing and an increasing number of Indian managers are influenced by international HRM 'best practices' and by models developed in leading Indian management institutes and international business schools. Evidence of 'convergence' is perhaps most visible in the emerging knowledge industries and thus it could be dangerous to assume that there are general rules for understanding working relationships that apply in all cases. The case of ANZ (see Box 2) illustrates the challenges and opportunities expatriate managers may encounter in India while managing work relationships.

Box 2: 'Learning to Live' in India: ANZ

ANZ, an Australian-based banking firm, entered the Indian market by acquiring a local banking network (Grindlays) in the 1990s. However, in 2000, after years of mixed fortunes in banking and local financial markets, ANZ sold its Indian banking operations. Despite this withdrawal, ANZ had still accumulated a great deal of local market knowledge over the years. More importantly, it retained a local software/IT firm (ANZIT) based in Bangalore (South India).

According to Dr Richard Tait, ANZ's head of customer technologies, the company 'learned to live with', and to solve, a number of fundamental challenges of working in India. Aside from problems with infrastructure (power, telecommunications) and the development of formal quality control and assurance programs, the company faced some very notable differences in terms of local, versus expatriate, cultural and workplace norms and management styles. In particular, there were differences in areas such as:

Degree of informality versus formality in personal interactions
General awareness and recognition of rank, functional level and status
The importance of family networks
Different perceptions of self-development and career advancement

By 2001, the firm had grown to around 500 employees who helped to service ANZ's global IT needs and develop financial services software. Moreover, ANZ announced plans to extend the capacities of ANZIT and to seek strategic partnerships with other financial-services software companies in Europe and the United States. The success of this venture was due to ANZ's willingness to identify and learn from the unique problems and opportunities of operating in India. One of the most crucial lessons for ANZIT, in an industry where there is considerable competition for skilled developers of software, was the need to focus on building relationships and adapting established management approaches to suit the local Indian context.

Sources: (Economic Analytical Unit, 2001; Tait, 2001)

Living in India: Easing the Transition

Developing Local Social and Business Networks

Perhaps no task is more essential for expatriates in India than developing local social and business networks. As one recent survey of business in India has noted:

> As in much of Asia, India business culture is strongly relationship based. Relationships are normally built over a long period of time and may extend to families. Developing an extensive network of relationships is a very worthwhile investment and may assist in dealings with bureaucracy, gathering market intelligence or identifying potential partners (Economic Analytical Unit, 2001, p. 52).

Aside from workplace related business contacts, the expatriate cultivates business networks by attending functions or conferences hosted by local industry-specific associations or the larger national industry associations, such as the Federation of Indian Chambers of Commerce and Industry (FICCI) or the Confederation of Indian Industry (CII). Additionally, many of India's leading business schools regularly host management development programmes and conferences, which could also serve as a potential means for developing national or cross-industry business networks. However, as with many aspects of life in India, investing time in building relationships is crucial, and it may be advisable to ask an Indian colleague to act as a facilitator and guide in developing these linkages.

Local social networks and business networks are likely to develop in tandem and the expatriate manager should to take care to nurture these developing links by accepting all possible social invitations, including important 'festival' occasions, such as weddings. Most expatriates, particularly those who relocate to India with their families, will develop informal and formal links with the local expatriate 'community'. In the latter respect, consulates and embassies should be able to provide information on expatriate associations, which operate in major cities such as Chennai, Mumbai and New Delhi. For example, for US nationals there are associations such as the American Women's Association (AWA) and the American Community Support Association (ACSA).

Cultural Adjustment

For many expatriate managers, the most difficult aspect of relocating to India is dealing with 'culture shock' as they engage with a social and environmental context that is profoundly different from their own home country. Culture shock is sometimes compounded when the expatriate manager is also relocating with his/her spouse and family, as different individuals will adapt to life in India at a different pace. One website with helpful guidance and tips on dealing with culture shock is http://www.indax.com/stayhlthy.html. Additionally, the website Indian Unlimited (http://asnic.utexas.edu/asnic/outreach/pages/dbimodule/iu1.html) provides an excellent range of resources on the social and practical dimensions of doing business in India.

Many HR managers are now implementing a more proactive approach to cultural adjustment. For instance, some companies and relocation consultants invite prospective expatriate professionals to come to India for a short visit before committing to relocation. This allows both the prospective expatriate employee and the local company to make some preliminary assessments as to how well they are likely to adjust to the challenge of a new cultural and organizational environment. Once relocated, some companies also choose to pair the newly arrived expatriate with a 'buddy' (either a fellow expatriate or an Indian colleague with international experience) to manage the transition in the workplace and assist in establishing a home and a welcoming social network (Prayag, 2002).

Cultural Engagement

As well as viewing relocation as a challenge, the expatriate should consider India as an *opportunity*. Aside from developing valuable experience in local business culture, working in India offers a tremendous opportunity to engage with a rich cultural heritage and a diverse natural environment. Cultural engagement might encompass visits to museums, art galleries, craft displays and important monuments in India's larger cities or short trips to India's many famous temples, forts and palaces. Popular religious festivals are a recurrent feature of life in both north and south India and Indian colleagues are likely to be more than willing to explain the significance and form of each major event.

> **Box 3: Relocation and Adjustment Agencies: Managing the Transition**
>
> The difficulties of adjusting to life in India and the rapid growth in the number of newly arrived expatriate workers and managers have led to new industry relocation and adjustment agencies. Typically, these agencies act as specialist consultants to the human resource sections of multinationals or domestic Indian corporations and manage virtually every aspect of the process of relocating an expatriate manager or employee in India. These agencies have become especially important in knowledge industry growth centres such as Bangalore, Hyderabad and Chennai and are reported to have acted for international corporate clients such as Chevron, Ford, Intel, Motorola, Hewlett Packard, Nokia and Procter & Gamble.
>
> Relocation agencies oversee introductory visits and short courses designed to allow prospective expatriate employees an opportunity to imagine their lifestyle in India and to begin the process of cultural adjustment by learning about the local culture and social system. Once relocation occurs, the agencies provide a range of assistance services to expatriates, including social introductions (local and expatriate networks), advice or active involvement in the search for rental property, establishing a home and local bank accounts, access to appropriate health care and education, and ongoing cultural adjustment training programs.
>
> *Sources:* Adapted from Prayag, 2002; various company websites.

While most expatriates are familiar with north Indian cuisine, there is again tremendous diversity to explore in terms of regional culinary specialities. Similarly, there is great diversity in the natural environment, from national parks and mountainous regions in the north to beaches in the south. Both the north and the south of India have renowned, generally peaceful 'hill stations', which expatriates can take advantage of as a respite from congested cities.

India is also characterized by linguistic diversity. The widespread use of English by the educated middle classes means that India is one of Asia's more accessible destinations in terms of international communication. However, learning a few simple phrases or words in Hindi or one of the major regional languages (Bengali, Tamil, etc.), will be a clear sign of cultural engagement and is likely to be warmly received.

Taxation Issues

In 2003, the Government of India announced some important changes to tax regulations on expatriate earnings. In the past, under long-standing provisions originally introduced to protect the foreign earnings of British executives and officials, expatriates and NRIs were largely shielded from paying tax on foreign earnings. In particular, expatriates and NRIs returning to India were afforded a nine-year exemption from paying tax on 'global earnings'. The changes introduced in 2003 cut the length of this exemption and stipulated that expatriates or 'returning' Indians, would be liable for tax on global earnings after three to four tax years (Merchant, 2003).

The revisions were viewed by taxation experts as having the greatest potential impact on the NRI community. However, given the uneven spread of dual bilateral taxation treaties and the relative inexperience of the local bureaucracy in dealing with global tax issues, some feared the possibility of 'double taxation' in both the home and host country (ibid.). The government and other observers offered a more optimistic interpretation of the implications of the changes, with one (Murlidharan, 2003) stating that:

> ...the apologists for the NRI have got it all wrong. It is not as if a ROR [Resident and Ordinarily Resident] ends up paying tax twice over, once in India where he pays tax on his global income and again in the source country. The Indo-US Double Taxation Avoidance Agreement (DTAA), for example, clearly precludes double taxation of the salary as well as fees for technical services.

Nonetheless, critics of the policy suggested that the regulatory changes would have a real impact on the general attractiveness and costs associated with expatriate postings in India, although the accuracy of this prediction remains as yet unclear.

Housing

Most expatriates will be based in the major cities of India, where a wide range of quality housing is available. The larger the city, the greater the choices, ranging from short- to long-term rental properties, to partially- or fully-furnished homes. Real estate agents or rental consultants will facilitate arrangements in a relatively short time frame and may even be able to arrange for domestic help (usually considered to be a necessity by middle-class Indians). Many large corporate employers will have already established furnished properties for expatriate workers. For further information on estimated costs, a number of agents now list properties on websites while expatriate Internet guides such as Indax (http://www. indax.com/) provide a general overview of the rental process.

Establishing a home in India involves more than merely considering the features of a property itself. Location is essential in terms of proximity to the place of employment (reducing the need to travel through often congested traffic), safety and local amenities such as parks, quality restaurants and well-stocked supermarkets. Feeling comfortable with the local neighbourhood is vital, so it is advisable to spend time exploring the area before committing to renting a property. The expatriate influx in certain desirable areas in cities such as New Delhi (which attracts international business, government and NGO workers) and Bangalore (in the wake of the IT boom) is driving up competition and prices for rental properties.

Health Services

Travel and medical guides will provide expatriates with adequate introductory information on basic health issues in India, including basics such as avoiding water that is not purified, the consumption of certain types of food and dealing with the climatic extremes of India's monsoon and summer. The most immediate and important task for an expatriate is to identify a reliable and trusted doctor or medical service. Employers and business colleagues will provide information on reliable medical services. In general, expatriates are often overly concerned about their ability to access adequate health care in India. In fact, private hospitals and medical centres, which claim to meet 'world class' standards and the achievement of ISO certification for their quality management systems, are now a feature of India's larger cities. The quality of many of these facilities and services, which are nonetheless low-cost in comparison to international prices, has led to recent attempts to promote India as a regional 'medical tourism' destination (Marcelo, 2003).

Education Services

India has been striving to make primary education compulsory across its regions and states in the last decade. Growing awareness of education as the essence, and schools as the centre of excellence, has led to the establishment of a number of public schools, independent schools, and government-aided schools. Selecting an appropriate school or college for children is often one of the most difficult decisions confronting an expatriate family in India. Again, the major cities have several options, and many expatriates opt for high quality international and diplomatic schools in these cities. Facilities and teaching staff in such schools are generally excellent and, as a result, there is competition for placement. If the employment location is comparatively remote, some consideration might also be given to elite international boarding schools. In general, it would also be advisable to thoroughly investigate the curriculum design in terms of compatibility with 'home' educational systems and the experience of teaching staff in assisting students to adjust to a new educational environment.

Many expatriates educate their children in prestigious boarding schools. Boarding schools admit children at the age of 11. Seven hundred students is the average size for a boarding school. The medium of instruction is English, although Hindi is compulsory until the tenth standard, while a third language is compulsory until the eight standard. The academic year consists of a spring and an autumn term, both lasting four months, with most boarding schools remaining closed over winter or summer, depending on the location.

Entertainment and Recreation

There are a variety of entertainment and recreation options in India's larger urban centres. India has an established golf tradition, and a number of new internationally designed courses have been developed over the last decade. Sporting clubs and leading hotels also provide recreational activities, including facilities for tennis, swimming and squash.

The larger cities also offer diverse culinary options, from international cuisine and fast food chains to regional Indian specialties. Multiplex cinema complexes, often showing newly-released English language films, alongside more traditional 'Bollywood' fare, are a new and rapidly proliferating feature of these cities. Satellite television channels, such as Discovery, BBC and Star TV, are available for entertainment in homes.

Cities such as Chennai, Bangalore, Kolkata, Mumbai and New Delhi also boast several excellent English language bookshops that stock international fiction titles and a wide range of non-fiction and scholarly texts on India's history and culture. Expatriates should also take advantage of international libraries and cultural centres such as the British Council Library and the American Information Resource Centers in these cities.

Bangalore, New Delhi and Mumbai also have an active nightlife with a number of bars and nightclubs. Local metropolitan English language newspapers and magazines also provide regular guides and feature articles on recreation and entertainment options.

Security Issues

As with other nations, there is a new security environment in India and security issues are now prioritized in the strategic planning of many international companies. In particular, many international companies and their HRM professionals have developed detailed contingency plans in the event of a security crisis. Typically, these plans envision the possibility of evacuating expatriate staff to a safe location in the event of a major security crisis. In a worst case scenario this might involve a chartered flight while in less demanding circumstances expatriates would be relocated to consular offices or placed on the first available standard commercial flight (Prayag, 2002). In considering the security scenario and in forming an accurate assessment of risk, there is an obvious need for close cooperation with relevant consular officials. For their part, it is essential for all expatriates to register with their embassy or consulate and keep this information updated.

During the 1999 'Kargil' low intensity war between India and Pakistan, some expatriate managers were reportedly evacuated to Singapore (Prayag, 2002). However, during renewed border tensions between the two countries in 2002, most multinational firms opted not to evacuate their staff from India (Bearak, 2002). Overall, many expatriate employers appear to be have the necessary strategic planning and organizational infrastructure in place to make realistic and considered 'risk assessments' and to act swiftly should the need arise.

References

Basu, I. (2003). 'India Calling' *The Washington Times*, 24 October.
Bearak, B. (2002). 'Many Americans, Unfazed, Go on Doing Business in India', *The New York Times*, 8 June.

Dhume, S. (2000). 'Bringing it Home', *Far Eastern Economic Review*, 163 (7): 44–46.

Economic Analytical Unit. (2001). *India: New Economy, Old Economy*, Canberra, Department of Foreign Affairs and Trade, Commonwealth of Australia.

Frazee, V. (1998) 'Working with Indians', *Workforce*, 3(4): 10–11.

Gopalan, S. and Rivera, J.B. (1997). 'Gaining a perspective on Indian value orientations: Implications for expatriate managers', *International Journal of Organizational Analysis*, 5(2): 156–80.

Lansbury, R.D., S.H. Kwon, W. Purcell and C. Suh. (2003). 'Korean Employment Relations Practices and Global Manufacturing Strategies: The Hyundai Motor Company in Canada and India', in *Proceedings of the 17th Conference of the Association of Industrial Relations Academics of Australia and New Zealand*, 4–7 February, Melbourne, 2003.

Marcelo, R. (2003). 'India Hopes to Foster Growing Business in 'Medical Tourism', *Financial Times*, 2 July.

Merchant, K. (2003). 'Indian Tax Change will Close Expatriate Loophole', *Financial Times*, 12 August.

Murlidharan, S. (2003). 'Why Shed Tears for the Well Heeled', *Business Line*, 23 August.

Patel, D. (2002). 'The Round Trip Brain Drain', *HR Magazine*, 47(7): 128.

Prayag, A. (2002). 'At Home in India', *Business Line*, 9 December.

Sharma, A. (2003). 'Come Home, We Need You', *Far Eastern Economic Review*, 166(3): 28–30.

Tait, R. (2001). Working in India: ANZ's Lessons of Experience, Presentation at launch of the Economic Analytical Unit Report, *India: New Economy, Old Economy*, Melbourne, Australia. Available at: http://www.dfat.gov.au/publications/india_new_old_economy/index.html

About the Editors and Contributors

About the Editors

Herbert J. Davis holds a joint professorship in the Schools of Business and International Affairs at The George Washington University, USA. He is concurrently Vice-President, South Asia, Middle-East, and Africa Affairs at the United States Chamber of Commerce in Washington, DC. He has extensive teaching and research experience in the area of management throughout South and South-East Asia. He has been a distinguished scholar at the East-West Centre in 1995 and a series Fulbright Scholar at the University of Dhaka, Bangladesh in 1984. Professor Davis has published extensively in the area of international management and national culture.

Samir R. Chatterjee is currently Professor of International Management at Curtin University of Technology, Australia. He has researched, consulted and taught in the USA, China, Japan, other countries in Asia and in Europe. He has served as an advisor to the UNDP and to the Asian Development Bank and is a frequent contributor to the literature on international management.

Mark Heuer is currently Federal Business Manager at Office Max, a management consulting company in the USA. He has served as a Visiting Assistant Professor at The George Washington University (2002-04). His research interests focus on stakeholder culture, national culture and managerial challenges.

About the Contributors

S.K. Chakraborty is the founder and former Convenor of the Management Centre for Human Values and Professor of Management at the Indian Institute of Management, Calcutta, India. A prolific writer, he has published 23 books and was the founding Editor of the *Journal of Human Values*.

Suresh Gopalan is an Associate Professor of Management and Director of T. Boone Pickens College of Business, West Texas A&M University, USA. His consulting interests are in the areas of cross-cultural management and ethics.

Cherif Guermat is a Lecturer in Economics at the University of Exeter, UK.

Ashok Gupta is the Charters G. O'Bleness Professor of Marketing at the Ohio University, USA.

Shveta Kakar is a Research Associate at INSEAD, France.

Sudhir Kakar is currently an Adjunct Professor at INSEAD, France. He served for many years as Professor of Organizational Behavior at the Indian Institute of Management, Ahmedabad, and Head of Humanities and Social Sciences at the Indian Institute of Technology, Delhi, India.

Devesh Kapur is an Associate Professor in the Department of Government, Harvard University.

Manfred F.R. Kets De Vries is the Director of the Leadership Centre and Professor of Leadership Development at INSEAD, France.

Pradip N. Khandwalla is the former Director and the L&T Professor of Organizational Behavior, Indian Institute of Management, Ahmedabad, India. His research interests include organizational design, management of excellence, innovative turnaround management, effective management of public enterprises and strategic organizations, individual and collective creativity, and innovation.

Manjulika Koshal is a Professor of Operations Management at Ohio University, USA.

Rajindar K. Koshal is a Professor of Economics at the Ohio University, USA.

Sarosh Kuruvilla is a Professor of Comparative Industrial Relations and Asian Studies at the School of Industrial and Labour Relations at Cornell University, USA.

Anil Mathur is the Associate Dean at the Frank G. Zarb School of Business and a Professor in the Department of Marketing and International Business at Hofstra University, New York. He received his Ph.D. in business administation from Georgia State University.

Kamel Mellahi is a Lecturer in International Business Strategy at Loughborough University, UK.

James P. Neelankavil is a Professor in the Department of Marketing and International Business, Frank G. Zarb School of Business, Hofstra University, New York. He received his Ph.D. in international business from Stern School of Business, New York University.

Cecil A. L. Pearson is a Senior Research Fellow with the School of Management, Curtin University of Technology, Australia.

Ravi Ramamurti is a Professor of General Management at North-Eastern University, USA.

Anil K. Sen Gupta is a former Professor of the Human Resource Group of the Indian Institute of Management, Calcutta, India.

P.K. Sett is Professor of Human Resource Management at the Indian Institute of Management, Calcutta, India.

B.N. Srivastava is Professor of Management at the Indian Institute of Management, Calcutta, India.

Angie Stahl is a Research Fellow at Texas A&M University, USA.

Monir Tayeb is a Reader in Management at the Heriot-Watt University, UK. She has researched and published widely on national culture and organizations.

Late Manab Thakur was a Professor of Management at the Craig School of Management, California State University, USA.

Pierre Vrignaud is a Research Scientist at the Institute of National Professional Conservatorium, France.

Yong Zhang is currently an Associate Professor of International Business at the Frank G. Zarb School of Business, Hofstra University, New York. He received his Ph.D. in business administration from the University of Houston.

Author Index

Subject Index

management by objectives (MBO), 391–92

Management Center for Human Values (MCHV), Indian Institute of Management (IIMs), 402, 405

management culture, 405

management education, 249

management information system (MIS), 341, 344, 349

management initiatives, diversity, 368

management of internal and external partnerships (MIEP), 147, 150

management skills of women managers, 295–96

management system, 401

management tools and techniques, 370

management, managerial values and practices, 28–29, 34–37, 49–69, 50–56, 101, 105–9, 121–22, 135, 140–41, 149, 152–54, 157, 158, 222, 240, 251, 369–71; diversity, 120; impact on managerial work, changing values, 122–30; of young and old managers, 150–51, 159

managerial challenge, 45

managerial culture, transition, 19–22

managerial factors/determinants, 50, 52

managerial job attitude, 52

managerial mindset, 23, 47, 252; shift, 122

managerial perceptions of ethical views, 222

managerial performance, 46–47, 49, 50, 56, 59–60, 62–65

managerial reorientations, 45

managerial satisfaction, 52

managing the expectations and perceptions of local managers and employees, 405–6

MANOVA, 62

manpower planning, 85

manufacturing, 282, 340

Marcos, 186, 187, 188, 189, 190

market culture, 120, 139, 213, 243, 346, 352

market economy, 22, 129, 139, 224, 247, 252–53, 368

market orientation, 66, 126, 248

market responsiveness orientation, 37, 130, 348

market segmentation, 218

marketing flops, 346

masculinity-femininity, 29–30, 31

material prosperity, 54, 227

mentoring, 309, 310; lack among women managers, 304, 305, 306

mercantilism, 331

mergers and acquisitions, 344, 347, 349

merit-based rewards, 36

meta-capabilities, 368

Microsoft, 16, 19, 262, 273

middle class, 20, 89

middle managers, 57–59, 66, 68, 321, 324

middle sector, 212

mind-set, 141, 226, 240, 289; change/shift, 1, 5; reorientation, 23, 131

mismanagement, 96

modeling, 111, 112, 113, 114, 115

modernity, modernization, 91, 107, 132, 240–41, 316

monetary policy, money and finance, 3–4

monitoring and control, 159

moral barriers, morale, 51, 54, 122, 226, 233–34

motivation, motivational practices, 30, 31, 32, 36, 52, 68, 167, 222, 240, 382, 388, 406

Motorola, 16, 20, 267, 273

multinational corporations (MNCs), 16, 21, 28, 30, 34, 37, 38, 39, 40,